With the

CH00809276

Also by Donald Davie from Carcanet

POETRY
Selected Poems
To Scorch or Freeze
Collected Poems
Poems & Melodramas

CRITICISM
*Under Briggflatts: a history of
poetry in Great Britain 1960–1985*

*Slavic Excursions: essays on
Polish and Russian literature*

Studies in Ezra Pound

*Older Masters: essays and reflections on
English and American literature*

Essays in Dissent

AUTOBIOGRAPHY
These the Companions

Donald Davie

....

With the Grain

....

ESSAYS ON

THOMAS HARDY

AND

MODERN BRITISH POETRY

Edited and introduced by
Clive Wilmer

CARCANET

Published in Great Britain in 1998 by
Carcanet Press Limited
4th Floor, Conavon Court
12-16 Blackfriars Street
Manchester M3 5BQ

A CIP catalogue record for this book is available from
the British Library.

ISBN 1 85754 394 7

The publisher acknowledges financial assistance from the
Arts Council of England.

Set in 10pt Bembo by XL Publishing Services, Tiverton
Printed and bound in England by SRP Ltd, Exeter

To Doreen
from the Publisher and Editor
with affection

Contents

III

Introduction

Donald Davie, who died in 1995, was a major figure in the literature of the later twentieth century. To the reading public at large, he was never as noticeable as certain of his contemporaries – Ted Hughes and Philip Larkin among poets, Raymond Williams and Frank Kermode among critics – but what makes him remarkable is precisely what disqualifies him from competition with them. He belongs to that comparatively rare category, the poet-critic: which means he competes with Eliot and Empson in his own century, with Johnson, Coleridge and Arnold in the past. It is unlikely that any poem in Davie's *oeuvre* will ever be loved like the best of Larkin's, but it is possible to argue that the *oeuvre* itself is more challenging than Larkin's and likely to be more fruitful in its effect. Part of that challenge derives from the way Davie's thoughts *about* poetry interact with the thoughts he expresses *in* poetry. No one in our era has thought longer or harder about what poetry can do in modern times, what it should do, what the implications are of doing or not doing those things. No one was better equipped to test such thoughts in practice.

For this reason, a handful of Davie's poems has been scattered through this collection of his prose. Certain of them pick up notions touched on in the essays and tease out their implications imaginatively. In some cases Davie made these connections explicit. The poem 'Widowers', for instance, was printed alongside the essay 'Hardy's Virgilian Purples' when they first appeared in a magazine he had guest-edited. Sometimes the traffic runs the other way: the essay title 'Remembering the Movement' was surely meant to recall the poem 'Remembering the Thirties'. Such parallels are more or less overt. Others perhaps run deeper.

The present collection is the first of several to be published by Carcanet that will help readers to draw such threads together. Davie was very prolific. The Collected Works he himself prepared for the press runs to six volumes, and another five are now projected. Moreover, the range of subjects he covered is notably wide: eighteenth-century poetry, in particular the congregational hymn; poetry in translation, especially from the Slavic languages; political and cultural questions that moved him to polemic; and twentieth-century poetry, British, American and post-colonial.

This book is concerned with a part of that last item, the poetry of the British Isles in modern times, though the last section of it extends, in a characteristic way, beyond the confines of national geography. It is not a representative collection. Davie precluded that possibility in 1989 when he published his *Under Briggflatts: A History of Poetry in Great Britain, 1960–1988*, for that book recycled the great mass of his articles on the subject. I have organized the present volume around one major book that has fallen out of print, *Thomas Hardy and British Poetry* (1972). Most of the remainder consists of periodical items which seemed to me important, but which had either eluded collection or been written later than 1989.

But none of the categories imposed on Davie's writings, whether by himself or his editors, can ever really circumscribe his subject. 'British poetry' is an arbitrary category as 'English poetry' probably is not. English is an international language, after all, and no longer the exclusive property of English people. And culture in the twentieth century is no longer nationally determined. It is no accident that the founders of modern poetry in English were two Americans and an Irishman, all of them living in the crucial years in London. Indeed, most serious readers of poetry would probably agree that it is the United States rather than Britain that has led the English poetry of our age, even if recently it has shown signs of falling back. It is equally no accident – as Davie was fond of pointing out – that modernism was responsible for a resurgence of verse translation as a major art, including (as on the whole it had not in previous eras) the translation of contemporary work in minority languages. These diverse phenomena have immeasurably expanded the range of 'English poetry', such that the blinkered concentration on the home-grown product encouraged by certain British poets must be seen as wilfully constricting.

This is not to argue that the home-grown product has ceased to be of interest or that one of the world's most impressive and durable traditions has come to an end. Nor is it to deny virtue to the local or provincial. It is noteworthy that modernism produced as many regional writers (MacDiarmid, Bunting) as international ones (Eliot, Pound), and it is characteristic of Davie that he sees no conflict between internationalism in the arts (or in his life) and his own emotions as an English patriot; no conflict either between English patriotism and local devotion to his native Yorkshire. On the contrary, his regional feelings provoke sympathy in him for those of others – for Roy Fisher's Birmingham, Thomas Hardy's Dorset or, elsewhere, Yvor Winters's California.

Thomas Hardy and British Poetry begins with the proposition

> that in British poetry of the last fifty years (as not in American) the most far-reaching influence, for good or ill, has been not Yeats, still less Eliot or Pound, not Lawrence, but *Hardy*.

The sense of having surprised himself which Davie's sentence enacts is a reflection, perhaps, on himself and his own poetry. One cannot avoid noticing – in Davie's quarrels with Hardy, Englishness and provincialism

— the shadow of some quarrel with himself. The literary aspect of that quarrel would appear to be near the surface. On the one hand, there is Davie the deliberate reactionary, the apostle of the Movement and admirer of Yvor Winters, who opposes reason and formal order to the dishevelments of 1940s neo-Romanticism. On the other, there is the champion of Ezra Pound, who is willing to contemplate the farthest reaches of modern experiment – who will speak up for American Objectivists such as Carl Rakosi and Lorine Niedecker or British post-modernists such as J.H. Prynne and Douglas Oliver. A chronological study of Davie's books might suggest that the reactionary steadily gave ground to the experimentalist, as the cautious 1950s turned into the daring 1960s. But closer examination of the early work reveals that the contradiction – if that is what it is – was there from the start and never went away. Moreover, far from being a flaw in Davie's intellectual system, this conflict is his greatest single strength. For of course, it is only the neurotically closed-minded who assume that nothing of value is attainable in whichever tradition they have decided to oppose. What is more, it's in the nature of things that what appear contraries often turn out to have more in common than they seemed to do at first. In his Conclusion to the Hardy volume, for instance, Davie movingly links himself with both Hardy and Pound as lovers of the hard and unchanging, lovers of stone, conservatives.

But it is Hardy who most often focuses the tension Davie felt in himself; and this is as much a matter of personal temperament as it is of poetry, as much a political issue as a critical one. It would therefore be as well at this juncture to reflect on Davie's background. He was born in industrial West Yorkshire in 1922. His family, wonderfully evoked in his memoir *These the Companions* (1982), was of modest social status, lower middle class, but, living in a largely working-class and Labour-voting area, proudly and stubbornly Tory. What they shared with their working-class neighbours, however, was a preference for religious non-conformity, as against the established church, which Conservative voters normally tend to favour. Despite his Cambridge education and subsequent academic distinction, despite his travels all over the world, despite his conversion in middle age to Anglicanism, Davie remained in temperament a northern Dissenter of Tory instincts and sympathies: a loyalist with a taste for rebellion and plain speaking.[1] That certainly defines the tone of his criticism: the tone of a man who is ready to convey certain blunt home-truths his compatriots may find discomforting.

Not much of this is likely to remind us, at first sight, of Thomas

---

1   The contradictions ran even deeper than this suggests. In practice he almost invariably voted Liberal and, though in the 1970s he joined the Anglican Communion, he did so via the non-established Episcopal Church of America, feeling a 'need to envisage [his] church as in tension with the state'.

xii   *With the Grain*

Hardy, for Hardy was a southerner, a countryman, an atheist of Anglican sympathies and a liberal humanist. Yet he too took on the role of awkward outsider and preacher of home-truths. He was also of modest social origins and deeply connected with a distinctive English region, a fact which never prevented him from contemplating the common human lot or from absorbing the literatures of other tongues. The most glaring difference between the two men would appear to be that between rural and industrial England. It is therefore one of the most striking features of Davie's book that he identifies Hardy the craftsman as a sort of industrial engineer and apostle of self-help: a rustic, no doubt, but also a child of the Victorian age, who saw his own social advancement in terms of the new industrial era and its new kind of achievement. This insight of Davie's – unlikely to have come from a rural writer or a metropolitan one – gives him access to qualities in Hardy that others of Davie's generation – Larkin, for instance – may have responded to on a less conscious level. At any rate, it is through this (in effect) enlargement of Hardy's range that Davie is able to trace his influence as a subterranean current running through much of modern English poetry and affecting the work of poets as various as Auden and Prynne, Lawrence and Roy Fisher.

Looking back over Davie's work, one can now see that a book on Hardy was inevitable, for Hardy is from the outset a persistent point of reference. His balancing point of reference is Ezra Pound, about whom Davie wrote two full-length studies: *Ezra Pound: Poet as Sculptor* (1964) and *Pound* (1975). In the latter, Davie makes much of Pound's brief correspondence with Hardy, whose work Pound evidently valued greatly. There is certainly a case for seeing Pound and Hardy as natural allies, with their shared respect for what Davie once called 'the irreducible Otherness of the non-human world... its being bodied against the senses'. This sets both poets, Davie has argued, against the symbolizing inwardness of Yeats and Eliot, neither of whom had much to say for Hardy. But for some readers this is to miss the more obvious distinction. For them, Hardy was the last great poet to have been unequivocally and uncompli-catedly part of a native English tradition. Many indeed, to Davie's exasperation, regard the Hardy current as a uniquely English one that, despite the modernist revolution, flows through such poets as Graves and Edward Thomas to surface in the work of Philip Larkin. To those who take this view, Pound is the most extreme representative of the international diversion the native line evades. What for Davie is an irrevocable change, brought about by the facts of modern life as much as by any poet's personality, is for Larkin and his supporters a betrayal of deep roots. Modernism, in Larkin's view, destroyed 'the strong connection between poetry and the reading public that had been forged by Kipling, Housman, Brooke and *Omar Khayyam*'. This is an attitude that disregards the Poundian insistence that poetry should be a learned art, that it should acknowledge its position among the other arts, and that it should consciously participate in what Eliot called 'the mind of Europe'. It may be that Pound acknowledges a world independent of his own imaginings, but he does so in a poetry that makes extreme demands on the intelligence, devotion and seriousness of the reader. In this he has been much more evidently followed by his fellow Americans than by the British, who, in preferring Hardy, are willingly accepting that poetry is (in Peter Porter's words) 'a modest art'. What Davie calls the 'diminished expectations' of modern British poetry cannot be blamed on Hardy exactly, but Hardy is the poet whose example appears to justify them.

As the early chapters of *Thomas Hardy and British Poetry* make clear, the poetry of 'diminished expectations' was something Davie the poet, at an early stage in his career, consciously opted for. It was, as he explains, a response to the horrors of the Second World War and the disastrously misjudged politics of the great modernists. Yet with his awareness of the poet's high calling, it was hard to settle for such reduced objectives. The compromise clearly irked him. He returns again and again throughout his life to Pound's ambitions for poetry and their connection in his case with an illusory and, in the outcome, brutally destructive politics. At the same time, there is a longing in Davie for some way of recovering that option. Hardy, in Davie's account of him, had a realistic understanding of the possibilities for poetry in the modern world, and he had a humaner sympathy with that world than the more ambitious of his junior contemporaries. But something other than realism and humane sympathy are called for in the artist; it is not a realistic understanding of modern circumstance that makes a great modern consciousness. Something less prudential, less resigned and more ruthless is required. The virtues we admire in one another as people, especially in modern democratic societies, are not necessarily the virtues that make for great art.

This awareness lies behind one of Davie's finest poems, 'To a Brother in the Mystery', which was first published in 1960. This poem, as Davie tells us in a note, explores his relationship with Charles Tomlinson and may be taken as in some sense addressed to him. In it he imagines Tomlinson and himself as medieval sculptors carving the foliate ornament for a cathedral chapter-house. He praises his fellow-artist's passion for the non-human – in the terms of the poem, for leaves and stone – and contrasts that passion with his own more human concerns. He acknowledges the influence of his friend's work on his own, at the same time noticing how 'the debt incurred' is 'Not all on the one side'. This leads him to warn the friend (Tomlinson, in effect) to be wary of his (Davie's) influence – not to be seduced by his humanity:

> And yet, take care: this cordial knack bereaves
> The mind of all its sympathy with leaves,

Even with stone. I would not take away
From your peculiar mastery, if I say
A sort of coldness is the core of it,
A sort of cruelty; that prerequisite
Perhaps I rob you of, and in exchange give
What? Vulgarity's prerogative,
Indulgence towards the frailties it indulges,
Humour called 'wryness' that acknowledges
Its own complicity.

Davie had just castigated the Movement poets for the 'wryness' and 'complicity' so characteristic of their poetry – his own as much as Larkin's or Amis's. This was in an essay called 'Remembering the Movement' (1959), which should now be read alongside a review of Charles Tomlinson's *Seeing is Believing* published a few months earlier. He praises Tomlinson for his sensuous alertness while objecting to 'irony' and 'social adaptiveness' in the Movement – both ways (as he saw it) of protecting writer and reader from the harsh glare of reality. If such devices, Davie suggests, defend us against 'cruelty', they also hold off the intensities of apprehension we associate with the greatest poetry. The critique is developed in the Hardy book when Davie distinguishes between the ironic stance of the writer towards reality, essentially self-insulating, and cosmic irony, 'the stance of reality as it confronts us'. Hardy's wholly justifiable preoccupation with the latter has been translated by Auden, Larkin and others into the former, Davie argues, and the result has been dilution, poetry as social compromise. It is against this that he sets what appears in Tomlinson an indifference to humanity and the human:

You, I fear,
Will find you bought humanity too dear
At the price of some light leaves, if you begin
To find your handling of them growing thin,
Insensitive, brittle. For the common touch,
Though it warms, coarsens. Never care so much
For leaves or people, but you care for stone
A little more. The medium is its own
Thing, and not all a medium, but the stuff
Of mountains; cruel, obdurate, and rough.

In so far as Davie's sculptors are poets in disguise, we must take it that stone stands for language, the poet's medium. In that case, leaves are the objects the language addresses, the 'outward and non-human things' which, Davie insists, are apprehended by the good poet 'crisply for their own sakes'. One of the great failings of the Movement, in Davie's view, was its apparent indifference to mere things. Behind such indifference he perceives an 'imperiousness towards the non-human [that] goes along with the excessive humility towards the human represented by the reader'. Charles Tomlinson, with his belief in the moral value of accurate sensation, seemed to offer Davie a way out of the Movement without betraying the principles that had led him there in the first place. For Tomlinson shared many Movement attitudes: repulsion from what he called the 'Freudian swamp' of 1940s neo-Romanticism and a commitment to verbal precision as the literary equivalent of personal responsibility. At the same time, he scorned the provincialism and occasional xenophobia of certain Movement poets. He had come to many of his convictions by foreign routes, many of them American, many European. Importantly, his American masters had all been Modernists and most of them were in one way or another followers of Ezra Pound. It must have been partly with Tomlinson's assistance that Davie drew his passion for Pound's verse closer to his own practice. In much the same way, Tomlinson's skills as a translator and his exploitation of various European models must have helped Davie absorb the work of Boris Pasternak, in many ways the key influence on his poetry of the 1960s.

Seeing is Believing was published in 1959. Subsequent books of Tomlinson's, notably *The Way In* (1974), extended the 'natural piety' of his early work to a world of industrial wastelands and mass production. But it cannot be said that he did more than modify the force of those youthful poems. The major contemporary challenge for Davie surprisingly came from a very much older man. Basil Bunting (1900–85) was rediscovered by the young poets of the 1960s, whose enthusiasm for the Beats and the Black Mountain school had led them to the less celebrated permutations of modernist experiment. Bunting was a disciple of Pound's, one of the two 'strugglers in the desert' to whom the master had dedicated his *Active Anthology*, but, unlike most Poundians, an Englishman. For Davie he had a further personal interest. He was a northerner, a provincial very much at odds with the metropolis, and in his religious background a Quaker – which is to say, another sort of Dissenter. His masterpiece, the long poem *Briggflatts*, was published in 1966 when he was already an elderly man. To many readers it had come as a sort of revelation: a major poem in the modernist tradition, wholly original, extremely English and appearing in the post-war era. It exhibited all the qualities Davie hoped for in contemporary poetry, confirming his critical stance and satisfying many of his deep personal needs. Thus, Bunting was rooted in his native Northumbria, yet having spent most of his life abroad, was free of provincialism and insularity. He was learned in music and visual art, both of which provided him with models for his writing: an approach which, following Pound, Davie had constantly argued for. *Briggflatts* sparkles with a sense of the world's multitudinous particularity, of things existing independently of human wants, not merely exploited for the poet's expressive needs. Yet it does not rest in its objects: it is a poem of great inwardness – about memory, guilt, rootedness and love. The natural processes it evokes are instances of universal laws and, as Davie came increasingly to believe, it includes a profound and searching metaphysic, indeed an unconventionally Christian insight into the invisible meanings of reality. This last point has been much disputed, but no one would disagree with Davie's account of Bunting's stylistic achievement: that the poem is intensely compressed – more so than most of Pound or Eliot – but that this economy is achieved, by and large, without violence to orthodox syntax. This modification to the Poundian programme appealed greatly to Davie with his respect for language as stone, an intractable substance whose grain must be observed and respected.

It is therefore no accident that this book includes as many as five articles on Bunting. *Briggflatts*, Davie contends in one of them, 'is where English poetry has got to, it is what English poets must assimilate and go on from'. The case is forcefully made but it has not been notably heeded. The exigencies of the publishing market and the unshakable complacency of academies have meant that Bunting's reputation is smaller today that it was when Davie set down that contention. Nevertheless, it provides a sort of prophetic climax to Davie's critical *oeuvre* and the force of the argument remains as compelling now as it did when those words were written in 1977.

Thomas Hardy and British Poetry was written in California. It is perhaps a commonplace that writers who expatriate themselves always return in thought and imagination to the scenes and situations with which they were once intimate. It is therefore not surprising that when Davie accepted a professorship at Stanford University, he soon turned his thoughts to the condition of British poetry and, through that, to the condition of Britain. This was in 1969 and the decision to join the 'brain drain' had been provoked less by the handsome salary than by a determination to go into voluntary exile. Five years earlier, his mood had been somewhat different. Then, forty-two years old and the rising star of the Cambridge English Faculty, Davie had been appointed to his first Chair at the new University of Essex. This was more than a wise career move. He had been offered the chance to create his own Faculty: it was to be a school of literature in which many of his enthusiasms and convictions were shaped into a single discipline. An interest in other arts and other languages was assumed – the study of poetry in translation, for instance, played a significant role, as never before in a British university. It was in effect a department of comparative literature, with the important difference that the practice and craft of writing were attended to and in a manner assuming that no single literary language possessed a monopoly of human wisdom and perception. To give substance to this aspect of the programme, writers in residence, many of them from abroad, played their part in the teaching: this again was a wholly new departure.

Davie was not a natural administrator and he was never again to accept so executive a role, but he relished the opportunity to build this new idea. In the year after his appointment, he committed himself still further by becoming the University's Pro-Vice-Chancellor. These were the early years of Harold Wilson's Labour government and, anti-socialist though he was, Davie was not out of sympathy with certain aspects of the government's outlook. He was in important ways a progressive and relished the chance to play his part in what Wilson saw as the modernization of Britain: the establishment of alternatives to the ancient universities, particularly in the undervalued provinces; the association of those alternatives with a radically modern architecture; the opportunity to free Britain from its circumscribing nostalgias and illusions. This was to be an institution that faced up to the simple fact, apparently so painful to many British citizens, that theirs was a country that for well over a century had been wholly dependent on manufacture and technology, yet one which consistently portrayed itself – in its poetry as in its popular mythology – as a green and pleasant land, the home of pastoral dreams and possibilities. Hand in hand with this illusion went another, as deeply engrained, that Britain cut much the same figure in the modern world as she had in the days of imperial supremacy and therefore had no need to attend to her allies and competitors. In his criticism Davie constantly returns to the ludicrous chauvinism so readily displayed by many of his fellow-countrymen and to the attenuation this has brought to what is otherwise recognised as one of the world's great literatures.

I stress the radicalism of Davie's approach because he is now very widely, and understandably, associated with a reactionary outlook. His instincts, as he reflects in the Hardy book, were for stability rather than reaction. With all the emotions of a patriot, he was determined that he and the art he loved should inhabit a real world rather than an illusion. (It is a curious fact that much the same motive lay behind his attacks, in his last years, on post-modernism: a tendency which understands literature as the product of desire and fantasy rather than truth and reality.) He was also, like his master Ezra Pound, fundamentally an optimist, who believed that well-rooted institutions and traditions could always be improved and made more productive, provided the will was there.

But at Essex, it seemed, the will was not there. Any educational innovator might expect opposition from hidebound colleagues. The surprise was that it came from the radical students. When student rebellion exploded across the world in the late 1960s, it made no fine distinctions between conservative and liberal, reactionary and progressive. These were the days of Herbert Marcuse and 'repressive tolerance': to the revolutionary young, the compromises of meliorists were merely subtler versions of the various hypocrisies behind which oppressive power concealed itself. Student revolt in Britain, widespread though it was, was rarely as alarming as in France or the United States. The University of Essex was one of two exceptions that proved that rule and, as Pro-Vice-Chancellor, Davie bore the brunt of the attack. That was painful enough. What was still more so, however, was the irrelevance of liberal education to the conflict. He was promoting progressive ideas, to which the rebels were indifferent. He acted on the principle of academic freedom, when they were determined to silence anyone touched by what they saw as repressive power. He believed there could be no knowledge or learning without authority; they regarded *all* authority as oppressive.

For Davie in those Essex years, the vandalism of the young seemed to conspire, not only with the pusillanimity of others in authority, but with the older and more widespread illusions of British society at large – the insularity, the philistinism, the sentimentality. 'England is a country,' he had written some years earlier, 'where even the poets are philistines without knowing it.' For a patriot, such confirmations of that earlier insight were anything but welcome. The consequent despair is almost certainly what lies behind the extraordinary 'Epistle' with which this volume concludes. Once these different strands are brought together, one can see it as almost inevitable that, when Davie was settled in California, he would need to reflect on the British attitude to authority and the elements that combine to form a culture of illusion.

Davie taught at Stanford for ten years. He then moved to Nashville. Tennessee, for a professorship at Vanderbilt University. For him and his family, these must have been years of relative ease and affluence, yet a tone of exasperation becomes frequent in his writing. His patriotism, in particular, nagged at him. As his publisher, the poet Michael Schmidt, has pointed out, there are two kinds of literary expatriate: those like Davie's friend and ally Thom Gunn, who sink into their new setting without regret for the old; and those like Davie, whose contentment is qualified by anxiety for the homeland. A number of essays from the 1970s, mostly polemical in tone; his advocacy of an older and intensely political poet, C.H. Sisson; his involvement with Schmidt and Sisson in the foundation of *PN Review*: all these suggest a preoccupation with the British body politic and its cultural effects. The more overtly political of his writings, in my judgement, suffer from the coarsening of tone that is the hallmark of the conservative driven against his will towards reaction. In many of them, whether in verse or prose, one has the sense of a writer angry with his native land, yet no longer as intimate with its doings as he might be. This is not to suggest a decline. On the contrary, much of Davie's best work belongs to these years, as the present collection perhaps bears witness, but the work is more uneven overall, and the impression some-times made – of irascibility, of puritanical gloom, of rigidity – is not true to the man as he really was.

He retired from Vanderbilt in 1988. After twenty mostly profitable years in the United States, he was none the less anxious to return to England and happy to stay put, for the most part, in the attractive Devon village of Silverton, where he and his wife Doreen had for many years owned a cottage. For the first part of his retirement, he proved as prolific as ever. In 1989 he published *Under Briggflatts*, the first volume of his Collected Works; it is a book to be read in conjunction with the present volume. In the same year appeared the most experimental of his books of verse, *To Scorch or Freeze*, a collection of religious meditations taking their bearings from the Psalms and, technically speaking, from Pound's *Cantos*. These were followed by *The Eighteenth-Century Hymn in England* (1993) and, posthumously, an anthology *The Psalms in English* (1996). With the publication of *To Scorch or Freeze*, it seemed to him that his career as a poet was over, yet when his *Collected Poems* (1990) appeared as a volume in the Collected Works, it included forty-three uncollected poems and, at his death, it was still possible to assemble a new book, *Poems and Melodramas* (1996). For most of this period, Davie was also productive as reviewer and essayist – some of what he wrote appears in the present volume – but by the mid-1990s his health had begun to fail and his consequent loss in mobility encouraged an inclination to despondency. Attacks on 'junk culture' and sexual depravity appeared in his letters and assaults on post-modernism in *PN Review* and other periodicals. But he was not an innately gloomy man and a temporary reprieve from illness in 1995 was accompanied by an uplift in his spirits and something like his old pattern of literary production, culminating in the finest of his religious poems, the sequence 'Our Father'. Shortly afterwards, however, cancer was unexpectedly diagnosed and he died within weeks of the news.

In a poem of the mid-1950s, 'Rejoinder to a Critic', Davie confronts a question that often recurs in his writings and which lies at the heart of *Thomas Hardy and British Poetry*. 'You may be right,' he begins to his interlocutor: 'How can I dare to feel?' and he goes on to argue that, in the era since the Second World War, no artist can claim the right to impose his personal feelings on other people:

> 'Alas, alas, who's injured by my love?'
> And recent history answers: Half Japan!
> Not love, but hate? Well, both are versions of
> The 'feeling' that you dare me to... Be dumb!
> Appear concerned only to make it scan!
> How dare we now be anything but numb?

Davie's combination of 'numb' rationality, technical precision, moral qualms and a distaste for the bohemian led imperceptive critics to imagine he not only dared not feel but could not. In his finest book of verse, the

Essex Poems of 1969, he confronted the problem again:

> The practice of an art
> is to convert all terms
> into the terms of art.
> By the end of the third stanza
> death is a smell no longer;
> it is a problem of style.
> A man who ought to know me
> wrote in a review
> my emotional life was meagre.
>
> ['July, 1964']

That problem of style – worried over to some profit in 'The Rhetoric of Emotion' (1972) – masks the personality of the poet writing the poem. It is right, and indeed necessary, that this should be so. If it were not, the making of art would become what naive persons seem to want it to be, the infliction of personality on the public. But art does not exist to prove that artists feel. It exists to enlarge our understanding and extend our sympathies, and to that end the artist must – to borrow some formulations from T.S. Eliot - sacrifice himself, escape from his personality. It is not always easy or even possible to do so, but the attempt is part and parcel of the creative process. In making this attempt, Davie seems to have obscured the fact – evident to his friends and to anyone who has read his books at all thoroughly – that he was a man of intense emotion and, therefore, immensely vulnerable. His warmth and loyalty made him, like most emotional people, prone to anger, contempt and even prejudice. It is necessary to see that his impatience with England derives from his love of it; that his need for external hardness, as he says in the poem 'Across the Bay', is the need of someone inwardly susceptible; that he values rationality and decorum with the passion of a man who knows they protect him from the pain of too much feeling. These fundamental tensions may account for the contradictions, the paradoxes, the internal arguments that characterize his critical work and for the occasions of misplaced rage and impatience, the failures of balanced judgement. But without these flaws and failures, there would be no heart to the matter. Re-reading the writings I have collected here, I am struck by the discipline which, despite the strains, gives balance and coherence to his thought, such that an insight from 1995 can complement one from 1955. But I also recognize that what holds me to Davie is the engagement that underpins his words. Without that engagement he would not seem – as he increasingly does in these few years since his death – the indispensable thinker about poetry of the later twentieth century.

CLIVE WILMER
Cambridge, 1998

I

Hardy's Virgilian Purples

Among Hardy's 'Poems 1912–13', there is 'Beeny Cliff', with below that title the dates, 'March 1870–March 1913':

i.

O the opal and the sapphire of that wandering western sea,
And the woman riding high above with bright hair flapping free –
The woman whom I loved so, and who loyally loved me.

ii.

The pale mews plained below us, and the waves seemed far away
In a nether sky, engrossed in saying their ceaseless babbling say,
As we laughed light-heartedly aloft on that clear-sunned March day.

iii.

A little cloud then cloaked us, and there flew an irised rain,
And the Atlantic dyed its levels with a dull misfeatured stain,
And then the sun burst out again, and purples prinked the main.

iv.

– Still in all its chasmal beauty bulks old Beeny to the sky,
And shall she and I not go there once again now March is nigh,
And the sweet things said in that March say anew there by and by?

v.

What if still in chasmal beauty looms that wild weird western shore,
The woman now is – elsewhere – whom the ambling pony bore,
And nor knows nor cares for Beeny, and will laugh there nevermore.

The poem has many features that are disconcerting to current taste – notably the unabashed *bravura* of alliteration, and the elaborately cunning metre. (The poem is in septenaries, but they are very artfully masked, especially near the start.) However, for present purposes, a single phrase in the poem will give us quite enough trouble to be going on with, and quite enough entertainment. I mean the five words in the third stanza, 'and purples prinked the main'. It is characteristic audacity: from the imperial splendour of 'purples' we are required, with 'prinks', to sidle through a boudoir or an aviary on our way to the no less imperial vastness of 'the main'. Such strenuousness is typical of Hardy. But not all his audacities are successful, he is not always strenuous to some purpose. And if we look for his purpose here, we are led far afield.

J.O. Bailey says, 'Hardy's description in the poem is accurate.'[1] And those who have visited Beeny will agree. In particular the rendering of the shifting tones as the little rain-squall passes over is recognizably from the same hand as scrupulously registered appearances in a notebook in 1872: 'August: At Beeny Cliff... green towards the land, blue-black towards the sea. Every ledge has a little, starved, green grass upon it: all vertical parts bare. Seaward, a dark-grey ocean beneath a pale green sky, upon which lie branches of red cloud...' And so we ask: could a slate-blue cliff under certain rainbow conditions cast a shadow so as to colour the sea at its foot in various shades of purple? Straining more than a little, we can just envisage how this might be so, can just about summon up the sense-impression which 'purples' seems to register. But in that case 'prink' confronts us just as startlingly as ever; and 'the main' necessarily invokes not the patch of the sea at a cliff's base but on the contrary, very insistently, the oceanic expanse of the Atlantic stretching to the horizon. And thus it is not enough merely to cite the Preface (1895) to *A Pair of Blue Eyes*, where Hardy evokes the same area, Beeny Cliff and its Cornish vicinity: 'The place is pre-eminently (for one person at least) the region of dream and mystery. The ghostly birds, the pall-like sea, the frothy wind, the eternal soliloquy of the waters, the bloom of dark purple cast, that seems to exhale from the shoreward precipices, in themselves lend to the scene an atmosphere like the twilight of a night vision.' If we are still looking for accurate register of sense-impressions, the 'bloom of dark purple cast', in this crepuscular scene where the sea is 'pall-like', does not help us at all with what the sea looked like on a clear-sunned day in March; and in any case this purple is not a shadow cast by the cliff but a bloom that seemed to exhale from it. The longer we look at this piece of prose, the more we realize that it is further from straightforward description than the verse is.

And yet the answer to the riddle is indeed in *A Pair of Blue Eyes*. For we read in chapter XXI of that novel another account of Beeny: 'What gave an added terror to its height was its blackness. And upon this dark face the beating of ten thousand west winds had formed a kind of bloom, which had a visual effect not unlike that of a Hambro' grape. Moreover it seemed to float off into the atmosphere, and inspire terror through the lungs.' This makes it plain that the purple of Beeny Cliff is on the one hand 'a visual effect' (the cliff-face *is* purple or purplish – as indeed it is), but on the other hand, in terms of what Beeny does to its ambience of sea and sky and land and the people who move there, the purple is not a

1 J.O. Bailey, *The Poetry of Thomas Hardy: A Handbook and Commentary* (Chapel Hill, 1970), p. 302.

visual effect at all (in, for instance, any shadow which the cliff casts upon the sea), but is spiritual – a seeming, a floating off, an exhalation; something which may at times inspire terror, at other times the quite different feelings that go along with 'prink'. And what those feelings might be we learn from chapter IV of the novel, where Hardy describes the effect made on a young man (such as Hardy was when he first met Emma Gifford, and in Beeny's vicinity) by Elfride, the heroine, who is physically very like Emma, as Hardy himself pointed out:[2] 'She looked so intensely *living* and full of movement as she came into the old silent place, that young Smith's world began to be lit by "the purple light" in all its definiteness.' This clinches it: the purples which prink the main as seen from Beeny Cliff are the spiritual light of sexual love – as indeed we should have guessed, for what but sexual passion is so likely to terrify and irradiate alternately or at the one time?

However, this is only the beginning. For the purple light which begins to irradiate the world of Stephen Smith is offered to us inside quotation-marks. Where is it quoted from? It is not hard to guess if we consider *A Pair of Blue Eyes* as a whole; if we note for instance, in chapter IX, that 'perhaps Stephen's manners, like the feats of Euryalus, owed their attractiveness in her eyes rather to the attractiveness of his person than to their own excellence'; or observe, in chapter XII, how the fingers of Elfride's step-mother 'were literally stiff with rings, *signis auroque rigentes*, like Helen's robe';[3] or if we envisage, in chapter XIV, 'Elfride, who like Aeneas at Carthage, was full of admiration for the brilliant scene'. This early novel is interlarded profusely with allusions to Virgil's *Aeneid*. And sure enough that is where the purple light comes from, from *Aeneid*, vi. 641: 'largior hic campos aether et lumine vestit / purpureo, solemque suum, sua sidera norunt'. Virgil's *purpureus* there is glossed by William Smith in his Latin-English Dictionary (19th ed., 1888) as 'brilliant, beautiful'. In fact, it is the 'purple' of Pope's *Pastorals* ('Spring', I. 28): 'And lavish Nature paints the Purple Year', on which Warburton notes in his edition (1751) '... used in the Latin sense, of the brightest, most vivid colouring in general, not of that peculiar tint so called.'

This is Hardy's 'purple', not just in *A Pair of Blue Eyes* and 'Beeny Cliff', but consistently. It is for instance the purple of 'The Revisitation', first published in August, 1904:

As I lay awake at night-time
In an ancient country barracks known to ancient cannoneers
And recalled the hopes that heralded each seeming brave and bright time
Of my primal purple years...;

2   Ibid., p. 303.
3   *Aeneid*, I, 648.

as also of 'The Change', dated 'Jan–Feb 1913':

> Out of the past there rises a week −
> Who shall read the years O! −
> Out of the past there rises a week
> Enringed with a purple zone.

And we realize that it was not any cartographer's colouring that Hardy had in mind, when he wrote in 'The Place on the Map', published 1913:

> I look upon the map that hangs by me −
> Its shires and towns and rivers lined in varnished artistry −
> And I mark a jutting height
> Coloured purple, with a margin of blue sea.

(The 'height' is either Beeny, if the poem is about Emma, or Portland, if it is about Tryphena.) So too in *The Woodlanders* (chapter XXIV), a woman reflects: 'But what an attenuation this cold pride was of the dream of her youth, in which she had pictured herself walking in state towards the altar, flushed by the purple light and bloom of her own passion…'[4] All these purples, we now realize, are Virgilian.

Which ought to remind us, if we hark back to where we started from, that 'Beeny Cliff' belongs in a sequence of poems that bears a Virgilian epigraph. We have been unaccountably reluctant to inquire what Hardy meant by this, and what bearing the epigraph has upon the poems which, as it were, it sponsors. Of recent commentators J. Hillis Miller has come nearest to grasping the nettle, and yet all he says is this:

> The epigraph for the whole group of poems is *Veteris vestigia flammae*: 'ashes of an old fire'. The phrase comes from *The Aeneid* (IV. 23), where it is part of Dido's statement that the love she once felt for her now dead husband is about to renew itself for Aeneas. Her love for Aeneas is of course doomed to end in separation and leads to her suicide. There is a complex relation between Hardy's poems about his dead wife and Vergil's story of Dido's betrayal by Aeneas. The analogy involves not only Dido's feelings for her dead husband, Sychaeus, but also the relation of Aeneas to Dido after her death. As Aeneas confronts in Book VI of *The Aeneid* the mute unforgiving ghost of Dido, so Hardy in the poems glimpses the voiceless ('After a Journey', *CP*, 328) ghost of his dead wife.[5]

This raises many more questions than it answers. For instance if in 'After a Journey' the ghost is voiceless, in 'The Haunter' she is a chatterbox, and in 'The Voice' she is 'calling'. Again, if we recall that Hardy in 1913 was

---

4   I owe this example, and some others, to Mrs Drew Cox.
5   J. Hillis Miller, *Thomas Hardy: Distance and Desire* (London, 1970), pp. 248–9.

presumably already attached to Florence Emily Dugdale, whom he was to take as his second wife in the next year, the 'complex relation' would work out: Hardy equals Dido; Emma equals Sychaeus; Florence Emily equals Aeneas. (We have already seen the sexes thus switched when Elfride in *A Pair of Blue Eyes* was said to be 'like Aeneas at Carthage'.) One thing certainly the epigraph supplies – an understanding of sexual passion as one undifferentiated energy running wild, fastening itself seemingly at random on this person or that one, and switching itself from one to another in a way that makes nonsense of all human vows of constancy. This is the classical and terrible conception which Racine recovered for later ages when he made Phèdre cry out, in appalled awareness of her own condition, 'C'est Vénus tout entiére á sa proie attachée'. And it is Hardy's conception also, as we can see from poem after poem and story after story. We must stop thinking of his classicism as no more than skin-deep, or as (worse still) the pathetic pretentiousness of the self-educated. J. Hillis Miller hurries us into *Aeneid* Book VI, but the striking thing is that Hardy goes for his epigraph not to Book VI (nor to Book II, where Aeneas meets the ghost of his first wife, Creusa)[6] but to the altogether more ambivalent and disturbing passage in Book IV. And this I shall return to.

As we have seen, however, it is indeed in Book VI that we find 'the purple light'. It comes more than a hundred and fifty lines later than Dido's celebrated silence when she turns from Aeneas towards the shade of Sychaeus. Aeneas has now penetrated the underworld as far as the abode of the blest, where he is to encounter the shade that he came to seek, his father Anchises:

> devenere locos laetos et amoena virecta
> fortunatorum nemorum sedesque beatas.
> largior hic campos aether et lumine vestit
> purpureo, solemque suum, sua sidera norunt.

William Morris in 1876 had rendered the lines:

> They came into a joyous land, and greensward fair and sweet
> Amid the happiness of groves, the blessed dwelling-place.
> Therein a more abundant heaven clothes all the meadows' face
> With purple light, and their own sun and their own moon they have.

---

6   See especially, with 'After a Journey' in mind, *Aeneid*, II, 793–4.

> *ter frustra comprensa manus effugit imago,*
> *par levibus ventis volucrique simillima somno.*

In Dryden:

> And thrice about her neck my arms I flung,
> And thrice deceived, on vain embraces hung;
> Or as a blast of wind, she rushed away.

Dryden gives, in that translation which Hardy's remarkable mother gave
to her son when he was eight years old:

> These holy rites performed, they took their way,
> Where long extended plains of pleasure lay.
> The verdant fields with those of heaven may vie,
> With ether vested, and a purple sky –
> The blissful seats of happy souls below:
> Stars of their own, and their own suns, they know.

But it is Robert Bridges's version which, grotesque though it is in both
diction and metre, rams home the fact that what Virgil is speaking of here
is not anything that can be dismissed as fanciful hyperbole:

> They came out on a lonely pleasance, that dream'd-of oasis,
> Fortunat isle, the abode o' the blest, their fair Happy Woodland.
> Here is an ampler sky, those meads ar' azur'd by a gentler
> Sun than th' Earth, an' a new starworld their darkness adorneth.[7]

Virgil's *purpureus* describes a light that is not any terrestrial light, however
preternaturally radiant and keen; it is preternatural through and through,
the light of an alternative cosmos, lit by another sun by day and other stars
by night. And it is this light, no other, that Hardy, agnostic and scientific
humanist, claimed to see from Beeny Cliff when 'purples prinked the
main'.

The unavoidable question is whether we can dismiss the matter as
hyperbole any more in Hardy's poem than we can in Virgil's. To put it
another way (a way that incidentally makes hyperbole more of a life-and-
death matter than we normally take it to be), do those 'purples' exist in a
psychological reality, or a metaphysical one? I am prepared to suggest that
this is the question that Hardy asks himself, and wrestles with, all through
'Poems of 1912–13'.

For consider: *veteris vestigia flammae*, sounding out of Virgil, had awakened other echoes in the poetry of Europe before the sound carried to
Thomas Hardy. In Canto XXX of the *Purgatorio* the pilgrim at last sees
Beatrice, the lode-star of all his pilgrimage. Overwhelmed, he turns to
share his transport, and with whom but Virgil, who has so far instructed
and protected him at every stage?

> volsimi alla sinistra col rispitto
> col quale il fantolin corre alla mamma
> quando ha paura o quando elli è afflitto,
> per dicere a Virgilio: 'Men che dramma
> di sangue m'è rimaso che non tremi:
> conosco i segni dell' antica fiamma'

7   Robert Bridges, *Ibant Obscuri* (Oxford, 1916).

The moment is superbly managed and poignant. For not only does the pilgrim find that Virgil, embodiment of pious and prudent reason, has at this moment withdrawn from him, ceding to the divinely inspired reason that is Beatrice; but the words which the pilgrim addresses to Virgil are Virgil's own, as the commentators do not fail to notice – *i segni dell' antica fiamma* is Dante's translation of *veteris vestigia flammae*. And so when Hardy meets the dead Emma in 'After a Journey', in the shadows which they cast not only does Aeneas meet the dead Dido but Dante meets the dead and transfigured Beatrice.

Because Hardy is as secretive and devious about his reading-habits as about his other habits and activities, there is I think no firm evidence that he ever read the *Purgatorio*. And yet it is inconceivable that he didn't. (After all, the reviewers had jeered at him for letting Tess Durbeyfield cite the *Inferno*.) And if Hardy knew the *Purgatorio* at least in Cary's translation, if he knew *i segni dell' antica fiamma* no less than *veteris vestigia flammae*, this vindicates us all over again in refusing to take the apparitions of the dead wife as no more than hyperbole, conventional machinery. The status of Emma's *being*, now that she is dead – more than ever this metaphysical question seems to be the question that the poems ask, and ask about.

Indeed, if we scan the pages that Erich Auerbach devotes to 'Dante's Early Poetry', one passage after another must strike us as applicable to Hardy's 'Poems of 1912–13' no less than to the poems of Dante. For instance:

> From the motif: my spirit often dwells with my dead beloved – a poet like Guinizelli would scarcely have made more than two lines; in order to write more, he would have had to move away from his point of departure, that is, from himself, and introduce something else, a related but new motif, perhaps a description of the condition of the departed, a message from her, in short an assortment of different elements. But when Dante's spirit wanders aloft, his vision of the event is all of a piece; there is nothing metaphoric about it; it is as though he were registering a real event in slow motion; the whole poem is a record of his spirit's ascent and return.[8]

Or again:

> Dante's whole striving is to intensify his feeling to the utmost by raising it above the sphere of subjectivity to which feeling is ordinarily confined... Even today we feel the power of this will, and the poem with all its unevenness still breathes the same magic. It is the magic

8   Erich Auerbach, *Dante als Dichter der iridschen Welt* (Berlin and Leipzig, 1929), translated by Ralph Manheim as *Dante, Poet of the Secular World* (Chicago and London, 1961) pp. 41–2. Subsequent quotations from this volume are from pp. 43–4, 44, 45.

exerted by Dante's passion for unity, by his striving to involve the whole cosmos in his own experience. The direction of his feeling is so definite that it cannot be deflected by the awkward rational order of the poem but operates, in the parts and in the whole, as a radiation of power, as a fiery enchantment.

Or:

he insists on being followed into the extreme particularity of the real situation that he conjures up. It would be inaccurate and perhaps unjust to say that his experience was stronger and more immediate than that of the earlier poets of the Middle Ages; and there is in his verses a considerable element of strain and exaggeration, which springs not from he prevailing taste but from his desire to express himself at any price. The truth is rather that the earlier poets tend to branch outward from their experience, to adduce, through association or logical connections, everything that is in any way related to the experience or likely to explain or ornament it metaphorically, whereas Dante holds firmly to his concrete point of departure and excludes everything else, whether alien, related, or similar. He never spreads himself thin but digs down.

And finally:

the composition of most of the poems has a cohesion and unity that may have seemed both bare and pedantic to the older generation. Seldom does one of the customary poetic ornaments appear; and when it does, it is not introduced with taste and charm, but is so immoderately exaggerated, so earnestly transposed into the realm of reality as to frighten and repel Dante's older contemporaries. By its insistence on the concrete, unique situation, by its unabashed disclosure of personal feeling, the poem takes on such an intensity that those who were not prepared to commit themselves with passion felt wounded and alarmed.

By 'one of the customary poetic ornaments… immoderately exaggerated', may we not understand that feature of 'Beeny Cliff' which we began by noting in a tone at once 'wounded and alarmed' – its *bravura* of alliteration?

However that may be, there is undoubtedly one respect in which Hardy stands closer to Dante than to Virgil. This is in his concern for locality and topography. The geography of Virgil's afterworld and other-world is vague (though it is true that his sense of the geography of southern Italy is not). On the other hand, Dante's afterworld – and particularly the mountain of Purgatory – is structured geographically very exactly indeed. As Auerbach says of *The Divine Comedy*,

In the eschatological sphere physics and ethics, or as we should say today, the natural and humane sciences, are no longer separate; here nature, too, is ordered by an ethical stand: and, the measure of its participation in divine Being, *every natural site has the ethical rank of the rational beings who dwell in it.* With that the meaning of landscape is defined. The vivid descriptions of landscape in which the great poem abounds are never autonomous or purely lyrical; true, they appeal directly to the reader's emotions, they arouse delight or horror; but the feelings awakened by the landscape are not allowed to seep away like vague romantic dreams, but forcefully recapitulated, for the landscape is nothing other than the appropriate scene or metaphorical symbol of human destiny.[9]

Whether we think of the landscape of the successive terraces on the purgatorial mount, or of the particular earthly terrains and catchment-areas which the dwellers on the terraces recall as soon as they are engaged in conversation, this is equally true – all the figures in Dante's poem tend to identify themselves by the landscapes which they inhabit now or have inhabited in their earthly past.

And so, if we say that the landscapes presented so insistently in 'Poems of 1912–13' are so many stations in a personal purgatory, we can mean something quite precise: we mean that each locality – and there are three of them, Dorset around Max Gate, Plymouth, and north Cornwall around Boscastle – is presented as the location, the haunt and habitat, of some one particular moral proclivity or principle. Max Gate is the land-scape of treason, Boscastle (Beeny Cliff, St Juliot) is the landscape of loyalty and love. (When Hardy says, in 'At Castle Boterel', that he will 'traverse old love's domain / Never again', he doesn't mean that he won't ever fall in love again, but that he won't come to Boscastle any more.) The half-way house of Plymouth is the questionable, the problematic location; but of that more in a moment. What is crucial is to realize that the Dantesque focus – by which 'every natural site has the ethical rank of the rational beings who dwell in it' – precludes not just the psychological analysis so brilliant in Meredith's *Modern Love*, but also any moral discrim-ination, any apportioning of blame between the two partners to a marriage that had gone disastrously wrong. Max Gate is simply the land-scape of treason; thereabouts he will betray her, she will betray him. North Cornwall is a landscape of loyalty; thereabouts he will be true to her, she will be true to him. The use of landscape is as starkly emblematic as that. The 'Poems of 1912–13' are sometimes said to be poems of remorse; through most of the sequence the chilling achievement is on the contrary that remorse is excluded from them. For remorse, and reproach also, are from the poet's point of view irrelevances; they only distract

9 Auerbach, op. cit. p. 95 (italics mine, for reasons that appear later).

from, and serve to obscure, the practice of Venus *à sa proie attachée*. Passion happens, Venus acts; and the ambivalence of her actions can be controlled only by locating the malevolence of her action in one place (Dorset) and its benevolence in another (Cornwall).

As for Plymouth, the problematical halfway house (where Emma grew up, where he promised to go visiting with her, but never did), Hardy does not take us there until late in the sequence, and then only that once. What J. Hillis Miller calls the 'wavelike pulsation of recovery and loss' through the sequence will no doubt be charted a little differently by each reader. To this one, the first sixteen poems rise very slowly from the desolation in which they start, at and around Max Gate. It is in the fifth poem, 'I found her out there', that the Cornish landscape first appears; and sure enough, it brings with it the first 'lift', the first movement towards recovery. This is in the 'maybe' of the last stanza:

> Yet her shade, maybe,
> Will creep underground
> Till it catch the sound
> Of that western sea
> As it swells and sobs
> Where she once domiciled,
> And joy in its throbs
> With the heart of a child.

(The grotesque literalness which sees, not Emma's spirit flitting to Cornwall, but her dead boy as it were *burrowing* thither, may strike us as genuinely Dantesque. For Hardy, resurrection must be of the body; as it would have to be for anyone who took location, in all its physicality, as seriously as Hardy did.) There follows a slump back. But the trough of renewed desolation ('Without Ceremony' and 'Lament') is quite soon over. 'The Haunter', in which the dead Emma assures the widower that she attends and listens, expresses a conviction that the first poems of the sequence had denied. In the next poem, 'The Voice' (which Bailey, on the strength of the 'air-blue gown', locates in Boscastle), the dead woman has found a voice which can carry to him – she is calling. But for a second time the flickers of hope are quenched, blasted by the landscape of Max Gate in 'His Visitor' and 'A Circular'. At this point, however, the pace quickens, through 'A Dream or No' to 'After a Journey', as this Aeneas plans and then undertakes his journey into the underworld. 'After a Journey' is a high point; though the ghost is voiceless, the man apprehends her meaning well enough, and the poem ends in an unprecedented serenity – naturally enough, for both are now firmly in the Cornish landscape of reciprocal loyalty, as Dido was when she turned to Sychaeus. Two poems later he has, with 'Beeny Cliff', penetrated the underworld or other-world as far as the abodes of the blest, as we have seen. The assurance and controlled excitement continue to mount, and 'At Castle Boterel' sees the poet making a measured affirmation: love triumphs over time. Only at this point, after five poems all set firmly in Cornwall, does the poet dare to try carrying his consoling revelation back into the upper air – outside of Cornwall, to Plymouth. The poem is called 'Places':

> Nobody says: Ah, that is the place
> Where chanced, in the hollow of years ago,
> What none of the Three Towns cared to know –
> The birth of a little girl of grace –
> The sweetest the house saw, first or last;
> > Yet it was so
> > On that day long past.
>
> Nobody thinks: There, there she lay
> In the room by the Hoe, like the bud of a flower.
> And listened, just after the bedtime hour,
> To the stammering chimes that used to play
> The quaint Old Hundred-and-Thirteenth tune
> > In St Andrew's tower
> > Night, morn, and noon.
>
> Nobody calls to mind that here
> Upon Boterel Hill, where the waggoners skid,
> With cheeks whose airy flush outbid
> Fresh fruit in bloom, and free of fear,
> She cantered down, as if she must fall
> > (Though she never did),
> > To the charm of all.
>
> Nay: one there is to whom these things,
> That nobody else's mind calls back,
> Have a savour that scenes in being lack,
> And a presence more than the actual brings;
> To whom today is beneaped and stale,
> > And its urgent clack
> > But a vapid tale.

The writing here, it must be admitted, is well short of masterly. Yet in the sequence this poem is irreplaceable; it is indeed the fulcrum on which the whole series turns. This appears, however, only if we append to it, as Hardy did, the firm dateline: 'Plymouth, March 1913'. On the one hand this makes it clear that the poem belongs on the way back from the pilgrimage. But it has a more crucial function: for it forces upon our attention (if we are attentive, as apparently most readers aren't) how, though the poem is thus insistently placed in Plymouth, the Plymouth places are continually called 'there', whereas it is the Cornish place, Boterel Hill, that is said to be 'here'. The superior reality of the domain of love and loyalty, over the domains of indifference and cold hatred, could hardly be asserted more pointedly; Cornwall is 'here' even when he is outside it, and somewhere else. This is a reach of spiritual conviction beyond any that he has reached earlier. As the next poem, 'The Phantom Horsewoman', declares, driving the point home:

> Not only there
> Does he see this sight,
> But everywhere
> In his brain – day, night,
> As if on the air
> It were drawn rose-bright –
> Yea, far from that shore
> Does he carry this vision of heretofore:

> A ghost-girl-rider. And though, toil-tried,
> He withers daily,
> Time touches her not,
> But she still rides gaily
> In his rapt thought
> On that shagged and shaly
> Atlantic spot,
> And as when first eyed
> Draws rein and sings to the swing of the tide.

And in this poem, which J.I.M. Stewart has called with entire justice 'a splendid taunt hurled at oblivion by the imagination', the execution is equal to the conception – witness the internal rhyme and sudden ripple of elated anapaests which make the last line so buoyant. The poem ends on a note of sublime assurance, of exultation even. And in its original form, in *Satires of Circumstance*, this was where the entire sequence ended – at the joyous tip of a long and climbing curve of spiritual apprehensions.

II

Leave Dante out of it. Hardy's contact with the *Purgatorio* is unproven. But his Virgilianism is another matter; he forces it on our attention. Why then have we never acknowledged it? (For Virgil rates not a single entry in the index to Bailey's *Handbook and Commentary*, all seven hundred pages of it.)

The answer I fear is too plain: we are determined to condescend to Hardy, to see in him what Yvor Winters saw – 'a naif'. Even when we mean to praise, we patronize; when Hardy's 'sincerity' is offered as a simple and straightforward value by F.R. Leavis and Douglas Brown and those who think with them, the implication is very plain that to Hardy – sturdily simple soul that he was – sincerity came more naturally than it did to his more sophisticated peers, or than it does (of course) to us. The great value of the biographical researches that have uncovered Tryphena Sparks and others is, quite apart from the illumination of certain poems otherwise obscure, that the biographers have exploded all notions of sturdy simplicity. What they have shown past any shadow of doubt is that Hardy on the contrary was a remarkably devious and tortuous man – just the sort of man who would at once convey and cloak his meanings with the allusive deviousness that I have been trying to demonstrate.

Even so, it is almost comically disconcerting that the past master we discern behind Hardy should turn out to be, of all people, Virgil. The idea of a Virgilian Hardy will not be readily or willingly entertained; it crosses too many wires, muddles too many of the alignments and counter-alignments that nowadays the studious reader clings to, in order to orient himself in the landscape of his reading. What! Hardy a Virgilian, he who was an admired eminence for two of our most redoubtable and influential deriders of Virgil's pretensions, Robert Graves and Ezra Pound? Hardy, who was singled out for untypically ferocious dismissal by Eliot, Virgil's eloquent champion? And anyway, isn't Tennyson, by common consent and for good or ill, the English Virgil *par excellence*? And isn't Hardy's Victorian allegiance quite conspicuously *not* to Tennyson, but to Browning?

So we could go on. But the case, all the same, is clear. From Ford's account of Hardy quoting at him from *Aeneid* Book II, through the characteristically laconic but repeated references to Virgil in the ghosted autobiography (Florence Emily's *Life*), there is sufficient evidence to support what the writings themselves prove – that Virgil was one writer from the past who was never far out of Hardy's mind. Improbably, it is the Public Orator of the University of Oxford who is in some sort vindicated. For the Orator in 1920, A.D. Godley, when presenting Hardy for an honorary degree, suggested: *Scilicet ut Virgilio nostro sic huic quoque 'molle atque facetum adnuerunt gaudentes rure Comenae'*. Perhaps what is most telling about this is that the author of the *Life*, that is to say Hardy himself in disguise, opens his chapter XXVI by quoting this, and obligingly provides a translation: 'Surely as with Virgil, so with him, have the Muses that rejoice in the countryside approved his smoothness and elegance.' If we balk at attributing smoothness and (of all things) elegance to Hardy, it may be because we have a too impoverished conception of elegance. More certainly, we have a drastically impoverished idea of Virgil if we think *his* elegance lies wholly within the compass of Tennyson.

Moreover, if for a moment we stop thinking about style, and lean back from the open page so as to think of Virgil as a whole, of Hardy as a whole, of the two personalities, their patterns of interest and allegiance, we can easily find so much in common between them that it becomes natural – it becomes, indeed, almost inevitable – that the modern poet should have responded intimately and keenly to the ancient one. To begin with, the Mantuan Virgil was, as everyone knows, profoundly a countryman and a provincial – as Hardy was. Bonstetten was the first to demonstrate that Virgil was moreover, in the late books of the *Aeneid*, a very scrupulous topographer – as was, of course, the writer who mapped 'Wessex'. Again, Virgil was in his time a devoted antiquarian and folk-lorist, almost indeed an anthropologist. G.M. Young remarked that, 'if you had asked a Roman what struck him most in Virgil he might have replied, "His profound knowledge of Italian antiquity".' (Italian, as against Roman.) And is that not what an Englishman of Hardy's day might have noticed first, about a writer who thought it no ignominious motive for either poem or story that it should commemorate a custom still remembered though no longer practised, or an episode only orally recorded? To abstract still further, to the point where one can talk of the cast of a temperament, who does not know that the cast of Virgil's temperament was melancholy? And what a difference it would make if, instead of arguing whether or not Hardy was 'pessimistic', we could agree that he was congenitally melancholy! (Some of Hardy's own exasperated impatience with the label 'pessimist' seems to point this way.) Finally, G.M. Young sees Virgil as 'too philosophic to believe in the gods and too Italian to do without them';[10] and does this not correspond to Hardy's position, non-Christian since the 1870s but throughout (as he testified himself, and as many a poem like 'The Oxen' is there to show) indelibly 'churchy'? All in all, there is quite enough of a 'rhyme in history' between Virgil's situation and Hardy's for the one to have served as paradigm for the other.

III

My story has an unhappy ending. For Hardy could not leave alone the 'Poems of 1912–13' as he had them in *Satires of Circumstance*. For the *Collected Poems* of 1919 he pulled in to the end of the sequence three additional poems; and this sequence of twenty-one poems, not the original eighteen, is what we now understand as 'Poems of 1912–13'. Henry Gifford has remarked that this extension of the sequence 'destroys the remarkable unity of Hardy's earlier design'. It certainly does. The first of the added poems, 'The Spell of the Rose', introduces the note of remorse that had been excluded, for good and necessary reason, from the original

10 G.M. Young, *Today and Yesterday: Collected Essays and Addresses* (London, 1948). My earlier quotation from Young is also from this source.

sequence. The second, 'St Launce's Revisited', recalls the Cornish landscape of constancy, only to deny it with a snarl:

> Why waste thought,
> When I know them vanished
> Under earth; yea, banished
> Ever into nought!

And with the third and last, 'Where the Picnic Was', the best we can do
is take some melancholy satisfaction in having J.O. Bailey show us that its
landscape is not, as Carl Weber thought, Cornwall, but – appropriately
enough for the spiritual inertness with which it brings the extended
sequence to a close – the landscape of betrayal and cold distrust, in Dorset.

It is from the perspective of 'Where the Picnic Was' that J. Hillis
Miller is able to detect

> the poet's gradual recognition, recorded explicitly in 'At Castle
> Boterel' and 'The Phantom Horsewoman', that Emma exists not as an
> objective ghost which any man might see, but in the poet's mind.
> Though the 'primaeval rocks' by a certain roadside record in their
> color and shape the fact that he and his lady passed there one March
> night long ago, this imprint of the transitory on the permanent is
> visible only 'to one mind', the mind of the poet in whose vision 'one
> phantom figure / Remains on the slope', though time, 'in mindless
> rote', has long since obliterated the reality.[11]

As should be clear from some of my earlier comments, I repudiate such a
reading totally, and with a sort of fury. What is more to the point is that
the poem itself repudiates the parody thus foisted upon it:

> It filled but a minute. But was there ever
>   A time of such quality, since or before,
> In that hill's story? To one mind never,
>   Though it has been climbed, foot-swift, foot-sore,
>   By thousands more.
>
> Primaeval rocks form the road's steep border,
>   And much have they faced there, first and last,
> Of the transitory in Earth's long order;
>   But what they record in colour and cast
>   Is – that we two passed.
>
> And to me, though Time's unflinching rigour,
>   In mindless rote, has ruled from sight

The substance now, one phantom figure
   Remains on the slope, as when that night
      Saw us alight.

I look and see it there, shrinking, shrinking,
   I look back at it amid the rain
For the very last time; for my sand is sinking,
   And I shall traverse old love's domain
      Never again.

The crucial word is 'quality' – ' a time of such *quality*'. For the qualitative has no existence outside of a mind that registers it. And quality is therefore invulnerable to time, since the 'rote' by which Time works is mindless. (All that time can destroy is 'substance' – a philosophical word to set against the other philosophical word, 'quality'.) Miller with bland audacity writes a minus for every plus in the poem, and a plus for every minus. When he speaks of 'this imprint of the transitory on the permanent', he takes as self-evidently transitory what the poem declares to be permanent – that is, quality; and he takes as permanent what the poem thinks of as comparatively transient – that is to say, the primaeval rocks, long-lasting though they are. 'Well, but' (I hear the protests) 'what happens to the quality when the one mind has gone, in which alone it had existence? What happens to it when Hardy is dead?' Who shall say? It's at this point that everything hinges on whether the reality that Hardy explores is psychological merely, or metaphysical. If Hardy is concerned only with psychological reality, as Miller and most other readers assume, then he is saying only that he will remember Emma, and the quality of this moment he shared with her, until the day he dies. Which is touching; but hardly worth saying at such length. But if the 'time of such quality' persists indestructible in a metaphysical reality, then it is *truly* indestructible – because a man's mind survives the death of his body, or because quality exists as perceived by a Divine Mind, or... The poet does not have to decide these matters; he does not have to decide the mode in which the quality will persist after his death, it is enough for him to affirm his conviction that persist it will. And here, as I read the poem ('The Phantom Horsewoman' also), Hardy makes that affirmation. My reading of 'At Castle Boterel' makes it a much more Virgilian poem, and a much greater one.

    The pity is that Hardy, by adding on 'The Spell of the Rose' and 'St Launce's Revisited' and 'Where the Picnic Was', himself psychologizes his own metaphysical insights, and so invites the sort of reading that Miller gives to 'At Castle Boterel'. It is as if, in the interim between *Satires of Circumstance* and *Collected Poems*, Hardy had remembered that he was a self-proclaimed infidel and scientific humanist, one who did not traffic in spiritual or metaphysical realities because he did not believe in them. That means that he did not believe in them *even though he had experienced them*; and that he pulled in the three extra poems so as to deny his own experience, to persuade himself and others that the experience had not happened.

This is an ugly imputation. (I must confess to finding it much uglier than the imputations of imperial time-serving that are cast at Virgil by Robert Graves and others.) But Hardy did not always live up to his vocation and his gifts; amid the deviousness of this devious man there was at times a capacity for selling short, for reneguing and defensive small-mindedness. In such a case we have the duty to save the works in which he lives up to his genius from the others in which he does not. 'At Castle Boterel' seems to me one of many works by Hardy that have this claim upon us; 'Beeny Cliff' is another.

Postscript: One thing that excited me in this investigation was the proof it seemed to give, that Hardy at his best proceeded in a way not wholly different from Pound's way, or Joyce's, or (I could have added) Eliot's. But in the years since, the sudden spate of books and essays about Hardy's poetry seems for the most part still impelled by a wish to prove that Hardy provides a viable insular alternative to the international 'modern movement'. I am quite out of sympathy with that sort of endeavour.

Agenda, 10: 2–3 (Spring–Summer, 1972); reprinted with postscript in *The Poet in the Imaginary Museum: Essays of Two Decades*, Ed. Barry Alpert (Manchester: Carcanet, 1977).

Widowers

'i segni dell' antica fiamma'

Atheist, Laodicean or
Whatever name our hand-to-mouth evasions
Earn for us, all of us have the thought
That states of soul in some uncertain sort
Survive us – sealed, it could be, in locations:
A yard, a coomb, an inn, a Cornish tor.

These leak their fragrances. To tap the fount
Of consolation calls on us for no
Dexterity at first; it isn't hard
To bruise a hip by falling in that yard
Or on that hillside. Hurt is all we know,
Stout alpenstock as we begin to mount

The purgatorial steeps, the terraces
Kicked back behind us. Then we sweat, we stink,
We fear that we forget. Our ancient haunts
Glow far above us, and the glimmer taunts
Our coming numbness. There she dwells, we think…
She does, although our need to think so passes.

Agenda, 10: 2–3 (Spring–Summer, 1972); first collected in *In the Stopping Train and Other Poems* (Manchester: Carcanet, 1977).

Thomas Hardy and British Poetry

Introduction

The poems I am to discuss in the following pages have been chosen so as
to illustrate a thesis: that in British poetry of the last fifty years (as not in
American) the most far-reaching influence, for good and ill, has been not
Yeats, still less Eliot or Pound, not Lawrence, but *Hardy*.

Pound, to be sure, unlike the others named, has declared himself
among the beneficiaries of Hardy; and indeed there is need of an essay or
a monograph that would map a way into the poetic universe of Pound by
the firmly interlinked stages of an English route that runs from Landor to
Hardy through Browning.[1] Such a study would necessarily swim against
the ever more rapid current that is flowing nowadays in the commentaries
toward what Daniel Pearlman hails with enthusiasm as 'the *dehistoriciza-*
tion of Pound'.[2] For Hardy has the effect of locking any poet whom he
influences into the world of historical contingency, a world of specific
places at specific times. Vernon Watkins realised this, when he asserted
that he and Dylan Thomas were both religious poets, who 'could never
write a poem dominated by time, as Hardy could'.[3]

Hardy appears to have mistrusted, and certainly leads other poets to
mistrust, the claims of poetry to transcend the linear unrolling of recorded
time. This is at once Hardy's strength and his limitation; and it sets him
irreconcilably at odds with for instance Yeats, who exerts himself repeat-

---

1   See Pound's tribute to Hardy in *Confucius to Cummings*, ed. by Ezra Pound and Marcella
Spann (New York, 1964), Appendix I.
2   *Agenda*, 8: 3–4 (Autumn-Winter 1970), p. 6.
3   *Letters to Vernon Watkins*, 1957, pp. 17–18, quoted by J. Press, *A Map of Modern English
Verse* (London, 1969), p. 222. It is worth saying that not all poets who have been influenced
by Hardy are prepared to acknowledge the fact, or are capable of recognising it. This applies
particularly to Irish, Scottish and Welsh poets, who do not care to be indebted to such an
intransigently *English* poet as Hardy. Elizabeth Huberman (*The Poetry of Edwin Muir*, New
York, 1971, pp. 54–6) is sure that Muir's *Chorus of the Newly Dead* (1926) is in many ways
manifestly indebted to Hardy. And I remain impenitently convinced that I detect Hardy
behind some early poems by Hugh MacDiarmid, though I have been reproved by Kenneth
Buthlay for saying as much. It is hard to believe that the scientific humanism to which the
Irishman Austin Clarke appears to vow himself in a poem such as 'Medical Missionary of
Mary' was arrived at without some appreciation of Hardy. And even R. S. Thomas, whose
dismissal of Hardy serves as epigraph to my next chapter, seems to me markedly Hardyesque
in for instance 'The Conductor' (from *Tares*, 1961).

edly to transcend historical time by seeing it as cyclical, so as to leap above it into a realm that is visionary, mythological, and (in some sense or to some degree) *eternal*. It ought to be possible for any reader to admire and delight in both Hardy and Yeats, if only because so much of the finest Yeats is concerned with the effort of transcendence rather than the achievement of it. But for any poet who finds himself in the position of choosing between these two masters, the choice cannot be fudged; there is no room for compromise. And so there is an emblematic significance to Philip Larkin's conversion (the word with its religious overtones seems not excessive) from Yeats to Hardy in 1946, after his very Yeatsian first collection, *The North Ship*.[4] Equally, there is perhaps tragic significance to the fact that Hardy is said to have been Dylan Thomas's favourite poet, whereas Yeats was his chosen master.

So much might be readily granted. To get beyond this point, we need to erase from our minds the image of (to use Henry James's unforgivable phrase) 'the good little Thomas Hardy'. None of Hardy's admirers has yet found how to make Hardy the poet *weigh* equally with Eliot and Pound and Yeats, in the image we have of the world that not just poets, but English-speaking intellectuals generally, have inhabited through the last half-century. Affection for Hardy the poet is general, and quite often (in Britain, at any rate) it is fervent; but it is ruinously shot through with protectiveness, even condescension. Hardy is not thought of as an intellectual force. When he is, rarely, considered from that point of view, it has been customary to say that whereas, as an imagination, he survives to instruct and challenge us, as an intellect he is *dated*, set into a late Victorian mould which the twentieth century finds not just outmoded but irrelevant. Herbert Spencer and Thomas Henry Huxley are old hat; and Hardy, who formed his ideas in the same climate of opinion, is therefore out of date. But quite apart from the question whether a man's images can be divorced from his ideas quite so cleanly (if they can, either the human imagination is being downgraded, or else the human intellect is), the second half of the twentieth century is surely much less confident than the first half was, of having outgrown Thomas Henry Huxley. The scientific humanism to which Huxley and Hardy gave their allegiances survives as a working ethic. The Second World War, which so discredited the reactionary or religious alternatives that had been promoted by the poets and the literary intellectuals, shook also – for instance, in the Oppenheimer case – the confidence of the scientific humanists, but not so radically. If 'we are all socialists now', we are all by that token scientific humanists also; and to just that degree the ideas of Thomas Hardy, even if we bitterly oppose them, are far more forces to be reckoned with than the ideas of T.S. Eliot. And political stances quite far to the right of program-

4   See his Introduction to the 1966 reprint of that book.

matic socialism are scientific-humanist no less. In the academies, the literary intellectual who in his classroom toys with the anti-democratic opinions of a Pound or Yeats or Wyndham Lewis, Lawrence or Eliot, transforms himself into a social democrat as soon as he attends his university senate, voting there, and perhaps speaking eloquently, in favour of 'freedom of inquiry' – a principle which his authors regarded without enthusiasm, if not indeed with animosity, much as some of them profited by it. And in standing by that principle, though he may call on authorities as old as Erasmus and Montaigne, the literary man knows that in a university senate, or a state senate either for that matter, the effective force behind it, which he needs to muster, is the ethic of the laboratory. In that way, scientific humanism is the ethic behind not just socialist positions in politics, but equally behind all those which may be called, or may call themselves, liberal.

Indeed, in all the worryings which in recent years have become so common, about the illiberal social and political ideas of the great literary imaginations of the present century (Pound and Eliot, Yeats and Lawrence), it is remarkable that to my knowledge no one has cited Hardy as the exception that proves the rule. For it could well be argued that Hardy is the one poetic imagination of the first magnitude in the present century who writes out of, and embodies in his poems, political and social attitudes which a social democrat recognises as 'liberal'. To take only one example, and incidentally to reveal liberalism in politics at its most vulnerable, Hardy's response to the First World War seems to have been liberal in a sense which does little credit to his shrewdness. The war seems to have taken him completely by surprise. Sceptical as he was in general, or was taken to be, he appears to have believed that European man, enlightened as he had been by scientific liberalism, had progressed beyond the point at which he would any longer have recourse to war. His less liberal and more coarse-grained contemporary, Rudyard Kipling, knew better – as of course did any number of observant journalists, who had seen the arms race gather momentum, and the balance of power tilt. But of international politics at that measurable and observable level Hardy appears to have been quite innocent – as the liberal tends to be.

He rallied from the shock of the war, and tried to make sense of it retrospectively, in a document which is central to my purpose. This is the 'Apology' (dated: 'February 1922'), with which he prefaced his post-war collection, *Late Lyrics and Earlier*.

Hardy had no talent for discursive prose, and this document cannot be read without exasperation. The trouble is not simply lack of talent for the marshalling and conduct of an argument. The way in which *Tess of the D'Urbervilles* and *Jude the Obscure* were received had rankled with Hardy over the years. And some of the discontinuities in the 'Apology' seem to represent an attempt to outwit and hoodwink the reader whom Hardy rancorously envisages. He wants to insinuate his argument so as to disarm the prejudices which he believes it would inflame were he to state it openly. A manoeuvre so complicated called upon urbane skills which Hardy did not possess; and his dislike and distrust of his readers peep through unattractively. For all these reasons, much of the piece is as if written in a clumsy code which we have to break. However, it is in its tortuous way explicit enough, at the point where he addresses the select few who will not mistake his 'evolutionary meliorism' for 'pessimism':

> looking down the future these few hold fast to the same: that whether the human and kindred animal races survive till the exhaustion or destruction of the globe, or whether these races perish and are succeeded by others before that conclusion comes, pain to all upon it, tongued or dumb, shall be kept down to a minimum by loving-kindness, operating through scientific knowledge, and actuated by the modicum of free will conjecturally possessed by organic life when the mighty necessitating forces – unconscious or other – that have 'the balancings of the clouds', happen to be in equilibrium, which may or may not be often.

The last part of this inelegant sentence makes it forgivable to think of Hardy, even today, as a pessimist; for introduction of the words, 'free will', and the immediate mournful qualification of them in clause after clause, phrase after phrase, mirror quite comically how in Hardy's system there is indeed a margin for human choice but the slimmest margin imaginable. Cramped and intermittent as that area of freedom may be, Hardy, however, is quite clear about what should motivate our actions within it – it is 'loving-kindness, operating through scientific knowledge'. This is what I have meant so far and shall mean in what follows, by 'scientific humanism'.

Why Hardy thought the position worth restating, and the plea worth making, appears near the end of the essay when, speaking of 'poetry, pure literature in general, religion',[5] he declares:

> these, I say, the visible signs of mental and emotional life, must like all other things keep moving, becoming; even though at present, when belief in witches of Endor is displacing the Darwinian theory and 'the truth that shall make you free', men's minds appear... to be moving backwards rather than on.

---

5   Hardy's uncharacteristic tenderness toward 'religion' in this essay – and institutional religion at that, as the context makes clear – derives from short-lived hopes he entertained at this time for 'modernism' in the Church of England. See *The Life of Thomas Hardy, 1840–1928*, by Florence Emily Hardy (London, 1962), p. 415. (This 'ghosted' autobiography by Hardy appeared first in two separate volumes, *The Early Life of Thomas Hardy, 1840–1891* (1928), and *The Later Years of Thomas Hardy, 1892–1928* (1930)).

If we remember Yeats's *A Vision* (1925) or *Per Amica Silentia Lunae* (1917) or Lawrence's *Fantasia of the Unconscious* (1922), we may be forgiven for associating them with that 'belief in witches of Endor' which Hardy, as a Darwinian, regards with such contempt and dismay.

The hidden or 'encoded' message of the piece supports this explicit message. The key to it is something to which Hardy himself draws attention, the extent to which the 'Apology' is interlarded with quotations from Wordsworth, some of them dragged in by the ears, others conspicuously 'wrenched'. The reason appears when we come to the last of them, when Hardy confesses to

> a forlorn hope, a mere dream, that of an alliance between religion, which must be retained unless the world is to perish, and complete rationality, which must come, unless also the world is to perish, by means of the interfusing effect of poetry – 'the breath and finer spirit of all knowledge; the impassioned expression of science', as it was defined by an English poet who was quite orthodox in his ideas.

What is alluded to is a famous passage among those which Wordsworth added to the Preface to *Lyrical Ballads*, for the edition of 1802. Familiar though it is (or should be), I shall give it in full:

> The knowledge both of the Poet and the Man of Science is pleasure; but the knowledge of the one cleaves to us as a necessary part of our existence, our natural and inalienable inheritance; the other is a personal and individual acquisition, slow to come to us, and by no habitual and direct sympathy connecting us with our fellow-beings. The Man of Science seeks truth as a remote and unknown benefactor; he cherishes and loves it in his solitude: the Poet, singing a song in which all human beings join with him, rejoices in the presence of truth as our visible friend and hourly companion. Poetry is the breath and finer spirit of all knowledge: it is the impassioned expression which is in the countenance of all Science. Emphatically may it be said of the Poet, as Shakespeare hath said of man, 'that he looks before and after'. He is the rock of defence of human nature; an upholder and preserver, carrying every where with him relationship and love. In spite of difference of soil and climate, of language and manners, of laws and customs, in spite of things silently gone out of mind and things violently destroyed, the Poet binds together by passion and knowledge the vast empire of human society, as it is spread over the whole earth, and over all time. The objects of the Poet's thoughts are everywhere; though the eyes and senses of man are, it is true, his favourite guides, yet he will follow wheresoever he can find an atmosphere of sensation in which to move his wings. Poetry is the first and last of all knowledge – it is as immortal as the heart of man. If the labours of men of

Science should ever create any material revolution, direct or indirect, in our condition, and in the impressions which we habitually receive, the Poet will sleep then no more than at present, but he will be ready to follow the steps of the Man of Science, not only in those general indirect effects, but he will be at his side, carrying sensation into the midst of the objects of the Science itself. The remotest discoveries of the Chemist, the Botanist, or Mineralogist, will be as proper objects of the Poet's art as any upon which it can be employed, if the time should ever come when these things shall be familiar to us, and the relations under which they are contemplated by the followers of these respective Sciences shall be manifestly and palpably material to us as enjoying and suffering beings. If the time should ever come when what is now called Science, thus familiarised to men, shall be ready to put on, as it were, a form of flesh and blood, the Poet will lend his divine spirit to aid the transfiguration, and will welcome the Being thus produced, as a dear and genuine inmate of the household of man.

Hardy's strategy was, we now realise, to buttress his case for scientific humanism as the only respectable working ethic for the poet, by enlisting as a scientific humanist *avant la lettre* an authority much more compelling than his own could be, bedevilled as his was (so he believed) by wilful misrepresentations of his own position as perversely 'unorthodox'. The elaborateness of the manoeuvre, however clumsily executed, shows how much Hardy took this cause to heart.

Yet if the buoyancy and generous certainty of Wordsworth's eloquence show up Hardy's manifesto as, by contrast, cramped and undermined by melancholy, it shows up hardly less damagingly the other literary authority from the nineteenth century whom Hardy cites: Matthew Arnold. For Hardy in his 'Apology' twice endorses Arnold's definition of poetry as 'the application of ideas to life'. And one virtue of Wordsworth's expansive but carefully indefinite formulations is that they leave room for relations between Science and Poetry altogether more intimate and less mechanical than the 'application' of the ideas of the one to the subject matter of the other. Hardy's most obviously Darwinian or post-Darwinian poems suffer from answering all too patly to Arnold's formula, disregarding the more intimate alliances with the sciences such as Wordsworth allowed for. (These were left for Hugh MacDiarmid to explore.)

On the other hand, the affirmative expansiveness of Wordsworth's welcome to the sciences, though appropriate to the first decade of the nineteenth century (when, however, the appropriateness was apparent only to unusually perceptive men, such as Wordsworth was), would have been quite out of place in the third decade of the present century, except for people much more unfeeling and much less perceptive than Thomas

Hardy. Hardy had seen, and had documented in a dozen novels and many poems, the strains and the outright damage which applied science, through industrialisation and urbanisation, had inflicted on the fabric of social and interpersonal relationships in the England that he knew. Indeed, sympathetic and perceptive readers have before now seen Hardy's entire career, in novels and poems alike, as an elegiac and indignant celebration of pre-industrial values which industrial technology had doomed.[6] In fact, I believe and hope to show that Hardy's attitudes were a great deal more complicated than that, and more ambiguous. For instance, 'The Convergence of the Twain', which some of us like to remember as a condemnation of technological presumption, in fact very markedly censures the vanity and luxury which created and inhabited the staterooms of the ocean liner, but not the technology which built the great ship and navigated her. Moreover, Raymond Williams has shown[7] that Hardy was well aware how the English peasantry, and the less fortunate among the yeomanry also, had been debased into an agricultural proletariat already, long before he was born. Thus, if Hardy finally pins what hopes he has upon science, and upon the industrial technology which is science's concomitant, he does so in full knowledge of a human cost which he has counted. And this ought to mean that Hardy speaks to these crucial issues with a weight and an authority perhaps greater than that of any imaginative writer of English, of comparable seriousness, in the present century. On the other hand, we have already come across grounds for thinking that Hardy will speak to these issues most cogently when he is concerned overtly with something quite different. Other things being equal, we should be prepared to listen to a Hardy poem most attentively when it is furthest from answering patly to Arnold's formula: the application of ideas to life. Hardy's attitude to technology will appear clearly, not from what he says about it (in his poems as a whole he says little), but from the formal dispositions of and in his verse style. His scientific humanism will be most influential on other poets, not as a set of propositions or a manifesto, but as an attitude informing his practice of his art.

Some of the features of later British poetry which have baffled and offended readers, especially in America – I have in mind an apparent meanness of spirit, a painful modesty of intention, extremely limited objectives – fall into place if they are seen as part of an inheritance from Hardy, an attempt to work out problems, especially social and political problems, which Hardy's poetry has posed for the twentieth century. And I hope to do more than merely excuse these characteristics of writing in

6   See Douglas Brown, *Thomas Hardy* (London, 1954).
7   Raymond Williams, 'Thomas Hardy', in the *Critical Quarterly*, 6: 4 (Winter 1964), pp. 341–51.

the Hardyesque tradition; I want to present them as challenging, and to ask in effect, 'Are not Hardy and his successors right in severely curtailing for themselves the liberties that other poets continue to take? Does not the example of the Hardyesque poets make some of those other poets look childishly irresponsible?'

1 Hardy as Technician

Then Hardy, for many a major
Poet, is for me just an old stager,
Shuffling about a bogus heath,
Cob-webbed with his Victorian breath.[1]

Hardy's poetry is a body of writing before which one honest critic after another has by his own confession retired, baffled and defeated. It is nothing short of comical that a criticism which can make shift to come to terms with Ezra Pound or Apollinaire, Charles Olson or René Char, should have to confess itself unable to appraise with confidence a body of verse writing like Hardy's, which at first glance offers so much less of a challenge to tested assumptions and time-honoured procedures. Irving Howe's confession is admirably explicit:

> Any critic can, and often does, see all that is wrong with Hardy's poetry, but whatever it was that makes for his strange greatness is much harder to describe. Can there ever have been a critic of Hardy who, before poems like 'The Going' and 'During Wind and Rain', did not feel the grating inadequacy of verbal analysis, and the need to resort to such treacherous terms as 'honesty', 'sincerity', and even 'wisdom'?[2]

Unless he has felt as Irving Howe describes, no critic of Hardy's poetry is qualified to speak. Equally, for the mere honour of the critical vocation, no one has the right to publish yet another essay on Hardy unless he thinks he can transpose the discussion into other terms than those which Howe rightly calls 'treacherous'. I write in that hope, or under that delusion.

Yvor Winters declared that Hardy was, 'like Emily Dickinson, essentially a naïf, a primitive, but one of remarkable genius'.[3] Yet neither 'naïve' nor 'primitive' is the word that comes first to mind to characterise

---

1 R.S. Thomas, 'Taste', *Poetry Review*, 61: 2 (Summer 1970).
2 Irving Howe, *Thomas Hardy* (New York, 1967), p. 164.
3 Yvor Winters, *Forms of Discovery* (Chicago, 1967), p. 189.

the most elaborate and considered of Hardy's few statements about his understanding of his own art. The statement is made in the third person because it comes from the very reticent autobiography which Hardy 'ghosted' through his second wife:[4]

> In the reception of this [*Wessex Poems*] and later volumes of Hardy's poems there was, he said, as regards form, the inevitable ascription to ignorance of what was really choice after full knowledge. That the author loved the art of concealing art was undiscerned. For instance, as to rhythm. Years earlier he had decided that too regular a beat was bad art. He had fortified himself in his opinion by thinking of the analogy of architecture, between which art and that of poetry he had discovered, to use his own words, that there existed a close and curious parallel, both arts, unlike some others, having to carry a rational content inside their artistic form. He knew that in architecture cunning irregularity is of enormous worth, and it is obvious that he carried on into his verse, perhaps in part unconsciously, the Gothic art-principle in which he had been trained – the principle of spontaneity, found in mouldings, tracery, and such like – resulting in the 'unforeseen' (as it has been called) character of his metres and stanzas, that of stress rather than of syllable, poetic texture rather than poetic veneer; the latter kind of thing, under the name of 'constructed ornament', being what he, in common with every Gothic student, had been taught to avoid as the plague. He shaped his poetry accordingly, introducing metrical pauses, and reversed beats; and found for his trouble that some particular line of a poem exemplifying this principle was greeted with a would-be jocular remark that such a line 'did not make for immortality'.

One may believe that this is a wrongheaded or foolish way of considering poetry, as is (so some think) any consideration of one art by analogy with another or with others. But in that case, surely, one regards it as over-sophisticated, not 'primitive'. And right or wrong, this way of looking at the arts was not an eccentric quirk in Hardy, but was shared by his contemporaries, including those, like Pater and Hopkins and Patmore, whose education had been both extensive and orthodox. Too much has been made of Hardy's provincialism, and his being self-educated; people still treat him with a sort of patronising indulgence on these false grounds, very much in the way that Hardy himself resented when he looked through the eyes of Jude Fawley.[5] If Hardy was self-educated, the education that he gave himself was in the end enviably thorough; and if for

---

4   *The Life of Thomas Hardy, 1840–1928*, pp. 300–301.
5   See, for instance, Samuel Hynes: 'Hardy went about the business of becoming a literary man with almost comic seriousness, like a burlesque of Milton at Horton.' (*The Pattern of Hardy's Poetry* (Chapel Hill, 1961), p. 21.) I perceive nothing comic, nothing of 'burlesque'.

instance we cannot make much use of the distinction Hardy made in the passage just quoted, it is because *our* education has been neglected, and has not included those texts of Pugin and Ruskin which Hardy and Patmore took for granted when they talked about the aesthetic of Gothic architecture. Nor is this the only field in which Hardy shames our ignorance; as a prosodist, for instance, he was immensely learned, with a learning that seems to be lost beyond recovery.

All the same, we should not fly to the other extreme. The autodidact *does* suffer, when set beside the man whose education has come to him without struggle against circumstance. My guess is that the autodidact suffers most from having had to discipline himself to depend too heavily on his own will, his own resolve to outwit circumstance and overcome it. And this is a very important element in Hardy's personality. Though he struck those who met him as a gentle and retiring man, the facts of his literary career speak for themselves: it is a Victorian success story, a model career on the lines of Samuel Smiles's self-help, with all that that involves of driving oneself hard with grim and clenched determination. And sometimes this is what offends us in Hardy's poetry – its form mirrors a cruel self-driving, a shape *imposed* on the material, as it were with gritted teeth. Edmund Blunden says something like this when he remarks: 'The faults of Hardy's verse are seldom those of the mediocre man, with his apparently easy measures, never quite full measures; they are those of a zealous experimenter, whose materials do not always obey the purpose or yield a restful completeness.'[6] An example is 'Lines to a Movement in Mozart's E-Flat Symphony':

> Show me again the time
> When in the Junetide's prime
> We flew by meads and mountains northerly! –
> Yea, to such freshness, fairness, fullness, fineness, freeness,
> Love lures life on.

> Show me again the day
> When from the sandy bay
> We looked together upon the pestered sea! –
> Yea, to such surging, swaying, sighing, swelling, shrinking,
> Love lures life on.

> Show me again the hour
> When by the pinnacled tower
> We eyed each other and feared futurity! –
> Yea, to such bodings, broodings, beatings, blanchings, blessings,
> Love lures life on.

6 Edmund Blunden, *Thomas Hardy* (London, 1942), p. 259.

> Show me again just this:
> The moment of that kiss
> Away from the prancing folk, by the strawberry-tree! –
> Yea, to such rashness, ratheness, rareness, ripeness, richness,
> Love lures life on.

Despite such incidental, characteristically audacious felicities as 'the pestered sea', this is surely not a poem we can admire. The musical air, as in a song, imposes the stanzaic symmetry; the air is sounded four times over, with only minimal change. But the rigidly symmetrical correspondence of the fourth lines in the stanzas, a symmetry rammed home by heavy-handed alliteration, was not required by the music of Mozart, but has been imposed by the poet. And the heavy-handedness drives any lived experience out of sight beneath the verbal surface. Where here is the 'cunning irregularity'? It is precisely what the poem needs, and suffers from the lack of. What one hears is not the chip-chip of a mason's chisel, but a clank of iron girders swung down from a crane; not Gothic architecture at all but specifically Victorian architecture, the iron bridges and railway stations of engineers like Brunel and Smeaton, who were indeed the accepted heroes of the self-help ethos. What destroys such a poem (and there are others like it) is not an all too stolidly planted rural provincialism, but just the opposite – its effective aesthetic is that of industrial technology in the age of heavy engineering. There is an essay to be written about Hardy the upwardly mobile *déraciné*; instead what we hear on every side is 'Hardy the countryman'.

It is Hardy the poet of technology, the laureate of engineering, who writes one of his most dazzling compositions, the poem on the sinking of the *Titanic*. The poem itself is an engine, a sleek and powerful machine; its rhymes slide home like pistons inside cylinders, ground exactly to fractions of a millimetre.

A more curious case from this point of view is a poem that Yvor Winters singled out, 'The Wind's Prophecy':

> I travel on by barren farms,
> And gulls glint out like silver flecks
> Against a cloud that speaks of wrecks,
> And bellies down with black alarms.
> I say: 'Thus from my lady's arms
> I go: those arms I love the best!'
> The wind replies from dip and rise,
> 'Nay; toward her arms thou journeyest.'
>
> A distant verge morosely gray
> Appears, while clots of flying foam
> Break from its muddy monochrome,

And a light blinks up far away.
I sigh: 'My eyes now as all day,
Behold her ebon loops of hair!'
Like bursting bonds the wind responds,
'Nay, wait for tresses flashing fair!'

From tides the lofty coastlands screen
Come smitings like the slam of doors,
Or hammerings on hollow floors,
As the swell cleaves through caves unseen.
Say I: 'Though broad this wild terrene,
Her city home is matched of none!'
From the hoarse skies the wind replies:
'Thou shouldst have said her sea-bord one.'

The all-prevailing clouds exclude
The one quick timorous transient star;
The waves outside where breakers are
Huzza like a mad multitude.
'Where the sun ups it, mist-imbued,'
I cry, 'there reigns the star for me!'
The wind outshrieks from points and peaks:
'Here, westward, where it downs, mean ye!'

Yonder the headland, vulturine,
Snores like old Skrymer in his sleep,
And every chasm and every steep
Blackens as wakes each pharos-shine.
'I roam, but one is safely mine,'
I say. 'God grant she stay my own!'
Low laughs the wind as if it grinned:
'Thy love is one thou'st not yet known.'

The grimness of this poem is quite extraordinary when we realise that the westward journey it describes is the one on which, in 1870, Hardy unexpectedly found his bride, Emma Gifford – the same journey, in fact, that produced the sweet lilt, 'When I set out for Lyonnesse'. It's true of course that the poem was almost certainly written long afterwards, when the marriage had turned out badly. What is uncanny is the way the elements are made to menace the traveller, and through associations with technology – the gulls 'glint' with a metallic glitter; when the sea comes into sight, its 'muddy monochrome' has a hint of the daguerreotype; and when the sea passes out of sight, the sound it makes is a slamming and a hammering. These industrial associations gather until we wonder whether the huzza-ing multitude of the penultimate stanza is not a dangerously mercurial proletariat. We know that Hardy was capable of such disparaging sentiments about the masses. In 1891 he had written in his diary something which he transcribed for his ghosted autobiography:

> Next day – wet – at the British Museum: 'crowds parading and gaily traipsing round the mummies, thinking today is for ever, and the girls casting sly glances at the young men across the swathed dust of Mycerinus (?) They pass with flippant comments the illuminated MSS. – the labours of years – and stand under Rameses the Great, joking. Democratic government may be justice to man, but it will probably merge in proletarian, and when these people are our masters it will lead to more of this contempt, and possibly to the utter ruin of art and literature!... Looking, when I came out, at the Oxford Music Hall, an hour before the time of opening, there was already a queue.'[7]

This is something that should be kept in mind when reading the poem written many years later, 'In Time of "The Breaking of Nations"':

> Yonder a maid and her wight
> Come whispering by:
> War's annals will fade into night
> Ere their story die.

The maid's and her wight's indifference to history is a fact; it is not necessarily reassuring. And as from Forster, so from Hardy, *two* cheers is all that Democracy deserves.

But in any case Lois Deacon's and Terry Coleman's revelations about Hardy's life,[8] up to the point where those eager sleuths launch into fraintly supported speculation, throw a quite different light on 'The Wind's Prophecy', and explain its otherwise inexplicable urgency and ominousness. (And it may as well be said here at once that, whatever the rights or wrongs of using biographical information to assist explication of other poets, in the case of an author so secretive as Hardy it has already proved itself indispensable.) They show conclusively that we read the poem right when we see it as dealing with Hardy's love for Tryphena Sparks, his cousin who in the end rejected him after he had see-sawed between her and Emma Gifford. Tryphena is the dark-haired girl behind the traveller eastward, whom he thinks of as his chosen; Emma is the blonde who, unknown to him, awaits him at his destination, St Juliot in Cornwall. Tryphena is a woman of his own social station exactly; Emma, whether or not Hardy thought her a cut above him socially, certainly herself thought she was, and, as we know, regarded Hardy's marriage to her as a

---

7　*The Life of Thomas Hardy, 1840–1928*, p. 236.
8　Lois Deacon and Terry Coleman, *Providence and Mr Hardy* (London, 1966). Miss Deacon and Mr Coleman prove that there was an affair with Tryphena; in my view they fail to prove that Tryphena bore a child to Hardy.

significant stage in his bettering of himself.[9] Thus the opposition between the two women, and the 'fated' switch from one to the other – matters that are explicitly at the centre of the poem – bring with them irrational feelings of guilt on the part of one who, upwardly mobile, is by that token 'a class-traitor'. And this explains much of the anxiety and foreboding which hang about the poem, otherwise unaccountably. But we may go, though hesitantly, a little further still, to account for the technological images. As we now read the poem, it is as if what separated Hardy from Tryphena were the Industrial Revolution itself, or at least as if the Nature which divided them (their relationship by blood was Tryphena's pretext for rejecting him) were itself a massive machine, of which sea and land and sky were components. And indeed, in a poem Hardy wrote about Tryphena's daughter after Tryphena died, Nature's manipulation of genetics is called 'her mechanic artistry', and the generation of children is seen as a sort of metallurgy:

> But niggard Nature's trick of birth
> Bars, lest she overjoy,
> Renewal of the loved on earth
> Save with alloy.[10]

The same trope – 'Every desired renewal of an existence is debased by being half alloy' – appears in *Jude the Obscure*, in what is, as Deacon and Coleman point out, an exactly parallel passage. Thus, one way to explain and vindicate the hoarse menace of 'The Wind's Prophecy' is to say that, whatever Hardy consciously meant to convey about the forces which drove him from Tryphena to Emma, his imagery presents them as the pressures of an advanced technological society. However Victorian man may have harnessed wind and sea ('as wakes each pharos-shine'), those elemental energies will retort 'like bursting bonds', and take their revenge where he can least resist them, in his sex and his sexual life. And in a devious remote way this is accurate enough about the relation between the young Hardy and his kinswoman Tryphena, as Deacon and Coleman permit us to reconstruct it. For Tryphena was no more the Dorset peasant than was her famous cousin. Like Sue Bridehead of *Jude the Obscure*, for whom in part Tryphena seems to have sat as model, Tryphena too was *déracinée* – having 'bettered herself' as her cousin had done, making herself a London-trained schoolmistress at just the time when the Education Act of 1870 was recognising the need, in an advanced technological culture,

---

9   See *Some Recollections by Emma Hardy*, ed. by Evelyn Hardy and Robert Gittings (London and New York, 1961). This indispensable and charming book had by 1970 been allowed to go out of print.

10   This poem first appeared in *Wessex Poems* (1898) as 'To An Orphan Child. A Whimsey'. It appears in *The Collected Poems of Thomas Hardy* (London, 4th edition 1930) p. 58, as 'To a Motherless Child'.

for virtually all the population to be, at an unambitious level, lettered and numerate.

Of course this is special pleading. The technological references in the poem are not so unambiguous, nor so insistent, as I have made out. And if this is, so far as I can see, the only way of reading the poem which accounts for all its components, the poem itself does not ask to be put together in this way. It is our reconstruction, as readers; the poem delivers to us, not an experience, but only the components of an experience – and indeed not all of those. Thus it fails to satisfy; and our interest in it is clinical.

A much better piece, yet one that still falls short of assured achievement, is 'Overlooking the River Stour':

> The swallows flew in the curves of an eight
>> Above the river-gleam
>> In the wet June's last beam:
> Like little crossbows animate
> The swallows flew in the curves of an eight
>> Above the river-gleam.
>
> Planing up shavings of crystal spray
>> A moor-hen darted out
>> From the bank thereabout,
> And through the stream-shine ripped his way;
> Planing up shavings of crystal spray
>> A moor-hen darted out.
>
> Closed were the kingcups; and the mead
>> Dripped in monotonous green,
>> Though the day's morning sheen
> Had shown it golden and honeybee'd;
> Closed were the kingcups; and the mead
>> Dripped in monotonous green.
>
> And never I turned my head, alack,
>> While these things met my gaze
>> Through the pane's drop-drenched glaze,
> To see the more behind my back....
> O never I turned, but let, alack,
>> These less things hold my gaze!

The 'cunning irregularity' which heedless readers have taken for clumsiness may be in a touch like the crowded stresses and consonants in 'the pane's drop-drenched glaze'. But once we have taken Hardy's word for it that such effects are the result of 'choice after full knowledge', the poem becomes throughout, and all too shiningly, the work of 'a superb technician' who dismays us precisely by his *superbia*. The symmetries, stanza by stanza, are all but exact to begin with; once we know that the occasional inexactitude is no less engineered, 'engineered' seems more than ever the only word to use. Once again there is an analogy with Victorian civil engineering, which topped off an iron bridge or a granite waterworks with Gothic finials, just as Hardy tops off his Victorian diction with an archaism like 'sheen' or 'alack'. Within its historically appropriate idiom, the poem is 'a precision job'; that is to say, its virtuosity is of a kind impossible before conditions of advanced technology.

Just this indeed could be the grounds on which to claim that Hardy, in a poem like this, is a very great poet indeed. Where else, we might ask, do we find among Hardy's contemporaries an imagination which has grasped with comparable force − not in what it says, but in how it addresses itself to the act of composition − the essential nature and life style of late-Victorian England, an England which rested on mechanical technology, on heavy engineering? I think this is the probably unanswerable case that should and must be made for 'The Convergence of the Twain'. If the same case cannot be made for 'Overlooking the River Stour', it is because its precision is more apparent than real. The poem raises issues which in the end it does not resolve nor account for. The bridge, when all is said and done, is faulty in its construction.

For whereas the poem presents itself as three stanzas running in parallel, with a last stanza that turns back upon them all, or runs across them all, in fact we experience a notable shift between the second stanza and the third. In the first two stanzas live creatures, the birds, are transformed into machines: the swallows into crossbows, and the moor-hen into some sort of lathe. (For the double sense of 'planing' is decisively tipped toward its mechanic sense, by 'ripped' and 'shavings'.) In the third stanza, however, the kingcups are presented in normal organic terms. The shift is notable. And yet the poet gives no indication that he has noticed it. Of course, we are ready to agree with him that neither perceiving organic things as mechanical nor perceiving them as organic is as important as the perception he has failed to make − of the human presence, Emma's, in the room behind him. He is right to reproach himself. But he has raised other questions which he seems to be unaware of.

Moreover, if the eye which fails to rest on Emma is the sharp and darting eye of the technician designing his next precision job on the basis of his finely honed perceptions, we get some sense of what it was like to be married to a Victorian engineer (whether in steel or in language), or to any man vowed to the Victorian ethos of self-help. We learn what strain may be laid on human relations, and what damage may be done to them, in an age of advanced technology. But this is very clearly our reflection, not the poet's; a reflection which the poem may prompt, but to which it does not lead us. Thus this poem, like 'The Wind's Prophecy', provides us with the components for an image of Victorian technological culture, but it does not assemble those components into the image. Where 'The Wind's Prophecy' failed to provide all the components that we find we need, 'Overlooking the River Stour' provides more components than it uses or takes account of.

I have two more comments to make. One is the wry confession that years ago when I used to read this poem, I was so won over by the brilliance of the descriptions by mechanical analogy in the first two stanzas, that I thought: 'Would that Hardy had written thus always!' 'Brilliance' is indeed the right word, but when I was younger I did not realise that 'brilliant' is double-edged; nor did I take account of the often stated truth that vivid exactness in descriptive images counts for nothing, unless moulded and if necessary subdued by a current of strong feeling through them. My second comment is more tentative, but may take us further. It concerns the word 'honeybee'd' which, in the rhyme position, draws attention to itself and its own audacity. It is an irregularity, in the sense that it is an ingenious coinage not vindicated by normal usage whether literary or spoken. But it is not one of Hardy's *cunning* irregularities, for those by his own account he contrives in metre, not in diction; and indeed of these frequent oddities in his diction he seems to have been largely unaware. If so, this word is less than masterly. It is not a seeming clumsiness, but a real one. This does not make it any better, nor is this poem any better for including it, but there *are* poems by Hardy which are redeemed by such oddities. Many critics of Hardy's poetry have found themselves in the uncomfortable and ultimately preposterous position of applauding him for his clumsiness. It may now be clear how we may be driven to such a desperate expedient: it is when we have to deal with an artist whose will is imperious, who claims by implication to be sharp-sightedly in command of every aspect of his undertakings, that we may in exceptional circumstances be grateful for the times when he shows himself fallible. For these are the times when the drilling and the riveting stop, and the eagle-eye descends from the gantry; when the civil engineer who was once a mason finds that he has to chip with his own chisel. What he does then will fall short of mechanical precision, but his artefact by its very faultiness will have something better, *virtù*, 'the light of the doer as it were cleaving to it'. (The words are Pound's.)

An instance springs to mind in what is often, and to my mind rightly, applauded as one of Hardy's greatest poems. This is 'The Voice':

> Woman much missed, how you call to me, call to me,
> Saying that now you are not as you were
> When you had changed from the one who was all to me,
> But as at first, when our day was fair.
>
> Can it be you that I hear? Let me view you, then,
> Standing as when I drew near to the town

Where you would wait for me: yes, as I knew you then,
Even to the original air-blue gown!

Or is it only the breeze, in its listlessness
Travelling across the wet mead to me here,
You being ever dissolved to existlessness,
Heard no more again far or near?

    Thus I; faltering forward,
    Leaves around me falling,
Wind oozing thin through the thorn from norward,
    And the woman calling.

Many years ago F.R. Leavis remarked of 'existlessness' (later it became 'wan wistlessness' – there is not much to choose between the two expressions) that it 'is a questionable word, a characteristic eccentricity of invention; and yet here it sounds right. The touch that there may still be about the poem of what would normally have been rustic stiffness serves as a kind of guarantee of integrity.' The nature of that 'guarantee' may now be clearer: the rustic stiffness guarantees integrity, only because it comes (as 'a touch') in a poem which is exerting itself, and with success, to be neither rustic nor stiff but elaborately and exactly tooled. 'And then,' says Dr Leavis, 'there is the exquisite modulation into the last stanza.' There is indeed. And the exquisiteness is registered with delight when the poem is read in isolation; but the keenness of the pleasure is heightened, and our sense of the integrity is further assured, when we consider the poem in the context of Hardy's poetry as a whole. For in that poetry it is an all but absolute rule for an intricately rigid symmetry, such as obtains between the first three stanzas, to be maintained throughout each poem. For the poet to have broken a rule he set such store by is another 'guarantee of integrity'. For nothing but fidelity to feeling could have caused him to do so.

Thus, in Yvor Winters's account of Hardy, one judgement that is wholly unacceptable comes, for me, when he remarks: '"The Haunter" and "The Voice" are companion pieces. The second has been often quoted; the first is by far the better.'[11] 'The Haunter' is an imperiously symmetrical piece in four eight-line stanzas, the rhyme words of the even lines in the first stanza reproduced exactly in each of the stanzas that follow. Winters does not tell us what he finds wrong with 'The Voice'; in view of his preference for 'The Haunter' one may suspect that he likes just that rigid symmetry which I have called technological, a symmetry which 'The Voice' departs from, whereas 'The Haunter' presses it home relentlessly. And sure enough, 'brilliant' seems to be always for Winters a term of unqualified approval.

---

11 Winters, *Forms of Discovery*, p. 192.

★   ★   ★

One critic after another complains that nearly 1000 poems are too many, and asks for a more or less agreed-upon select few, a canon on which Hardy's reputation shall rest, about which disagreements shall circle. But even on this point there are dissenting voices; Mark Van Doren's, for instance: 'No poet more stubbornly resists selection... There is no core of pieces, no inner set of classic or perfect poems, which would prove his rank... It is the whole of him that registers and counts...'[12] And Philip Larkin has declared that he delights in Hardy's poems because one can have read for years up and down in the *Collected Poems*, and still be surprised by something newly discovered or previously overlooked. As the years pass, I for one find myself more and more of Van Doren's and Larkin's way of thinking. Nothing supports their case so much as the half-dozen selections of Hardy's poems that have in fact appeared; and one of them in particular, the selection made by John Crowe Ransom.[13] Ransom – what could be better? It seemed a splendidly appropriate conjunction: Ransom, the author of 'Piazza Piece' and 'Spectral Lovers', seemed the one poet in English since Hardy who could be relied upon to have a temperamental sympathy with Hardy's concerns and Hardy's style, and a just sense of how to discriminate between Hardy's strong poems and his weak ones. And yet, when the book appeared, among the 125 pieces printed by Ransom one looked in vain for 'After a Journey', 'At Castle Boterel', 'The Voice', 'My Spirit will not haunt the mound', 'Under the Waterfall'. Of 'the five great elegies' which, according to another critic,[14] were 'the summit of Hardy's achievement', Ransom had selected just one, 'The Going'. And yet Ransom had not scamped his assignment. When we study his selection, and in particular his valuable introductory essay, we are forced to realise that his assessment of Hardy is not at all perfunctory. It is not at all clear, even, that it is eccentric. And indeed, as much must be said of the other selections that have been made by editors, or hinted at by critics. Cast about as one may, and measure one authority against another, one perceives no consensus emerging as to what is centrally significant in Hardy's poetry, still less therefore as to what is the canon of his secure achievements. And if no one can determine where the centre is, no one reading of the corpus can be more eccentric than any other.

This points to something that is very important. What defeats the attempt to discriminate the better from the worse among Hardy's poems is not just the great number of the poems, and their variousness. It is not even the impossibility, for the most part, of categorising the poems as 'early' or 'late'; nor the almost equal difficulty of categorising them according to genre, except in the broadest and most impressionistic way.

---

12 Quoted by Howe, *Thomas Hardy*, p. 168.
13 *Selected Poems of Thomas Hardy* (New York, 1960; in Collier Books 1966).
14 Brown, *Thomas Hardy*, p. 176.

These impediments to taking Hardy the poet as a whole, the good with the bad, do not come about by accident. Behind them is the curious paradox that Hardy, who imposes himself so imperiously upon his medium, imposes himself on his reader hardly at all. On every page, 'Take it or leave it', he seems to say; or, even more permissively, 'Take what you want, and leave the rest'. This consciousness of having imposed on his reader so little is what lies behind Hardy's insistence that what he offers is only a series of disconnected observations, and behind his resentment that he should be taken as having a pessimistic design upon his reader, when in fact he so sedulously respects the reader's privilege not to be interested, not to be persuaded. It is on this basis – his respect of the reader's rights to be attentive or inattentive as he pleases – that one rests the claim for Hardy as perhaps the first and last 'liberal' in modern poetry. And it is because we are so unused to liberalism as a consistent attitude in a poet, that we have so much difficulty with the poetry of Hardy.

But the outcome is that every new reader of Hardy's poetry finds there what he wants to find. And in the event this means, for the most part, that each reader finds in the poems what he brings to them; what he finds there is his own pattern of preoccupations and preferences. If this is true of every poet to some degree, of Hardy it is exceptionally true. And this is the justification for attending in particular to Ransom; since Ransom on the evidence of his own poems is an exceptionally intelligent and sophisticated reader.

What Ransom most esteems in Hardy's poetry are the poems which, after canvassing other possibilities, he finally decides to call 'fables'. Irving Howe, who agrees with Ransom in esteeming this kind of poem, points out:

> For having written such poems Hardy has been severely rated by critics in the Eliot line, who regard them as tritely heretical and intellectually feckless. They look with distaste upon what one of them, R.P. Blackmur, called Hardy's lack of 'emotional discipline and the structural support of a received imagination' (by which immensity I take Blackmur to mean the complex of symbols and myths associated with the Christian tradition). Yet it might be remembered that we cannot always choose the situation in which we live out our lives; that for Hardy, as for many other nineteenth century writers, the loss of faith was an experience of the utmost consequence, not a mere frivolity or pretext for a wanton emotionalism; and that his effort to improvise voices, personifications and fables which might replace Christian authority was undertaken in a spirit of humility testifying not merely to the hold Christianity continued to exert upon his mind but also the depth to which its values had penetrated his very being.[15]

15 Howe, *Thomas Hardy*, p. 175.

There is a minor puzzle here, for Ransom might well be taken as a critic 'in the Eliot line', who would therefore dislike the sort of poem represented at its best by 'Channel Firing' or 'The Subalterns'. But anyone who knows Ransom's beautiful poems can soon solve this puzzle; it was the poet in Ransom, not the critic, who wrote appreciatively of such poems:

> They offer natural images of the gods in action or, sometimes unfortunately, in inaction. The sharp and homely detail of the country naturalist in Hardy is not compromised by the presence of deity and his ministers; these are made to answer in his own language to the naturalist or his spokesman in the poem. The tone of the composition may be altogether grave and earnest. But fable is a self-confessed fiction by an independent thinker, therefore very free in its images. As if to allow in advance for the failure of human speculations, including his own, Hardy often gives them a sporting or rowdy turn which makes them comic in their irony.[16]

'A sporting or rowdy turn...' Well, this is forcing the note a little. It is true that in 'Channel Firing' the dead Parson Thirdly is made to say, 'I wish I had stuck to pipes and beer.' But this is not the note that Hardy's poem ends on; whereas Ransom's poem 'Armageddon' does indeed come to rest on lines which are 'comic in their irony':

> The immortal Adversary shook his head:
> If now they fought too long, then he would famish;
> And if much blood was shed, why, he was squeamish.
> 'These Armageddons weary me much,' he said.

All the same, 'Armageddon' is, like other fine poems by Ransom, Hardyesque. And we must agree that Hardy's sense of humour is not asleep even in 'The Subalterns':

> I
>
> 'Poor wanderer,' said the leaden sky,
>   'I fain would lighten thee,
> But there are laws in force on high
>   Which say it must not be.'
>
> II
>
> ' – I would not freeze thee, shorn one,' cried
>   The North, 'knew I but how
> To warm my breath, to slack my stride,
>   But I am ruled as thou.'

---

16 Ransom, *Selected Poems of Thomas Hardy*, p. x.

III

' – Tomorrow I attack thee, wight,'
   Said Sickness. 'Yet I swear
I bear thy little ark no spite,
   But am bid enter there.'

IV

' – Come hither, Son,' I heard Death say;
   'I did not will a grave
Should end thy pilgrimage today,
   But I, too, am a slave!'

V

We smiled upon each other then,
   And life to me had less
Of that fell look it wore ere when
   They owned their passiveness.

Ransom's account of this poem is scrupulous, exhaustive, and compelling. He notes for instance the firm symmetry by which each of the subalterns except the first employs a figure out of the traditional rhetoric of Christian devotion – the shorn lamb, the ark, the pilgrim; and yet he sees that this and other symmetries are those of the mason, not the engineer:

> The ecclesiastical architect in Hardy must have liked to find the poem looking this way; he would have been familiar with the series of members precisely equal in weight and function, yet different individually, in a good structure of masonry.[17]

We think of masonry rather than engineering because here both metre and rhyme are by Hardy's standards, sober; and so the mastery can manage symmetries of both without advertising itself as 'brilliant'. It is noteworthy and regrettable that 'The Subalterns' does not appear among the 175 poems chosen by W.E. Williams for his 'Thomas Hardy' in the Penguin Poets.

On the other hand, once we have admitted 'Channel Firing' and 'The Subalterns' as fine achievements in this kind, it is not clear from either Ransom or Howe what others we should set beside them. Irving Howe indeed cites two examples of failure in this kind: 'The Masked Face' and 'New Year's Eve'. The latter poem is printed by both Williams and Ransom, though by Ransom it is unaccountably deprived of its last three stanzas. It is very unattractive, doubtless (as Howe suggests) because the intellectual difficulty which provoked it has not fired the poet to any 'remembered or imagined situation which serves him as an emblem of the

---

17 Ransom, *Selected Poems of Thomas Hardy*, p. xiv.

difficulty'. As Howe says, 'Despite the dogmas of certain critics, a poetry of statement can be written, and written well: but not by Hardy.' From time to time such poetry, turning on the same intellectual difficulties as troubled Hardy and out of a mood very like Hardy's in 'New Year's Eve', was written by the author of *A Shropshire Lad*; and in fact a poem like 'New Year's Eve' challenges, and fails to sustain, comparison with Housman.

Indeed Housman it is who comes insistently to mind when Ransom declares: 'Hardy the poet rates for us as decidedly the principal Voice of Irony among the poets of his age.' Housman surely merits that description far more than Hardy. Only in his weaker poems, like 'New Year's Eve', is Hardy content to settle for irony. And indeed Ransom delivers himself of this judgement on Hardy at precisely the time when he is chiding him for not letting Irony have the last word, but reserving it for 'the Spirit of Pity'. This happens in the fable poem, 'And There Was a Great Calm', on which Ransom's comments are very odd indeed. Can 'one of the noble war poems in our language, or any language', afford such lines as these?

> The feeble folk at home had grown full-used
> To 'dug-outs', 'snipers', 'Huns', from the war-adept
> In the mornings heard, and at evetides perused;
> To day-dreamt men in millions, when they mused –
> To nightmare-men in millions when they slept.

('Day-dreamt' for 'day-dreaming' is surely inexcusable.) But it appears that Ransom praises the poem in general thus extravagantly, only so as to object in particular that 'Hardy is constitutionally so much under the domination of Pity, and so close to the event when he writes the Armistice poem, that he disparages the tone of the Spirit of Irony', and so fails 'to represent a great Spirit according to his honours'. And so we realise what was involved for Ransom when he insisted that Hardy often gave his speculations 'a sporting or rowdy turn which makes them comic in their irony'. This is what Ransom does himself in a poem like 'Armageddon'; and what he wants to do is to take over Hardy's irony while dispensing with Hardy's pity. Accordingly, he ingeniously over-reads the last stanza of 'Channel Firing', so as to find an irony where I think there is none.[18] If irony matters so much to Ransom he ought to prefer Housman to Hardy; but we may take it he knows very well the price he would have to pay for that exchange, how much there is in Hardy that we have to agree not to ask Housman for, how much of variety and tangible particularity must be given up for the sake of Housman's irony. (A better fable poem, incidentally, is one provoked by the Boer War, 'The Souls of the Slain', which has the same setting as

18 Ransom, *Selected Poems of Thomas Hardy*, p. xii.

Housman's 'The Isle of Portland'.)

Since the First World War, through and since the Great Depression until the day before yesterday, an ironical stance before experience has been much favoured and highly extolled in literature by various sorts of humanist, including those sorts that call themselves, or may be called, 'tragic', or even 'Christian'. But to the scientific humanist, who pins his faith as Hardy did on 'loving-kindness operating through scientific knowledge', irony can never have more than a subordinate place in the moral economy. And indeed in those words Hardy declared that for him the Spirit of Pity, not Irony, would always have the last word. Moreover, the irony of Hardy and Housman alike is in any case quite different from most modern irony; the older poets do not recommend irony as a secure or dignified stance from which to confront reality, rather it is the stance of reality as it confronts *us*. Their irony is cosmic, where an Auden's is provisional and strategic. Armoured in irony, the liberal may be, though ineffective, invulnerable; but Hardy's poems open a window on a world where liberalism may yet be a passion – as, one likes to believe, it always has been in the laboratories.

A comparison of Hardy with Housman may be taken a stage further. For when a reader so scrupulous and sensitive as Ransom reads a poem askew, it's likely we have to do with a sort of misreading that will be persistent unless we can scotch it. We may consider, then, a poem by Housman and a poem by Hardy which offer themselves for comparison for an unusually good reason, in that each of them is clearly a variation on a classic poem by Wordsworth, the eight-line masterpiece, 'A Slumber Did My Spirit Seal'. Here is the Housman:

> The night is freezing fast,
> 　　Tomorrow comes December;
> 　　　　And winterfalls of old
> Are with me from the past;
> 　　And chiefly I remember
> 　　　　How Dick would hate the cold.
>
> Fall, winter, fall; for he,
> 　　Prompt hand and headpiece clever,
> 　　　　Has woven a winter robe,
> And made of earth and sea
> 　　His overcoat for ever,
> 　　　　And wears the turning globe.[19]

Hardy's poem is called, 'While Drawing in a Churchyard':

19　A.E. Housman, *Last Poems* (London, 1922), xx, p. 43.

'It is sad that so many of worth,
　Still in the flesh', soughed the yew,
'Misjudge their lot whom kindly earth
　　Secludes from view.

'They ride their diurnal round
　Each day-span's sum of hours
In peerless ease, without jolt or bound
　　Or ache like ours.

'If the living could but hear
　What is heard by my roots as they creep
Round the restful flock, and the things said there
　　No one would weep.'

'"Now set among the wise,"
　They say: "Enlarged in scope,
That no God trumpet us to rise
　　We truly hope."'

I listened to his strange tale
　In the mood that stillness brings,
And I grew to accept as the day wore pale
　　That show of things.

Ransom or anyone else could readily explicate the irony in 'show' in Hardy's last line. But the 'sporting or rowdy turn' is all Housman's, in his veering from 'robe' to 'overcoat'. The irony is what Housman is working for, and attains; when we have taken the force of it, we have taken the force of Housman's poem. In Hardy, the irony is acknowledged and allowed for; and yet, for all that the irony comes in the last line, the total response worked for and earned by Hardy, though it thus incorporates irony, goes beyond it or envelops it. It is only when we rate the ironical vision less highly than Ransom does, that we appreciate the human breadth of Hardy's feeling, and how far – on this showing at least – he transcends Housman.

All the same, this comparison prompts other reflections. John Wain, comparing Housman's poem unsympathetically with its Wordsworth model, complains that 'the over-artful stanza form seems vulgar by comparison'.[20] And this may be true. But metrically, of course, Housman's stanza is quite straightforward, and its intricate look on the page is merely a typographical device for showing how it is structured according to rhyme; it is Hardy's stanza that is artful *metrically*. And is it not true that by the side of the Wordsworth original (which Hardy must have had in mind no less than Housman – the word 'diurnal' says as

---

20 John Wain, 'Housman', in *Preliminary Essays* (London, 1957); reprinted in *A.E. Housman: A Collection of Critical Essays*, ed. by Christopher Ricks (Englewood Cliffs, N.J., 1968), p. 31.

much), it is Hardy's stanza that seems over-artful? Formally, Hardy's little poem is ambitious; inwardly or humanly, though Hardy's poem is more ambitious than Housman's, it falls almost as short as that does of the masterly succinctness of 'A Slumber Did My Spirit Seal'.

And this is a crucial point. A great deal of the trouble we have with Hardy comes of our wanting to consider as an ambitious poet like Wordsworth a poet who was very unambitious indeed, as we know from external as well as internal evidence. If we read 'While Drawing in a Churchyard' as a relaxed and leisurely though formally adroit gloss on a great poem by Wordsworth, it may be that this is as much as the poet hoped for. As with other sorts of poem by Hardy, so with these verse fables, we are in no time at all looking at poems which are 'all right in their way' or 'very good of their kind' – poems like 'God-forgotten', 'By the Earth's Corpse', 'To the Unknown God' and 'God's Education'. Hardy was very ambitious technically, and unambitious every other way – like, once again, the Victorian architect, who knew he could construct an Early English chancel more elaborately exact than the thirteenth century could manage, but didn't (unless he was stupid) suppose that he had thereby recovered the spirituality of the Age of Faith. The implications of this are far-reaching for the poets who come after Hardy and take him as their model or their master.

For what we are saying is that, except in the ill-starred and premature *Dynasts*, Hardy the poet comes before us as 'the honest journeyman', highly skilled indeed but disablingly modest in his aims. We reached this recognition as soon as we noticed how little Hardy imposes himself on his reader. On page after page he bows and retires at just the point where another poet would, for good or ill, advance and take us by the throat. At first we are so disconcerted that we cannot believe our eyes or our ears; then we are won over by such unaccustomed civility. And yet we remain disconcerted, because so completely disarmed. (The effect is not created by any quality of Hardy's conception or of his images, but by his formal disposition of verse lines; his symmetrical stanzas lie on the page demurely self-contained.)

Very much to the point here are the many poems by Hardy which may be called 'occasional'. The honest journeyman rises dutifully to public occasions, like an unofficial poet laureate. Witness his *Poems of the Past and Present*, where a loyal homage to Queen Victoria lately dead introduces a dozen poems on the Boer War. These include 'Drummer Hodge', and we realise how disarming Hardy is when we see this poem esteemed by some who would castigate Rupert Brooke's '1914', though the senselessness of war is glossed over by the same means in the one poem as in the other. Similarly, though John Crowe Ransom was right to reprove the reader who thought 'Channel Firing' was mere sabre-rattling, it is disingenuous to remember this poem and 'In Time of "The Breaking of Nations"', while forgetting several other poems by Hardy that are indeed sabre-rattlings or morale-builders or worse.

Yet the Boer War sequence included 'The Souls of the Slain', which is important and memorable. And in fact Hardy scored some of his most notable successes with occasional poems. R.P. Blackmur notes some of these:

> such poems as those (sic) about the loss of the *Titanic*, with its extraordinary coiling imagery... such poems as those on Leslie Stephen and Swinburne, each ending with a magnificently appropriate image, Stephen being joined to the Schreckhorn which he had scaled, and Swinburne joined with the waves –
>
> > Him once their peer in sad improvisations,
> > And deft as wind to cleave their frothy manes –
>
> and again such poems as 'Channel Firing' and 'In Time of "The Breaking of Nations"', which need no comment; and finally in such poems as 'An Ancient to Ancients' with its dignity and elegance making the strength of old age. But these poems are or ought to be too generally received to permit their being looked at as anything except isolated, like something in the Oxford Book of English Verse.[21]

Here Blackmur begins with occasional poems and ends with anthology pieces – 'like something in the Oxford Book of English Verse'. And I think this is right; for the same 'honest journeyman' attitude lies behind both sorts of poem. And indeed the two sorts of poem are really one. Consider 'The Darkling Thrush'. This is the poem with which, in *The Times* at New Year 1900, Hardy greeted the new century. But surely it is also contrived so as to earn just the fate which has come upon it – of being in all the anthologies.

I do not know that anyone has defined the term 'anthology piece', or explained and justified the disparaging inflection which hangs about it. If we remember 'The Lake Isle of Innisfree' as Yeats's anthology piece, and recall how bitterly Yeats came to resent its notoriety, we may approach a definition: an anthology piece is a poem which, whether by luck or design, and whatever its other virtues, cannot give offence. 'The Darkling Thrush' answers to this description, as does (I'm afraid) that other favourite of the anthologists, 'The Oxen'. And who can think that the innocuousness of 'The Darkling Thrush' on New Year's Day 1900 was arrived at by luck, by being for instance luckily abstracted from a context which would have cast a guilty shadow on its innocence? A modern enthusiast for the poem, John

21 R.P. Blackmur, 'The Shorter Poems of Thomas Hardy', in *Language as Gesture* (London, 1954), p. 75.

Berryman,[22] makes much of the irony latent in the last line:

> Some blessèd Hope, whereof he knew
> And I was unaware.

(That is to say, the hope is an illusion.) But can we doubt that the reader of *The Times* in 1900, and the readers of the anthologies ever since and at present, read the lines quite differently, to mean: 'I, the notorious pessimist and author of *Jude the Obscure*, humbly confess myself foolish beside the sanguine and resolute wisdom of this bird'? And – a nastier question – can we doubt that Hardy, either when he wrote the poem for this occasion or else when he mailed it to *The Times* to meet the occasion, counted upon the editor and the regular readers of the newspaper to take it in just that up-beat, unexceptionable way? Such are the dishonesties, or the opportunities for dishonesty, which attend a poet who, like Hardy, declares that his highest ambition is to place one or two poems in an anthology like *The Golden Treasury*.

We must not be unfair. We have every reason to believe that Hardy's respect for Queen Victoria, and for a Victorian institution like Palgrave's *Golden Treasury*, was sincere. There is no reason to think that Hardy had misgivings about his country and his nation, which he ignobly stifled. Quite the contrary indeed. A technician such as Hardy was, and conceived himself to be, needs to believe that decisions are being wisely taken elsewhere about what the ventures are to which his technical expertise shall be applied. Others decide whether the railway bridge is necessary; the engineer is responsible only for building it safely, elegantly, strongly. Major issues of national policy were among the matters that Hardy was too modest to concern himself with; and his modesty was that of the expert technician, imperious within his expertise, diffident or indifferent outside it.

Accordingly, in most of the senses of 'great' as we apply it to poets, Hardy is not a great poet at all. He is not 'great' because, except in *The Dynasts*, he does not choose to be, does not enter himself in that competition. This is the burden of R.P. Blackmur's essay of 1940, 'The Shorter Poems of Thomas Hardy'. Blackmur insists that, tot up as we may the sum of admirable poems by Hardy, what stops him short of greatness is something in the quality of his attention to experience and to the poetic rendering of it. It is not a matter of his having only so many admirable poems to plead his case for him, but of something that is built into his poems even at their most admirable. If we say that even at his best Hardy was not enough the craftsman, we certainly do not mean what Yeats meant when he said (incredibly) that Hardy's work 'lacked technical

---

22 John Berryman, in *Master Poems of the English Language*, ed. Oscar Williams (New York, 1966), pp. 788–90.

accomplishment'.[23] (In sheer *accomplishment*, especially of prosody, Hardy beats Yeats hands down.) We mean that Hardy failed to be a craftsman to just the degree that he insisted on being the triumphant technician. As Blackmur put it, 'what Hardy really lacked was the craft of his profession – technique in the wide sense'. Hardy too often lacked craft, to just the extent that he had expertise; he lacked technique 'in the wide sense', to just the degree that he exulted in possessing it in its narrower senses. The honesty of the honest journeyman may be dishonest in his master.

It may not be clear how Hardy the technician is related to Hardy the scientific humanist and Hardy the 'liberal'. But the relation is one that is familiar enough, though we seldom encounter it, or any analogue of it, in poetry. It is the relation between pure science and applied science, a crucial relation for any advanced technological culture, and one which throws up in many aspects of that culture – for instance, in its politics – precisely the contradiction that I am struggling to define in Hardy's attitude to his art, and his practice of it. For we accuse the corporate enterprise of science and technology of being insufferably and perilously arrogant in the way that it manipulates and conditions us and our environment. And yet the individual scientist or engineer often sees himself, quite sincerely, as very modest, merely an honest worker at specific tasks and problems. It is not he, but the literary man or the philosopher, who has the presumption to question the whole cultural design, and offer to set the whole world to rights! In just the same way the liberal in politics usually contends that he addresses himself to each question 'on its merits'; and he rejects as intolerably presumptuous the radical's contention that each and every question – for instance, whether a university should harbour an officers' training corps – must be related to the ultimate issues of how, if at all, mankind is to survive on this planet. At the scientist in his laboratory, as at the earnest liberal in his committee, the radical throws the angry word 'cop-out' – meaning by that precisely that the individual's modesty is what makes possible the corporate presumption. And Hardy in his poetry is this sort of cop-out, a modest (though proudly expert) workman in a corporate enterprise which from time to time publishes a balance-sheet called *The Golden Treasury* or *The Oxford Book of English Verse*.

These are harsh words, but it may be that harshness is what is called for. For it begins to look as if Hardy's engaging modesty and his decent liberalism represent a crucial selling short of the poetic vocation, for himself and his successors. For surely the poet, if any one, has a duty to be radical, to go to the roots. So much at least all poets have assumed through the centuries. Hardy, perhaps without knowing it, questions that assumption, and appears to reject it. Some of his successors in England, and a few out of England, seem to have agreed with him.

23 W.B. Yeats, Introduction to *The Oxford Book of Modern Verse* (London, 1937), p. xiv.

2 Hardy Self-Excelling

In five-score summers! All new eyes,
New minds, new modes, new fools, new wise;
New woes to weep, new joys to prize;

With nothing left of me and you
In that live century's vivid view
Beyond a pinch of dust or two;

A century which, if not sublime,
Will show, I doubt not, at its prime,
A scope above this blinkered time.

— Yet what to me how far above?
For I would only ask thereof
That thy worm should be my worm, Love![1]

But does not Hardy quite often excel himself, and escape from the limitations which we have gracelessly insisted upon, and laboured, through the last chapter? Indeed he does. Time and again he writes in ways that it seems his declared intentions and his professed ideology would have ruled out.

To be sure, there are certain ranges of poetic fiction which he will never stray into. For instance, when he wrote scornfully in 1922 how 'belief in witches of Endor is displacing the Darwinian theory', must we not believe that among those 'witches of Endor' Hardy would have included mythological ladies like Demeter and Artemis? And if so, there can be no doubt of his impatience with a declaration by one of his younger contemporaries, Ezra Pound:

Speaking aesthetically, the myths are explications of mood: you may stop there, or you may probe deeper. Certain it is that these myths are only intelligible in a vivid and glittering sense to those people to whom they occur. I know, I mean, one man who understands Persephone and Demeter, and one who understands the Laurel, and

---

1   Thomas Hardy, '1967'. The poem was written in 1867.

another who has, I should say, met Artemis. These things are for them *real*.[2]

Hardy would surely have responded to this very much as would his disciple Philip Larkin, who thirty years later in a strident phrase which has become famous, impatiently declared his disbelief in 'a common myth-kitty'. It is easy to share their impatience when Pound strikes into this way of talking, as he does (to give another example) in his essay of 1915, 'Arnold Dolmetsch':

> The first myths arose when a man walked sheer into 'nonsense', that is to say, when some very vivid and undeniable adventure befell him, and he told someone else who called him a liar. Thereupon, after bitter experience, perceiving that no one could understand what he meant when he said that he 'turned into a tree', he made a myth – a work of art that is – an impersonal or objective story woven out of his own emotion, as the nearest equation that he was capable of putting into words. That story, perhaps, then gave rise to a weaker copy of his emotion in others, until there arose a cult, a company of people who could understand each other's nonsense about the gods.[3]

But then, writing about Pound would be a great deal more responsible, and hostile readers like Philip Larkin would get the attention they deserve, if critics, when they quote passages like these, would pause long enough to say explicitly whether from their own experience they know what it means to 'meet Artemis', to 'turn into a tree', to 'walk sheer into nonsense'. I will confess at once that my own experience provides me with not an inkling of what these expressions mean.

And accordingly I owe it to myself to refuse the trust which I am asked to give, that for other persons 'these things are... real'. Does this seem very illiberal? Or is it not the merest prudence, and of a firmly liberal kind, to refuse, without supporting evidence from one's own experience, the claim of others to have private revelations of a supra-rational sort? After all, on the basis of such revelations, do we not hear it contended that the Elders of Zion have planned world conquest; that black and brown peoples must be servants of the whites; that peasants and artisans are happy in Mao's China; that the German nation is called to rule over Europe, the Japanese over Asia... ? In short, who is to persuade me – and how – that the man who says he has met Artemis or turned into a tree is not danger-ously self-deluded or self-intoxicated? And is not this in fact the central and unavoidable question about Pound's poetry, as about Charles Olson's and Robert Duncan's? One would not think so, scanning the many pages of criticism already devoted to these poets. It would certainly have been

2   Pound, 'Psychology and Troubadours' (1916), reprinted as Chapter V of *The Spirit of Romance* (New York reprint 1968), p. 92.
3   *Literary Essays of Ezra Pound*, ed. by T.S. Eliot (London, 1954), p. 431.

the question raised by Hardy.

However, in Pound's theory and practice there is a range of supra-rational apprehensions which falls short of the take-it-or-leave-it of 'he turned into a tree'. Pound writes, for instance, in his essay, 'Mediaevalism':

> The Tuscan demands harmony in something more than the plastic. He declines to limit his aesthetic to the impact of light on the eye... This really complicates the aesthetic. You deal with an interactive force: the *virtù* in short.
>
> And dealing with it is not anti-life. It is not maiming, it is not curtailment. The senses at first seem to project for a few yards beyond the body. Effect of a decent climate where a man leaves his nerve-set open, or allows it to tune into its ambience... The conception of the body as perfect instrument of the increasing intelligence pervades.[4]

And this is immediately related to a crucial passage, later in the same ambitious essay, which is quoted, and rightly, by every commentator. It comes where Pound is characterising the lost world of Cavalcanti, a world which Cavalcanti's poems take for granted:

> the radiant world where one thought cuts through another with clean edge, a world of moving energies '*mezzo oscuro rade*', '*risplende in se perpetuale effecto*', magnetisms that take form, that are seen, or that border the visible, the matter of Dante's *paradiso*, the glass under water, the form that seems a form seen in a mirror, these realities perceptible to the sense, interacting... this 'harmony in the sentience' or harmony of the sentient, where the thought has its demarcation...[5]

Are there people, poets indeed and readers of poetry, to whom 'one thought cuts through another with clean edge', and 'a man leaves his nerve-set open', and 'the thought has its demarcation', are propositions as meaningless − as little corroborated by personal experience − as is for others the statement, 'He met Artemis'? My experience suggests that there are people thus disadvantaged. And, without taking too seriously Pound's reference to 'a decent climate' (for we may suspect that the perceptions described are more common among Nordic travellers to Italy, than among Italians), still we may believe that people to whom both sets of propositions seem meaningless are often English.

English or not, what are such readers to do, in all honesty and the merest prudence? Finding that 'one thought cuts through another with clean edge' is (after self-scrutiny and some patient exercise) meaningless to them, must they not declare that this range or level of the poet's experi-ence is as closed to them, and just as suspect, as the mythological level is

4   Ibid., pp. 151–2.
5   Ibid., p. 154.

closed and suspect to others? I believe they must, and do; though they need to notice, as they seldom do, that they thereby declare themselves shut out not just from much of Pound's poetry, nor just from a Poundian though English poet such as Basil Bunting or Charles Tomlinson, nor from an Italianised one like Rossetti, but also from English poets thought of as thoroughly insular. The last stanza of Philip Larkin's 'The Whitsun Weddings' is, or ought to be, equally meaningless to a reader who does not know from experience how thoughts can be 'magnetisms that take form, that are seen, or that border the visible'. And those last phrases from Pound seem to be the very stuff of 'After a Journey', by Larkin's master, Hardy:

> Hereto I come to view a voiceless ghost;
> > Whither, O whither will its whim now draw me?
> Up the cliff, down, till I'm lonely, lost,
> > And the unseen waters' ejaculations awe me.
> Where you will next be there's no knowing,
> > Facing round about me everywhere,
> > > With your nut-coloured hair,
> And gray eyes, and rose-flush coming and going.

The status of Hardy's ghosts is very hard to determine. On the one hand, they seem to be merely Virgilian stage properties, in Hardy as in his contemporary and friend Masefield. But Masefield does not come before us as an atheistic humanist, as Hardy does; and in any case some of Hardy's ghosts are more 'real' than others, as we shall see. Hardy is disingenuous; we encounter in his poems things that are not dreamed of in his philosophy. And this is troublesome. But of course we must trust the poem, not the poet.

If, still with Hardy in mind, we range Ezra Pound's poems and perceptions on a scale of diminishing complexity and increasing accessibility, we find other levels of poetic experience treated by Pound, each of them less exacting than either the mythological or the level we have just been discussing. We find, that is to say, the experiences comprised within, or lying on the frontiers of, Imagism.

Even with Imagism the English reader has had great difficulties, and has them still, being by no means helped by seemingly wilful darkenings of counsel on the part of some whom he had every right to take as authorities – influential academic critics in England who have used 'imagism' as a blanket term to cover all developments in Anglo-American poetry since French *symbolisme* made its impact, or else as merely an Anglo-American variant on Symbolist doctrine and practice. There is an amusing irony here because, as Herbert Schniedau and others have hinted,[6] the influen-

---

6   Herbert Schniedau, *Ezra Pound: The Image and the Real* (Baton Rouge, 1969).

tial figure behind at any rate Pound's imagism is the Englishman, Ford
Madox Ford (whom, to be sure, the English for the most part refuse to
read); and moreover – a very nice point which I think is original with
Schniedau – the characteristic and much prized terseness of the Imagist
poem seems to owe something to the laconic understatement of the
English upper classes, a linguistic or rhetorical phenomenon which fasci-
nated the Americans among the original Imagists.

Pound, it will be recalled, speculated that a myth came into being
when a man who had 'turned into a tree', despairing of finding a hearer
for direct narration of this experience, made instead 'an impersonal or
objective story woven out of his own emotion, as the nearest equation
that he was capable of putting into words'. This mathematical analogue –
the 'equation' – was used by Pound in other contexts, and sometimes he
elaborated the analogy into specific parallels between poetry and algebra
(much as, across the Channel, Valéry was doing, and was to do, in
explaining to himself the procedures of Mallarmé). Schniedau makes it
clear that for Pound this was a great deal more than just a modish flourish.
As used by Pound, this algebraic analogue puts at the centre of Imagist
aesthetic the device of the *synecdoche*, the part that stands for the whole (in
happy cases, the particular that stands for the universal). Indeed this marks
the point at which, in Pound's most considered thinking about Imagism,
he goes beyond his mentor Ford, and raises Ford's novelistic impres-
sionism to the power and tension of poetry. What Pound learned from
Ford (not without pain, for it involved abandoning his own earlier styles
as well as much instruction from his other mentor, Yeats) was the superiority to mere 'description' of that 'presentation' which Pound and Ford
alike associated above all with Stendhal or Flaubert. The 'equation',
sparer and more demanding of the reader even than 'presentation', represents a tightening of the screw beyond Ford's stories and poems. Thus
Imagism strictly speaking is concerned with *equations* for emotional experience, not presentations of it through images, still less implications or
evocations of it through cumulative description of attendant physical
properties.

This argument supplies us with three further levels of poetic artifice, in
descending order of exactingness – equation, presentation, description.
And Hardy exerted himself on all three levels. Here, for instance, is what
I take to be an Imagist equation, 'Snow in the Suburbs':

> Every branch big with it,
> Bent every twig with it;
> Every fork like a white web-foot;
> Every street and pavement mute:
> Some flakes have lost their way, and grope back upward, when
> Meeting those meandering down they turn and descend again.

The palings are glued together like a wall,
And there is no waft of wind with the fleecy fall.

A sparrow enters the tree
Whereon immediately
A snow-lump thrice his own slight size
Descends on him and showers his head and eyes,
And overturns him,
And near inurns him,
And lights on a nether twig, when its brush
Starts off a volley of other lodging lumps with a rush.

The steps are a blanched slope,
Up which, with feeble hope,
A black cat comes, wide-eyed and thin
And we take him in.

And here is a 'presentation', 'A Spellbound Palace' (subtitled 'Hampton Court'):

On this kindly yellow day of mild low-travelling winter sun
The stirless depths of the yews
Are vague with misty blues:
Across the spacious pathways stretching spires of shadow run,
And the wind-gnawed walls of ancient brick are fired vermilion.

Two or three early sanguine finches tune
Some tentative strains, to be enlarged by May or June:
From a thrush or blackbird
Comes now and then a word,
While an enfeebled fountain somewhere within is heard.

Our footsteps wait awhile,
Then draw beneath the pile,
When an inner court outspreads
As 'twere History's own asile,
Where the now-visioned fountain its attenuate crystal sheds
In passive lapse that seems to ignore the yon world's clamorous clutch,
And lays an insistent numbness on the place, like a cold hand's touch.

And there swaggers the Shade of a straddling King, plumed,
sworded, with sensual face,
And lo, too, that of his Minister, at a bold self-centred pace:
Sheer in the sun they pass; and thereupon all is still,
Save the mindless fountain tinkling on with thin enfeebled will.

(Ghosts are frequent denizens of Hardy's poems; but these shades of

Henry VIII and Wolsey are, in no derogatory sense, conventional, as the woman's ghost in 'After a Journey' certainly is not.)

As for a poem by Hardy that is brilliantly descriptive, no more, we have looked at one such already, 'Overlooking the River Stour', a poem which itself confesses, guiltily, that its composition did not engage the full attention of its author. It thus proclaims its own minor or marginal status; and yet of course, so long as description is so vividly exact and inventive as in that poem, we cannot wish to deny to description a place, if perhaps a humble one, within the legitimate endeavours and performances that we call poetry. A rung or many rungs beneath description, and beneath the dignity of poetry, is inert observation (however accurate) and enumeration, such as are found allegedly in a young British poet perhaps unfairly parodied:[7]

> Down in Rowntree Road
> Motorbikes, dogshit and girls
> Are words, words, words,
> Not *motorbikes, dogshit* and *girls*...
>
> When thou hast Dunn
> Thou hast not done,
> For he has more
> Words like motorbikes, dogshit, girls.

My point is to suggest that the now five-fold scale, from description through presentation to equation, and thence through the ghostly to myth — a scale perhaps of mounting intensity, certainly of increasing scope and ambitiousness — is one upon which to place quite a lot of poems by Hardy. Of course, the distinctions within it are not clear-cut; and it may raise problems that are sterile because mechanical. For instance *The Dynasts* is offered rather plainly as 'myth'; if it fails to satisfy on that level, does it — or can it — earn our esteem on some other? (I would guess not.)

No distinction is more crucial than that between presentation and Imagist equation. Pasternak wrote, in 1922:

> People nowadays imagine that art is like a fountain, whereas it is a sponge. They think art has to flow forth, whereas what it has to do is absorb and become saturated. They suppose that it can be divided up into means of depiction, whereas it is made up of the organs of perception.[8]

An English critic, Martin Dodsworth, noting this declaration, was discon-

7 *Expostulations*, by Teddy Hogge, and *The Wooden Muse*, Part One, by Alec Pope (London, 1970), p. 13.
8 Pasternak, Neskol'ko polozhenii (1922); see *Sochineniya* [*Works*] (Ann Arbor, 1961), III, 152.

certed to come across poems by Pasternak where a quality of sparseness, even meagreness, in the scene which the poem renders is registered appreciatively or at least without reprobation.[9] But Pasternak seems to have been as much of an Imagist as Pound was, at least in the sense that he sought to give not presentations of experience, still less descriptions, but equations for it. And in poetry as in mathematics an equation is above all economical, elegantly spare. The Imagist poem, like the short poems of Pasternak, epitomises experience by anatomising it; as Schniedau says, it is characteristic of the Imagist poem to be skeletal. The Pasternakian 'saturation' in no way denies this; at the cost of mixing metaphors let us say that only when the poet is saturated with an experience is he in a position to anatomise it, to distill from it not a description nor even a presentation but an anatomy, an equation. (When Wordsworth speaks of 'emotion recollected in tranquillity', the 'tranquillity' stands for the saturation, the 'recollecting' for the distillation.)

And in fact Pasternak is very Poundian indeed, but very Hardyesque also, when he opts for poetry as sponge, not as fountain. Poets and students of poetry do not need phenomenologists to tell them that any successful encounter between subject and object, certainly any such encounter that is at once fine enough and resonant enough to germinate a poem, has to be marked above all by reciprocity, by a giving that is equal (and no more than equal) to a taking. But, that once said, it makes a difference from which point of view we regard the transaction, from the point of view of the subject or of the object; in short, which way the traffic is run, from inside out or from outside in. And Pasternak's figure of the sponge ranges him firmly with Pound, with Williams, with George Oppen – in fact with the whole Imagist and post-Imagist tradition in American poetry, which envisages the traffic run from outside in, not the other way around. It is probably as true now as it was in 1922 that 'people nowadays imagine art is like a fountain'. Doubtless, even in a freed Russia, Blok and Mayakovsky would be more popular than Pasternak; just as on both sides of the Atlantic, Ginsberg and Lowell are, and will continue to be, more popular than George Oppen and Charles Tomlinson. For readers, it seems, will always take more readily to the subjective making demands on the objective, than to any traffic the other way. And for this reason most readers, even in England, will always find Hardy's poetry, however estimable and touching, insufficiently exciting. For Hardy, though he seems to have lived through the Imagist Movement and its immediate aftermath without being aware of them, is certainly among those who see poetry as sponge rather than fountain – as both 'Snow in the Suburbs' and 'A Spellbound Palace' should have shown.

9   Martin Dodsworth, in *The Review*, No. 22 (June 1970), pp. 46–7.

In something like the lyric sequence 'Razryv' ('The Break'), as in many other places, Pasternak can be seen to have moved beyond Imagist anatomising.[10] And Hardy moves there also; as I have contended, the author of 'Wessex Heights' was one of those 'certain men' who, as Pound said, 'move in phantasmagoria; the images of their gods, whole country-sides, stretches of hill and forest travel with them':

> There's a ghost at Yell'ham Bottom chiding loud at the fall of the
> night,
> There's a ghost in Froom-side Vale, thin-lipped and vague, in a
> shroud of white,
> There is one in the railway train whenever I do not want it near,
> I see its profile against the pane, saying what I would not hear.

Hardy's 'gods' are always ghosts; but certainly as he travels, whole countrysides travel with him. Of poem after poem by Hardy, as of story after story, we can say that what occasions them is topography, a reality of place rather than time. Carl Weber has worked out that the cycle of the Wessex novels and stories is devised in such a way as to span, decade by decade, the course of the nineteenth century through that area of south-west England. But of course what most insistently strikes the reader of Hardy's prose is not this charting of historical time, but a mapping of physical space. What the reader of Hardy first needs – and this is as true of the poems as of the stories – is not a history of nineteenth-century England, but a map. Significant is the presence of poems entitled 'In Front of the Landscape' and 'The Place on the Map'. Time brings in its revenges, and now that Edwin Muir in Britain has despairingly protested, 'Nothing can come of history but history', now that in the United States, Charles Olson and other poets have set themselves to learn from geographers like Herodotus and C.O. Sauer and J. Tuzo Wilson,[11] it should be easier to understand how and why, in the poems of bereavement after the death of his first wife, Hardy's imagination turned continually on the

10 It is also true that in some poems Pasternak moves on or up to that level of *myth*, where as I have confessed I cannot follow him nor Pound nor any poet – the level on which Pound is able to say, in his obituary of Ford, 'he saw quite distinctly the Venus immortal crossing the tram tracks'. Since I have followed Herbert Schniedau gratefully in a great deal, I ought to make it clear that this is where I depart from him. The point may be crucial. For it's on the assumption that 'myth' is the central business of the *Cantos* that Schniedau rests his ingenious case that the *Cantos*, being essentially a compendium of myths like Ovid's *Metamorphoses*, had to deny themselves that 'unity of surface' which Pound once found 'boring' in Pope, Racine, Corneille. What we are offered instead is that current shibboleth, 'composition by field'. The argument, however, is unsound; for in one of its aspects Pope's *Dunciad*, for all its 'unity of surface', is a compendium of myth, as Aubrey Williams and others have shown. True to my predilections or my limitations, I esteem that dimension of Pope's masterpiece much less than its magnificently sustained and curious phantasmagoria.
11 See, for topography in contemporary American poetry, my lecture, 'The Black Mountain Poets', in Martin Dodsworth (ed.), *The Survival of Poetry* (London, 1970); also 'Landscape as Poetic Focus' in *The Southern Review* 4: 3 (July 1968), pp. 685–91.

difference between her native Cornwall and the Dorset he took her to, where she lies buried. It will be noticed, with newly heightened sympathy, how in his poems for Leslie Stephen and Swinburne, Hardy identified both men with patches of physical space which in their lives they attached themselves to – in Swinburne's case, the Channel coast, in Stephen's the Alpine peak of the Schreckhorn. And it will be noticed too that location matters so much, and it changes into phantasmagoria, only for a man who is on the move; on the move, for instance, between *cultures*, mobile in more than a physical sense.

★　★　★

When Hardy excels himself, what happens to Hardy the technician? We may recall that the trademark of that technician was an often intricate symmetry between stanzas. And if we are right about that, we can begin to answer the question by noticing that both of the admirable poems by Hardy quoted in this chapter are conspicuously asymmetrical. Another finely asymmetrical poem is 'The Voice', as we have noticed. And yet there are very few such poems by Hardy. If it is true, as I think it is, that we see him excel himself when he breaks stanzaic symmetry, we cannot expect to have that breaking away into asymmetry manifested for us, as it is in these poems, by the look of the verse on the page. We must learn to look through apparent symmetry to the real asymmetry beneath. Let us look at the body of Hardy's poems which can be designated, in some sense, as love lyrics.

One such is 'An Upbraiding', which is like 'The Haunter' in that it is put in the mouth of the woman's ghost; it is better than 'The Haunter' simply because it is more brief, and shaped much more simply. Of other poems supposedly spoken by the woman, the most imperiously 'engineered' is 'A Man Was Drawing Near To Me', the most winning is 'I Rose and Went To Rou'tor Town', and the most painful is 'Love Lost':

> I play my sweet old airs –
>   The airs he knew
>   When our love was true –
>   But he does not balk
>   His determined walk,
> And passes up the stairs.
>
> I sing my songs once more,
>   And presently hear
>   His footstep near
>   As if it would stay;
>   But he goes his way,
> And shuts a distant door.

So I wait for another morn,
  And another night
  In this soul-sick blight;
  And I wonder much
  As I sit, why such
A woman as I was born!

There are many poems like this, mostly short, mostly remorseful, written immediately out of the torments that Hardy and Emma inflicted on each other through the last twenty years of their life together. It is distasteful to have to admit that of recent years the biographers, picking apart the cloak of Hardy's reticence, have helped us greatly with small but important poems such as this.[12] These poems are not conspicuously engineered, and taken together they make up a notable achievement. They are of a sort that is nowadays called 'confessional', and often esteemed very highly. Indeed, we sometimes hear it said that such poetry, which seems to be written immediately out of the jangle of agonised nerves, is the only poetry that nowadays we can afford to attend to. There are those of us who cannot agree, for whom such confessional poetry is a valid and valuable kind but not the highest. In Hardy's generation Patmore, a head-strong and too fervent critic, nevertheless makes the case for us in his essay, 'Emotional Art' (Essay V of *Principle in Art*), when he insists, traditionally enough, on the importance for high art of *repose* – something that confessional poetry by its nature cannot attain to. Thus, to call these poems 'painful' is to recognise their achievement but also to limit it. To see that limit transcended, we need only turn to 'My Spirit Will Not Haunt the Mound':

My spirit will not haunt the mound
  Above my breast,
But travel, memory-possessed,
To where my tremulous being found
  Life largest, best.

My phantom-footed shape will go
  When nightfall grays
Hither and thither along the ways
I and another used to know
  In backward days.

12 A far from exhaustive list would be: 'The Rift', 'Once at Swanage', 'Without, not Within Her', 'I Look into My Glass', 'You Were the Sort that Men Forget', 'Lost Love', 'The End of the Episode', 'Tolerance', 'The Last Performance', 'The Peace-Offering', 'The Prophetess', 'The Walk', 'Without Ceremony'.

> And there you'll find me, if a jot
>   You still should care
> For me, and for my curious air;
> If otherwise, then I shall not,
>   For you, be there.

Yvor Winters points very justly to 'the very quiet and very skilful final stanza'. Just so. Between 'very skilful' and 'brilliantly engineered' there is a world of difference, and most of the difference is in 'quiet'. Multiple meanings crowd in upon the word 'curious'. And the last lines, by confessing that the ghost is only subjectively real, forestall objections that must be made to the use of the ghost convention in inferior poems like 'The Haunter'. The completeness of the loss, the irremediable finality of it, is insisted on no less in this poem than in others more painful; the fact of its being irremediable, which is the source of the pain, is also, paradoxically, the reason for repose. The poem recognises this paradox, as the more painful poems do not; we know that it does so chiefly by the way that its movement – syntax and metre interwoven – works upon us.

Of such poems by Hardy, Irving Howe has said finely:

> These have been called poems of mourning, and so they are. But they are also something else, perhaps more valuable. Hardy's ultimate concern is not with any immediate emotion, but with the consequences of emotion, survival beyond emotion: how a man lives through what it seems he cannot, and how he learns not to tamper with his grief and not even to seek forgiveness in his own eyes. The kindness Hardy characteristically shows to all creatures he does not deny to himself, for he is free of that version of pride which consists in relentless self-accusation. The speaker in these poems is a man, perhaps a little better or a little worse than others, but not, in any ultimate reckoning, very different. He moves through emotion, for there is no way to live and avoid that, but then he moves a little past it, toward the salvage of poise. And thereby this figure free of the impulse to moralise becomes a moral example, such as few among the more brilliant or complex sensibilities of our age could provide.

This I take to be a valuable gloss on Coventry Patmore's 'repose'.

Thus it may appear that we have a rule of thumb by which to recognise Hardy's best love poems: they will be poems in which repose transcends pain (or pleasure, for that matter – but in Hardy that is seldom the problem[13]) as human skill transcends technique.

---

13 Seldom, and yet sometimes. For instance, 'Louie':

> I am forgetting Louie the buoyant;
> Why not raise her phantom, too,
>   Here in daylight

'After a Journey', for instance, has been singled out for praise by nearly all commentators in the years since F.R. Leavis examined it memorably in *Scrutiny*.[14] And yet there is a general reluctance to locate the convincingness of this poem in the aspect of it where, surely, the conviction is most carried – that is to say, in the metre. For this is, of all Hardy's poems, the one that most triumphantly vindicates the plea he entered for himself in his comment about 'the Gothic art-principle in which he had been trained'. The 'cunning irregularity', achieved by 'metrical pauses, and reversed beats', permeates this poem from first to last; it is not to be located in this 'touch' or in that, and accordingly – so far is it from being *appliqué* or deftly engineered – we experience it no longer as technical expertise, but as human and as it were manual skill, as 'fingering'. With that word, we seek our analogies no longer in architecture, but in music; and this is very significant. For Edmund Blunden's deceptively casual chapter on Hardy's poems is nowhere so perceptive as when he compares Hardy's practice in verse with Gautier's 'L'Art':

> Oui, l'oeuvre sort plus belle
> D'une forme au travail
>   Rebelle,
> Vers, marbre, onyx, émail...

For Hardy, as we see from his choosing the architectural analogy, is, like Gautier, one of the late nineteenth-century poets who find analogies for their art in the arts that dispose masses in space not (as music does) in time. And yet, in 'After a Journey', the architectonic symmetries between stanzas, though they persist exactly and the sensitive prosodist can elicit them,[15] are so overlaid by cunning irregularities that what we apprehend

> With the elect one's?
> She will never thrust the foremost figure out of view!
>
> Mid this heat, in gauzy muslin
> See I Louie's life-lit brow
>   Here in daylight
>   By the elect one's. –
> Long two strangers they and far apart; such neighbours now!

Though the scene is a graveyard, here the repose is radiant.

14 *Scrutiny*, 19: 2 (1952–3).
15 So I must suppose, at any rate; though I've met no one yet who could scan the poem. The best I can do is to scan the lines as four-foot trochaic-dactylic. But the 4th line of the last stanza does not conform. And the short 7th line has two feet in the first two stanzas, three feet in the later two. Hardy tells us that he 'spent some time in hunting up Latin hymns at the British Museum', hoping to 'enrich' English prosody 'by adapting some of the verse-forms of these'. We may note that, according to Schipper (*History of English Versification*, 1910), tail-rhymed and other elaborate stanza forms may have come into English from Provençal as well as from Latin hymns. Thus Pound's Provençal interests would have enabled him to respond readily to the many elaborate stanzas in Hardy which ask to be analysed in terms like *frons* and *cauda*. I suspect now that the whole of 'After a Journey', except for the penultimate 'bob' line in each stanza, is to be understood as written in English hendecasyllables.

is the musical form shaped in time from first through to last, not the architectural form which reproduces a shape three times over. The rigid symmetry, though it holds firm and could be disclosed by sufficiently erudite scansion, cedes – in our experience of the poem as we read it – to the fluid, musical, and narrative shape of the poem as it starts, goes on, and ends. One remembers, very much to the point, how Leavis was driven to a musical analogy – 'the exquisite modulation into the last stanza' – in the case of a comparable piece, 'The Voice'. And as for the reposefulness of the irremediable, 'After a Journey' almost spells it out:

> Trust me, I mind not, though Life lours,
>   The bringing me here; nay, bring me here again!

It is a great poem, and it is phantasmagoria:

> Hereto I come to view a voiceless ghost;
>   Whither, O whither will its whim now draw me?
> Up the cliff, down, till I'm lonely, lost,
>   And the unseen waters' ejaculations awe me.
> Where you will next be there's no knowing,
>   Facing round about me everywhere,
>   With your nut-coloured hair,
> And gray eyes, and rose-flush coming and going.
>
> Yes: I have re-entered your olden haunts at last;
>   Through the years, through the dead scenes I have tracked you;
> What have you now found to say of our past –
>   Scanned across the dark space wherein I have lacked you?
> Summer gave us sweets, but autumn wrought division?
>   Things were not lastly as firstly well
>   With us twain, you tell?
> But all's closed now, despite Time's derision.
>
> I see what you are doing: you are leading me on
>   To the spots we knew when we haunted here together,
> The waterfall, above which the mist-bow shone
>   At the then fair hour in the then fair weather,
> And the cave just under, with a voice still so hollow
>   That it seems to call out to me from forty years ago,
>   When you were all aglow,
> And not the thin ghost that I now fraily follow!
>
> Ignorant of what there is flitting here to see,
>   The waked birds preen and the seals flop lazily;
> Soon you will have, Dear, to vanish from me,
>   For the stars close their shutters and the dawn whitens hazily.
> Trust me, I mind not, though Life lours,

The bringing me here; nay, bring me here again!
    I am just the same as when
Our days were a joy, and our paths through flowers.

'The Going', written the previous year (1912), is often grouped with 'After a Journey' and 'The Voice' – for instance by Douglas Brown. I am inclined to think of it, rather, as the most ambitious and memorable of the poems that I have called 'confessional' and 'painful'. It is very elaborately symmetrical indeed, on a twofold alternating plan, seven verse lines taking one shape in stanzas 1, 3 and 5, and another in stanzas 2, 4, 6. Given a pattern thus rocking and repetitive, it is very difficult for us to feel the poem unfolding itself, moving us through from first to last, as 'After a Journey' does. And yet Hardy seems to have intended the poem to end, as it were, quite a long way from where it began. The 'Going' of the title is picked up by 'be gone' in the first stanza; this is linked with 'your great going' in the next; and all these variations on 'go' and 'going' and 'gone' are consummated six lines from the end in the utterly characteristic, audacious, and harrowing line: 'Unchangeable. It must go.' It asks a poet, not just a great and daring technician, to ring such changes on so common a word, and by his changes to graph the progress of a pain from first to last through his poem. And yet if this is the nerve of the poem, the hidden form of its unfolding, that form is (I think) not merely hidden and decently cloaked but positively *impeded* by the overt form with its intricate symmetries. Accordingly, though with the greatest hesitation, I find the imperious verbal engineer still, even here, thwarting the true and truly suffering poet.

On the other hand, as nearly every critic has agreed, there can be no doubt at all about 'During Wind and Rain'. This is one of Hardy's greatest achievements. The characteristically exact and intricate symmetry between the four elaborate stanzas of this poem is transcended, as it is in the four stanzas of 'After a Journey', by the cunning variations of the accomplished metrist; but the crucial variation can be located and identified, whereas in 'After a Journey' it works all through and all over. In 'During Wind and Rain' the variation that is decisive is on the seventh and last line of each stanza:

    'How the sick leaves reel down in throngs!'

    'See, the white storm-birds wing across!'

    'And the rotten rose is ript from the wall.'

    'Down their carved names the rain-drop ploughs.'

Rhythmically so various, the lines are metrically identical. Though anapaests are twice substituted for iambs in the line about the rose, the expectation of symmetry proves that this line too is iambic tetrameter like the others. And the rhythmical variations testify only to a wonderfully fine ear,[16] not to any special expertise in prosody; in other words, to a human skill, not technical virtuosity. The effect is that when we reach the refrain at the end of the third stanza, though symmetry is maintained between that stanza and the first two, it is so masked by the rhythmical variation that, instead of checking back to register how this stanza reproduces the earlier ones, we are propelled forward to see what will happen in the last. And thus we experience an unfolding from first to last, not a folding back three times over. The feeling flows into each stanza, brims, and three times pours into the next. Repose transcends pain, as manual skill transcends mechanical technique.

There are other poems by Hardy of which one wants to speak admiringly in such terms. One is 'Beeny Cliff', and another is 'At Castle Boterel', in which the musical flow through the symmetrically sculpted stanzas is signalised with unusual plainness, by a carry-over of sense and grammar from the first stanza to the second. But it is more important to insist that these poems to which we give unqualified praise are, when all is said and done, thoroughly of a piece with others about which we have qualms or hesitations. On the one hand this means (to reiterate) that we cannot add to the list of thoroughly approved pieces until we arrive at a Selected Poems that will stand in place of the Collected. For the range – or, better still, the *ranging-ness* – of Hardy's imaginative activity is one of the most impressive things about him, and no weeding out of imperfections can be allowed to obscure this. On the other hand, when we find Hardy excelling himself, this is not quite the same as saying that he transcends himself and those professed principles of his which we have called 'liberal' and 'scientific humanist'. It still matters that the gods in Hardy's phantasmagoria are all ghosts. The apparition of the dead Emma in 'After a Journey' is certainly not conventional, like the apparition of Wolsey in 'A Spellbound Palace'; but this doesn't mean that the experience recorded in the poem should have been submitted to the Society for Psychical Research. And indeed, if the Hardy of 1922, the scientific humanist, were to say that the apparition and the dialogue in 'After a Journey' were only a manner of speaking, we should not need to quarrel with him.

This must be my excuse for trying to connect Hardy with his younger contemporaries, Pasternak and Pound. Though we can find things that they have in common with him, in the end what must strike us is how different he is. Pound and Pasternak (and Yeats and G.M. Hopkins and Eliot) are radical in a sense that Hardy isn't. All these other poets claim, by implication or else explicitly, to give us entry through their poems into

16 I am sorry and surprised to find Irving Howe perpetuating an old error when he says of Hardy: 'His ear was uncertain: many of his lines drag and crumble…' (Howe, *Thomas Hardy*, pp. 162–3).

a world that is truer and more real than the world we know from statistics or scientific induction or common sense. Their criticism of life is radical in that they refuse to accept life on the terms in which it offers itself, and has to be coped with, through most of the hours of every day. In their poems, that quotidian reality is transformed, displaced, supplanted; the alternative reality which their poems create is offered to us as a superior reality, by which the reality of every day is to be judged and governed. But neither in 'After a Journey' nor anywhere else does Hardy make that claim. For him, 'criticism of life' means 'application of ideas to life' – the two formulations by Matthew Arnold are two ways of saying the same thing. And so his poems, instead of transforming and displacing quantifiable reality or the reality of common sense, are on the contrary just so many glosses on that reality, which is conceived of as unchallengeably 'given' and final. This is what makes it possible to say (once again) that he sold the vocation short, tacitly surrendering the proudest claims traditionally made for the act of the poetic imagination. Whether this was inevitable, given his intellectual convictions and the state of the world in his time, is an interesting question. Some poems by a later atheist and scientific humanist, Hugh MacDiarmid, suggest that it was not. In any case, it happened; and the consequences of it, for some of Hardy's successors, have been momentous.

3 Landscapes of Larkin

Let there be treaties, bridges,
　　Chords under the hands, to be spanned
Sustained: extremity hates a given good
　　Or a good gained. That girl who took
Her life almost, then wrote a book
　　To exorcise and to exhibit the sin,
Praises a friend there for the end she made
　　And each of them becomes a heroine.
The time is in love with endings. The time's
　　Spoiled children threaten what they will do,
And those they cannot shake by petulance
　　They'll bribe out of their wits by show.[1]

I shall take it for granted that Philip Larkin is a very Hardyesque poet; that Hardy has been indeed the determining influence in Larkin's career, once he had overcome a youthful infatuation with Yeats. Larkin has testified to that effect repeatedly, and any open-minded reader of the poems of the two men must recognise many resemblances, though Larkin, it is true, has shown himself a poet of altogether narrower range – it is only a part of Hardy that is perpetuated by Larkin into the 1960s, but it is a central and important part.

The narrowness of range, and the slenderness of Larkin's record so far (three slim collections of poems, and of those only two that are relevant) might seem to suggest that he cannot bear the weight of significance that I want to put on him, as the central figure in English poetry over the last twenty years. But in fact there has been the widest possible agreement, over most of this period, that Philip Larkin is for good or ill the effective unofficial laureate of post-1945 England. Some may have criticised what Larkin does with the truths he discovers, what attitudes he takes up to the landscapes and the weather of his own poems; but those landscapes and that weather – no one, I think, has failed to recognise them. And this is

---

1　Charles Tomlinson, 'Against Extremity', *The Way of a World* (London, 1969). The allusion appears to be to Anne Sexton and the late Sylvia Plath.

just as true if we think of landscapes and weather metaphorically; we recognise in Larkin's poems the seasons of present-day England, but we recognise also the seasons of an English soul – the moods he expresses are our moods too, though we may deal with them differently. On the literal level at any rate, no one denies that what Larkin says is true; that the England in his poems is the England we have inhabited. We may compare Ted Hughes, who – in America especially – is Larkin's chief rival for the unofficial laurels. We all know that England still has bullfrogs and otters and tramps asleep in ditches; yet because in the landscape of Hughes's poems these shaggy features bulk so large, it may strike us as more an Irish landscape than an English one. The congested England that we have inhabited day by day is Larkin's England:

> A slow and stopping curve southwards we kept.
> Wide farms went by, short-shadowed cattle, and
> Canals with floatings of industrial froth;
> A hothouse flashed, uniquely: hedges dipped
> And rose: and now and then a smell of grass
> Displaced the reek of buttoned carriage-cloth
> Until the next town, new and nondescript,
> Approached with acres of dismantled cars.[2]

Those slow canals have wound through many a poem about England since T.S. Eliot's *Waste Land*, but never under such a level light as this. For in the poem as a whole ('The Whitsun Weddings'), the tone of the describing voice is scrupulously neutral; it affords no handle at all for reflections like 'A canal, not a river', or 'Tainted water, not fresh'. There is no meaning, no 'placing', in the way pre-industrial things like farms, cattle, hedges, and grass are interspersed with industrial things like chemical froth and dismantled cars. And for Larkin indeed this seems to be one of the rules of the game; there is to be no historical perspective, no measuring of present against past. Canals and smashed cars come along with hedges and cattle simply because they come along like that in any railway journey through England, as we all know. And precisely because poem after poem since *The Waste Land* has measured our present (usually seen as depleted) against our past (usually seen as rich), Larkin's refusal to do this is thoroughly refreshing – at last, we recognise with relief, we can take all that for granted, take it as read. It's in this that Larkin differs from John Betjeman, whom he admires; Betjeman is the most nostalgic of poets, Larkin the least.

And yet this poet who speaks so levelly of 'Canals with floatings of industrial froth' is the author also of 'Water':

2   Philip Larkin, *The Whitsun Weddings* (London, 1964).

If I were called in
To construct a religion
I should make use of water.

Going to church
Would entail a fording
To dry, different clothes;

The litany would employ
Images of sousing,
A furious devout drench,

And I should raise in the east
A glass of water
Where any-angled light
Would congregate endlessly.[3]

This is less distinctive writing than 'The Whitsun Weddings', but not therefore less distinguished. And the mere fact of its existence proves, if proof be needed, that when Larkin in more ambitious pieces refuses to recognise any special dignity or sanctity attached to elemental presences like water, it is not because this sort of sentiment about the natural is foreign to his experience. He mostly refuses to allow such sentiments into the peopled landscapes of his England because they would impede his level-toned acceptance of that England as the only one we have, violated and subtopianised and poisoned as it is. To put it more pointedly, Larkin makes himself numb to the non-human creation in order to stay compassionate towards the human. Thus, near the end of 'The Whitsun Weddings', when

I thought of London spread out in the sun,
Its postal districts packed like squares of wheat...

the collision between the organicism of wheat and the rigidity of 'postal districts' is calculated. It is the human pathos of the many weddings he has seen from the train which spills over to sanctify, for the poet, the postal districts of London, the train's destination; the human value suffuses the abstractly schematised with the grace of an organic fertility.

This makes Larkin into one sort of extreme humanist. And no doubt it lays him open to the antihumanist objection which, for instance, Leo Shestov brought against Chekhov, that if so little is asked of the human person before he deserves sympathy, then the sympathy is not worth having. If the persons in the landscape were thought to be in some degree the makers as well as the victims of the history which has polluted the landscape round them, they would gain in dignity by just as much as they forfeited compassion. What cannot be doubted, I think, is that Larkin has foreseen this objection and decided to risk it; that he does not lower his sights without counting beforehand those experiences (for instance, natural piety about water) which, when the sights are lowered, must go out of focus.

Larkin therefore would understand, though he might not like, a poem called 'Hardly Anything Bears Watching' by Mairi MacInnes:

> Hardly anything bears watching.
> Bricks and stone
> Have lost their intense surprise.
> For years I kept my trust in things.
>
> Even beyond the last parishes
> Fringed with refuse,
> Hills drawn beneath the surveyor's rod.
> They too lie perfectly numb.
>
> The old parabolas of socialism,
> Spirals of love,
> Make hope the habitat of the soul.
> But hope's not native to the blood.
>
> No comfort from the boy who draws
> Upon my memory of bombs.
> The man recalls
> Brave days on a far-off sea.
>
> Picture after picture fails.
> When I was young,
> The pavement kerbs were made of stone
> A substance like my finger-nails.
>
> It is not like that any more.
> I do not see
> The essential life of inorganic things.
> Humanity has covered all.[4]

In this surely admirable poem, it is once again the curiously level tone of voice which can carry off the big blunt words like 'inorganic' and 'humanity' and 'hope' and 'the soul'. Mairi MacInnes is counting the cost more explicitly than Larkin does; and rather plainly in the lines about 'The old parabolas of socialism' she comes nearer repenting of her bargain than ever Larkin does – though for that matter I have my own ideas about

4 Mairi MacInnes, 'Hardly Anything Bears Watching', quoted from *The Spectator*, 16 August 1963.

what causes the powerfully ugly and vicious poems that our laureate sometimes disconcerts us with, poems like 'A Study of Reading Habits' or 'Send No Money'. Miss MacInnes's poem says that to buy sympathy with the human, at the price of alienation from the non-human, is a hard bargain at best.

However, not many English poets think so. For most of them, 'nature poetry' (since that after all is what we are talking about) is a world well lost. The reviewer who said that Ted Hughes's 'Pike' was at bottom a Georgian nature poem thought he had scored a shrewd hit. And conversely, when A. Alvarez (introducing the Penguin *New Poetry*) wants to establish that Hughes's poem about horses is better than Larkin's 'At Grass', on the same subject, he does so to his own satisfaction by arguing that Hughes's poem isn't about horses at all; that the horses are 'symbolic' – and symbolic of what? Why, of something in the human psyche, of course. In other words, it's only when what seems to be a nature poem can be converted into a human-nature poem that we begin to take it seriously. This is a humanism like Larkin's, but less respectable because it does not count the cost, seems not to know that there is any cost incurred. A poem by Alvarez proceeds on the same assumption – an account of the killing of an animal by a drinking pool is deliberately blurred into an evocation of the sexual act between two people; in other words, the encounter between human and non-human has no value and no significance until it can be made an allegory of an encounter between humans. One recalls the cries of satisfaction with which the modern reader approaches that one of Wordsworth's nature poems, 'Nutting', in which the imagery conveys a submerged metaphor of rape. 'All value is in the human, and nowhere else.' It is a possible point of view, and may be sincerely held. For the English it has the great advantage of anaesthetising them to the offensiveness of their own landscapes and removing any sense of guilt at having made them offensive. It is D.H. Lawrence's constant guilt and horror at what the English had made of England which makes it certain that, breeder as he was of his own symbolic horses (in *The Rainbow*, in *St Mawr*), he certainly counted the cost and mostly he thought it extortionate.

Kingsley Amis, an Englishman in Wales, sets the scene for the amours of Mr Evans and Mrs Rhys in 'Aberdarcy, the Main Square':

> The journal of some bunch of architects
> Named this the worst town centre they could find;
> But how disparage what so well reflects
> Permanent tendencies of heart and mind?
>
> All love demands a witness: something 'there'
> Which it yet makes part of itself. These two

Might find Carlton House Terrace, St Mark's Square,
A bit on the grand side. What about you?[5]

This is not a level tone at all. The ugliness that it is, piled on to the ugliness it talks about, sets us veering crazily between disgust and self-disgust
as we oscillate without guidance between the two possible answers to the
last question. Either, 'Yes, I too should find it too grand (or too beautiful)' – in which case we confess that our own amours, and by implication everybody's, are as squalid and furtive as Evans's; or else, 'No, I
deserve something better than Aberdarcy' – in which case we are being
superior and unfeeling toward the Evanses of the world, and perhaps
hypocritical as well.

It is the same dilemma – either we accept that we deserve no better
than the gracelessness of scene which surrounds us, or else we shut
ourselves off from our neighbours who seem to ask nothing better and are
doing their best to make it worse. Like Richard Hoggart as regards literature, Larkin, as regards landscape and architecture and indeed literature
also, agrees to tolerate the intolerable for the sake of human solidarity
with those who don't find it intolerable at all. Rather than put up with
the intolerable, Lawrence forfeited the solidarity – and with a clearer
sense of what he was doing, of the price he was paying. As for Amis, he
leaves us to answer a question he cannot answer himself. Exploiting the
facile irony of that veering tone which Auden reinvented for us, he
contrives to be, in the brilliantly baleful words of Auden himself, 'paid on
both sides' – though in a devalued currency. And this is the irony so
readily applauded in British writing today; it refuses to answer questions
which need answering.

To give Amis his due, the question he asks is no longer open by the
time he has finished with it; at the end of his sequence, 'The Evans
Country', he contrives (though in wretchedly bad writing) an effect of
hysterical brutality which leaves us still in the dark about Evans's motives,
but not about Amis's attitude to him. The last two stanzas of 'Welch
Ferry, West Side' can only mean that we are all alike, each of us is Evans
at heart, and none of us therefore deserves anything better than
Aberdarcy:

> ... all the smog had lifted, and more stars
> Than he knew what to do with filled the sky,
> And lighted lighthouse, civic centre, quay,
> Chimneys, the pony's pasture, cooling-towers;
> 'Looks beautiful tonight', he muttered,

---

5   Kingsley Amis, 'Aberdarcy, the Main Square', *A Look Round the Estate* (London, 1967).

> Then raised his voice: 'Eurwen, get moving, do,
> You think I want to hang round here all night?
> Free over the week-end, are you? I'm not;
> I'm boozing with the boys on Saturday,
> Sunday's the club... All right, then – never.'⁶

The self-disgust of this crowds out compassion; yet in his twisted way Amis too opts for solidarity – St Mark's, with all the grace and grandeur of an architectural setting fit for human action of dignity, is the price that must be paid for fellow feeling with the Evanses.

And all this has political implications. There is nothing gratuitous about Mairi MacInnes's word, 'socialism'. For this readiness to opt in the last resort for solidarity at all costs, to trade the non-human for the human, to lose dignity and beauty and elegance for the sake of supposedly more tangible and general benefits – this is the distinguishing mark of the British Left. Indeed, in the astonishing way that life has of imitating literature, Amis's sequence on his squalid amorist Evans was no sooner published than we saw English intellectuals of the Left making the late Stephen Ward (one of the minor actors in the Profumo scandal) into love's martyr, happy to overlook the squalid tastelessness of his life as a procurer for the sake of the humaneness which (arguably) shone through it. And if this is the choice of the Left, the only possible alternative – a moral fastidiousness which cannot help but seem arrogant – certainly finds no home in the British Conservative party; it must look for its politics much further to the Right, as the case of Lawrence shows. In fact, I suppose, all parliamentary politics in Britain belongs in the broad band of the political Centre, which corresponds to the ironist's evasion of the choice, his wish to be paid on both sides though at reduced rates – and just as well perhaps, for the open-minded ironist is worth more in politics than he is in poetry. (And that's a reflection to make any poet pause and disconsolately wonder.)

Looked at in this way, Larkin's poetry of lowered sights and patiently diminished expectations can be justified, and the British poetic scene in which he figures makes no bad showing. Larkin and others like him, in the '50s and '60s, seem to have been facing, in different ways and with different degrees of honesty and awareness, an issue which the anthologists and editors and commentators of that period hardly perceived at all. And of course this is as it should be – the respectable poets should always be several jumps ahead of their readers. (And yet throughout the period there was a common and totally unacceptable assumption that there existed an English audience – a mass audience, said the Left; an *élite*, said the Right – which deserved better poets than it was getting.)

---

6   Kingsley Amis, *A Look Round the Estate.*

Commentary came nearest engaging with this issue that concerned the poets when, in the early 1960s, it began to consider the allegation that writing like Larkin's was damagingly insular and provincial. At different levels of urbanity and perceptiveness this was discussed in Robert Conquest's introduction to his anthology, *New Lines 2* (London, 1963), in Alvarez's introduction to his anthology, *The New Poetry* (Harmondsworth, 1962; 2nd ed., 1966), and in John Press's *Rule and Energy* (London, 1963). But none of these approached the question at the level that seems to be called for; nor did the medicine prescribed and rather timidly taken – respectful reading of foreign poets in translation, and of some Americans – seem to cure the disease, if disease was what it was. For surely the distinctive quality and the distinctive task of poetry in Britain were defined, and are still to be defined, by the fact that Britain as a whole is the most industrialised landscape in the world; that there the non-human has been exploited and violated by the human more consistently and over a longer period than anywhere else. It was English poetry (with Wordsworth) that in modem times first expressed ideas of elemental sanctity and natural piety; and it seems it must be English poetry which asks what to do with these ideas in a landscape where virtually all the sanctuaries have been violated, all the pieties blasphemed. Though this is essentially a British theme, it is not therefore insular. For industrialisation, with the suburbia that is its corollary, is coming to other parts of the globe only a little less fast than it has come to England and South Wales, Northern Ireland and much of Scotland. Larkin, who deals with this issue (explicitly in 'Water', obliquely in 'The Whitsun Weddings'), may be insular in other ways; but certainly this theme of his is central to the contemporary experience of readers far outside the British Isles.

The difficulty of confronting this theme in poetry cannot be overestimated. The poet confronts it even when he writes on quite other themes, for he knows it in the damage it has done to the language he has to use. Our poetry suffers from the loss, or the drastic impoverishment, of the traditional images of celebration. Consider only Larkin's images of this kind, wheat and water; or Mairi MacInnes's image, worked stone ('The pavement kerbs were made of stone'). Can we believe that it makes no difference to the potency of these ancient images, when more and more, as poets and readers, we know water only as it flows from a tap; when we can go from one year's end to the next without seeing a wheatfield, and when the bread we eat – chemically blanched, ready-sliced, untouched by human hand – bears no perceivable relation to the wheat-ear; when we walk and live no longer amid stone but amid concrete? Can we trust any longer the celebratory, hallowing potency which these images and others like them (laurel and nightingale, rose and oak) have manifested in poetry of the past? It is questions like these that are involved when one conceives of a poetry that should survive in a wholly urbanised and industrialised society. And if, as seems likely, it is British poets who are called on first to write such a poetry, their task is dauntingly difficult. A poem such as 'The Whitsun Weddings', though it may be written from a standpoint we cannot endorse, is heartening evidence of how the British poet might rise to this historically unprecedented challenge.

The foregoing pages on Larkin, except for some touchings up and second thoughts, were already in print in 1963, when I had not begun to think about the significance of Hardy for the English poets who came after him. But plainly what I have called Larkin's lowering of his sights represents a further withdrawal or surrender beyond those that Hardy had made already. And yet Larkin has more excuse than Hardy, so much excuse that we cannot in justice call him a cop-out, though plenty of people have done so. If his range is obviously narrower than Hardy's, in the sector that we are concerned with his analysis goes, or is pushed by historical circumstances, much deeper. As concerned as Hardy is with landscape, he never, so far as I know, confronts the exploitation and poisoning of landscape by industry. On the one hand he could not do so because of his ambiguous sympathy with technology and with his sense of himself as technician. (And, incidentally, there is nothing of this in Larkin – the stanzaic and metrical symmetries which he mostly aims at are achieved skilfully enough, but with none of that bristling expertise of Hardy which sets itself, and surmounts, intricate technical challenges.) On the other hand, the landscapes of Hardy's England were not yet quailing so defencelessly before technology as they are now, after fifty years of the cheap motor car. And this rape of the sanctuaries provokes in Larkin a sense for what has been ravished – the elemental sanctity of water and wheat, something else that Hardy never invokes, devout Wordsworthian though he was. (Would he have thought it one sort of belief in 'the witches of Endor'? One hopes not.)

But it is in the political implications of their poetry that the two poets are most alike. Each of them settles for parliamentary democracy as a shabby, unavoidable second-best. Do they persuade us that it is indeed unavoidable? Larkin apparently does not persuade Colin Falck.[7] Mr Falck, taking issue with my essay of 1963 (though really it is Larkin he is quarrelling with), declares at the end of a careful scrutiny of Larkin's poems:

> In rejecting Larkin's particular brand of 'humanism' I may seem to be asking for the kind of 'right wing' violence to which D.H. Lawrence was sometimes led. I think perhaps I am. The last and truest humanism in art is the truthful expression of emotion, and this is something prior to all questions of politics: it concerns only the honesty or the corrup-

7   Colin Falck, 'Philip Larkin', *The Review*, No. 14, reprinted in *The Modern Poet: Essays from The Review*, ed. by Ian Hamilton (London, 1968), pp. 101–10.

tion of our consciousness. If this means barbarism, then let us have
barbarism.

Falck goes on to say that barbarism 'has come to be associated with obscurity', whereas what he asks for is 'lucid barbarism' – which forces me to
recognise that I don't know what 'barbarism' means as he uses the word.
More mysteriously still, he says of this lucid barbarism, 'If we cannot face
it in art, we shall have to face it soon enough in life', then speaks in his
next sentence of 'this post-Nazi age'. My mystification is complete; for I
should have thought that the experience we have had, thanks to the
Nazis, of what a right-wing alternative to parliamentary democracy is like
– an experience available to Larkin but not to Hardy – is what should
impel us to acknowledge that the shabby second-best we have is indeed
unavoidably our choice, the alternative having turned out so much
worse. The alternatives currently on offer of course come not from the
Right but the Left; and one would like to know what Colin Falck thinks
of *their* violence. But in fact I think he is speaking of a violence that has
nothing to do with political arrangements at all: a barbarism and a
violence merely of rhetoric and gesture. One does not have to be any sort
of dogmatic Marxist to be dumbfounded when he asserts that 'the last and
truest humanism in art' is 'prior to all questions of politics'. How can this
be so? That 'truthful expression of emotion' which he asks for has to
express the emotion of an individual, the poet. And is not that individual
conditioned, at least in part, by the politics he lives among and has
suffered through? Are the emotions which Larkin seeks to express in no
way conditioned by his being a post-Nazi poet, whereas Thomas Hardy
wasn't? Hardy and Larkin, it appears, accept responsibility for the political
implications of what they say in their poems; and Colin Falck wishes they
wouldn't. Indeed the poet, as Falck conceives of him, is a highly
specialised creature. For he has said earlier in his essay:

> No doubt it is always important to maintain some general sense of
> what most other people's lives are like. But the poet cannot be content
> with this, and it might even be argued that it is not really his business
> *qua* poet at all, whatever might be expected of him as a novelist or as a
> human being.

Hardy and Larkin may have sold poetry short; but at least neither of them
sold it so short as to make the poet less than a human being. And part of
being human is being a citizen of some commonwealth. I can sympathise
with Falck's outraged refusal of the diminished world which Larkin's
poetry proffers as the only one available to him; but he cannot escape that
world as easily as he thinks.

I don't know that any of us can escape it. I have spent some time on
Colin Falck only to introduce a far more sustained and tormented attempt

to break out of the greyly constricting world of Larkin, and (I fear we must say) the not much less constricting world of Hardy. This attempt has been Charles Tomlinson's. Ever since 1957 Tomlinson has been lucidly angry at what he pungently calls the 'suburban mental ratio' which Larkin and other poets have imposed on their experience. And he has not failed to realise that his quarrel with these contemporaries is in part a political quarrel, or at least that it has immediate political implications. He has written, for instance, with evident and explicit sympathy, about the *élitist* and hierarchical politics which W.B. Yeats was drawn to from his youth when he responded with enthusiasm to Nietzsche.[8] It is the more remarkable that, as I read him, Tomlinson has lately – though with unabated anger and contempt – settled for Larkin's world as indeed *politically* the only one that we dare conceive of for ourselves. This is the acknowledgement he makes at the end of 'Prometheus':

> Summer thunder darkens, and its climbing
>   Cumulae, disowning our scale in the zenith,
> Electrify this music: the evening is falling apart.
>   Castles-in-air; on earth: green, livid fire.
> The radio simmers with static to the strains
>   Of this mock last-day of nature and of art.
>
> We have lived through apocalypse too long:
>   Scriabin's dinosaurs! Trombones for the transformation
> That arrived by train at the Finland Station,
>   To bury its hatchet after thirty years in the brain
> Of Trotsky. Alexander Nikolayevitch, the events
>   Were less merciful than your mob of instruments.
>
> Too many drowning voices cram this waveband.
>   I set Lenin's face by yours –
> Yours, the fanatic ego of eccentricity against
>   The systematic son of a schools inspector
> Tyutchev on desk – for the strong man reads
>   Poets as the antisemite pleads: 'A Jew was my friend.'
>
> Cymballed firesweeps. Prometheus came down
>   In more than orchestral flame and Kérensky fled
> Before it. The babel of continents gnaws now
>   And tears at the silk of those harmonies that seemed
> So dangerous once. You dreamed an end
>   Where the rose of the world would go out like a close in music.

---

8   See Tomlinson, 'Yeats and the Practising Poet', in *An Honoured Guest*, ed. by Denis Donoghue and J.R. Mulryne (London, 1965), pp. 1–7. Predictably, Hardy felt for Nietzsche nothing but contempt; see Hardy's letters to the press in 1914, reprinted in *Life and Art*, ed. by Ernest Brennecke (New York, 1925), pp. 137–9.

Population drags the partitions down
    And we are a single town of warring suburbs:
I cannot hear such music for its consequence:
    Each sense was to have been reborn
Out of a storm of perfumes and light
    To a white world, an in-the-beginning.

In the beginning, the strong man reigns:
    Trotsky, was it not then you brought yourself
To judgement and to execution, when you forgot
    Where terror rules, justice turns arbitrary?
Chromatic Prometheus, myth of fire,
    It is history topples you in the zenith.

Blok, too, wrote The Scythians
    Who should have known: he who howls
With the whirlwind, with the whirlwind goes down.
    In this, was Lenin guiltier than you
When, out of a merciless patience grew
    The daily prose such poetry prepares for?

Scriabin, Blok, men of extremes,
    History treads out the music of your dreams
Through blood, and cannot close like this
    In the perfection of anabasis. It stops. The trees
Continue raining though the rain has ceased
    In a cooled world of incessant codas:

Hard edges of the houses press
    On the after-music senses, and refuse to burn,
Where an ice-cream van circulates the estate
    Playing Greensleeves, and at the city's
Stale new frontier even ugliness
    Rules with the cruel mercy of solidities.[9]

This is not Tomlinson's characteristic style. The poem is in a collection called *The Way of a World* (1969), and the only British reviewer who did justice to the book rightly remarked, in 'Prometheus' and some other poems, 'a less private voice, a controlled rhetoric which claims and commands a wider space, ranges over a more impressive variety of tones than ever before'.[10] But though his more characteristic style is different from this, it is no nearer than this to any style that could be called Hardyesque. Tomlinson's styles always transform and displace the realities

9   Charles Tomlinson, 'Prometheus', *The Way of a World*.
10 Ronald Hayman, 'Observation Plus', in *Encounter* (December 1970), p. 73.

known to science, to statistics, to the bleared eye of every day; he refuses the Hardyesque surrender, by which those realities are the unquestionable texts which poetry can only gloss. Tomlinson is a poet for whom an expression like 'one thought cuts through another with clean edge' is abundantly meaningful. The realm of experience which such an expression refers to, the realm of the *phantastikon*,[11] a realm which Hardy and Larkin infrequently break into without meaning to and without noticing, is the world which Tomlinson's imagination lives in and ranges over continually.

And yet Tomlinson stops short of myth. If he characteristically transforms and displaces quotidian reality, it is not in order to supplant that reality, but on the contrary only to do it justice by defining and following through with patience the articulations of it – articulations which our bleared eyes miss, resonances which our dulled ears slide over without noticing. And it is this tough-minded grasp upon the actual which enables and indeed compels him, here, to settle for the canned music of 'Greensleeves' from an ice-cream van, as symbolising *politically* something at least solid and merciful, whereas Scriabin's tone poem, 'Prometheus', orchestrates a politics which has proved itself both merciless (the murder of Trotsky) and nebulous. Thus Tomlinson, when he thinks politically, lowers his sights and settles for second-best just as Larkin and Hardy do – but more impressively than either because so much more aware of, and pained by, the cost.

Hardy, it is true, predicted what the cost would be and was pained by it in prospect: 'Democratic government may be justice to man, but it will probably merge in proletarian, and when these people are our masters it will lead to more of this contempt, and possibly be the utter ruin of art and literature!' This marks off Hardy from Larkin very sharply: Hardy moved at ease and as of right in the bourgeois culture which he had made his own by strenuous self-education. Catullus and Voltaire, Gibbon and Aeschylus, Clement and Origen, *La Bohème* and *II Trovatore*, the painters Eddy and Maclise, are named on the pages of Hardy with as little embarrassment as Scriabin and Blok, Van Gogh and Constable and Maillol, are named by Tomlinson. Larkin at best ignores such names, at worst he turns upon them snarling:

(He once met Morgan Forster) ...

Books are a load of crap.

11 See Pound, 'Psychology and Troubadours' (1916), now printed as chapter V of Pound's *The Spirit of Romance* (New York reprint, 1968, p. 92): 'We have about us the universe of fluid force, and below us the germinal universe of wood alive, of stone alive. Man is – the sensitive physical part of him – a mechanism... As to his consciousness, the consciousness of some seems to rest, or to have its centre more properly, in what the Greek psychologists called the *phantastikon*. Their minds are, that is, circumvolved about them like soap-bubbles reflecting sundry patches of the macrocosmos.'

In fact on this issue Hardy's gloomy forebodings have not been borne out: it is not the proletarians, 'our masters', who have heaped contempt on Hardy's art and literature, but the masters of those masters, the black-leg intellectuals who direct and use 'the media' (including, of course, newsprint). It is these, the self-appointed spokesmen for a proletarian culture not theirs, who will not forgive poems like Tomlinson's which are webbed together by specific allusions to music, literature, and history. And their strategy is always the same, apocalyptic; somewhere – on the Somme, in Petrograd, at Katyn or Buchenwald, over Dresden, in Algeria, or at My Lai (the list is endless) – something has happened of such momentous enormity that, so they would persuade us, it has removed our right any longer to frequent the artistic and intellectual monuments of the past, having made those monuments irrelevant to our condition. It is to challenge these apocalyptic voices that Tomlinson, elsewhere in *The Way of a World*, writes 'Against Extremity', declaring 'extremity hates a given good/Or a good gained', and 'The time is in love with endings'. Hardy, especially if we measure him against his contemporary Yeats, is of Tomlinson's way of thinking. But Larkin is a different case. His is not an apocalyptic voice; on the contrary those who fly to extremes cannot forgive him his mostly level tone. And yet, he is certainly in love with endings. Moreover he is so ready to lower his sights – to a point where artistic monuments go out of focus, no less than elemental presences and sanctities – that we begin to think he does so under pressure not from 'the age', but only from some compulsion in himself. Certainly, if the lowered sights can be vindicated in 'The Whitsun Weddings', there are other poems in which they cannot.

One such poem is 'Here', which seems to be a portrait of the city of Hull and its environs:

> Swerving east, from rich industrial shadows
> And traffic all night north; swerving through fields
> Too thin and thistled to be called meadows,
> And now and then a harsh-named halt, that shields
> Workmen at dawn; swerving to solitude
> Of skies and scarecrows, haystacks, hares and pheasants,
> And the widening river's slow presence,
> The piled gold clouds, the shining gull-marked mud,
>
> Gathers to the surprise of a large town:
> Here domes and statues, spires and cranes cluster
> Beside grain-scattered streets, barge-crowded water,
> And residents from raw estates, brought down
> The dead straight miles by stealing flat-faced trolleys,
> Push through plate-glass swing doors to their desires –

Cheap suits, red kitchen-ware, sharp shoes, iced lollies,
Electric mixers, toasters, washers, driers –

A cut-price crowd, urban yet simple, dwelling
Where only salesmen and relations come
Within a terminate and fishy-smelling
Pastoral of ships up streets, the slave museum,
Tattoo-shops, consulates, grim head-scarfed wives;
And out beyond its mortgaged half-built edges
Fast-shadowed wheat-fields, running high as hedges,
Isolate villages, where removed lives

Loneliness clarifies. Here silence stands
Like wheat. Here leaves unnoticed thicken,
Hidden weeds flower, neglected waters quicken,
Luminously-peopled air ascends;
And past the poppies bluish neutral distance
Ends the land suddenly beyond a beach
Of shapes and shingle. Here is unfenced existence:
Facing the sun, untalkative, out of reach.[12]

Here every non-urban thing comes along with a negating or cancelling epithet – leaves are 'unnoticed', waters are 'neglected', distance is 'neutral'. And if existence is 'unfenced', it is also 'out of reach'; if it is 'untalkative', it is by that token noncommittal, unhelpful. The insistence seems excessive – as if the poet were *determined* not to be helped nor instructed by things that plainly he responds to keenly. (For obviously the leaves do not go unnoticed by him, so by whom are they 'unnoticed'? By the cut-price crowd, or by the country dwellers? And if by both or either, is this a good thing or a bad?) It was not thus that Hardy responded to the waked birds that preen, the seals that flop lazily, in 'After a Journey'. And in 'Beeny Cliff', though 'The woman now is – elsewhere – whom the ambling pony bore,/And nor knows nor cares for Beeny, and will laugh there never more', it is as a source of mysterious comfort, not in mocking irrelevance, that 'Still in all its chasmal beauty bulks old Beeny to the sky.'

In Larkin's poem one detects a perverse determination that the ultimate ('terminate') pastoral shall be among the cut-price stores, and nowhere else. And the pity felt for the denizens of that pastoral, the 'residents from raw estates', is more than a little contemptuous. A political analogue might be the petty bourgeois who, aspiring to the cultural goods and sylvan retreats of the *haut bourgeois*, finds himself overtaken by the proletarians, and resentfully throws in his lot with them, a dedicated iconoclast such as they have no wish to be. This is unfair – it defines some of Larkin's critics more than it defines Larkin; but it shows how little resis-

---

12 Philip Larkin, 'Here', *The Whitsun Weddings*.

tance his world, and his cast of mind, can muster against such iconoclasts. If he is Hardy's heir, he sells out or sells off a great deal of his inherited estate. Yet Hardy had provided the precedent for such a sell-out. And of course in the interim between Hardy and Larkin (or Tomlinson) the pressures to make such surrenders had increased.

4 Lucky Jim and the Hobbits

> *Forgive me Sire, for cheating your intent,*
> *That I, who should command a regiment,*
> *Do amble amiably here, O God,*
> *One of the neat ones in your awkward squad.*[1]

It would be unfair to Kingsley Amis to leave an account of his poetry with my rude remarks in the last chapter about 'The Evans Country'. In the years before that poem Amis had written several pieces very cleanly and solidly composed, which are too little known and too little respected. Amis the novelist, Amis the polemicist, and latterly Amis the personality on radio and television, have crowded out of attention Amis the poet; and this sufficiently illustrates the relative importance given in modern Britain to writing in verse, writing in prose, and unconsidered remarks by way of 'the media'. Amis's poetry, however, is much to our purpose, since far more than his novels it concerns itself quite explicitly with political issues. It does so not under Hardyesque but rather under Gravesian auspices; and so this chapter must be regarded as a digression – though a necessary one – for the understanding of the climate of political ideas in which British poets since Hardy have been working.

The political idea that Amis has been particularly concerned with is that crucial one, the concept of authority. For instance:

THE VOICE OF AUTHORITY: A LANGUAGE GAME

> Do this. Don't move. O'Grady says do this,
> You get a move on, see, do what I say.
> Look lively when I say O'Grady says.
>
> Say this. Shut up. O'Grady says say this,
> You talk fast without thinking what to say.
> What goes is what I say O'Grady says.
>
> Or rather let me put the point like this:
> O'Grady says what goes is what I say
> O'Grady says; that's what O'Grady says.

1   Norman Cameron, 1905–1953. 'Forgive Me, Sire', from his *Collected Poems* (London, 1957).

By substituting you can shorten this
Since any god you like will do to say
The things you like, that's what O'Grady says.

The harm lies not in that, but in that this
Progression's first and last terms are I say
O'Grady says, not just O'Grady says.

Yet it's O'Grady must be out of this
Before what we say goes, not what we say
O'Grady says. Or so O'Grady says.[2]

This piece is what it says it is, 'A language game'. There is an obvious sense in which it isn't a poem. The game 'O'Grady', familiar to me from my childhood, and I believe sometimes used by drill-sergeants to enforce alertness in the training squad, depends upon a simple rule: the listener obeys the orders which are prefixed by the phrase 'O'Grady says', but disobeys or ignores orders given without that prefix. Sooner or later, one 'jumps to it', responding to the imperative tone, though the essential prefix has not been given. Amis uses the device of this exercise to explore the nature of authority, as we know it, and its relation to power. Thus, after the first six lines we read from the poem the statement: 'Authority is hollow; a thin cloak for the only naked face, power.' But after the next three lines we read from the poem: 'No. Authority is real; it genuinely exists to legitimise power, and not merely as rhetorical subterfuge.' The next three lines say: 'But since we have lost any confidence (it would have to be a religious or metaphysical confidence) that we can locate the one source of genuine authority in the world, it is as if there were no one such source but many.' But, the poem goes on, this would not matter if the several sources were agreed to be objectively real. But we cannot agree or believe that this is the case, and a subjectively arrived at authority is equivalent to arbitrary power. The last three lines of the poem suggest that the answer to the conundrum is to acknowledge that the source of authority is human (some men have it, others haven't), but that this does not make it any less real. Indeed, the last four words – 'Or so O'Grady says' – may be taken to mean that the location of authority in some men rather than in others may in fact have a divine or metaphysical sanction.

   Amis was not alone among British poets of the 1950s in concerning himself with such matters. Here are the first three stanzas of a poem of my own which I wrote in 1953, called 'Creon's Mouse':

Creon, I think, could never kill a mouse
When once that dangerous girl was put away,
Shut up unbridled in her rocky house,
Colossal nerve denied the light of day.

2   Kingsley Amis, from *A Case of Samples* (London, 1956).

> Now Europe's hero, the humaner King
> Who hates himself, is humanised by shame,
> Is he a curbed or a corroded spring?
> A will that's bent, or buckled? Tense, or tame?
>
> If too much daring brought (he thought) the war,
> When that was over nothing else would serve
> But no one must be daring any more,
> A self-induced and stubborn loss of nerve.

This poem was seriously meant, and much of it I still subscribe to. A loss of nerve is what has saved us time and again in the years since 1953. It was what averted world war over Budapest in 1956, as also in 1968 over Prague, in which latest case it was in fact, and rightly, taken for granted. On the other side of the balance, an alarming recovery of nerve, 'too much daring', was what took Britain into the Suez crisis and America into Vietnam. But I ask myself now, as apparently I didn't in 1953, 'How much daring is too much?' What I didn't envisage then, which there is no excuse for not envisaging now, is that there would be people who would think it too daring of Creon to be a king at all, however self-limited and vowed to consultation and compromise. It is possible, I now have to realise, to think that it is audacious presumption for a man to get into any position of authority over his fellows, to take on any kind of institution-alised responsibility for directing them.

If I am challenged on this, I can point, for instance, to a letter which appeared in *The Listener* in 1968. Headed 'End of the anti-university', the letter declared that that venture ran aground on precisely this rock. Mr John Rowley, the writer of the letter, expostulated with his ex-colleagues in the anti-university: 'But you need a "place" and an "organisation" within it, however small and flexible, that is recognisable by all. Nobody seemed to be able to accept this. It meant an organisation and that meant "power", which was anathema.' Even at that point, Mr Rowley said, the anti-university might have been saved if 'some reluctant capitalist' had written a cheque; but this was impossible because 'we are unable to tell him who to send it to'. The difficulty, one would have thought, could have been foreseen. But apparently not. The anti-university was full of Antigones, not a Creon among them; and no one would take, or could be given, the authority to receive a cheque on behalf of the rest. For that would have been to acknowledge that the anti-university had been insti-tuted and was therefore (insupportable word) an institution. When people behave like this, Creon's nerve has been buckled indeed.

Other people in 1968 were reading political lessons out of Sophocles' *Antigone*. Conor Cruise O'Brien, writing in the same issue of *The Listener* in which John Rowley's letter appeared, reminded us that Antigone had a sister, Ismene, who resented Creon's order but would not flout it; and he applied the situation between Creon and Antigone and Ismene to the disturbance then occupying the headlines in the news from Northern Ireland:

> There are many, even among the victims of the present conditions, who feel that the price of change would be too high: the spiritual children of Ismene are more numerous than those of Antigone, in Ulster as elsewhere. And their arguments, as always, are reasonable. The disabilities of Catholics in Northern Ireland are real, but not overwhelmingly oppressive; is their removal really worth attaining at the risk of precipitating riots, explosions, pogroms, murder? Thus Ismene. But Antigone will not heed such calculations: she is an ethical and religious force, an uncompromising element in our being, as dangerous in her way as Creon, whom she perpetually challenges and provokes.

My sympathies have always been with Ismene, and they are even more fervently with her in view of what has happened in Northern Ireland since 1968. I have always thought that she had more reason to lose patience with Antigone than ever Creon had, though neither Sophocles nor his commentators seem to have thought so. Creon and Antigone understand each other rather well, they have a great deal in common, more than either of them has with unheroic, painfully reasonable Ismene. So it is no surprise if Amis has played Antigone in his time. As he did, I think, in a poem of his called 'Masters', which must have been written about the same time as my 'Creon's Mouse':

> That horse whose rider fears to jump will fall,
> Riflemen miss if orders sound unsure;
> They only are secure who seem secure;
> 　　Who lose their voice, lose all.
>
> Those whom heredity or guns have made
> Masters, must show it by a common speech;
> Expected words in the same tone from each
> 　　Will always be obeyed.
>
> Likewise with stance, with gestures, and with face;
> No more than mouth need move when words are said,
> No more than hand to strike, or point ahead;
> 　　Like slaves, limbs learn their place.
>
> In triumph as in mutiny unmoved,
> These make their public act their private good,
> Their words in lounge or courtroom understood,
> 　　But themselves never loved.

> The eyes that will not look, the twitching cheek,
> The hands that sketch what mouth would fear to own,
> These only make us known, and we are known
>   Only as we are weak:
>
> By yielding mastery the will is freed,
> For it is by surrender that we live,
> And we are taken if we wish to give,
>   Are needed if we need.[3]

I think this is an enviably well-written poem until the last stanza, where the cadence smoothes itself out with disconcerting slickness. And not just the cadence, surely. For what follows if we take the argument seriously and try to follow it through? Surely one thing that might follow, one moral we might draw, is to act like Mr Rowley's anti-university colleagues. For if the only way to be known and loved is not to act or speak with authority, then shouldn't we at all costs refuse authority and neither sign nor receive cheques on anyone's behalf? Always be in the Opposition, never in the Government? Always refuse office? There is nothing else that Antigone can do, if she is to remain Antigone.

The interesting thing about Amis's poem is that his Antigone refuses above all the supposed loneliness of office. In Sophocles' play Antigone is the intransigent individual, a loner. But the Antigones that tangle with the police on or off campus, or in the streets of Derry and London, are always in the plural, and think of themselves thus, as the speaker of 'Masters' does. The price that our Antigones won't pay in order to take authority is the price of detachment from the collective. Of course, mass action is the only weapon they have. But their slogans and rallying cries, and their cooler statements also, make it clear that for most of them identification with the mass isn't just a strategic necessity but an emotional need, as witness their remarkable jumpiness about any allegations of a personality cult surrounding any of their leaders. Sophocles' Antigone could not be a social democrat; our Antigones are.

Conor Cruise O'Brien insists that Creon and Antigone and Ismene are universal types, or at least that the Creon-stance, the Antigone-stance, the Ismene-stance are constants of political action, in any place at any time. Doubtless this is right. Nikita Creon loses his nerve in the Cuban missile crisis, as Uncle Sam Creon loses his nerve over Budapest in 1956, as alas he doesn't lose it over Vietnam. But when we think that Russian Antigones are called Larisa Daniel and Pavel Litvinov, we are forced to remember how circumstances alter cases. There is nothing disingenuous nor hypocritical about admiring the Antigone-stance in certain situations and in certain societies, while deploring it in others. If Communism is not

---

3   Kingsley Amis, 'Masters', from *A Case of Samples*.

monolithic, neither is 'protest'. So the British Antigone can be seen and judged only if we separate her from Antigones elsewhere; she belongs and is to be understood only in the context of British society.

Amis's name for Antigone is 'Lefty'. Amis describes 'the lefty' in one of his best poems, 'After Goliath', which one can think of as 'After Creon'. In the poem, David, having laid the giant out cold, exults briefly over Goliath's adherents:

> … aldermen, adjutants, aunts,
> Administrators of grants,
> Assurance-men, auctioneers,
> Advisers about careers

– all Creon types, of the sort hilariously pilloried in Amis's novels, *Lucky Jim* and *That Uncertain Feeling*. Lucky Dave then pauses:

> But such an auspicious debut
> Was a little too good to be true,
> Our victor sensed; the applause
> From those who supported his cause
> Sounded shrill and excessive now,
> And who were they, anyhow?
> Academics, actors who lecture,
> Apostles of architecture,
> Ancient-gods-of-the-abdomen men,
> Angst-pushers, adherents of Zen,
> Alastors, Austenites, A-test
> Abolishers – even the straightest
> Of issues looks pretty oblique
> When a movement turns into a clique,
> The conqueror mused, as he stopped
> By the sword his opponent had dropped:
> Trophy, or means of attack
> On the rapturous crowd at his back?[4]

And in the years since, we have seen how Amis the giant killer settled that last question: the weapon of his fame, wrenched from the giant Establishment, has been turned on those who most applauded that assault. A sword taken from Creon has been used against Antigone. And, allowing for the comic-dramatic convention of the poem (the catalogue gets more vehement and more random as David's exasperation mounts), it is plain who Amis's Antigone is: she is the British intelligentsia. If he calls her 'Lefty', this is because the British intelligentsia has virtually no right wing at all. Indeed, the delayed result of Fascism and of the Second

4   Kingsley Amis, 'After Goliath', from *A Look Round the Estate*.

World War has been to taint or smear the whole right wing of the political spectrum in England, so that for the most part the range of permissible and expressible political attitudes in Britain since 1945 has run only from the centre to the left. Thus, any talk of the Labour party or the Conservative party can only muddle the issue. And it is an issue too important to be muddled; nothing less than: what is an intelligentsia? Or what has it come to be in British society? What are the social privileges and obligations of an intelligentsia, and are these the privileges it enjoys, and the obligations it honours, in Britain today?

But we sometimes find it said that there is no such thing as a British intelligentsia, and that Britain is the poorer for the lack of it. When this view is expressed in academic circles, it is usually the preamble to a stirring call to university teachers to abandon the view of their function which Matthew Arnold had articulated for them. In the words of one exponent of this point of view, the professors must 'abandon the status of Arnoldian defenders of culture', and 'accept the distortions and special pleadings... involved in any attempt to make the past genuinely available to the present'. According to the same authority, the British intellectuals must on the contrary 'accept their role... as Sartre has accepted it in his brilliant and polemical literary studies'. But of course no one who has been involved in recent disturbances on British campuses – for instance at the University of Essex in 1968, when Sartre, that eagle eye in its Paris eyrie, intervened impudently by telegram – can doubt that we already have in England a politically conscious intellectual class in principled opposition to the national society, and ready on that principle to purvey 'distortions and special pleadings' to the nation's student youth.

Surely, not only does Britain have in this deplorable sense an intelligentsia; it has had one for a long time, perhaps forty years, from just about the time in fact when Thomas Hardy died. All through that time, to be a British intellectual and yet not a socialist has meant swimming against the tide. What was new in the 1960s was the election to office of a socialist government which disappointed the hopes of most of the left-wing intellectuals who had helped to get it elected. But even if the Wilson government had chalked up a better record, the British intelligentsia would still have deserted it. For an intelligentsia, being on this showing a perpetual opposition, cannot be other than irresponsible. Like Antigone, it cannot afford ever to be responsible for the consequences of the actions it has demanded. And so it seems that any socialist government in Britain, however effective and honourable it might be, will always be disowned by the socialist intelligentsia of Britain, which will always move to the left so as to resume its oppositionist role.

Thus, one asks for an intelligentsia in the sense of a perpetual opposition only if one assumes intellectuals have a right to be politically irresponsible. As an intellectual myself I have never understood why any society should be expected to recognise that right, or be reproached for not conceding it. Czarist Russia, the society in which the concept of an intelligentsia was generated, never recognised nor conceded that right; nor did the Russian intelligentsia expect that it should.

Thus, when Isaiah Berlin argues that there is not a British intelligentsia, he means something quite different from what I have just been describing, and something altogether more acceptable. When Isaiah Berlin says that Britain has not and cannot have an intelligentsia, he means that British intellectuals have not earned, and cannot claim, the right to that privileged irresponsibility which the Russian intelligentsia could justly claim, not from Czarist society but, as it were, before posterity. If a society is so repressive that it will not let its intellectuals exercise any political responsibility at all, not even the responsibility that is incurred by openly debating political alternatives in the public prints, it forfeits its right to require its intellectuals to be responsible. Americans, in particular black Americans, are currently asking themselves whether American society is repressive enough (in more devious ways than were known to Czarist Russia), to justify them in taking or advocating politically irresponsible action. But only a lunatic fringe believes that British society is, or has been for at least a hundred years, repressive enough to give the British intellectual that justification. Yet there clearly is in Britain a class of people who assume and act upon this right which they have not earned, a body of educated persons who demand and act upon the right to be politically irresponsible; Antigones whose 'colossal nerve' becomes more impudent wherever Creon's nerve is first bent and then broken. These are the people whose type is the Lefty as Amis defines him: 'an intellectually disreputable and morally desensitised person'.

How has it come about that British society not only tolerates such an intelligentsia (for that is what any democratic society has to do), but applauds it and is proud of it? No democratic society has yet found a way to restrict the influence that such people exert, and perhaps within a democracy no way can be found. But British society, so far from wishing to curtail the influence, encourages its intelligentsia and rewards it. In many areas of the national life it has sometimes seemed as if proven irresponsibility was the surest qualification for positions of responsibility and influence. It is foolish to start gobbling and hectoring about conspiracies and self-perpetuating cliques. The answer must be looked for somewhere else. I propose that the Antigones are so powerful in Britain because there are virtually no Creons left, and precious few Ismenes. Amis's Lefty gets his own way so often because he has us half converted before he starts. Those who should play Creon's role, or Ismene's, and conceive themselves to be doing so, believe in their hearts that Antigone is right. Lefty turns out to have involuntary sleepwalking allies in the most unlikely places. The poet who wrote 'Masters' was such an involuntary accomplice, so I have suggested; and the poet who wrote 'Creon's Mouse' was another. Yet another is the author of *The Hobbit* and *The Lord of the Rings*. And he is a specially instructive case.

For all we know, J.R.R. Tolkien may be a Labour voter. On the face of it, nothing seems much less likely. A Roman Catholic born in South Africa who has spent nearly all his professional life as fellow of an Oxford college, specialising in Old English – nothing could be much farther from the Lefty stereotype, or from the type of the British intelligentsia as I have tried to define it. (For to be a scholar does not automatically put you in the intelligentsia, nor does being a poet, a sculptor, or a painter put you there – but that is another argument.) Yet I read *The Lord of the Rings* as a parable of authority, a parable pointing in one direction – towards the conviction that authority in public matters, because it is always spiritually perilous to the person it is vested in, can be and ought to be resisted and refused by anyone who wants to live humanely. And this is the conviction that the anti-university was based on; it is Antigone's conviction.

The Lord of the Rings is one of the most surprising products of British literature since 1945, and one of the most serious. Edmund Wilson's attack on the book, though it heteningly insisted on the obvious – for instance that Tolkien's prose is as undistinguished as his verse – quite fails to account for the seriousness of the undertaking, for the pressure that drove the author through these thousand or more pages, as it has driven many readers (this reader among them) to follow through the same pages eagerly. The avidity with which *The Lord of the Rings* is read, the appeal of it and the loyalty it evokes among admirers – these are self-evident facts which cannot be explained convincingly by talk of frivolity and escapism.

At first sight there seems an obvious solution: the book answers to a hunger for the heroic. And to some degree this must be true; *The Lord of the Rings* is a grown-up's *Superman*. But the driving force of the book is unheroic, even anti-heroic. The logic of the plot (which is very logical and tidy, not at all like medieval romance) is quite unequivocal; heroes are not to be trusted, only anti-heroes. The heroes have the style of authority. They are always looking 'stern' or 'grave'. And so Tolkien's narrative seems to contain many portentous images of civic authority taken and exercised – for instance, by Gandalf the wizard, and Aragorn the lost king who comes into his own. But though these heroes have the style of authority, they never have the fact of power. Tolkien asks us to admire them precisely because, when they are offered power, Gandalf and Aragorn refuse it. The villains are those, like another wizard, Saruman, who when they see a chance of power to back their authority, attempt to take it. And the contrast between Gandalf and Saruman is particularly interesting, because in the world that Tolkien has made the wizards are intellectuals. They are superhuman, however; and so, really, is Aragorn. He is called a man, but he is of superhuman mould, with an 'elfish' admixture' and he lives much longer than normal men. Indeed the point of leverage for the whole of Tolkien's creation is an assumption the sourness of which is surprisingly little noticed, still less resented – the assumption that the hobbits, who are less than human, are the only beings in Tolkien's world that a human reader can, as we say, 'identify with'. We are forced to go along with this assumption because of the language that is put in the mouths of the hobbits, as contrasted with the more elevated and literary language that is spoken by everyone else. Though the language that the hobbits speak is not convincingly the language which the common Englishman does use (and sometimes, as in the case of the loyal servitor, Samwise, is quite embarrassingly wide of that mark), it is plainly meant to be so, and we register it as at least nearer to live spoken English than the archaic and rhetorical language given to all others.

What the narrative says is that neither Gandalf nor Aragorn can be trusted with the power of the magical Ring – a power which on the contrary can be entrusted safely only to the hobbit, Frodo. The idealistic and devotedly heroic capacities of men cannot be trusted with power; power can safely be invested (and even so not with complete safety, for even Frodo is tempted and falls, right at the end) only in those 'halfling' men who, lost in a sleep of modestly sensual gratification, can rise to idealism only reluctantly and mistrustfully under the pressure of outrageous events, who behave heroically as it were in spite of themselves and to their own surprise, without premeditation. Thus the whole vast work tends to one end – to the elevation of the common man, of the private soldier over his officers and the schoolboy over his schoolmasters, of the sensual man over the intellectual, and of the spiritually lazy man over the spiritually exacting and ambitious. This is 'the Dunkirk spirit', or 'Theirs not to reason why':

> 'Still we shall have to try,' said Frodo. 'It's no worse than I expected. I never hoped to get across. I can't see any hope of it now. But I've still got to do the best I can…'[5]

Although no hobbit can be imagined as fornicating, an American admirer of *The Lord of the Rings* got the message when he was moved to 'memories of War, when unlettered, fornicating, foul-mouthed Tommies were heroes, pure and simple, on occasion…'

When a narrative calls up images so charged with sentiment as the fornicating Tommy and the Dunkirk beaches, anyone who carps at it has to be ready for trouble. So it is prudent to say that these images are charged for me too. A work of literature that calls them up, not explicitly but I think insistently, is Edwin Muir's poem, 'The Combat', which in

5 J.R.R. Tolkien, *The Return of the King*, Book VI, ch. II., *The Lord of the Rings*, Part III (Boston, 1956).

my opinion grasps more austerely than Tolkien everything in Tolkien's vision that can be made true and moving.

Amis's 'Masters' is nearer to *The Lord of the Rings* than to 'The Combat'. All the same there are differences between Amis's concerns in his poem, and Tolkien's in his romance; differences that are important and also troublesome. They have to do with the difference between authority and power. Amis's poem is entirely concerned with authority, and in fact with the *style* of authority – with whatever it is in some sorts of behaviour that makes such behaviour authoritative. Tolkien is concerned with this, but he is also concerned with power. Gandalf and Aragorn have authority without power; and this, it seems, is all right. Frodo the hobbit has power without authority; and it seems that this is all right too. What is not all right, in Tolkien's scheme of things, is to be like Saruman the wicked wizard who wants power *and* authority, both at the same time, the one to back the other. Creon and even Ismene would find this hard to understand. And so do I. Power without authority, unauthorised power, is the power of the gangster. Authority without power, impotent authority, is the authority of the figurehead, the merely nominal head of state. But this is not the worst of it. If, as Amis does explicitly and Tolkien by implication, you identify authority with *style* ('They only are secure who seem secure'), then power without authority means power where we least expect it, power that is exerted upon us without manifesting itself: the power, for instance, of the advertiser and the media-manipulator – power which is all the more dangerous for not having any of the external marks by which we might recognise it, a power which operates under wraps or under the mask of the entertainer and the discreet or fawning servant. And authority without power, when authority is identified with style, becomes the magnetic or hypnotic authority of the great performer and the charismatic leader, the authority of a Hitler, whose authority is his power, and a very great power indeed. This authority is personal; it is conceded, and the power of it is exerted, in every classroom of any university or anti-university. 'Your personal authority as a good teacher is unalienable; why do you need to have it registered in a title like Professor, and in privileges that go with that title?' Thus the campus rebels, speaking in the very accent of Antigone, and of J.R.R. Tolkien too. They do not understand, or they do not believe us, if we reply: 'Because power that is authorised, and is seen to be authorised, is the only sort of power that can be controlled and allowed for and if necessary guarded against – by the man who wields it, but also and more urgently by those he wields it over, who may suffer by it.'

Tolkien, it is well known, is far more popular with American youth than with British; and among radicals and dissidents as much as with the squares. The manager of the Berkeley campus bookstore told the *New York Times* (15 January 1967), 'This is more than a campus craze. It's like a drug dream.' A vision so British as *The Lord of the Rings* cannot help but be distorted in the enthusiastic imagination of an American sophomore; and so one is sympathetic as well as amused, reading of Tolkien's distaste for things like the campaign buttons reading, 'SUPPORT YOUR LOCAL HOBBIT' or 'GO, GO, GANDALF'. All the same, an editor for the American publishers of Tolkien in paperback was obviously in the right when he told the *New York Times*, 'Young people today are interested in power and they are interested in working out the conflict of good and evil. Here it is worked out for them.' It is indeed; perhaps perversely, but certainly with impressive consistency. Antigone is right to be grateful. And although American campus rebels are very different from the British rebels, it's reasonable to think that when they cry 'Pigs!' at the representatives of authority on and off campus they, like their British counterparts, are conceiving of a society from which authority shall seem to have vanished, where at any given moment overt authority shall be vested in no one at all. *The Lord of the Rings* endorses such hopes, and feeds them.

William Ready, who wrote *The Tolkien Relation*, speaks for a quite different section of Tolkien's American public. He is irritated and embarrassed by 'the children and those who cherish simplicity, the wooden-beads-and-sandals set, in whom he [Tolkien] has aroused enthusiasm...' And he admits, in some bewilderment, 'This is a surprising cult, this campus trend, because Tolkien is all conservative, traditional and rigid...' But, of course, no British reader need be bewildered. The Dunkirk spirit brings a lump to a Tory throat as soon as a cheer from a Labour conference; Antigone is as ready to sprinkle regretful dust on the graves of our war dead as Creon is to deliver an oration over them. And British society, in entrusting itself ever since 1939 to the principle that has been called 'a lot of weak government', has come perhaps as near as any society can to making itself into a society from which overt authority shall be absent; that is to say, just the sort of society which *The Lord of the Rings* incites us to realise.

For in practice a social organisation based on the conviction that no man can be trusted with authority has to take the form of government by committee; and thus *The Lord of the Rings* can figure as an elaborate apology for the rule by bureaucracy which Britain has invited and endured for the last thirty years, under coalition and Conservative governments as well as under Labour. The committees have the authority. As for the power, that is with the advertisers and the commentators and the trend-setters, and with those members of committees – ministers, professors of economics, vice-chancellors, trades-union leaders, others – who hurry from the committee rooms to the TV studios.

They are all Antigones really; Creon's is such a thankless role in modern Britain that there is no one left to play it with conviction.

This is what Amis says in a poem called 'Autobiographical Fragment', which in its angry irony expresses an altogether more sympathetic attitude towards the authoritarian personality than had appeared in 'Masters'.

> When I lived down in Devonshire
>   The callers at my cottage
> Were Constant Angst, the art critic,
>   And old Major Courage.
>
> Angst always brought me something nice
>   To get in my good graces:
> A quilt, a roll of cotton-wool,
>   A pair of dark glasses.
>
> He tore up all my unpaid bills,
>   Went and got my slippers,
> Took the telephone off its hook
>   And bolted up the shutters.
>
> We smoked and chatted by the fire,
>   Sometimes just nodding;
> His charming presence made it right
>   To sit and do nothing.
>
> But then – those awful afternoons
>   I walked out with the Major!
> I ran up hills, down streams, through briars;
>   It was sheer blue murder.
>
> Trim in his boots, riding-breeches
>   And threadbare Norfolk jacket,
> He watched me frowning, bawled commands
>   To work hard and enjoy it.
>
> I asked him once why I was there,
>   Except to get all dirty;
> He tugged his grey moustache and snapped:
>   'Young man, it's your duty.'
>
> What duty's served by pointless, mad
>   Climbing and crawling?
> I tell you I was thankful when
>   The old bore stopped calling.[6]

Though Constant Angst back in 1956 represented irresponsible withdrawal from social concerns (he takes the telephone off the hook) rather than irresponsible intervention in them, his name is plainly Lefty, just as the Major (who has already 'stopped calling') is Creon before his nerve

6   Kingsley Amis, 'Autobiographical Fragment', *A Case of Samples*.

was broken. For 'the old bore' is surely a phrase that is meant to reflect back discreditably on the speaker. Such uneasily retrospective admiration for the vanished authoritarian figure is to be found in other writings of the late '50s, notably in the plays of John Osborne. One of Osborne's unattractive heroes complains, in an excuse which has been much quoted, that there are no causes left to die for. But Amis's poem suggests that it is not so much a matter of having no International Brigade to enlist in, as of having no Captain Tom Wintringham to advance behind – and equally no Orde Wingate to obey, no Captain Sherwood of the Royal Navy, above all no Churchill. I find Amis's diagnosis more plausible, because less self-congratulating, than Osborne's.

The virtues of Amis's writing in 'Autobiographical Fragment' are those of Robert Graves at his best. The dry unshadowed silhouette of the Gravesian emblematic fable is also what pleases and carries conviction in 'After Goliath'. But in Amis's poems since 1957 'After Goliath' stands alone; no Gravesian virtues redeem any other poem in *A Look Round the Estate*, which is subtitled 'Poems 1957–1967'. This collection is deplorable; and if we are still looking in our poets for the presence of Hardy, we cannot be happy to think we catch a glimpse of him in the shrill and sentimental blasphemies of a poem called 'New Approach Needed':

> People have suffered worse
> And more durable wrongs
> Than you did on that cross
> (I know – you won't get me
> Up on one of those things),
> Without sure prospect of
> Ascending good as new
> On the third day, without
> 'I die, but man shall live'
> As a nice cheering thought.[7]

However, it is not Hardy's remonstrances against his Creator – thin and brittle stuff as those Hardy poems are – which lie behind such an excess as this. The figure in the shadows is the more elegant blasphemer whom Amis has elsewhere honoured in accomplished and frigid pastiche:

A.E.H

> Flame the westward skies adorning
> Leaves no like on holt or hill;
> Sounds of battle joined at morning
> Wane and wander and are still,

7   Amis, 'New Approach Needed', *A Look Round the Estate*.

> Past the standards rent and muddied,
> Past the careless heaps of slain,
> Stalks a redcoat who, unbloodied,
> Weeps with fury, not from pain.
>
> Wounded lads, when to renew them
> Death and surgeons cross the shade,
> Still their cries, hug darkness to them;
> All at last in sleep are laid.
>
> All save one, who nightlong curses
> Wounds imagined more than seen,
> Who in level tones rehearses
> What the fact of wounds must mean.[8]

Loose lips and tight lips tell the same story: the Yahoo bluster of the one, the professorial curtness of the other, provoke in us (admiringly, if all works out right) the tone which is insistently present to just the degree that it is conspicuously choked back or shouted down – the tone of whining self-pity. For Housman's Spirit of Irony easily accommodates self-pity, whereas Hardy's Spirit of Pity does not. (It is looking the other way).

It gives me no pleasure to write of Kingsley Amis in this way. But anyone who thinks me unfair when I detect self-pity, ought to turn to other pieces in *A Look Round the Estate*, like the distressingly explicit 'A Chromatic Passing-Note'. And there is more to be said of the failure of *A Look Round the Estate*. For it cannot be coincidence that the only good poem in that collection, 'After Goliath', is also the only poem that is political. As a polemicist Amis has been politically active of recent years – notably, and valuably, in the struggle (doubtless foredoomed, but a fight that must be fought) to maintain a modicum of authority for at least one representative figure in one situation, that is to say, for the teacher in his schoolroom. Yet this concern for authority, which was the nerve of the best of Amis's earlier poems, has of late expended itself entirely in such polemic and public action, leaving the poems to expostulate not with public servants like 'aldermen' and 'administrators of grants', but only with the figure of straw that atheists label 'God'. Of course Amis's master had gone the same way long before; Graves, once the social historian of *The Long Week-End*, withdrew forty years ago to Majorca and has since found a retreat even more securely insulated from British social and polit-ical realities – the mythological Never-Never Lands ruled over by goddesses, white and black, where lately he seems to have been joined in mumbo-jumbo by Ted Hughes.[9] Amis is too responsible to take that way

---

8   Amis, 'A.E.H.', *A Look Round the Estate*.
9   Ted Hughes, in *The London Magazine* (January 1971), p. 6.

out. And if we want to seduce him from a Housmanesque allegiance to another more sturdy and comprehensively humane, we may tempt him by citing Hardy at his most liberal and least socialist, least 'Lefty':

> I find that my politics really are neither Tory nor radical. I may be called an intrinsicalist. I am against privilege derived from accident of any kind, and am therefore equally opposed to aristocratic privilege and democratic privilege. (By the latter I mean the arrogant assumption that the only labour is hand-labour – a worse arrogance than that of the aristocrat, – the taxing of the worthy to help those masses of the population – who will not help themselves when they might, etc.) Opportunity should be equal for all, but those who will not avail themselves of it should be cared for merely – not be a burden to, nor the rulers over, those who do avail themselves thereof.[10]

In these comments of 1888 there speaks plainly the self-made man, the hero (or the martyr) of self-help. But they take on a more generally applicable resonance when set beside some observations of three years before:

> History is rather a stream than a tree. There is nothing organic in its shape, nothing systematic in its development. It flows on like a thunderstorm-rill by a road side; now a straw turns it this way, now a tiny barrier of sand that. The offhand decision of some commonplace mind high in office at a critical moment influences the course of events for a hundred years. Consider the evenings at Lord Carnarvon's, and the intensely average conversation on politics held there by average men who two or three weeks later were members of the Cabinet. A row of shopkeepers in Oxford Street taken just as they come would conduct the affairs of the nation as ably as these.
>
> Thus, judging by bulk of effect, it becomes impossible to estimate the intrinsic value of ideas, acts, material things: we are forced to appraise them by the curves of their career. There were more beautiful women in Greece than Helen; but what of them?[11]

That last question – 'more beautiful women in Greece than Helen; but what of them?' – is unanswerable in terms of the right-wing mythological politics of Pound or of Yeats. But it is no more answerable in terms of the historically determinist politics of Marx; for 'judging by bulk of effect, it becomes impossible to estimate the intrinsic value of ideas, acts, material things', or, we must add, of persons – among whom, as Amis has bemusedly noticed, some have innate authority, whereas others haven't.

Amis has many years yet in which to redeem the calamity of *A Look*

10　*The Life of Thomas Hardy 1840–1928*, p. 204.
11　*The Life of Thomas Hardy 1840–1928*, p. 172.

Round the Estate. One way to do so would be to resume in his poems the investigation of the fact of authority, instead of letting his concern with it lead him, as a public figure, into excusing the inexcusable, for instance the presence of the Americans in Vietnam. Unless he or some one else does this, the British will have to concur in the saturnine analysis of *The Lord of the Rings*, and subscribe themselves, when all is said and done, not men but hobbits.

5 The Hawk's Eye

> *Since I must hold to the gradual in*
> *this, as no revolution but a slow change*
> *like the image of snow. The challenge is*
> *not a moral excitement, but the expanse,*
>   *the continuing patience*
>   *dilating into forms so*
>   *much more than compact.*[1]

If we were right to think that the unusual rigidity and intricacy of Hardy's metres and stanza patterns had something to do with the phase of Victorian culture which he lived through, that of heavy engineering, we shall not expect to find this characteristic transmitted to any of his successors. For we need not subscribe to the comically confident assertions of some authorities, who would have it that because our technology is now electronic, there is a sort of necessity for the poet to compose 'by field'; but we may well feel that indeed the way in which Hardy rivets one verse line to another by clanging exact rhymes and builds up in this way a finely tooled metrical machine, is inappropriate to our sense of what really conditions and keeps running the world in which we live now.

However, there is the exceptional case of John Betjeman. For in Betjeman's poetry we do find, in the decades since Hardy died, something approaching the rigidity and intricacy of Hardy's metrical procedures. If the particular model in some of Betjeman's poems is Kipling rather than Hardy, this does not alter our sense that in any case the forms are inappropriate to the historical circumstances in which the poet is using them, and indeed that Betjeman is in many instances attracted to them for just this reason; in other words, that there is an air of antiquarianism and connoisseurship which hangs heavily around many of Betjeman's poems which are most expert and intricate as metrical constructions.

Thus, I find Betjeman most successful and most moving when his writing least reminds me of anything one might find in Hardy or Kipling

---

1 J.H. Prynne, 'Moon Poem', from *The White Stones* (Lincoln, 1969). J.H. Prynne, born 1936, is Fellow of a Cambridge college. His publications are *Force of Circumstance & Other Poems* (London: Routledge & Kegan Paul, 1962); *Kitchen Poems* (London: Goliard, 1968); *Aristeas* (London: Ferry Press, 1969); *The White Stones* (Lincoln: Grosseteste Press, 1969); and *Brass* (London: Ferry Press, 1971).

or another poet of their generation. This holds true even when the master that we hear Betjeman's poem allude to is a poet of an earlier generation yet, for instance Tennyson. The effect is more valuable still when Betjeman has asserted his independence of Hardy not just in his verse forms but also in what he chooses to say; for instance, when he is as straightforwardly and unaffectedly Christian as Hardy is atheist. One of Betjeman's most touching and valuable poems is one that qualifies on both these counts, 'Sunday Afternoon Service in St Enodoc's Church, Cornwall'. This poem, in skilful but unobtrusive and unambitious blank verse, is too long to quote in full; this is a pity, because a great deal of the impressiveness of the poem depends upon the way in which it sustains itself through easy modulations of tone and feeling. But something of the sure and fine transitions can be seen even in an excerpt:

> Where deep cliffs loom enormous, where cascade
> Mesembryanthemum and stone-crop down,
> Where the gull looks no larger than a lark
> Hung midway twixt the cliff-top and the sand,
> Sun-shadowed valleys roll along the sea.
> Forced by the backwash, see the nearest wave
> Rise to a wall of huge, translucent green
> And crumble into spray along the top
> Blown seaward by the land-breeze. Now she breaks
> And in an arch of thunder plunges down
> To burst and tumble, foam on top of foam,
> Criss-crossing, baffled, sucked and shot again,
> A waterfall of whiteness, down a rock,
> Without a source but roller's furthest reach:
> And tufts of sea-pink, high and dry for years,
> Are flooded out of ledges, boulders seem
> No bigger than a pebble washed about
> In this tremendous tide. Oh kindly slate!
> To give me shelter in this crevice dry.
> Those shivering stalks of bent-grass, lucky plant,
> Have better chance than I to last the storm.
> Oh kindly slate of these unaltered cliffs,
> Firm, barren substrate of our windy fields!
> Oh lichened slate in walls, they knew your worth
> Who raised you up to make this House of God.
> What faith was his, that dim, that Cornish saint,
> Small rushlight of a long-forgotten church,
> Who lived with God on this unfriendly shore,
> Who knew He made the Atlantic and the stones
> And destined seamen here to end their lives

Dashed on a rock, rolled over in the surf,
And not one hair forgotten. Now they lie
In centuries of sand beside the church.
Less pitiable are they than the corpse
Of a large golfer, only four weeks dead,
This sunlit and sea-distant afternoon.
'Praise ye the Lord!' and in another key
The Lord's name by harmonium be praised.
'The Second Evening and the Fourteenth Psalm'.[2]

Even here of course the coy or quizzical allusions to past idioms,
Tennyson's and earlier, sink the poem away from us behind a glaze of
knowledgeability in the poet; and there will always be readers to whom
that sort of knowing play with one idiom poised against another will seem
antipathetic. However, there are many other poets beside Betjeman, and
poets who are much greater, who will by that token be beyond such a
reader.

When W.H. Auden was introducing Betjeman to an American audience, in 1947, he faced the matter of this compulsion in Betjeman always
to quiz his readers:

I will content myself with asserting dogmatically that, this season, the
man of good will will wear his heart up his sleeve, not on it. For better
or worse, we who live in this age not only feel but are critically
conscious of our emotions... and, in consequence, again for better or
worse, a naive rhetoric, one that is not confessedly 'theatrical', is now
impossible in poetry. The honest manly style is today only suited to
Iago.[3]

But this prophecy was no sooner uttered than events disproved it. In the
years since 1947, on both sides of the Atlantic, naïve rhetorics and manly
tones have been very much in evidence. The quizzical and evasive ironies
which are favoured by both Auden and Betjeman now seem to be a
peculiarity of their age group, not a condition of 'this age'. In any case, in
'Sunday Afternoon Service in St. Enodoc's Church, Cornwall', the
reader is quizzed by the poet only from time to time, and then gently and
with tact; the poet's eye (and therefore the reader's) is elsewhere − on the
matter being contemplated, not on the relations of the poet-performer
with his audience.

As much cannot be said, however, of poems in which Betjeman draws
nearer to the Hardyesque. There is, to take a blatant example, a poem

2 John Betjeman, 'Sunday Afternoon Service in St Enodoc's Church, Cornwall', *John Betjeman's Collected Poems* (London, 1958, 2nd ed., 1962).
3 W.H. Auden, Introduction to *Slick But Not Streamlined: Selected Writings of John Betjeman* (New York, 1947).

called 'Dorset', which is an imitation of Hardy's 'Friends Beyond':

> Light's abode, celestial Salem! Lamps of evening, smelling strong,
> Gleaming on the pitch-pine, waiting, almost empty evensong:
> From the aisles each window smiles on grave and grass and
>   yew-tree bough –
> While Tranter Reuben, Gordon Selfridge, Edna Best and
>   Thomas Hardy lie in Mellstock Churchyard now.[4]

And a coy and maddening footnote by the author tells us that the names in the last line of this stanza and in the corresponding line of the two earlier stanzas – T.S. Eliot, H.G. Wells, Edith Sitwell, Mary Borden, Brian Howard, Harold Acton – are 'put in not out of malice or satire but merely for their euphony'. The self-conscious 'tease' of performing the parody at all, compounded by the double-take to which this disingenuous footnote invites us, puffs such a dense vapour of self-consciousness about the poet's relationship to his readers that behind it the lineaments of the poem as in any way a considered utterance entirely disappear.

A much less obvious case, but one which in the end we have to regret more bitterly, is a poem called 'The Heart of Thomas Hardy':

> The heart of Thomas Hardy flew out of Stinsford churchyard
> A little thumping fig, it rocketed over the elm trees.
> Lighter than air it flew straight to where its Creator
> Waited in golden nimbus, just as in eighteen sixty,
> Hardman and son of Brum had depicted Him in the chancel.
> Slowly out of the grass, slitting the mounds in the centre
> Riving apart the roots, rose the new covered corpses
> Tess and Jude and His Worship, various unmarried mothers,
> Woodmen, cutters of turf, adulterers, church restorers,
> Turning aside the stones thump on the upturned churchyard.
> Soaring over the elm trees slower than Thomas Hardy,
> Weighted down with a Conscience, now for the first time fleshly
> Taking form as a growth hung from the feet like a sponge-bag.
> There, in the heart of the nimbus, twittered the heart of Hardy
> There, on the edge of the nimbus, slowly revolved the corpses
> Radiating around the twittering heart of Hardy,
> Slowly started to turn in the light of their own Creator
> Died away in the night as frost will blacken a dahlia.[5]

The extremely difficult verse line, one sort of English hexameter, is handled here with something approaching Hardy's inventiveness and finesse in similarly ringing the changes upon rare and difficult metrical

4   Betjeman, 'Dorset', from the *Collected Poems*.
5   Betjeman, 'The Heart of Thomas Hardy', from *Collected Poems*.

arrangements. One notes admiringly how fast the poem gathers speed, to take off with 'rocketed' in the second line; and how Betjeman uses the rapidity of spoken rather than written syntax, in a touch like the adverbial 'thump' of line 10. And the grotesque literalness of the image created, a myth rendered with the effect of hallucination, can without self-evident foolishness, and appropriately enough considering the subject, be described as Dantesque. If for the first and even the second reading the direction of the poem, and the intention behind it, remain equivocal – is the poem a tribute to Hardy, or an attack on him? – we are ready to believe that the ambiguity faithfully reflects the struggle of emotions in a reverently believing poet when regarding the spectacle of his loved and admired master who is infidel and blasphemer. In fact I take the poem to be a hyperbolical compliment to Hardy, in that his fictional creations at least *start* to turn around him, as the souls of God's creations turn around Him continually in eternal adoration and love. Indeed we should have to say that the admiration for Hardy and the pity for him are in this poem adjusted one to the other most memorably, were it not for a single betraying phrase – 'various unmarried mothers'. Everything else in the poem, certainly including the makers of the Brummagem sacred furniture, if it is appropriate to the character or the *persona* of John Betjeman, is appropriate no less to the character and the historical circumstances of Thomas Hardy. The image of the conscience made physically present, 'hung from the feet like a sponge-bag', is magnificent. But... 'various unmarried mothers'! At that point in the poem, quite needlessly and ruinously, there intrudes a flippantly knowing and heartless voice out of some shallowly competitive conversation at a college high table. The failure of nerve is lamentable and irredeemable: and the chance of a more splendid compliment to Hardy than anyone else is likely to pay has been irretrievably muffed and missed. This is what happens when the cosmic irony with which, in Hardy or Housman, the universe confronts man, becomes the evasive and defensive irony with which the poet confronts the universe, including that part of the human universe which he envisages as his readers.

If I propose that this sort of evasive obliquity in the poet's stance toward his audience was forced upon Betjeman by the inappropriately rigid forms which he adopted from Hardy, rather than from some psychological or social maladjustment in himself, I am giving him the benefit of the doubt. I am happy to do so, however; it is a sort of giving to which critics are not much prone. The point to be made is in any case one that does not depend upon this particular illustration, though this may enforce it. The rigidly intricate metrical and stanzaic arrangements of Hardy could be used, in the years after his death, only by poets who were willing or eager to stand obliquely to their audience. This is not the same as saying (what I do not believe) that the traditional accentual-syllabic metres of English have been self-evidently superseded by *vers libre*; it is a quality of curious tenacity in the handling and elaboration of those metres which seems to be appropriate to the generation of Hardy and Hopkins, Patmore and Kipling, but inappropriate to every generation since.

*   *   *

If this can be granted, it raises the possibility that the sort of verse style which I have called Hardyesque can survive into, and be detected in, verse writing which obeys none of the criteria – of symmetry, parallelism, and rigorous equivalence – which normally governed Hardy's own writing in verse. And in 'Sunday Afternoon Service in St Enodoc's Church, Cornwall', the play that Betjeman makes with Cornish slate suggests one way in which this may be true. For a parallel, there is an indifferent poem by Hardy, entitled 'Green Slates (Penpethy)':

> It happened once, before the duller
>   Loomings of life defined them,
> I searched for slates of greenish colour
>   A quarry where men mined them;
>
> And saw, the while I peered around there,
>   In the quarry standing
> A form against the slate background there,
>   Of fairness eye-commanding.
>
> And now, though fifty years have flown me,
>   With all their dreams and duties,
> And strange-pipped dice my hand has thrown me,
>   And dust are all her beauties,
>
> Green slates – seen high on roofs, or lower
>   In waggon, truck, or lorry –
> Cry out: 'Our home was where you saw her
>   Standing in the quarry!'

These slates, and more generally, the geological and topographical features of landscape which play such a major role in Hardy's poems particularly of bereavement, are among those images which Raymond Williams allows for, even as he argues that Hardy's vision is more precisely conditioned historically than most critics are willing to admit:

> It is also obvious that, in most rural landscapes, there are very old and often unaltered features, which sustain a quite different time-scale. Hardy gives great importance to these, and this is not really surprising, when we consider his whole structure of feeling.[5]

5 Raymond Williams, 'Thomas Hardy', in the *Critical Quarterly*, 6: 4 (Winter 1964), pp. 341–51.

Hardy's feeling for topography and locality, as somehow conditioning the human lives lived under their influence more powerfully than any theory available to him or to us can allow for, is something that can and does persist, as a tradition, quite athwart the evident discontinuities, between him and us, in the way that artistic form, and specifically poetic form, is conceived. The poet who wrote 'Green Slates', or, in 'The Going', 'You were she who abode/By those red-veined rocks far West', or 'Primaeval rocks form the road's steep border,/And much have they faced there, first and last,/Of the transitory in Earth's long order' ('At Castle Boterel'), is not outside the range of sympathy of a contemporary poet who responds with elation to the possibility of placing himself according to geological, rather than humanly historical, time:

> Age by default: in some way this must
> be solved. The covenants that bind
> into the rock, each to the other
> are for this, for the argon dating
>   by song as echo of the world.
>   O it runs sweetly by, and prints over
>   the heart; I am supremely happy,
> the whole order set in this, the
> proper guise, of a song. You can hear
> the strains from so far off: withdrawn
>   from every haunted place
>   in its graveness, the responsive
>   shift into the millions of years.
> I am born back there, the plaintive chanting
> under the Atlantic and the unison of forms.
> It *may* all flow again if we suppress the
>   breaks, as I long to do,
>   at the far end of that distance
>   and tidings of the land...[6]

And yet the author of these lines, J.H. Prynne, is a poet as vowed to the open-ended and diffusive forms of verse as Hardy was to the constrictive.

Though Prynne appears to have taken instruction from American practitioners of 'composition by field', like Charles Olson and Edward Dorn, who share his and Hardy's concern with defining human beings by the topographical location which they occupy, he could also – and I would guess he did – take his bearings from a native source, that is to say, from Hardy. For certainly, Prynne's emphasis is frequently on patience, on lowering the sights, settling for limited objectives. And all of this side of what he says is as far as possible from the sanguine expansiveness of the

6 Prynne, 'The Wound, Day and Night', in *The White Stones*.

American poets whom he has read and emulates. In 'The Holy City', he writes:

> Where we go is a loved side of the temple,
> a place for repose, a concrete path.
> There's no mystic moment involved: just
>   that we are
>   is how, each
>   severally, we're
>   carried into
> the wind which makes no decision and is
> a tide, not taken. I saw it
>   and love is
>   when, how &
>   because we
>   do: you
> could call it Ierusalem or feel it
> as you walk, even quite jauntily, over the grass.[7]

I take this to mean: love of others is a matter of recognising their right to exist, and that comes about from accepting them and yourself in relation to elemental and uncaring presences like wind and sun. Similarly, Prynne has his own poem 'against extremity':

> Finally it's trade that the deep changes
> work with, so that the lives are heavier,
> less to be moved from or blunted. The city
> is the language of transfer
>   to the human account. Here
>   the phrases shift, the years
>   are an acquiescence.
> This isn't a wild comment: there's no
> good in the brittle effort, to snap the pace
> into some more sudden glitter of light:
>   hold to this city or the slightly pale
>   walking, to a set rhythm of
>   the very slight hopefulness. That
> is less than patience, it's time or more clearly
> the sequence of years; a thickening in the words
> as the coins themselves wear thin and could
>   almost balance on the quick
>   ideal edge. The stirring is so
>   slight, the talk so stunned, the

city warm in the air, it is a
too steady shift and life as
it's called is age and the merest impulse,
    called the city and the deep
    blunting damage of hope.
    That's where it is, now
as the place to be left and the last
change still in return: down there
in the snow, too, the loyal city of man.[8]

The structuring principle of this poetry, which makes it difficult (sometimes too difficult), is the unemphasised but radical demands it makes
upon English etymologies, so that to follow the logic we have to
remember 'trade' as meaning traffic, for instance pedestrian traffic in the
streets, also exchange and interchange, as of current coin and current
language in human as well as commercial transactions and transfers. And
though Hardy like any good poet may go for his effects into that dimension of language, of course his poetry does not work in that dimension at
all so constantly as Prynne's does. Other differences between the two
poets are too obvious to be worth commenting on. And yet the sentiment on which Prynne's poem comes to rest is not far from one that
Hardy expresses, especially when he contemplates features of topography.
An example (in which the first line is unfortunate self-parody), is
'Yell'ham-Wood's Story', dated 1902:

    Coomb-Firtrees say that Life is a moan,
        And Clyffe-hill Clump says 'Yea!'
    But Yell'ham says a thing of its own:
          It's not 'Gray, gray
          Is Life alway!'
        That Yell'ham says,
      Nor that Life is for ends unknown.

    It says that Life would signify
      A thwarted purposing:
    That we come to live, and are called to die.
        Yes, that's the thing
        In fall, in spring,
        That Yell'ham says: –
    'Life offers – to deny!'

           ★   ★   ★

8 'In the Long Run, To Be Stranded', in *The White Stones*. The poem is given in full.

If it still seems, as no doubt it does, that only special pleading can bridge the evident discrepancies between Hardy's way of writing and J.H. Prynne's, incredulity may be eased a little by considering as representative of the intervening generations a figure more substantial than John Betjeman; that is to say, Auden. Auden has more than once paid homage to Hardy as his own first master, though seldom without a faint air of condescension. Yet no one I think has yet succeeded in locating the Hardyesque contribution to Auden's subsequent styles and concerns; and where others have failed, I may be allowed to guess. Accordingly, I will guess that part of the continuing inheritance from Hardy in Auden's poetry is the importance for the later poet of topography, the frequency with which specific landscapes (particularly those of his native Pennine limestone) serve as the provocation for Auden's imagination, and the focus of some of his most delicate and feelingful writing. Introducing Betjeman's poems, Auden coined the words 'topophil' and 'topophilia' to characterise the sort of topographical poet that Betjeman is, and the sort of habit of mind which in Betjeman gets poetic expression. He remarked:

> Topophilia differs from the farmer's love of his home soil and the litterateur's fussy regional patriotism in that it is not possessive or limited to any one locality; the practiced topophil can operate in a district he has never visited before. On the other hand, it has little in common with nature-love. Wild or unhumanised nature holds no charms for the average topophil because it is lacking in history; (the exception which proves the rule is the geological topophil). At the same time, though history manifested by objects is essential, the quantity of the history and the quality of the object are irrelevant; a branch railroad is as valuable as a Roman wall, a new tudor teashop as interesting as a Gothic cathedral. America is so big, the countryside not actually under cultivation so wild, that the automobile is essential to movement. Topophilia, however, cannot survive at velocities greater than that of a somewhat rusty bicycle. (Hence, Betjeman's obsession with that vehicle.)[9]

Those last sentences look forward twenty years to 'Prologue. The Birth of Architecture', where Auden tells John Bayley:

> From gallery-grave and the hunt of a wren-King
> to Low Mass and trailer camp
> is hardly a tick by the carbon clock, but I
> don't count that way nor do you:

9   Auden, from his Introduction to *Slick But Not Streamlined: Selected Writings of John Betjeman* (New York, 1947).

already it is millions of heartbeats ago
    back to the Bicycle Age,
before which is no *After* for me to measure,
    just a still prehistoric *Once*.

And we may certainly reflect that in Hardy's poems as much as in Betjeman's the commonest and most favoured vehicle is the bicycle. However, Auden declares, having defined the sort of topophil poet that he takes Betjeman to be: 'It is one of my constant regrets that I am too short-sighted, too much of a Thinking Type, to attempt this sort of poetry, which requires a strongly visual imagination.' And yet, however we may regard this deprecating modesty on Auden's part, it is plain that he has left himself a valuable niche in the parenthetical room he has left for 'the geological topophil'. For in Auden's poetry, from those early poems which make such ominous play with images of flooded mine shafts and abandoned mine workings, through to 'In Praise of Limestone' and beyond, there is a steady concern with the stony bones of various land-scapes. And this is something which Prynne has in common with Auden, as we shall see.

No one would maintain that Hardy lacked 'a strongly visual imagina-tion', or, more generally and more pertinently, a capacity to occupy a particular scene or situation with all his senses alert. Descriptions like 'Overlooking the River Stour' or 'On Sturminster Foot-Bridge', or such magnificent presentations as 'A Spellbound Palace' or 'The Sheep Boy', spring at once to mind. And yet in Hardy's more ambitious poems, those which approach and achieve the condition of phantasmagoria, the poet is content to be impressionistic and use a broad brush. For instance, in 'Wessex Heights' the different kinds of landscape comprised in Wessex – its hills, its lowlands, and its plain – are rendered by an imagination which has abstracted the main and determining features of each:

There are some heights in Wessex, shaped as if by a kindly hand
For thinking, dreaming, dying on, and at crises when I stand,
Say, on Ingpen Beacon eastward, or on Wylls-Neck westwardly,
I seem where I was before my birth, and after death may be...

I cannot go to the great grey Plain; there's a figure against the moon,
Nobody sees it but I, and it makes my breast beat out of tune...

The different kinds of landscape are adverted to in turn, chiefly so as to bring out the sort of emotional and social life which each of them seems to require of the speaker of the poem. And this is precisely the interest, requiring the poet's imagination to abstract and generalise, which we find for instance in Auden's 'Bucolics'. It is almost as if each of Auden's long poems under this title – 'Mountains', 'Lakes', 'Islands', 'Plains', 'Streams'

– were an elaboration and development of a perception starkly indicated by different stanzas in Hardy's poem, with the characteristic difference, however, that the deprecating category, 'Bucolics', permits or requires Auden to descend to moments of bumpkin bathos: 'Just reeling off their names is ever so comfy', or 'Five minutes on even the nicest mountain/Is awfully long.'

Neither in Hardy nor in Auden is there any sign of that determination to render the particular scene, experience, or topic in all its particularised quiddity which we find in Ruskin, in Hopkins's poems (and his theories of 'inscape' and 'instress'), and, in the present day, in characteristic poems by Charles Tomlinson. As for Prynne, he has a poem, 'For a Quiet Day', in which he appears to consider this way of encountering the non-human creation as he might have met it in Tomlinson, and firmly though respectfully to reject it:

> There are some men that focus
> on the true intentness, as I know
> and wouldn't argue with: it is
> violent, the harp – I will not do it
>> though, and the time is
>> so gentle, in the shadow
>> that any youth might
>> sleep. But I will
> not do it, with the gilded harp
> and of all things, its pedals, for
> the nice touch. As the curves too
> are sometimes gentle, where we shall be
>> in the succession of
>> light, hope, the
>> evening
> distracts: and it is always too
> fine, too hopeless and will not let
> the gentle course – by the chance
> rise of a voice.
>> And if the intentness
>> is the more true, then
>> I want the gentler
>> course, where
> the evening is more of what we are:
> or the day as well – moist, casual,
> broken by inflictions of touch. This
> is the resting-place, out in the street.
>> That we are so, and
>> for the other thing

> I will not do it, will
> not; this is a quiet day.[10]

Though the extremes that are here being guarded against and excluded include those which Tomlinson also has ruled out in 'Against Extremity', Prynne's poem exorcises also that Ruskinian or Hopkinsian extreme of anguished perception to which Tomlinson is subject, to which indeed he seems to have vowed himself. What Prynne most values would be broken by, would experience as an infliction, the 'nice' (the precisely and exactly discriminating) 'touch'. The 'curves' which Prynne here holds before us as the image of a longed-for civil and equable way of life and behaviour, are embodied in his own sentences which, strung as they are across his hesitant short lines, very frequently change direction in mid-course. But, as other poems in *The White Stones* make clear, the curves are also – and even principally – those of a gently undulating countryside, its shallow contours ground down by glacial erosion during one or another ice age. An elaborate and beautiful poem by Prynne, 'The Glacial Question Unsolved', seems to say this, among other things. In Hardy and Auden and Prynne alike the long temporal perspectives of geology induce a quietness which, though it is undermined by apprehension, seems like a liberation:

> So I am found on Ingpen Beacon, or on Wylls-Neck to the west,
> Or else on homely Bulbarrow, or little Pilsdon Crest,
> Where men have never cared to haunt, nor women have walked
>   with me,
> And ghosts then keep their distance; and I know some liberty.

However, the political implication or analogue is plain and dismaying. It is quietism, an impasse, inaction; as Prynne says elsewhere, in a passage which there seems to be no point in printing as verse: 'Contentment or sceptical calm will produce instant death at the next jolt & intending suicides should carry a card at least exonerating the eventual bystanders...' Thus, if all these poets are scientific humanists (for neither in Prynne nor in Auden is the science of geology merely a source for illustrative metaphor), plainly what we have is scientific humanism at the end of its tether. Of course if it were in any other condition, we should rightly refuse to listen to it; and for that matter Jeremy Prynne is not being listened to in any case.

Meanwhile, the geological or geographical time scale at least serves to reveal the absurdity of all forms of Utopian revolution:

> ... what is anyone waiting
> *for*, either resigned or nervous or frantic from
> time to time? Various forms dodge through

10 Prynne, 'For a Quiet Day', in *The White Stones*.

the margins of a livelihood, but so much talk
about the underground is silly when it would require a constant effort to keep below the surface,
when almost everything is exactly that, the
mirror of a would-be alien who won't see how
much he is at home. In consequence also the
idea of change is briskly seasonal, it's too cold
& thus the scout-camp idea of revolution stands
in temporary composure, waiting for spring. All
forms of delay help this farce, that our restrictions
are temporary & that the noble fiction is to have
a few good moments, which represent what we know
ought to be ours. Ought to be, that makes me
wince with facetiousness: we/you/they, all the
pronouns by now know how to make a sentence
work with *ought to,* and the stoic at least saves
himself that extremity of false vigilance.[11]

The wince of exasperation makes for good impatient prose, if not for anything that we can usefully call verse.

Already in 1939 Cleanth Brooks decided that 'the central impulse of Auden's poetry' could be located in some early verses which Brooks quoted:

And all emotions to expression came,
Recovering the archaic imagery:
The longed for assurance takes the form

Of a hawk's vertical stooping from the sky;
These tears, salt for a disobedient dream,
The lunatic agitation of the sea;

While this despair with hardened eyeballs cries
'A Golden Age, a Silver... rather this,
Massive and taciturn years, the Age of Ice.'

Brooks commented:

Auden's surest triumphs represent a recovery of the archaic imagery – fells, scarps overhung by kestrels, the becks with their potholes left by the receding glaciers of the age of ice. His dominant contrast is the contrast between this scene and the modern age of ice: foundries with their fires cold, flooded coal-mines, silted harbours – the debris of the new ice age. The advent of the new age of ice, a 'polar peril', supplies the background for his finest poetry.[12]

11 'Questions for the Time Being', from *The White Stones* (Lincoln, 1969).
12 Cleanth Brooks, *Modern Poetry and the Tradition* (Chapel Hill, 1939); reprinted in *Auden: A Collection of Critical Essays*, ed. by M.K. Spears (Englewood Cliffs, 1964), pp. 17–18.

So much has happened to Auden in the past thirty years that no doubt Cleanth Brooks would not hold to the same confident judgement now, or not without qualifications. What is striking is that the same description – of humankind seen as inhabiting a span between an ice age long past and another which is imminent – fits exactly Prynne's collection *The White Stones*, as well as particular pieces in that connection, such as 'The Glacial Question, Unsolved'.

The landscapes of those early poems by Auden are so insistently those of Craven in the Yorkshire Pennines that one would not think of connecting them with the chalk landscapes of Hardy's Wessex.[13] Yet we have Auden's own word for it that such a connection exists. Looking back from 1940 at the period of his youthful apprenticeship to Hardy, Auden wrote:

> What I valued most in Hardy, then, as I still do, was his hawk's vision, his way of looking at life from a very great height, as in the stage directions of *The Dynasts*, or the opening chapter of *The Return of the Native*. To see the individual life related not only to the local social life of its time, but to the whole of human history, life on the earth, the stars, gives one both humility and self-confidence. For from such a perspective the difference between the individual and society is so slight, since both are so insignificant, that the latter ceases to appear as a formidable god with absolute rights, but rather as an equal, subject to the same laws of growth and decay, and therefore one with whom reconciliation is possible.[14]

This can only mean that Auden is aware of Hardy as a presence brooding over poems where to us he is hardly, if at all, perceptible – for instance over the justly famous piece in *Poems, 1930*:

> Consider this and in our time
> As the hawk sees it or the helmeted airman...

– in which Auden addresses the 'supreme Antagonist':

> In Cornwall, Mendip, or the Pennine moor
> Your comments on the highborn mining captains,
> Found they no answer, made them wish to die
> – Lie since in barrows out of harm.
> You talk to your admirers every day

---

13 I cannot forbear noting with a chuckle the astonishing consistency of A. Alvarez who predictably, as it now must seem, disapproves of just those 'silted harbours' which Cleanth Brooks singles out for approval. See Alvarez, *The Shaping Spirit* (London, 1958), p. 94. Alvarez's hatred for unpeopled landscape is insatiable!
14 W.H. Auden, 'A Literary Transference', in *The Southern Review*, 6: 1 (Summer 1940), p. 83.

> By silted harbours, derelict works,
> In strangled orchards, and the silent combe
> Where dogs have worried or a bird was shot.

And sure enough Monroe K. Spears, examining a collection of twenty-six poems which predates even *Poems, 1930* (*Poems, 1928*, printed by Stephen Spender in Oxford), located there a Hardyesque style, laconic and in short lines, which he calls 'the clipped lyric'; and he exemplifies it by some verses in which Auden already walks before us as geological topophil:

> I chose this lean country
> For seven day content,
> To satisfy the want
> Of eye and ear, to see
> The slow fastidious line
> That disciplines the fell...[15]

The last two lines survive into *Poems, 1930* in a poem beginning, 'From scars where kestrels hover'.

Spears usefully singles out two poems by Hardy written in a verse form which could have taught Auden this laconic yet lyrical style; they are 'Rain on a Grave' and 'In Tenebris I'. Yet rather than any terseness of diction or versification, what on this showing constitutes the Hardyesque for Auden is what Auden himself points to – 'his way of looking at life from a very great height'. And in 1940 in 'A Literary Transference', Auden did not shirk from pointing out the political implications of this angle of vision:

> No one who has learned to do this can ever accept either an egocentric, overrational Humanism which fondly imagines that it is willing its own life, nor a pseudo-Marxism which rejects individual free-will but claims instead that a human society can be autonomous.

Much angry ink has been spilt on the question whether Auden in 1940 had earned the right to this lofty dismissal of alternatives by which, a few years before, he had seemed to be seduced himself. What is more to our purpose is to remark that this political statement, like others that could be read out of the early poems we have been looking at, seems much less quietistic than the logically identical statement implied by the 'Bucolics'.

And yet it is plain that the angle of vision of Hardy looking down from a towering height at Wessex Heights and Salisbury Plain, if it is the angle of vision from which Auden, in the 'Bucolics', looks down at mountains and lakes, woods, islands and plains, is also the angle from which the

15 See Monroe K. Spears, *The Poetry of W.H. Auden: The Disenchanted Island* (New York, 1963), p. 23.

young Auden had inspected the England of 1930 'as the hawk sees it or the helmeted airman'. In the case of a poet so protean as Auden this constancy is remarkable. And it becomes even more striking when in his most recent collection we encounter 'Amor Loci':

> I could draw its map by heart,
> showing its contours,
> strata and vegetation,
> name every height,
> small burn and lonely shieling,
> but nameless to me,
> faceless as heather or grouse,
> are those who live there,
>
> its dead too vague for judgement,
> tangible only
> what they wrought, their giant works
> of delve and drainage
> in days preterite: long since
> their hammering stopped
> as the lodes all petered out
> in the Jew Limestone.
>
> Here and there a tough chimney
> still towers over
> dejected masonry, moss,
> decomposed machines,
> with no one about, no chance
> of buttering bread,
> a land postured in my time
> for marginal farms.
>
> Any musical future
> is most unlikely.
> Industry wants Cheap Power,
> romantic muscle
> a perilous wilderness,
> Mr. Pleasure pays
> for surf-riding, claret, sex;
> it offers them none.
>
> To me, though, much: a vision,
> not (as perhaps at
> twelve I thought it) of Eden,
> still less of a New
> Jerusalem but, for one,

>   convinced he will die,
>   more comely, more credible
>   than either daydream.
>
>   How, but with some real focus
>   of desolation
>   could I, by analogy,
>   imagine a Love
>   that, however often smeared,
>   shrugged at, abandoned
>   by a frivolous worldling,
>   does not abandon?[16]

This poem seems to be a revision of 'In Praise of Limestone', which, first published in 1948, was subsequently included in the collection *Nones*. And, although that earlier poem has had many admirers, 'Amor Loci' seems to be in nearly every way an improvement.

Nearly every way; but not quite. For, to begin with, most readers will find 'In Praise of Limestone' more entertaining. And where Auden is concerned, this is important. For he deserves our sympathy when he tells the poet, in a poem of 1954:

>   Be subtle, various, ornamental, clever,
>   And do not listen to those critics ever
>   Whose crude provincial gullets crave in books
>   Plain cooking made still plainer by plain cooks.[17]

Entertainment is something that we should be grateful for, from our poets; and those critics look foolish who have refused to take Auden seriously because he has been high-spirited, not sufficiently glum. We may object, not to being entertained, but to being cajoled. And quirky cajolings have been typical of Auden's writing from very early in his career until very recently indeed. What I mean is something that we recognised in Betjeman – an inability on the part of the poet to stand squarely in front of his reader, a defensive obliquity. And there is a good deal of this in 'In Praise of Limestone', as in the slightly later 'Bucolics'. That said, however, it must be agreed that there is in the earlier poem a delightful variety, a quality of invention and surprise which is present, if at all, only in a very muted way in the fiercer and more intense 'Amor Loci'.

'In Praise of Limestone' contrives, by what is really sleight of hand, to superimpose landscapes of Ischia and even perhaps of Greece on the limestone landscapes of Craven; in 'Amor Loci' the landscapes are those native Pennine landscapes which, as we have seen, were the natural habitation

16 Auden, 'Amor Loci', in *City Without Walls* (New York, 1969).
17 'The Truest Poetry Is the Most Feigning', in *The Shield of Achilles* (New York, 1955), p. 44.

for Auden's imagination from his earliest youth. With this change goes another; whereas the earlier, more expansive poem set up a 'we' against a 'they' (and John Fuller interestingly identifies the 'we' with 'intellectuals'), in 'Amor Loci' there is only an 'I'. 'We' were called 'The Inconstant Ones', and it was said in the earlier poem that we responded to a limestone landscape because of the treacherous inconstancy of that kind of rock. In 'Amor Loci' that treachery is registered altogether more blankly and fiercely in the astonishing phrase 'the Jew Limestone'. This expression must certainly give offence. For Auden to use it at a time when for instance Eliot is on every side being censured for his use of 'the Jew' in 'Gerontion', is an act of brutal defiance. And Auden, though in the past he has been often foolhardy and consistently impudent, has never up to this point been defiant. Auden here confronts his reader bleakly and boldly. If we compare these taut syllabics with the indulgent inclusiveness of the looping accentual lines of 'In Praise of Limestone', we are compelled to realise that Auden is being graceful no longer, but intense and savage. And for this reason the modulation into the expression of Christian faith at the end of 'Amor Loci' cannot help but strike us as altogether more in earnest than the corresponding modulation at the end of 'In Praise of Limestone'.

It is against this background of sweeping and violent change in Auden's stance and tone of voice that we must account for an unusually pointed allusion to Hardy in this poem. For such I take to be the phrase, 'in days preterite'. It is a phrase that I can persuade myself I have read in Hardy's *Collected Poems* (perhaps I have). At all events, it is – in its uncompromising inversion of noun and adjective and in the exact Latinate pedantry of 'preterite' – unmistakably Hardyesque. In a rhetorician so adept as Auden, this does not happen by accident. And we have seen why, from Auden's point of view, a grim brief bow in Hardy's direction would seem appropriate in a poem like this which after so long reverts without equivocation to the Pennine landscape, and looks at it moreover from a height where its contours, strata, and vegetation are laid out before the poet's eye as on a map. Seen from that height, the inhabitants of the landscape are inevitably 'faceless as heather or grass'. And so the poem has no political implications. Though it acknowledges historical perspectives (for the mining captains were gone, the Pennine slopes had reverted from heavy industry to marginal farming, already 'in my time', in the bicycle age, the poet's boyhood), the poem is set outside history; because it is not concerned to make sense of historical change, it can have no political dimension – as indeed the last stanza makes clear, by insisting that the experience makes emblematic meaning only in a religious perspective.

'Amor Loci' is not of course an open-ended poem. Auden's forms – various as they are, and despite the enormous elbow room which he claims and can manage in one form after another – are always closed forms. Indeed, one may suspect that there is no call for the 'open' forms, and really no possibility of using them, so long as human capacities are seen on a vertical scale from high to low. The open forms, from the time of Whitman who for our purposes invented them and first made them current, envisage man as transcending himself by moving outward and on. If he is figured as transcending himself by rising to the altitude of the hawk, or of hiding himself by delving as deep as the lowest gallery of a mine (and it is thus that Auden thinks, as does Tolkien, whom Auden is known to admire), there is every reason why poetic forms should exhibit unity, regularity, and repetition. Conversely, J.H. Prynne has earned the right to the open forms which he uses; for in Prynne's poems man saves or at least preserves himself always and only by moving patiently on and over the surface of a landscape. Among the many shamanistic poems which have been such a feature of recent years in Anglo-American poetry, only Prynne's 'Aristeas, in Seven Years' seems to make significant play with the profound difference in spatial relations which we encounter when we move into understanding the shamanistic religions from those we are more used to, such as Christianity. For in fact it seems to be the case that the shaman's dream journey is not up or down a vertical axis as in Dante, or even in Homer, but along the level. At most, the shaman's soul, when it is conceived of as having left the body, moves up or down only in the sense of upstream or downstream – a habit of spatial perception natural enough to the hunting or pastoral nomadic cultures in which shamanism, whether in Asia or America, has been chiefly practised. (Accordingly, Prynne is right to take as his fable the epic journey of the Pontic Greek Aristeas into the Asian hinterland of Scythian and other tribes. For whereas C.M. Bowra in *Heroic Song* persuasively saw the Western epic as emerging from and superseding shamanism, the epic journey of Aristeas represents a reversal of this.)[18] If it is true that the distinction between the open-ended and the closed forms goes as deep as this, then it is doubtless true that the Hardyesque tradition in British poetry cannot after all survive a translation into the open forms; that between Hardy's precedent and Whitman's there can be no compromise. But then, of course, there can be little doubt that Thomas Hardy would have thought the Asiatic or Amerindian shaman first cousin to the witches of Endor.

18 See E.D. Phillips, 'The Legend of Aristeas: Fact and Fancy in Early Greek Notions of East Russia, Siberia, and Inner Asia', *Artibus Asiae*, 18: 2 (1955), pp. 161–77.

6 A Doggy Demos: Hardy & Lawrence

If this book had been an exercise in literary history, observing more or less chronological order, I should have had at an early stage to give attention to a number of English poets active in the 1920s who are known to have set their sights very deliberately by the model which Hardy, then still living, seemed to afford them. (Equally, I should have needed at some stage to notice how C. Day Lewis moved in the 1940s into using very explicitly Hardyesque forms and styles.) Sydney Bolt's annotated anthology, *Poetry of the 1920s*, one of the most intelligent and valuable of recent pieces of literary criticism (though not acknowledged as such, because modestly issued as a textbook for British secondary schools), is the most sympathetic attempt known to me to place the poets of the 1920s in the context of their contemporaries, and to explain why the precedent of Hardy served such poets as Edmund Blunden, Siegfried Sassoon, and Robert Graves less well than the alternative models offered, though at that point hardly ever emulated, by Ezra Pound and T.S. Eliot. Bolt points out that the three poets just named, although they 'all started their poetic careers under the kindly wing of Sir Edward Marsh', in the 1920s were united for a time in following, not the precepts of Edward Marsh or any other, but the precedent of Hardy. In all these poets the sensibility had been seared, and in some cases one might almost say cauterised, by their experience in the trenches of the First World War, and they came home determined to put English poetry to the test of rendering completely and truthfully that appalling experience. Sydney Bolt's conclusion is that the precedents afforded by Hardy were inadequate to accommodate and register the horrific experiences which these poets needed to get into focus:

> The critical question was whether new tests did not demand new forms, and here the influence of Hardy was conservative. Advising the young Graves that '*vers libre* would come to nothing in England' he added: 'All we can do is to write on the old themes in the old styles, but try to do a little better than those who went before us'. The implication that the old styles were linked with old themes is clear and whether or not they recognised the fact, the themes of these poets

were too new to be accommodated by minor modifications of the style they inherited. As a result, the honesty which they all had in common sometimes exposed the limitations of their verse, inviting a stylistic irony which they could not entertain. Thus, when Sassoon begins a sonnet – 'When I have lost the power to feel the pang' – he invites specific comparisons with sonnets by Shakespeare, Milton and Keats which expose weakness, but which Eliot could have used as a source of sardonic strength. The only poet of the twenties who practised what he regarded as an inherited craft without exposing himself to such irony was Graves, and the reason for his immunity was, quite simply, that his version of Standard English poetry was entirely new.[1]

Sydney Bolt's contention is abundantly borne out by the poems that he prints from these authors, together with his comments upon them. (And incidentally he turns up poems by Blunden and Sassoon, both nowadays unjustly neglected writers, which are – despite the limitations which he points out – memorable and beautiful.)

When Bolt speaks of the 'sardonic strength' that Eliot might have achieved out of those echoes of previous English poetry which exist in Sassoon's sonnets all too vulnerably, he is pointing to the alternative tradition, that of Pound and Eliot, which (so he contends) would have served Sassoon and Blunden better, had they been able and ready to learn from that tradition rather than from Hardy. In Bolt's anthology Blunden, Sassoon, and Graves appear under the category 'established form', while Eliot and Pound, also Yeats and (more surprisingly) William Empson, appear under the alternative rubric 'dramatic form'. For our purposes, and in line with terminology we have used already, for Bolt's word 'dramatic' we might substitute 'ironical'. For in Eliot's 'Prufrock' and 'Gerontion', still more in Pound's *Hugh Selwyn Mauberley*, we perceive the cosmic ironies of Hardy and Housman supplanted by the strategic ironies whose later development (and decrepitude) we have seen in Betjeman and Auden. This is an important distinction to keep in mind, for cosmic irony, the ironical look on the face of the universe as it confronts man, was precisely what Sassoon and Blunden had experienced in the trenches, precisely what they wished to express in their post-war poetry. Sydney Bolt takes the point very well, speaking of Sassoon:

> Hardy's *Satires of Circumstance* was the only literary source which Siegfried Sassoon could suggest for the satirical war poems which had made him the best-known 'new poet' in 1920. Indeed, his poems deserved the title more than Hardy's did. The irony of the satire does not rely upon the reader's literary tact, sense of literary tradition, or

1 Sydney Bolt, *Poetry of the 1920s* (London, 1967), pp. 41–2.

sense of values in any form: it depends upon the reader's sense of fact. Sassoon's target, in his war poetry, was cant: he exposed cant by relating it to stark reality. Reality provided the best comment. The vision of a real tank in the stalls exposes the chorus 'We're sure the Kaiser loves our dear old tanks' (in 'Blighters'). The spectacle of 'the intolerably nameless names' exposes the legend 'Their name liveth for ever' on the New Menin Gate. Nothing more needs to be said.

Thus, if we describe the early poems of Eliot and Pound as 'ironical', it must be clear that we mean, not the irony in a poem by Sassoon, but the strategic irony which relies upon 'the reader's literary tact, sense of literary tradition, or sense of values'.

In 1947, when Auden declared that 'a naive rhetoric, one that is not confessedly theatrical, is now impossible in poetry', and for many years after 1947, it seemed clear that the ironical style of Eliot and Pound had indeed conclusively superseded the relatively 'naïve' rhetoric of styles derived from Hardy. But even Auden, as we have seen, was by 1970 winning through intermittently to an 'honest manly style', now in the voice of Iago (see his 'Song of the Devil' from *City Without Walls*), now in the voice of Thersites. And in fact time has brought in its revenges so sweepingly that the style of the early Eliot and early Pound, strategically sidestepping behind a pasteboard persona or mask, quizzing a reader always kept off balance, is nowadays heartily and intemperately disliked by readers and poets alike. This means that the issue, as between a Hardyesque style on the one hand and an Eliotic style on the other, is by no means such an open and shut case as it seemed until a few years ago. And indeed there were at least two British poets active in the 1920s whose careers as a whole would in any event have complicated the argument. One of them Sydney Bolt has acknowledged: it is Robert Graves. The other is D.H. Lawrence, who similarly emerged upon the literary scene from under the shadow of Eddy Marsh, and who similarly acknowledged Hardy as one of his masters (Whitman, however, being another).

Accordingly, since the tide changed, both these poets have been treated with a new respect – Lawrence more conspicuously than Graves. Indeed it has become possible, and not uncommon, to have Lawrence presented to us as the one honest and straightforward voice sounding to us out of the early years of this century, a voice which (so the argument goes) reveals as craven and unnecessary the 'Byzantine' intricacy or 'Alexandrian' evasiveness of Pound and Eliot and the poets who have followed their lead.

It is generally agreed, however, that Lawrence's verse, where it is memorable and successful, is almost all written in his own version of that *vers libre* which Hardy had declared 'would come to nothing in England'.

In fact, it is hard to see the presence of Hardy behind any of Lawrence's worthwhile poems. And we cannot even be sure that it was Hardy who steered Lawrence, as for good or ill he steered Sassoon and Blunden, away from Eliot's and Pound's poetry of the ironical persona.

What must be our astonishment, however, to find a critic presenting Hardy as a poet who hides behind a *persona!* Yet this is just what Kenneth Rexroth maintains, urging Lawrence's superiority to Hardy on just these grounds − that whereas Hardy needed to shield himself behind an assumed mask, Lawrence didn't:

> Hardy could say to himself: 'Today I am going to be a Wiltshire yeoman, sitting on a fallen rock at Stonehenge, writing a poem to my girl on a piece of wrapping paper with the gnawed stub of a pencil', and he could make it very convincing. But Lawrence really was the educated son of a coal miner, sitting under a tree that had once been part of Sherwood Forest, in a village that was rapidly becoming part of a world-wide disemboweled hell, writing hard, painful poems, to girls who carefully had been taught the art of unlove. It was all real. Love really was a mystery at the navel of the earth, like Stonehenge. The miner really was in contact with a monstrous, seething mystery, the black sun in the earth.

And again:

> Hardy was a major poet. Lawrence was a minor prophet. Like Blake and Yeats, his is the greater tradition. If Hardy ever had a girl in the hay, tipsy on cider, on the night of Boxing Day, he kept quiet about it. He may have thought that it had something to do with 'the stream of his life in the darkness deathward set', but he never let on, except indirectly.[2]

This is outrageous. In part, it is meant to be. It is monstrously unfair to Hardy. But then, fairness is what we never find from anyone who at any time speaks up for what Rexroth is speaking for here. Are prophets fair-minded? Can we expect Jeremiah or Amos or Isaiah to be *judicious?* Lawrence was often unfair; so were nineteenth-century prophets like Carlyle and Ruskin; so was William Blake unfair to Reynolds and to Wordsworth. And some of them, some of the time − perhaps all of them, most of the time − know that they are being unfair, as doubtless Rexroth knows it. Fair-mindedness, the prophet seems to say, is not his business; if judiciousness is necessary to society, it is the business of someone in society other than the prophet or the poet. It is Lawrence's lofty disregard for mere fair-mindedness, a loftiness readily adopted by his admirers, which makes it so difficult to be fair to him.[3]

2 Introduction to *Selected Poems of D.H. Lawrence* (New York, 1959), pp. 3−4.
3 Since I have taken issue with A. Alvarez on other topics, I ought to give credit to his

Lawrence certainly at times assumed the mantle of a prophet, on the old-fashioned Carlylean model. But if he did, this has nothing to do with the distinction that Rexroth tries to draw between Hardy and Lawrence. The distinction as Rexroth presents it is quite simply that when 'I' appears in a poem by Lawrence, the person meant is directly and immediately D.H. Lawrence, the person as historically recorded, born in such and such a place on such and such a date; whereas when 'I' appears in a poem by Hardy, the person meant need not be the historically recorded Thomas Hardy, any more than when King Lear in Shakespeare's play says 'I', the person meant is William Shakespeare.

When Rexroth introduces the notion of a tradition of *prophecy*, above all when he puts in that tradition the most histrionic of modern poets (W.B. Yeats), he is shifting his ground abruptly and very confusingly. What he is saying to start with is simply and bluntly that Lawrence is always sincere, whereas Hardy often isn't; and Lawrence is sincere by virtue of the fact that the 'I' in his poems is always directly and immediately himself. In other words, the poetry we are asked to see as greater than Hardy's kind of poetry, though it is called 'prophetic' poetry, is more accurately described as *confessional* poetry. Confessional poetry, of its nature and necessarily, is superior to dramatic or histrionic poetry; a poem in which the 'I' stands immediately and unequivocally for the author is essentially and necessarily superior to a poem in which the 'I' stands not for the author but for a persona of the author's – this is what Rexroth asks us to believe.

In asking us for this he is asking us, as he well knows, to fly in the face of what seemed, until a few years ago, the solidly achieved consensus about poetry and the criticism of poetry. That consensus seemed to have formed itself on the basis of insights delivered to us by the revolutionary poets of two or three generations ago. It had taken the idea of the persona from Ezra Pound, and the closely related idea of the mask from W.B. Yeats, and it had taken from T.S. Eliot the ideas that the structure of a poem was inherently a *dramatic* structure, and that the effect of poetry was an impersonal effect. It had elaborated on these hints to formulate a rule, the rule that the 'I' in a poem is *never* immediately and directly the poet; that the-poet-in-his-poem is always distinct from, and must never be confounded with, the-poet-outside-his-poem, the poet as historically recorded between birthdate and date of death. To this rule there was a necessary and invaluable corollary: that the question 'Is the poet sincere?' – though it would continue to be asked by naïve readers – was always an impertinent and illegitimate question. This was the view of poetry asso-

temperate and persuasive and justly influential essay on Lawrence's poetry in *The Shaping Spirit* (pp. 140–61). Alvarez goes out of his way to reject Rexroth's sort of enthusiasm: 'Lawrence is not a mystic; his poetry has to do with recognitions, not with revelations.' It has nothing to do with 'the cant of "dark gods"' or 'the stridency of *The Plumed Serpent*'.

ciated in America with the so-called New Criticism, and (although it has been challenged from directions other than the one we are concerned with) it is still the view of poetry taught in many classrooms.

We must now abandon it – or rather, we may and must hold by it for the sake of the poetry which it illuminates; but we can no longer hold by it as an account which does justice to *all* poetry. It illuminates nearly all the poetry that we want to remember written in English between 1550 and about 1780; but it illuminates little of the poetry in English written since. And the question has been settled already; it is only in the university classrooms that anyone any longer supposes that 'Is he sincere?' is a question not to be asked of poets. Confessional poetry has come back with a vengeance; for many years now, in 1972, it is the poetry that has been written by the most serious and talented poets, alike in America and Britain. Consider only the case of Robert Lowell, probably the most influential poet of his generation. It is a very telling case: trained in the very heart of New Criticism by Allen Tate, Lowell made his reputation by poems which were characteristically dramatic monologues, in which the 'I' of the poem was hardly ever to be identified with the historical Robert Lowell. Then in the mid-'50s came his collection called *Life Studies* in which the 'I' of the poems nearly always asked to be taken, quite unequivocally, as Robert Lowell himself. At about the same time, from under the shadow of Rexroth himself, came Allen Ginsberg's prophetic-confessional poem, *Howl*! And ever since, confessional poems have been the order of the day, with the predictable consequences – the poem has lost all its hard-won autonomy, its independence in its own right, and has once again become the vehicle by which the writer acts out before his public the agony or the discomfort (American poets go for agony, British ones for discomfort) of being a writer, or of being alive in the twentieth century. Now we have once again poems in which the public life of the author as author, and his private life, are messily compounded, so that one needs the adventitious information of the gossip columnist to take the force or even the literal meaning of what, since it is a work of literary art, is supposedly offered as public utterance.

For these reasons, one may regret the passing of that less dishevelled world in which the concept of the ironical persona was paramount. But indeed it has passed, as it had to. And yet, what has all this to do with Thomas Hardy? His reputation should have profited by this change of sentiment, as in England indeed it has. For Hardy, as we have noticed, is a thoroughly confessional poet, though his reticence about his private life concealed this to some extent until lately. What poems by Hardy could Rexroth have had in mind when he imagined the poet deciding, 'I am going to be a Wiltshire yeoman…'? Hardy has indeed some poems which are spoken through the mouth of an imagined character, but in such cases he intimates as much very clearly, usually in his title. And much more frequently the 'I' of his poems is as unequivocally the historically recorded Thomas Hardy as the 'I' of Lawrence's poems is David Herbert Lawrence.

Hardy, I have contended, writes at his best when he can coerce the painfully jangled nerves of the confessional poem into some sort of 'repose'. And, little as the notion will appeal to perfervid Lawrencians like Rexroth, the same is true of Lawrence, as he moves from the too rawly confessional poems of his first two collections into his more mature writing of the early 1920s, in which the repose, the saving distance, is achieved in several ways, notably by way of emblematic fables or descriptions out of a personal bestiary or herbal.

However, if Lawrence (and Graves also) could turn to profit the confessional mode which Hardy bequeathed to them, only by transcending and distancing it in ways for which Hardy provided no precedent; if Sassoon, moreover, because he found no such way out, thereupon ceased to be a poet of significance – it seems we must conclude, with Sydney Bolt, that in the 1920s the models which Hardy provided were not very useful. Eliot's ironical modes were more fruitful. And so it looks as if the long spell of Eliot's ascendancy as a formative influence on poets, and at the centre of an elaborately systematic criticism, was not fortuitous, nor could it have been avoided. It was not an unnecessary aberration from which British poetry could have escaped if it had followed a Hardy or a Lawrence or a Graves, nor could American poetry have been spared the expense if it had attended to William Carlos Williams.

★   ★   ★

I have spent so much time on Kenneth Rexroth because it is worthwhile asking what animus impelled him to argue a case so inaccurate and tendentious. And I think the answer is fairly clear: Rexroth detects in Hardy a quality of timorousness, a sort of 'cop-out', which he dislikes and derides. Against it, what he admires and responds to in Lawrence is a quality of risk clearly foreseen and fearlessly taken. In Alvarez as well as in Rexroth, in all of us to some degree, it is this in Lawrence which compels our attention, if not always our admiration. And such a way of thinking was very familiar to Lawrence himself throughout his career. Very early in that career, in 1911, he reviewed an anthology of modern German poetry:

> The Germans in this book are very interesting, not so much for the intrinsic value of the pieces of poetry here given, as for showing which way the poetic spirit trends in Germany, where she finds her stuff, and how she lifts it. Synge asks for the brutalising of English poetry.

Thomas Hardy and George Meredith have, to some extent, answered. But in point of brutality the Germans – and they at the heels of the French and Belgians – are miles ahead of us; or at the back of us, as the case may be.

With Baudelaire, Verlaine, and Verhaeren, poetry seems to have broken out afresh, like a new crater. These men take life welling out hot and primitive, molten fire, or mud, or smoke, or strange vapour. But at any rate it comes from the central fire, which feeds all of us with life, although it is gloved, clotted over and hidden by earth and greenery and civilisation. And it is this same central well of fire which the Germans are trying to tap. It is risky, and they lose their heads when they feel the heat. But sometimes one sees the real red jet of it, pure flame and beautiful; and often, the hot mud – but that is kin. Why do we set our faces against this tapping of elemental passion? It must, in its first issuing, be awful and perhaps, ugly. But what is more essentially awful and ugly than Oedipus? And why is sex passion unsuited for handling, if hate passion, and revenge passion, and horror passion are suitable, as in Agamemnon, and Oedipus, and Medea. Hate passion, horror passion, revenge passion no longer move us so violently in life. Love passion, pitching along with it beauty and strange hate and suffering, remains the one living volcano of our souls. And we must be passionate, we are told. Why, then, not take this red fire out of the well, equally with the yellow of horror, and the dark of hate? Intrinsically, Verhaeren is surely nearer the Greek dramatists than is Swinburne.[4]

On the one hand, this reminds us that in 1911 the Hardy of the 1890s, the author of *Tess of the D'Urbervilles* and *Jude the Obscure*, was still to he thought of as an author who had risked a very great deal – as he continued to do, in certain poems. On the other hand, in 1972 can we say with any confidence that 'hate passion, horror passion, revenge passion no longer move us so violently in life'? In any case, it gives us a valuable sense of how Lawrence at the start of his literary career saw the challenge presented to him: the one of his masters, Hardy, no less than the other, Whitman, had pioneered a path of risk which it was his duty, historically, to follow beyond the point at which they had lost heart, or had erected a sign saying, 'Thus far and no farther.'

Among the risks which Lawrence saw as presented to him, as a challenge to his poetic vocation, are certainly some which must be called political. In view of the several sentimental and embarrassing poems which Hardy addressed to dogs or wrote about dogs, it is appropriate to

4   *The English Review*, November 1911, pp. 721–24; reprinted by Carl E. Baron, 'Two Hitherto Unknown Pieces by D.H. Lawrence', in *Encounter*, 33: 2 (August 1969), p. 4.

illustrate the political risks which Lawrence took, from his poem about a
bitch which he and Frieda owned in New Mexico. The poem is called
'Bibbles', and it is virulently antidemocratic:

> And even now, Bibbles, little Ma'am, it's you who appropriated me,
>   not I you.
> As Benjamin Franklin appropriated Providence to his purposes.
>
> Oh Bibbles, black little bitch,
> I'd never have let you appropriate me, had I known.
> I never dreamed, till now, of the awful time the Lord must have,
>   'owning' humanity,
> Especially democratic live-by-love humanity.
>
> Oh Bibbles, oh Pips, oh Pipsey,
> You little black love-bird!
> *Don't* you love *everybody!*
> Just everybody.
> You love 'em all.
> Believe in the One Identity, don't you,
> You little Walt-Whitmanesque bitch?

Towards the end of the poem (so we may call it, though the merely
provisional and rhetorical disposition of line endings can only embarrass
Lawrencians who want to defend his *vers libre*), we have:

> Me or the Mexican who comes to chop wood
> All the same,
> All humanity is jam to you.
>
> Everybody so dear, and yourself so ultra-beloved
> That you have to run out at last and eat filth,
> Gobble up filth, you horror, swallow utter abomination and fresh-
>   dropped dung.
>
> You stinker.
> You worse than a carrion-crow.
>
> Reeking dung-mouth.
> You love-bird.
>
> *Reject nothing*, sings Walt Whitman.
> So you, go out at last and eat the unmentionable,
> In your appetite for affection.
>
> And then you run in to vomit in my house!
> I get my love back.
> And I have to clean up after you, filth which even blind Nature
>   rejects

From the pit of your stomach;
But you, you snout-face, you reject nothing, you merge so much in
    love
You must eat even that.

Then when I dust you a bit with a juniper twig
You run straight away to live with somebody else,
Fawn before them, and love them as if they were the ones you had
    really loved all along.
And they're taken in.
They feel quite tender over you, till you play the same trick on
    them, dirty bitch.

Fidelity! Loyalty! Attachment!
Oh, these are abstractions to your nasty little belly.
You must always be a-waggle with LOVE.
Such a waggle of love you can hardly distinguish one human from
    another.

You love one after another, on one condition, that each one loves
    you most.
Democratic little bull-bitch, dirt-eating little swine.

And by the end of the piece the anti-democratic demand for authority
becomes quite clear:

> So now, what with great Airedale dogs,
> And a kick or two,
> And a few vomiting bouts,
> And a juniper switch,
> You look at me for discrimination, don't you?
> Look up at me with misgiving in your bulging eyes,
> And fear in the smoky whites of your eyes, you nigger;
> And you're puzzled.
> You think you'd better mind your P's and Q's for a bit,
> Your sensitive love-pride being all hurt.
>
> All right, my little bitch.
> You learn loyalty rather than loving,
> And I'll protect you.[6]

It is intriguing to wonder how Lawrence, the author of these sentiments,
would have responded to the loyalty of that ideal batman, Tolkien's Sam
Samwise. A related but much better poem, from Lawrence's emblematic
bestiary, is 'St Mark'.

---

6   D.H. Lawrence, 'Bibbles', in *The Complete Poems of D.H. Lawrence* (New York, 1964).

There was a lion in Judah
Which whelped, and was Mark.

But winged.
A lion with wings.
At least at Venice
Even as late as Daniele Manin.

Why should he have wings?
Is he to be a bird also?
Or a spirit?
Or a winged thought?
Or a soaring consciousness?

Evidently he is all that,
The lion of the spirit.

Ah, Lamb of God,
Would a wingless lion lie down before Thee, as this winged lion lies?

The lion of the spirit.

Once he lay in the mouth of a cave
And sunned his whiskers,
And lashed his tail slowly, slowly
Thinking of voluptuousness
Even of blood.

But later, in the sun of the afternoon,
Having tasted all there was to taste, and having slept his fill
He fell to frowning, as he lay with his head on his paws
And the sun coming in through the narrowest fibril of a slit in his
    eyes.

So, nine-tenths asleep, motionless, bored, and statically angry,
He saw in a shaft of light a lamb on a pinnacle, balancing a flag on
    its paw,
And he was thoroughly startled.

Going out to investigate
He found the lamb beyond him, on the inaccessible pinnacle of light.
So he put his paw to his nose, and pondered.

'Guard my sheep,' came the silvery voice from the pinnacle,
'And I will give thee the wings of the morning.'
So the lion of the senses thought it was worth it.

Hence he became a curly sheep-dog with dangerous propensities,
As Carpaccio will tell you:

Ramping round, guarding the flock of mankind,
Sharpening his teeth on the wolves,
Ramping up through the air like a kestrel
And lashing his tail above the world
And enjoying the sensation of heaven and righteousness and
    voluptuous wrath.

There is a new sweetness in his voluptuously licking his paw
Now that it is a weapon of heaven.
There is a new ecstasy in his roar of desirous love
Now that it sounds self-conscious through the unlimited sky.
He is well aware of himself
And he cherishes voluptuous delights, and thinks about them
And ceases to be a blood-thirsty king of beasts
And becomes the faithful sheep-dog of the Shepherd, thinking of
    his voluptuous pleasure of chasing the sheep to the fold
And increasing the flock, and perhaps giving a real nip here and
    there, a real pinch, but always well meant.

And somewhere there is a lioness,
The she-mate.
Whelps play between the paws of the lion,
The she-mate purrs,
Their castle is impregnable, their cave,
The sun comes in their lair, they are well-off,
A well-to-do family.

Then the proud lion stalks abroad alone,
And roars to announce himself to the wolves
And also to encourage the red-cross Lamb
And also to ensure a goodly increase in the world.

Look at him, with his paw on the world
At Venice and elsewhere.
Going blind at last.[7]

This is not exclusively nor chiefly an anti-Christian poem. It is an anti-philanthropist poem. It is directed against the do-gooder, whether he exerts himself to do good *de haut en bas* under Christian auspices or some other. In 1972 we well may think first of a militantly or complacently secular philanthropist, a Fabian expert in the behavioural sciences called in as a consultant, a social engineer, by a British or for that matter American government or municipality. What the poem is about is the devious compensation which the lion of aggressiveness can earn when he persuades himself that he is the protective sheepdog, serving the higher

7   From *The Complete Poems* of *D.H. Lawrence*.

purpose of social cohesiveness and amelioration. The poem could be directed indeed against the Thomas Hardy who wrote poems to and for the Royal Society for the Prevention of Cruelty to Animals. The distinctive snarling and taunting tone, here informing the disposition of free-verse lines as well as the dextrous shifts from one level of diction to another, still stings and hurts; for Lawrence's target in such a poem is just that form of government and social organisation which the British have increasingly, since his death, come to accept as normal. And to set Lawrence against Hardy at this point is to raise immediately the urgent question for the modern Englishman: Do we have to accept the insistent presence of the semi-official busybody, in order to ensure what we regard as a minimal level of social and political justice? Lawrence, it is clear, wants his countrymen to answer that question with a resounding No! But of course the answer since his death has been, sometimes grudgingly and resentfully, Yes. We have given Hardy's answer, not Lawrence's.

★   ★   ★

R.P. Blackmur, a critic of the Eliotic persuasion who gave a more considered account of Lawrence's poetry than any other from that inevitably hostile point of view, gives three good examples of early poems by Lawrence in which the influence of Hardy is apparent. These are 'Lightning', 'Turned Down', and the two quatrains called 'Gipsy':

> I, the man with the red scarf,
>> Will give thee what I have, this last week's earnings.
> Take them and buy thee a silver ring
>> And wed me, to ease my yearnings.
>
> For the rest, when thou art wedded
>> I'll wet my brow for thee
> With sweat, I'll enter a house for thy sake,
>> Thou shalt shut doors on me.[8]

Blackmur remarks, 'Hardy would have been ashamed of the uneven, lop-sided metrical architecture and would never have been guilty (whatever faults he had of his own) of the disturbing inner rhyme in the second quatrain.' This is true, and it is well said. It is also quite irrelevant. The whole notion of 'metrical architecture', all the cluster of metaphors and analogies which lies behind such an expression, was entirely foreign to Lawrence's way of thinking about what it was he did when he wrote poems. It is not just that Lawrence rejected the architectural analogy which was so important to Hardy. He rejected also the finding of analo-

8   Lawrence, 'Gipsy', from *The Complete Poems*.

gies for poetry in any of the other arts, including music, and insisted on the contrary, as anyone who has read even a little of him must recognise, on taking as the only reliable analogues for the act of poetic creation various biological processes of copulation, parturition, generation, metamorphosis.

This is what makes the case of Lawrence unique. It is still not pointed out sufficiently often that Lawrence's use of free verse or of 'open form' is in no way a paradigm of what has been and is still normal practice in these modes. It should be plain for instance that J.H. Prynne, when he writes free verse in open form, is using a dense and elaborate rhetoric, as are those American writers such as Olson and Dorn whom Prynne is to some degree emulating. In considering these writers we can, and indeed must, talk of skill, of craftsmanship, even perhaps of 'technique'. Lawrence on the other hand meant just what he said in 1913 when, in a much-quoted letter, he wrote to Edward Marsh: 'I have always tried to get an emotion out in its own course, without altering it. It needs the finest instinct imaginable, much finer than the skill of craftsmen'; and when a line later he exhorted Marsh to 'remember skilled verse is dead in fifty years'.

If we remember how necessary we found it, when speaking of Hardy's poems, to bear hard upon a distinction between 'technique' and 'skill', we have to say that Lawrence will tolerate poetic skill as little as poetic technique. 'Technique', with its inevitably metallic and mechanical overtones in our age of technology and technocracy, is anathema to Lawrence, as it is to all free-verse poets and perhaps to all poets in our time whatever (though certainly, as I have argued, not at all so unambiguously to Hardy); but also *skill*, bringing with it a quite different range of associations (for instance with worked or incised or sculptured stone), is anathema to Lawrence no less. In Lawrence's poetry we encounter a man who is eager to junk not just industrial civilisation, but also the pre-industrial civilisation which expressed itself in ashlar and marble, even perhaps in brick. One of the most moving of his letters, written in 1917, laments the death of the inherited English culture in images of the stonework of Garsington Manor; but Lawrence seems to have believed in all seriousness that an end had come to that culture of stonework, as it must be made to come to the culture of metal girders. To be sure, when Lawrence wrote his essay 'Poetry of the Present', as his introduction to the American edition of his *New Poems*, he contrived a distinction between poetry of the past and the future, and his own poetry of the present, in such a way as to mask very engagingly the enormity of the challenge he was throwing down to his readers. But this is adroitly tactful, rather than convincing; and we have not measured up to the challenge which Lawrence throws down, we have not measured the risk which Lawrence is prepared to take with the inherited cultural goods of our civilisation, if we think we can take Lawrence on Lawrence's own terms while still keeping Shakespeare or Donne unshaken in their honoured niches. Lawrence would deny to such masters from the past any room at all so spacious as the generations before him had agreed to allow them. Either there are in artistic forms some kinds of fixity and finality which we are right to value as satisfying, instructive, and invigorating; or else on the contrary, as Lawrence would have us believe, there is no kind of fixity, no finality, which is other than an impediment and an obstruction to the vital apprehension which is always fluid, always in flux.

Thus Lawrence's metaphors from biology are in no way on a par with the metaphors from topography and geology which we find in Auden or in Hardy – as indeed everyone acknowledges; since no one, I think, has ever claimed Lawrence as any sort of scientific humanist. From Lawrence's extreme and exacerbated point of view, the humanistic liberal and the religious authoritarian are condemned alike and without distinction, as are all images of strain and fixity, whether in stone or in metal. The clearest example of this is a poem called 'The Revolutionary':

Look at them standing there in authority,
The pale-faces,
As if it could have any effect any more.

Pale-face authority,
Caryatids;
Pillars of white bronze standing rigid, lest the skies fall.

What a job they've got to keep it up.
Their poor, idealist foreheads naked capitals
To the entablature of clouded heaven.

When the skies are going to fall, fall they will
In a great chute and rush of débâcle downwards.
Oh and I wish the high and super-gothic heavens would come down
    now,
The heavens above, that we yearn to and aspire to.

I do not yearn, nor aspire, for I am a blind Samson
And what is daylight to me that I should look skyward?
Only I grope among you, pale-faces, caryatids, as among a forest of
    pillars that hold up the dome of high ideal heaven
Which is my prison,
And all these human pillars of loftiness, going stiff, metallic – stunned
    with the weight of their responsibility
I stumble against them.
Stumbling-blocks, painful ones.

To keep on holding up this ideal civilisation
Must be excruciating: unless you stiffen into metal, when it is easier
   to stand stock rigid than to move.
This is why I tug at them, individually, with my arm round their
   waist,
The human pillars.
They are not stronger than I am, blind Samson.
The house sways.

I shall be so glad when it comes down.
I am so tired of the limitations of their Infinite.
I am so sick of the pretensions of the Spirit.
I am so weary of pale-face importance.

Am I not blind, at the round-turning mill?
Then why should I fear their pale faces?
Or love the effulgence of their holy light,
The sun of their righteousness?

To me, all faces are dark,
All lips are dusky and valved.

Save your lips, O pale-faces,
Which are lips of metal,
Like slits in an automatic-machine, you columns of give-and-take.

To me, the earth rolls ponderously, superbly
Coming my way without forethought or afterthought.
To me, men's footfalls fall with a dull, soft rumble, ominous and
   lovely,
Coming my way.

But not your foot-falls, pale-faces,
They are a clicketing of bits of disjointed metal
Working in motion.

To me, men are palpable, invisible nearnesses in the dark
Sending out magnetic vibrations of warning, pitch-dark throbs of
   invitation.

But you, pale-faces,
You are painful, harsh-surfaced pillars that give off nothing except
   rigidity,
And I jut against you if I try to move, for you are everywhere, and I
   am blind,
Sightless among all your visuality,
You staring caryatids.

See if I don't bring you down, and all your high opinion
And all your ponderous, roofed-in erection of right and wrong,
Your particular heavens,
With a smash.

See if your skies aren't falling!
And my head, at least, is thick enough to stand it, the smash.

See if I don't move under a dark and nude, vast heaven
When your world is in ruins, under your fallen skies.
Caryatids, pale-faces.
See if I am not Lord of the dark and moving hosts
Before I die.[9]

It is quite beside the point that by the end Lawrence had more hopes of a revolution from the Right than from the Left; in the light of a poem such as this, his revulsion was against all forms of instituted authority whatever, and the direction from which the wind should come that would topple them from their pediments is to him almost indifferent – as indeed is acknowledged by his most enthusiastic readers today, who are most often ranged upon the political Left. Even his preference for loyalty over love – announced in 'Bibbles' and developed in a poem in *Pansies* called 'Fidelity' (where the rock, fidelity, is preferred to the flower, love) – is nowadays, when the revolutionary ardour of the Left is focused upon charismatic leaders like Mao and Che Guevara, as acceptable and exciting to the Left as to the Right.

But further argument is needless. If we are still a little contemptuous of Hardy's political cop-out, if we respond more vividly to Lawrence's reck-lessness, if we are eager to join in his condemnation of the bureaucratic philanthropist, he for his part offers us no political standing point short of wholesale and open-ended revolutionary upheaval. More even than he is a revolutionary, Lawrence is an iconoclast. *All* the graven images must be cast down and powdered – the bull of St Luke no less than the lion of St Mark, no less than even the biologically graven image on the horny shell of the tortoise. By the time he wrote the poem in *Pansies* called 'Give us Gods', Lawrence had gone beyond all these. It is not surprising, and it is certainly not disgraceful, that English poets have refused to take that risk and pay that price.

For it needs to be asserted, now when the air is thick with voices like Rexroth's demanding that all poetry be *prophetic* (like Blake's, like Lawrence's), that prophetic poetry is necessarily an inferior poetry. The reason has emerged already. The prophet is above being fair-minded – judiciousness he leaves to some one else. But the poet will absolve himself

9   D.H. Lawrence, 'The Revolutionary', from *The Complete Poems*.

from none of the responsibilities of being human, he will leave none of those responsibilities to 'someone else'. And being human involves the responsibility of being judicious and fair-minded. In this way the poet supports the intellectual venture of humankind, taking his place along with (though *above*, yet along with) the scholar and the statesman and the learned divine. His poetry supports and nourishes and helps to shape *culture*; the prophet, however, is outside culture and (really) at war with it. The prophet exists on sufferance, he is on society's expense account, part of what society can sometimes afford. Not so the poet; he is what society cannot dispense with.

7 Roy Fisher: An Appreciation

> *Sombre mood*
> *in the presence of things,*
> *no matter what things;*
> *respectful sepia.*[1]

Roy Fisher's principal publications are *City* (Worcester, Migrant Press, 1961), *Ten Interiors with Various Figures* (Nottingham, Tarasque Press, 1967), *The Memorial Fountain* (Newcastle-upon-Tyne, Northern House, 1967), and *Collected Poems: The Ghost of a Paper Bag* (London, Fulcrum Press, 1969). The names of his publishers are significant; Fisher has published with provincial and more or less fugitive presses, just as he has been printed for the most part only by magazines with a limited or specialised readership, far from the reputation-making centres of Oxford and Cambridge and London. In the literary life of England, despite several state-instituted attempts to stimulate and help artistic activity in the provinces, the blindness or condescension of the metropolis to writing which is provincial in its origins or its subject matter is not much less scandalous now in the 1970s than it was forty years ago. Fisher, like many other writers, has suffered from this; and it is not surprising that those readers and editors who have recognised the worth of his work should have resented how little he is known in the metropolis (and consequently outside England, for until lately the metropolitan circles had the monopoly of what English authors and reputations were promoted abroad), or that an admirable enterprise like the Fulcrum Press, when it does handsome justice to a writer like Fisher, should seem in doing so to be the organ of an underground, or a counterculture. And indeed, though 'underground' and 'counterculture' are both words too fashionably theatrical to be accurate, it cannot be doubted that there are in literary England two distinct circles or systems of literary activity and literary reputation, and that there is a sometimes rancorous rivalry between them. Of recent years the cause of the literary counterculture in England has been strengthened in many ways, notably by the activities of Fulcrum Press and a few similar enterprises, still more by the fact that the

---

1 Roy Fisher, 'The Memorial Fountain', *Collected Poems, 1968* (Fulcrum Press, 1969).

counterculture has established its own relations with literary activity in America, and – most momentously of all – by the fact that the most senior of England's provincial and outsider poets, Basil Bunting, has lately published what is undoubtedly his masterpiece, *Briggflatts*, by any account one of the greatest achievements of English poetry in the last forty years.

The existence of a literary culture and counterculture, of an establishment and an anti-establishment, is damaging to all English poets whatever, and obfuscating for readers of poetry. There are few enough such readers in any case; and it is gratuitously unfortunate for any poet that the small public he may hope to communicate with should be split into two halves which hardly communicate one with the other. (To give an example of the damage that is done, it is almost true to say that the full range of current American verse writing is known to no one in England, since the American writing most esteemed by the counterculture – Olson, Snyder, Levertov – is quite different from the American writing – Lowell, Berryman, Sylvia Plath – recognised and admired by the 'establishment'.) Moreover, as reviewers and anthologists align themselves with the one camp or the other, there is inevitably much darkening of counsel. The reader who conscientiously seeks enlightenment from these authorities will find himself being asked to take sides, and being persuaded that for instance no one can like equally Roy Fisher, who writes in free verse and in open forms, and Larkin, who characteristically uses closed forms and writes in metre. And yet this is not the case; Fisher and Larkin are very much alike, as I shall hope to show. In particular, though I think there is no evidence internal or external that Roy Fisher has ever read any of Hardy's poems with attention, his temperament is, like Larkin's, profoundly Hardyesque. If I can show this, it will support one of my principal contentions – that the Hardyesque tone in so much British writing is the result of social and political circumstances, which bear in upon and condition writers who perhaps are not directly influenced by Hardy's poems at all.

To begin with, however, what strikes the reader is the gulf between Roy Fisher's imagination and Hardy's. In an early poem, 'The Intruder',[2] Fisher, encountering suddenly the image of 'a young girl… doing some household work, a couple of generations ago', confesses in the poem that he does not know what to do with this image, what (as it were) the image asks of him. When he says in mild bewilderment, 'it's as if I had walked into somebody else's imagination', we feel that that somebody else could well have been Hardy, for whom the image of a woman thus mysteriously arising from a past scene recurred time and again to provoke some of the best poetry he ever wrote. When Roy Fisher decides, in the last line of his poem 'to retire discreetly, and leave the sulky bitch to it', he is

---

2   Roy Fisher, *Collected Poems*.

in effect refusing, with a somewhat shrill fierceness, to let his imagination walk in one of Hardy's favourite paths.

Accordingly, it comes as no surprise to find that in another early poem, 'The Hospital in Winter',[3] the attempt at rhyme and metre (those enabling constrictions so invaluable to Hardy) is quite plainly an embarrassing obstruction and impediment to Fisher, as it is in the early rhyming poems of Lawrence. And indeed, again among the early poems is one, 'Why They Stopped Singing',[4] which may be read as a defiant apology for abandoning such 'traditional forms'. The alternative open forms to which even so early Fisher vows himself are finely justified in a piece called 'Linear':

> To travel and feel
> the world growing old on your body
>
> breathe and excrete
> perpetually the erosion that makes the world
>
> a caravan the little city
> that has the wit to cross a continent
>
> so patiently it cannot help but see
> how each day's dust lay and shifted and lies again
>
> no forgotten miles or kinks
> in the journey other than cunning ones
>
> to pass through many things acquisitively
> and touch against many more
>
> a long line without anything
> you could call repetition
>
> always through eroded
> country amused by others and other worlds
>
> a line like certain snail tracks
> crazily long and determined.[5]

That last image of the snail tracks might be usefully compared with the ending of 'Considering the Snail', by another British poet, the scrupulous expatriate, Thom Gunn.

But the most important of Fisher's early poems is 'Toyland' which, if it is worlds away from Hardy, is just as far from anything one could think of as Lawrencian:

---

3   Roy Fisher, *Collected Poems*.
4   *Collected Poems*.
5   *Collected Poems*. The poem is quoted in full.

Today the sunlight is the paint on lead soldiers
Only they are people scattering out of the cool church

And as they go across the gravel and among the spring streets
They spread formality: they know, we know, what they have been
    doing,

The old couples, the widowed, the staunch smilers,
The deprived and the few nubile young lily-ladies,

And we know what they will do when they have opened the doors
    of their houses and walked in:
Mostly they will make water, and wash their calm hands and eat.

The organ's flourishes finish; the verger closes the doors;
The choirboys run home, and the rector goes off in his motor.

Here a policeman stalks, the sun glinting on his helmet-crest;
Then a man pushes a perambulator home; and somebody posts a
    letter.

If I sit here long enough, loving it all, I shall see the District Nurse
    pedal past,
The children going to Sunday School and the strollers strolling;

The lights darting on in different rooms as night comes in;
And I shall see washing hung out, and the postman delivering letters.

I might by exception see an ambulance or the fire brigade
Or even, if the chance came round, street musicians (singing and
    playing).

For the people I've seen, this seems the operation of life:
I need the paint of stillness and sunshine to see it that way.

The secret laugh of the world picks them up and shakes them like
    peas boiling;
They behave as if nothing happened; maybe they no longer notice.

I notice. I laugh with the laugh, cultivate it, make much of it,
But I still don't know what the joke is, to tell them.[6]

By the end of this poem, though nothing presents itself to the poet as an
alternative to what he adumbrated in 'Linear', there is the honest confession of some dissatisfaction with the inconclusiveness which that sort of
open form brings with it.

In his long poem, *City*, there are some sections, for instance 'The Hill
Behind the Town', in which the exigencies of verse writing still seem to

be more of a hindrance than a help to Fisher. And although this is not true of other sections in verse (for instance 'The Poplars'), still the most distinguished parts of this poem – and they are very distinguished indeed – are those which are interspersed in continuous prose. For instance:

> In the century that has passed since this city has become great, it has twice laid itself out in the shape of a wheel. The ghost of the older one still lies among the spokes of the new, those dozen highways that thread constricted ways through the inner suburbs, then thrust out, twice as wide, across the housing estates and into the countryside, dragging moraines of buildings with them. Sixty or seventy years ago there were other main roads, quite as important as these were then, but lying between their paths. By day they are simply alternatives, short cuts, lined solidly with parked cars and crammed with delivery vans. They look merely like side-streets, heartlessly overblown in some excess of Victorian expansion. By night, or on a Sunday, you can see them for what they are. They are still lit meagrely, and the long rows of houses, three and four storeys high, rear black above the lamps enclosing the roadways, clamping them off from whatever surrounds them. From these pavements you can sometimes see the sky at night, not obscured as it is in most parts of the city by the greenish-blue haze of light that steams out of the mercury vapour lamps. These streets are not worth lighting. The houses have not been turned into shops – they are not villas either that might have become offices, but simply tall dwellings, opening straight off the street, with cavernous entries leading into back courts.
>
> The people who live in them are mostly very old. Some have lived through three wars, some through only one; wars of newspapers, of mysterious sciences, of coercion, of disappearance. Wars that have come down the streets from the unknown city and the unknown world, like rainwater floods in the gutters. There are small shops at street corners, with blank rows of houses between them; and taverns carved only shallowly into the massive walls. When these people go into the town, the buses they travel in stop just before they reach it, in the sombre back streets behind the Town Hall and the great insurance offices.
>
> These lost streets are decaying only very slowly. The impacted lives of their inhabitants, the meaninglessness of news, the dead black of the chimney breasts, the conviction that the wind itself comes only from the next street, all wedge together to keep destruction out; to deflect the eye of the developer. And when destruction comes, it is total: the printed notices on the walls, block by block, a few doors left open at night, broken windows advancing down a street until fallen slates

appear on the pavement and are not kicked away. Then, after a few weeks of this, the machines arrive.[7]

This is description at its most impressive, able to move with ease into analysis on the one hand and into mournful poetry on the other, and at no point subsiding into mere limp enumeration. One responds to it in the first place as one responds to Larkin's 'Whitsun Weddings': this is how it is! At least, so one feels if one knows any of the industrial cities built or greatly enlarged in the nineteenth century in the English Midlands and North – cities like Leeds, Nottingham, Birmingham, Salford. The truth is, however, that not only foreign visitors to England but also many Englishmen from the Home Counties have never visited such cities; and accordingly Roy Fisher's scrupulousness is lost upon them.

It would not have been lost upon Hardy. Hardy never frequented industrial landscapes, and formally no doubt Fisher's *City* would have seemed to Hardy a very odd production indeed. Yet we can be sure that he would have responded very promptly and sympathetically to what is Fisher's central concern in this poem, the large-scale demolitions (in Fisher's Birmingham as in other industrial cities) which, gratuitously inaugurated by German bombs during the Second World War, were pursued enthusiastically through the post-war years by civic authorities. Fisher's protest against such 'slum clearance', though it may owe something to what was an agitated talking-point of the 1950s, Young's and Willmott's study of the social and human implications of slum clearance in Bethnal Green,[8] is thoroughly in the spirit of Hardy's address when, in 1910, he was made a freeman of the borough of Dorchester:

> … An American gentleman came to me the other day in quite a bad temper, saying that he had diverged from his direct route from London to Liverpool to see ancient Dorchester, only to discover that he knew a hundred towns in the United States more ancient-looking than this (*laughter*). Well, we may be older than we look, like some ladies; but if, for instance, the original All-Saints and Trinity Churches, with their square towers, the castle, the fine mansion of the Trenchards at the corner of Shirehall Lane, the old Three Mariners Inn, the old Greyhound, the old Antelope, Lady Abingdon's house at the corner of Durngate Street, and other mediaeval buildings were still in their places, more visitors of antiquarian tastes would probably haunt the town than haunt it now. Old All-Saints was, I believe, demolished because its buttresses projected too far into the pavement. What a reason for destroying a record of 500 years in stone! I knew the

7   *Collected Poems.*
8   Michael Young and Peter Willmott, *Family and Kinship in East London* (London, 1957).

architect who did it; a milder-mannered man never scuttled a sacred edifice. Milton's well-known observation in his *Areopagitica* – 'Almost as well kill a man as kill a good book' – applies not a little to a good old building; which is not only a book but a unique manuscript that has no fellow.[9]

Probably none of the Birmingham buildings whose demolition is mourned by Roy Fisher reached back as far as 500 years, and (a more important point) none or few of them were in *stone*. But this does not affect the principle, which is identical in Hardy and in Fisher:

Brick-dust in sunlight. That is what I see now in the city, a dry epic flavour, whose air is human breath. A place of walls made straight with plumbline and trowel, to desiccate and crumble in the sun and smoke. Blistered paint on cisterns and girders, cracking to show the priming. Old men spit on the paving slabs, little boys urinate; and the sun dries it as it dries out patches of damp on plaster facings to leave misshapen stains. I look for things here that make old men and dead men seem young. Things which have escaped, the landscapes of many child-hoods. Wharves, the oldest parts of factories, tarred gable ends rearing to take the sun over lower roofs. Soot, sunlight, brick-dust; and the breath that tastes of them.[10]

It may be objected that Hardy as an architect takes it for granted, as Fisher plainly doesn't, that the buildings which are to be saved from demolition are artistically valuable, beautiful, monuments to the shaping imaginations of architects. But this is not the case, as we see quite clearly from a document of cardinal importance for understanding Hardy, his 'Memories of Church Restoration', originally delivered as an address to the Society for the Protection of Ancient Buildings in 1906.[11] Here Hardy is speaking out against not literal demolition, but the more abstract and devious demolition that is called 'restoration'. After arguing in the first place that reproduction of an ancient feature by the restorer is an impossibility (if only because the restorer will avail himself of technical resources unknown to the original builder, since for instance 'curves were often struck by hand in mediaeval work'), Hardy goes on:

The second, or spiritual, attribute which stultifies the would-be repro-ducer is perhaps more important still, and is not artistic at all. It lies in human association. The influence that a building like Lincoln or Winchester exercises on a person of average impressionableness and

9   *The Life of Thomas Hardy, 1840–1928*, p. 352.
10 Fisher, *Collected Poems*.
11 Published in *Cornhill Magazine*, July 1906. See Hardy, *Life and Art*, ed. E. Brennecke (New York, 1925).

culture is a compound influence, and though it would be a fanciful attempt to define how many fractions of that compound are aesthetic, and how many associative, there can be no doubt that the latter influence is more valuable than the former. Some may be of a different opinion, but I think the damage done to this sentiment of association by replacement, by the rupture of continuity, is mainly what makes the enormous loss this country has sustained from its seventy years of church restoration so tragic and deplorable. The protection of an ancient edifice against renewal in fresh materials is, in fact, even more of a social – I may say a humane – duty than an aesthetic one. It is the preservation of memories, history, fellowships, fraternities. Life, after all, is more than art, and that which appealed to us in the (maybe) clumsy outlines of some structure which had been looked at and entered by a dozen generations of ancestors outweighs the more subtle recognition, if any, of architectural qualities.[12]

It is not hard to envisage the devoted architect who might angrily denounce Hardy on this showing as, in this field as in others, a 'cop-out'. And in such a passage he does indeed lay himself open to the charges we have found ourselves levelling at his disciple, Larkin – of being too ready to do without distinction (artistic and other) for the sake of imaginative sympathy with the undistinguished and anonymous many. It is no more than appropriate that these sentiments should be expressed in remarkably inelegant and slipshod language. But at least the passage makes it clear that when Hardy considers the obliteration of buildings and townscapes he, no more than Roy Fisher, is concerned with the presence or absence of aesthetic quality in what is being obliterated.

On the other hand, if Hardy believes that the old is to be preserved whenever possible simply for its oldness, he is not therefore merely obstructive, sentimentally opposed to all change. In his address on receiving the freedom of Dorchester, after the tartness of 'a milder-mannered man never scuttled a sacred edifice', he says surprisingly:

> And when all has been said on the desirability of preserving as much as can be preserved, our power to preserve is largely an illusion. Where is the Dorchester of my early recollection – I mean the human Dorchester – the kernel – of which the houses were but the shell? Of the shops as I first recall them not a single owner remains; only in two or three instances does even the name remain. As a German author has said, 'Nothing is permanent but change.' Here in Dorchester, as elsewhere, I see the streets and the turnings not far different from those of my schoolboy time; but the faces that used to be seen at the doors, the

---

12 Brennecke, *Life and Art*, pp. 105–6.

inhabitants, where are they? I turn up the Weymouth Road, cross the railway-bridge, enter an iron gate to 'a slope of green access', and there they are! There is the Dorchester that I knew best; there are names on white stones one after the other, names that recall the voices, cheerful and sad, anxious and indifferent, that are missing from the dwellings and pavements. Those who are old enough to have had that experience may feel that after all the permanence or otherwise of inanimate Dorchester concerns but the permanence of what is minor and accessory.

Change must come, and so must demolitions. But in every case (so Hardy seems to say) let the cost be counted – as it certainly is not counted by town-planners nor by civil engineers nor by connoisseurs of architecture and townscape, nor even by sociologists. An old church may have to be demolished; but let it be for some better reason than that 'its buttresses projected too far into the pavement'.

And this seems to have been what Roy Fisher meant to say in *City*. But if so, he was at that stage unable to say it clearly, because his verse writing let him down. In the midst of *City* there are for instance six lines headed, 'By the Pond':

> This is bitter enough: the pallid water
> With yellow rushes crowding toward the shore,
> That fishermen's shack,
>
> The pit-mound's taut and staring wire fences,
> The ashen sky. All these can serve as conscience.
> For the rest, I'll live.[13]

And these lines (which have, incidentally, a distracting resemblance to Hardy's 'Neutral Tones') cannot be understood with the help of anything elsewhere in *City*. To understand them, in particular to understand what they mean to convey by 'conscience', we have to turn to a later poem called 'For Realism', which evokes the scenes in the workers' streets when the local factory has discharged its shift of workers on a summer evening. On these scenes the poet comments:

> there presses in
> – and not as conscience –
> what concentrates down in the warm hollow:
>
> plenty of life there still,
> the foodshops open late, and people
> going about constantly, but not far;

13 Fisher, *Collected Poems*.

there's a man in a blue suit
facing into a corner,
straddling to keep his shoes dry;
women step, talking, over the stream,
and when the men going by call out, he answers.

Above, dignity. A new precinct
comes over the scraped hill,
flats on the ridge get the last light.

Down Wheeler Street, the lamps
already gone, the windows have
lake stretches of silver
gashed out of tea green shadows,
the after-images of brickwork.

A conscience
builds, late, on the ridge. A realism
tries to record, before they're gone,
what silver filth these drains have run.[14]

This suggests that when, in 'By the Pond', 'conscience' is seen as something apart from life, what is meant is, as in this later poem, the social conscience of the confident demographer and humanitarian administrator who has demolished acres of the inner city and rehoused their denizens in high-rise apartment-blocks on the ridge above their old dwellings, at whatever cost to the human associations that those demolished dwellings had for them. And if this is so, other sections of *City* fall into place, as expressing, like Lawrence's 'St Mark', distrust and dislike of the civic conscience as embodied in the philanthropist, the officially designated do-gooder. For instance:

At the time when the great streets were thrust out along the old highroads and trackways, the houses shouldering towards the country and the back streets filling in the widening spaces between them like webbed membranes, the power of will in the town was more open, less speciously democratic, than it is now. There were, of course, cottage railway stations, a jail that pretended to be a castle out of Grimm, public urinals surrounded by screens of cast-iron lacework painted green and scarlet; but there was also an arrogant ponderous architecture that dwarfed and terrified the people by its sheer size and functional brutality: the workhouses and the older hospitals, the thick-walled abattoir, the long vaulted market-halls, the striding canal bridges and railway viaducts. Brunel was welcome here. Compared

14 *Collected Poems.*

with these structures the straight white blocks and concrete roadways of today are a fairground, a clear dream just before waking, the creation of salesmen rather than of engineers. The new city is bred out of a hard will, but as it appears, it shows itself a little ingratiating, a place of arcades, passages, easy ascents, good light. The eyes twinkle, beseech and veil themselves; the full, hard mouth, the broad jaw – these are no longer made visible to all.[15]

And this is followed by a very fine evocation of a monument surviving from the city's more brutal age – a railway station; a description informed with an uneasy and unwilling nostalgia, in prose that once again is infinitely more poetic than Fisher's verse. The animus against the new breed of city fathers, who are ingratiating and paternalistic, more like salesmen than engineers, is patent. The nostalgia is for an image of naked authority, however brutal; and it is carried in images of stone.

It would be foolish to translate this into political sympathies or a political stance, arguing that Fisher wants to regain a society governed by unrestricted capitalist competitiveness. What Fisher expresses in these passages is only a mood, almost an aberration. Apart from anything else, he says, 'I am not able to imagine the activity that must once have been here. I can see no ghosts of men and women, only the gigantic ghost of stone.' All the same we certainly have at this point moved into the area of what we can legitimately decipher as Fisher's politics. We may deduce as much from a later poem called 'Seven Attempted Moves'.[16] The third of these 'moves' is:

> Crisis –
>
> a man should be able
> To hope for a well made crisis,
> Something to brace against.
>
> But see it come in rapidly and mean
> along some corridor
> In a pauperous civic Office.

And the last of them reads:

> It is a shame. There is
>   nowhere to go.
> Doors into further in
>   lead out already
> To new gardens

15 *Collected Poems*.
16 *Collected Poems*.

> Small enough for pets' droppings
>   quickly to cover:
> Ceilings
>   too soon, steps curtailed;
> The minibed; minibath;
>   and jammed close
>   the minican.
>
> Confinement,
>   shortness of breath.
> Only a state of mind.
>   And
> Statues of it built everywhere.

The writer of these verses, in which at last the curtness of the verse-line and the choice of diction (for instance, the sardonic 'It is a shame') enact the bitter distaste of the speaker, plainly is less than enthusiastic about social democracy as it has evolved in Britain since 1945. His 'minibed... minibath... minican' is his way of endorsing Charles Tomlinson's angry contempt for 'that suburban mental ratio which too many... poets attempt to impose on their experience'. What is remarkable is that Fisher, unlike Tomlinson, comes by this hostile perception while restricting himself as self-denyingly as Larkin to the urbanised and industrialised landscapes of modern England.

The resemblance between Fisher and Larkin is sometimes very striking indeed. For instance, Fisher's 'As He Came Near Death', one of the finest short poems to come out of England these many years, begins:

> As he came near death things grew shallower for us:
> We'd lost sleep and now sat muffled in the scent of tulips, the
>   medical odours, and the street sounds going past, going away;
> And he, too, slept little, the morphine and the pink light the curtains
>   let through floating him with us,
> So that he lay and was worked out on to the skin of his life and left
>   there...[17]

And no one who has read Larkin with sympathy can fail to be reminded, by Fisher's fourth line, of the end of Larkin's justly admired 'Afternoons', about young mothers bringing their children to play in the civic recreation ground:

> Their beauty has thickened.
> Something is pushing them
> To the side of their own lives.[18]

---

17 *Collected Poems.*
18 Philip Larkin, 'Afternoons', in *The Whitsun Weddings.*

Behind 'worked out on to the skin of his life' and 'pushing them to the side of their own lives', the act of the imagination is identical. It is not, I think, anything that can be found in Hardy. And indeed Fisher at any rate seems to have had to go far afield to discover it – so far indeed that the terms 'underground' and 'counterculture', with their populist implications (that tedious and perennial nonsense about bringing poetry 'back to the people'), are seen to be grotesquely inappropriate to his case. For he has described himself as 'a 1920s Russian modernist'.[19] And in fact 'As He Came Near Death' ends chillingly with a fine deployment of that 'making strange' which the Russian modernists found adumbrated for them already by Tolstoy:

> Then the hole: this was a slot punched in a square of plastic grass rug,
>   a slot lined with white polythene, floored with dyed green gravel.
> The box lay in it; we rode in the black cars round a corner, got out
>   into our coloured cars and dispersed in easy stages.

> After a time the grave got up and went away.

'Making strange', however (basically the slow-motion dismemberment of a ritual or routine action into its bizarre components), is only the simplest of the devices which Fisher took over when he set himself to school to the Russian modernists of the '20s. And when the full battery of their resources is deployed, as in Fisher's 'Three Ceremonial Poems' or in his prose piece, *The Ship's Orchestra* (which Edward Lucie-Smith has described – admiringly, I think – as 'perhaps the most hermetic text to have been published in England in recent years'), it seems that the game is hardly worth the candle. Whether in English or in Russian – even in the hands of Pasternak, who practised this mode, though infrequently – this Russian-type modernism seems mannered and wasteful. In the 'Three Ceremonial Poems',[20] for instance, Fisher seems to be on the brink of making definitive judgements (about metals and stone and urine-loosened brick as alternative media for human expression and association) which only a perverse allegiance to a non-discursive poetics prevents him from promulgating. The 'realism' to which from time to time Fisher vows himself, seldom without sardonic emphasis, is constantly in danger of deteriorating into the mere enumeration of 'motorbikes, dogshit, girls'. And to escape this trap (which he has always escaped in his prose, but not in his verse), Fisher has taken this wide circuit into Mayakovsky and Mandelstam. Yet one cannot help but remember how surely Larkin has escaped the same pitfall, using devices no more recondite than the choice epithet and the strategically reversed foot in a metrical scheme.

19 *Contemporary Poets of the English Language*, ed. Rosalie Murphy (London and Chicago, 1970), p. 374.
20 Fisher, *Collected Poems*, pp. 76–8.

Thus, although the fruits of his apprenticeship to foreign models manifest themselves impressively in 'Seven Attempted Moves' and 'As He Came Near Death', Fisher remains most challengingly the author of *City*, imperfect as that poem is.

And, as regards the imperfections of *City*, Michael Shayer was not wrong, though he was admirably bold, when he recalled in this connection the not much less manifest imperfections of *The Waste Land*, of Pound's *Cantos*, of (most pertinently) Joyce's *Ulysses*. On the one hand there is no doubt that Fisher was technically much less adroit when he embarked upon *City* than were Eliot and Pound and Joyce when severally they addressed themselves to their masterpieces. But on the other hand the terms of the problem posed were no longer the same: in the first place, the industrial metropolis could be seen by Fisher, as not by the earlier writers, as strangled by its own waste or else as built on stratum after stratum of such waste − a perception carried in *City* by Fisher's almost obsessive image of urine-loosened brick; and in the second place, the political climate had changed radically since Eliot wrote *The Waste Land* and Joyce wrote *Ulysses:*

> What follows seems to me a ruined work of art. It lies around as a series of sketches might lie around a studio waiting in vain for the total act of sculpture they were drawn to serve. Yet I am glad the writer has made no attempt to give it a bogus unity, but has preferred to leave it as it stands. What it has to say it will say to those who can see where it was aiming: if it had been tidied up the gesture it does make towards a total structure would have got obscured.
>
> Unity is hard to come by, anyway, at the depth at which this writing is operating. There are cases where love of humanity best shows itself in a desperate exposure of personal nakedness − Lear's Fool and Edgar in the storm − than in a willed uplift. The world of the last forty years is one in which whatever unity was achieved in Central Europe was at the expense of the suffering and ultimate death of six million people in concentration camps, and in which the unity of the communist world would have been impossible without the continuous presence of twenty million people in forced labour camps, and the premature death, by starvation or worse, of at least as many as were exterminated by the Germans. These things must not be forgotten in talking politics or sociology. Even in my placid area south-west of Birmingham the intake into the mental hospital is such that in a twenty-year period a fifth of the population will have had some treatment either as inpatients or outpatients. Modern industrial society seems to need its scapegoats. At their best the writers of the West have had this kind of knowledge in their bones, and their struggles after

unity can no more be written off as due to their faulty politics than can the suicides of Mayakowsky, Esenin, or Tsvetayeva.[21]

It was thus that Michael Shayer wrote about *City*, when it first appeared. It is the sort of thing that is said every day by our advertisers of apocalypse, the journalistic prophets of exciting doom who on these grounds excuse much dishevelled and egotistical writing, and attack any writing which aspires to be different. If I am not disposed to put Michael Shayer in that category, it's because in the case of Fisher the struggle towards unity is so evident.

Fisher's very thorough and unsparing revision of *City* for his *Collected Poems* is further evidence of this. The two versions are very different; originally, for instance, 'Toyland' was part of *City*, whereas now it is printed as an independent poem. *City* has been much improved by the revision – the prose sections, in particular, are made much tighter and cleaner. Yet some things about the poem, or behind it, emerge much more clearly when the two versions are compared. Originally, for example, the poem ended with a piece, now discarded, called 'Do Not Remain Too Much Alone':

> There was a hole in the floorboards;
>   I called it poetry
> Because it covered a void,
>   A dusty mystery,
> And also because it had
>   An orifice of form
> Whose draught about my bed
>   Kept me from lying warm.

Later stanzas describe how the poet tried to fill up the hole by stuffing down it bread and sand, water and milk,

> Lead shot, nail parings, currants,
>   Torn-up paper bags,
> Splinters that once were furniture
>   And my clothes cut into rags;
>
> And so, morsel by morsel,
>   Till its last trick was sprung
> I poked my life away into
>   The bland English tongue.

– whereupon, in this first version, *City* tails away in a raucous chorus:

---

21 Michael Shayer, Preface to *City* (Worcester: Migrant Press, 1961), p. 3.

> 'O once I went a courting
> of a girl called Mary May;
> But I poked my life away boys,
> I poked my life away.'

Fisher was right to eliminate this in revision (for if his poem had to remain dishevelled, at least he could stop it from being egotistical); yet the image of the hole in the floor has the effect of making salient an earlier passage which in the revised version can easily be passed over inattentively, especially because in revising Fisher has pared it down and made it less explicit. I quote it in its first version:

> Yet whenever I am forced to realise that some of these people around me, people I have actually seen, whose hopeful and distended surface I have at moments touched, are bodily in love and express that love bodily to dying-point, I feel that it is my own energy, my own hope, tension and sense of time in hand, that have gathered and vanished down that dark drain; that it is I who am left, shivering and exhausted, to try and kick the lid back into place so that I can go on without fear. And the terror that fills that moment or hour while I do it is a terror of anaesthesia: being able to feel only vertically, like a blind wall, or thickly, like the tyres of a bus.
>
> Lovers turn to me faces of innocence where I would rather see faces of bright cunning. They have disappeared for entire hours into the lit holes of life, instead of lying stunned on its surface as I, and so many, do for so long, or instead of raising their heads cautiously and scenting the manifold airs that blow through the streets. Sex fuses the intersections of the web where it occurs into blobs that drag and stick; and the web is not meant to stand such weights. Often there is no web.[22]

Neither here nor anywhere else in *City*, in either of its versions, is there any hint of an ironical intention, any grounds for thinking that the 'I' of the poem is a persona behind which the poet conceals himself. And this makes these un-Lawrencian, indeed *anti*-Lawrencian, sentiments all the more startling. Vowed to a realism which consists of 'scenting the manifold airs that blow through the streets', this is an art which sees the intensities and ecstasies of the sexual and personal life only as so many dangerous distractions. The poem is concerned with a social reality, to the exclusion of the human. And this must mean that it denies itself the possibility of tragedy, the better to render pathos. The poet is fully aware of the bargain he is striking, and he agrees to its humiliating terms. Larkin, as we have seen, lowers his sights and settles for second-best in just the same way, and just as consciously; and Hardy had sometimes done the

22 *City* (1961).

same, though less consciously and under less provocation. Fisher's exclusion of tragedy along with ecstasy is particularly clear from a passage which in the original *City* immediately follows the passage just quoted:

> Once I wanted to prove the world was sick. Now I want to prove it healthy. The detection of sickness means that death has established itself as an element of the timetable; it has come within the range of the measurable. Where there is no time there is no sickness.

And so it comes as no surprise that the best moments in Fisher, as in Larkin, are moments of piercing pathos. Indeed 'moments' gives the wrong impression; for *City* is a work of sustained pathos throughout, constructed carefully in that mode around a centre – the grotesque and touching section called 'Starting to Make a Tree' – in which the pathos is at its most intense.

Thus it appears that, however often Fisher may feel surges of anger at the obsequious or ingratiating meanness of the public life in his city, however he may at times hunger for more naked images of power, more monumental images of authority, more dramatic images of conflict, yet he will and does settle (with admirable consistency indeed) for Larkin's and Tolkien's hobbit-world of reduced expectations, its wistfulness regarded with an undemanding compassion. Though technically and formally Roy Fisher derives from traditions which have nothing to do with Hardy, he is a Hardyesque poet in the cast of his sensibility, or at any rate in the attitudes he takes up towards the English society that he moves in. And Michael Shayer was surely right to suggest that those attitudes, in particular Fisher's opting for pathos and compassion as his objectives, have everything to do with the history of our times, which has shown that the political alternatives to social democracy on the British model – mean-spirited as that undoubtedly is – are too costly in terms of human suffering for any man of humane feeling, least of all a poet, to find them real alternatives any longer.

8 A Conclusion

The flux, the endless malleability of life – have there been people in every age to whom this was the nightmare that it is for some of us today? Doubtless every age can show them, persons hungry for rigid certainties, just as every age throws up their opposites, the people for whom flux is excitement and freedom. But what is clear, surely, is that in the present century the rigidifiers are on the defensive as never before, frustrated and dissatisfied as never before; whereas the melters-down, the moulders and manipulators, the apostles of the fluid, are now in the ascendant and in the saddle. Freedom itself – not the fact of it, but the unchallengeable prestige of it as a slogan and a rallying cry that no one can afford not to rally to – is one card in the hand of the melter-down which by itself sweeps the board; once freedom is invoked, the rigidifier has to throw in his hand at once. And everything in the nature of our age conspires in the same direction; the unprecedented speed of change (technological in the first place, demanding moral and psychological change thereafter) compels anyone who has even a minimal grasp of the actual to acknowledge that the only feasible policy for him as for all others must be fluid, plastic, experimental, provisional. Yet there are people for whom this goes against the grain, who are by temperament drawn to the rigid, the hard, the resistant. For such people the present is a very hard time to live in; and the correspondence columns of any local newspaper show them protesting, crying out in pain, seeking ever more hysterical and irrational ways to break out from the impasse in which they find themselves. The more they become hysterical, as their plight forces them to envisage ever more patently foredoomed false alternatives, the more they play into their opponents' hands; and the more plausible becomes the allegation which those opponents contemptuously throw at them – that they are stupid as well as afraid, that a yearning for the rigid and the certain is to be found in any age only among the unintelligent.

Yet this is surely not the case. In another age than ours those who now seek the rigid would have settled for the stable; they would have been conservatives rather than reactionaries. For stability, in the physical and the moral universes alike, might be defined as a controllable proportion between rigid elements and fluid elements, between the persistent and the unprecedented. Nowadays what drives the naturally intelligent conservative into reactionary postures is the way in which the fluid has totally overborne the rigid, the impossibility of finding grounds for thinking that any persistent element in his life is other than an anachronistic survival, a removable impediment. Changeability seems to be total, as universal law; not only the tempo of change, but the scope of it, appears to be uncontrollable because illimitable. And in this case, the man who is stupid is not he who, however vainly, tries to resist change, but rather the many pragmatists among the apostles of change, those who think that they can ride with the wave only to that point in the future where they can stop it rolling, can alight, and can rigidify life in the momentary shape it will then have taken, a shape which conforms to their interests or their principles.

What provokes me to these reflections is thinking about sculpture. And sculpture has led others who are not sculptors into thinking along the same lines. Théophile Gautier, in 'L'Art', for instance:

> Tout passe. – L'art robuste
> Seul a l'éternité;
> > Le buste
> Survit à la cité.
>
> Et la médaille austère
> Que trouve un laboureur
> > Sous terre
> Révèle un empereur.
>
> Les dieux eux-mêmes meurent.
> Mais les vers souverains
> > Demeurent
> Plus fort que les airains.
>
> Sculpte, lime, cisèle;
> Que ton rêve flottant
> > Se scelle
> Dans le bloc résistant![1]

For Shakespeare and many another poet before Gautier, sculptors' work in brass or bronze seemed in this way the token and the guarantee that art at any rate, the poet's no less than the sculptor's, could stem and survive the flux; that art was one element of life which persisted, changing its forms only within controllable limits, answerable to controls which were its own and embodied in its traditions. In the century since Gautier wrote, this ancient conviction has been battered and eroded; and the

1   Théophile Gautier, 'L'Art'.

progressives, enamoured of the flux, have been at pains to show that art forms, like all forms, are expendable, and must be thought of henceforward as provisional merely. In Michael Ayrton's novel *The Maze Maker*, the traditional assurances are given to the young sculptor Daedalus by his master:

> Another time he said to me that we were the keepers of memory. 'Our work will live when the warriors lie in their tombs and our work lies with them,' he said. 'They will be dust and what we make will lie among their bones as whole as when we made it.'[2]

But it is not clear by the end of the astonishing narrative which Michael Ayrton puts into Daedalus' mouth, whether this assurance has been vindicated. It is not what Michael Ayrton is centrally concerned with, and after all he is writing a novel, not a fable, still less a tract for the times. It is the urgency of our own concerns which makes us want to schematise it, to make an intricately rigid model out of what is tantalisingly protean.

So it is, at least if one is of those who hanker for the rigid in a world of flux. Gautier was such a one. Another was Ezra Pound, notably in a famous essay, 'The Hard and the Soft in French Poetry', in which, fifty years ago, he explicitly aligned himself with Gautier. Another such was Thomas Hardy, as Edmund Blunden realised. And, if I can diagnose myself, I am another of the same kind.

In many ways Pound is the most instructive, the exemplary case, and this for all sorts of reasons. In the first place his career demonstrates all too neatly how a liking and a need for the rigid, for what he calls 'the hard', may nourish at the present day extremely authoritarian politics, and of the Right, rather than the Left. Less obvious, but more intriguing, is the seeming paradox by which this poet, enamoured of the hard, devotes his major poem *The Cantos* to celebrating a world of metamorphosis. Like his master Ovid, Pound, at the times when he is in control of his material in the *Cantos*, combines maximum hardness in the execution with maximum fluidity in the conception. For the world that he renders is above all things protean, malleable, in process, ceaselessly metamorphic.

And yet there is no paradox. Or if there is paradox it is one that is the very *raison d'être* of one kind of art – the art that as it happens Michael Ayrton, in his book as in his own sculptures, has chiefly been concerned with: the art of casting bronze. For those cast bronzes which Gautier and Pound respond to so eagerly, as showing how art can be durable and rigid, in fact are fashioned out of the most fluid material; the molten bronze is *poured* into the mould. The rigidity and hardness of the end product are in direct proportion to the fluid malleability in the process of production. Most exegesis of Pound's *Cantos is* wide of the mark because

2   Michael Ayrton, *The Maze Maker* (London, 1967), p. 19.

by its very nature exegesis pursues what is said, at the expense of *how* it is said; and this means that the exegetes lead us into a world of continual flux and change which does not at all correspond to our experience as readers, of responding to the hard bright surfaces which Pound's language, when he is in control, presents to us as a sequence of images, each sharp-edged and distinct. The exegetes are necessarily concerned with the process, not with the product; with the bronze while it is still molten, not with the rigid surfaces of the finished bust. For mythology, whether we encounter it in the archaic records which served as source for Ovid, subsequently for Pound, or as updated and internalised in the psychological diagrams of Freud or Jung, is above all a fluid world, in which for instance Hathor, Circe, and Aphrodite are only different names for one archetypal female presence. And it is for this reason that the man I have called the rigidifier, the devotee of the hard, the seeker after the certain and the unchanging, is the man who will most resist psychological explanations for art, who will most anxiously deny that the artist is imprisoned within the maze of his own personality, from which he can never break out to explore any nature other than his own. For we do not need Freud or Jung to tell us that, however the individual psyche may be in the last analysis rigidly determined by heredity or in infancy, it is, as we experience it by introspection, a realm above all protean and malleable, a world of metamorphosis, of merging and self-transforming shapes and fluid contours. Not in those subterranean wynds and galleries, nor in the kneaded wax and the poured bronze which seem their natural concomitant, shall we find what some of us will always want more than anything else – the resistant and persisting, the rigid and the hard, everything that poets have yearned for naïvely in the image of the stone that resists the chisel and confronts the sunlight.

Accordingly it is Hardy, so much the stonemason in his poetic imagination and so resistant to the temptations of the mythological and the mythopoeic, who can seem, more than Pound, the emblem and the exemplar in our time of what Pound meant by 'the hard' in poetry. This is not how Hardy is usually envisaged. He is thought of as a crepuscular poet, the voice of those half-lit hours in which phantoms and apparitions glimmer uncertainly at the edge of vision. But this is once again to mistake the process for the product; the poems as they lie on the page, or utter themselves from it, speak for themselves – they are dry, angular, hard-edged. Sometimes their angles are so sharp and so many that, as I pointed out in Chapter 1, they make us think of industrial metalwork rather than carved stone. And to that extent such poems are inferior to Hardy at his best. But between stone and metal, the distinction is not always important. Both can be images of authority, as they are, interchangeably, in the first line of Eliot's 'Coriolan':

> Stone, bronze, stone, steel, stone, oakleaves, horses' heels…

And the wish for the hard in art doubtless goes along with a wish for authority in public life. Hardy satisfies both demands, the one in fact, the other in fantasy.

Nevertheless, the prehistoric shift from the stone age to the bronze age can still, in certain imaginative circumstances, be alive for modern man as distinguishing at least two different kinds of power, or even, it may be, of authority. Theorists of the Left have pointed out for instance that once the techniques of mining and working metals had been mastered, the way was opened towards coinage, towards a 'money economy' as opposed to a 'natural economy', and therefore to the forms of mercantile power, an altogether more abstract sort of power since the wielder of it gives no visible sign, for instance by any weapon that he may carry, of possessing it. Some of the implications of this contrast have been teased out, with a mannered terseness, by J.H. Prynne. Prynne sees the shift from stone to metals at the start of the bronze age as a shift from 'substance' to 'quality'. But he hastens to qualify the starkness of this contrast:

> That's a deliberately simplified sketch, because it may well be that this theorising of quality, with its control over weaponry and tillage and hence over life, induced a deeper cultural adherence to substance as the zone of being in which the condition was also limit: the interior knowledge of dying… So that stone becomes the power substance marking the incorporated extensions of dying, and is still so as a head-stone is the vulgar or common correlative of a hope for the after life.[3]

So many of Hardy's most moving poems are set in graveyards that this comment certainly seems to fit his case.

But it may well be that the modern experience can no longer define itself in the different fantasies, whether complementary or opposed, adhering to stone on the one hand, metals on the other. For it might be said that the characteristic material of modern civilisation is neither stone nor metal, but composites and plastics. Certainly in both Prynne[4] and Fisher[5] we find an attempt to grapple imaginatively with the frightening perception that while the products of an industrial society may be demolished and dismembered, they cannot be destroyed. We find in them – less in what they say than in how they manipulate their medium – a recognition of what the ecology crisis has taught us to call 'recycling'; that is to say, the way in which, if our civilisation is not to be strangled by the detritus of its own waste products, we have to learn to live with our own

---

3   See Prynne, 'A Note on Metal', in *Aristeas* (Ferry Press, 1968), p. 14.
4   See 'L'Extase de M. Poher', in J.H. Prynne, *Brass* (Ferry Press, 1971).
5   See Roy Fisher, *The Ship's Orchestra*, pp. 30, 36 38; and also 'Three Ceremonial Songs'.

waste and use that waste over and over again. Of course, to the devotee of the rigid and the hard, this vision of a world in which nothing can be destroyed though it can interminably change its shape and its function, is a new nightmare of that flux from which he continues to hope that art will save him. On the other hand, to the intelligentsia, to the moulders of opinion (that fluctuant medium which it is their interest and their nature to keep fluctuating), 'ecology crisis' is a godsend; and its minatory vision of a civilisation choked and poisoned by its own waste is the new stock in trade of the salesmen of apocalypse. In 'The Ideal Star-Fighter', the only one of his recent poems which I think I understand, Prynne with just indignation rejects the moral blackmail which the ecologist's propaganda exerts and depends upon.

Hardy's recycling poem is one that he entitles, with a typically haughty clumsiness, 'Voices from Things Growing in a Churchyard':

> These flowers are I, poor Fanny Hurd,
> > Sir or Madam,
> A little girl here sepultured.
> Once I flit-fluttered like a bird
> Above the grass, as now I wave
> In daisy shapes above my grave,
> > All day cheerily,
> > All night eerily!
>
> – I am one Bachelor Bowring, 'Gent',
> > Sir or Madam;
> In shingled oak my bones were pent;
> Hence more than a hundred years I spent
> In my feat of change from a coffin-thrall
> To a dancer in green as leaves on a wall,
> > All day cheerily,
> > All night eerily!
>
> – I, these berries of juice and gloss,
> > Sir or Madam,
> Am clear forgotten as Thomas Voss;
> Thin-urned, I have burrowed away from the moss
> That covers my sod, and have entered this yew,
> And turned to clusters ruddy of view,
> > All day cheerily,
> > All night eerily!
>
> – The Lady Gertrude, proud, high-bred,
> > Sir or Madam,
> Am I – this laurel that shades your head;
> Into its veins I have stilly sped,

And made them of me; and my leaves now shine,
As did my satins superfine,
          All day cheerily,
          All night eerily!

– I, who as innocent withwind climb,
          Sir or Madam,
Am one Eve Greensleeves, in olden time
Kissed by men from many a clime,
Beneath sun, stars, in blaze, in breeze,
As now by glowworms and by bees,
          All day cheerily,
          All night eerily!

– I'm old Squire Audeley Grey, who grew,
          Sir or Madam,
Aweary of life, and in scorn withdrew
Till anon I clambered up anew
As ivy-green, when my ache was stayed,
And in that attire I have longtime gayed
          All day cheerily,
          All night eerily!

– And so these maskers breathe to each
          Sir or Madam
Who lingers here, and their lively speech
Affords an interpreter much to teach,
As their murmurous accents seem to come
Thence hitheraround in a radiant hum,
          All day cheerily,
          All night eerily!

If we think of each of these stanzas as a headstone standing in that 'slope of green access' which Hardy evoked when he was given the freedom of Dorchester (though the churchyard in fact was Stinsford, not Dorchester), perhaps the symmetrical filigree of each should make us think of those eighteenth-century headstones in the old iron-mining areas of the Kentish and East Sussex Weald which are in fact not *stones* at all but iron plates. It hardly matters. The imperious energy which forced 'little girl' along with 'sepultured', and made that learned word cohabit through rhyme with 'bird', strikes us no longer as the masterful presumption of man as technician or technologist, or else, if it does thus strike us, it is subsumed in the sense of man making what hard stay he can against the temporal flux, and (if he is technological man) using his technological symmetries and precisions to serve that perennial need.

'Cheerily'… 'eerily' – was a more eerie rhyme ever perpetrated? If it draws attention to itself, it draws attention only to the yawning gulf between opposite strains of feeling, which agnostic man must bridge, with correspondingly energetic and audacious exertion of nervous energy, if he is to compass the fact of death. The agnosticism, one perceives, is indeed the crux. *Ars est celare artem* – but not when the art, and the human energy that makes it, can rely upon nothing outside themselves to make sense of the experience which they celebrate. By contrast, Roy Fisher's 'As He Came Near Death' relies, for its effect, upon the felt absence of a rite which could have made death meaningful. Hardy knows on the contrary that no rite except the one that he makes up as he goes along will do the trick; and the solemnity of the occasion requires that the rite thus composed be elaborate and imperiously manipulated.

And thus it is not true that it is merely the passage of time, and of atrocious history, which makes Roy Fisher or Philip Larkin unable to rise to Hardy's at once playful and mournful serenity. The attainment of pathos does *not* mean the exclusion of tragedy; the fidelity to the social need *not* mean the scanting of the human (Fanny Hurd was a real girl called Fanny Hurden, as Hardy told Walter de la Mare after they had walked Stinsford churchyard together,[6] and Eve Greensleeves was Eve Trevillian or Trevelyan, 'the handsome mother of two or three illegitimate children', as we are told in a note to the *Collected Poems*); and neither Auschwitz nor Katyn Forest makes the least difference to Hardy's poem. Facing (and out-facing) death is as necessary in socialist Britain as in capitalist America or communist Russia; and there, in the fact of death and the term it sets to all our exertions, is the place where we escape at last the attentions of the bureaucrats, the philanthropists, and the moulders of opinion, and need the hard rigidity which only monumental art can give us.

---

6   *The Life of Thomas Hardy, 1840–1928*, pp. 413–14.

An Afterword for the American Reader

'English poetry is presently at a very low point.' Thus, in 1969, an American reviewer with respectable standards (Richard Tillinghast), writing moreover in a journal (*The Southern Review*) which has shown itself indulgent towards British writing. The English poet from whom the American reader was warned thus firmly not to expect very much was Charles Tomlinson, who has behind him twenty years of scrupulous and fiercely independent writing and verse translating on both sides of the Atlantic. Tillinghast confessed that Tomlinson 'has always struck me as just another of those dull English poets'. And not much in the collection he had before him (Tomlinson's *American Scenes & Other Poems*) made him want to change his mind. What *did* interest him a little was – guess what? – that Tomlinson had profited from a year in New Mexico to learn something from American poets, specifically from the late William Carlos Williams and from Robert Creeley, about how to handle free verse: 'At this point Mr Tomlinson's use of the line lacks grace and subtlety. But he has made a beginning. Perhaps Charles Tomlinson will be the one to lead his fellow countrymen out of the wilderness.'

It is encouraging for the countrymen of Chaucer to realise that from the standpoint of Albuquerque they have just made a beginning, or rather have had it made for them. If I object that grace and subtlety are not necessarily the highest values in poetry, but that in any case Creeley's exquisite if pernickety melodies seem to me less graceful and subtle, as well as infinitely more restricted in range, than the tunes that Tomlinson has been playing these many years, I don't see what Tillinghast and I can do except smile and shrug and go our separate ways. And indeed we'll be lucky if we can maintain that much civility; for it looks as if, in poetry as in diplomacy, a good neighbour policy gives more offence than straightforward hostility. Anyway, it's obvious that Tillinghast is hearing what I don't hear, and vice versa.

And this is typical. One is tempted to say that for many years now British poetry and American poetry haven't been on speaking terms. But the truth is rather that they haven't been on *hearing* terms – the American reader can't hear the British poet, neither his rhythms nor his tone of voice, and the British reader only pretends to hear the rhythms and the tone of American poetry since William Carlos Williams. And so what we have had for some years now is a breakdown in communication between these two English-speaking poetries, though for civility's sake the appearance of a continuing dialogue between them is maintained.

This failure of a dialogue – the historians can explain it, as they can explain everything: which is to say, after the fact, too late to help. The American's contemptuous tolerance, the Englishman's resentful fascination – they have shown up in areas other than poetry. What is it but a reflection of the changed relationship of the English-speaking partners in other fields – in politics, in economics? And of course there is truth in this, in fact a very important and sourly paradoxical truth. For American poetry by and large has been very notably on the side of those elements in American society which most deplore American chauvinism, which reject the overweening presumption that sets out, from an unquestioned faith in American virtues, to set the world to rights; and yet American poetry is itself very chauvinistic nowadays, convinced that the rendering of American reality into poetry is a task so special that the American poet can go nowhere outside America to get assistance. This will be denied. Do not Stephen Berg and Robert Mezey, in an anthology called *Naked Poetry* (from which all British poets are excluded), go for a title to Jimenez, and for an epigraph to Mandelstam? Indeed they do; and doubtless it is only sour grapes on the part of an Englishman to wonder aloud if Jimenez and Mandelstam can be recruited so peremptorily, torn so brusquely out of their contexts, Spanish and Russian – to wonder, in fact, if this wholesale appropriation of foreign authorities isn't a reflection in poetry of the imperious rapacity which created just those banana republics that American poets are ashamed of, and inveigh against.

But there is another explanation. Culturally, the United States remained a colony of Britain long after they had broken the colonial ties politically and in other ways. Until well into the present century most American writers still looked timorously to London for appreciation and esteem. This is why, through two generations after Whitman's death, his massive innovations were not taken advantage of by the American poets who were his ungrateful heirs. For the colonialist dependence of American literature upon English, already anachronistic in 1900, was artificially protracted thereafter through the lifetime of T.S. Eliot, that naturalised Englishman from St Louis, Missouri, who wielded his influence (unparalleled through the last twenty-five years of his life) always to obscure and suppress Whitman's bequest to American writing.

And yet Eliot himself, as he acknowledged, found his feet in poetry from study of French poets, not English ones. And this was true, by and large, of a whole generation of American poets; as has been noted before, American poetry came to splendid maturity in the present century when American poets, if they needed to look outside America for guidance, at least looked elsewhere than to London – to Paris, to Vienna, Rapallo, even Tokyo. Vienna was particularly fruitful. For out of Vienna came a voice which assured the American writer that historical time could be transfigured and displaced – and is, afresh in every generation – by Everyman (social democracy is vindicated!) as he endures the Oedipal or some other timeless mythical action between ego, superego, and id. Ever since, just as diluted Marxism has been characteristic of British culture, poetic and other, so diluted Freudianism has been characteristic of American. And at the present day this difference in allegiance, so diffused in each case that it is unconscious, accounts for one crucial difference between the English and the American poet. The Englishman supposes he is trying to operate in some highly specific historical situation, conditioned by manifold contingencies (hence his qualifications, his hesitancies, his damaging concessions), whereas the American poet, conditioned since the Pilgrim Fathers to think in utopian terms, is sure that he is enacting a drama of which the issues are basically simple and permanent, and will be seen to be so once we have penetrated through their accidental, historical overlay.

Thus what speaks in Richard Tillinghast, when he writes of Charles Tomlinson, is the voice of a post-colonialist backlash, speaking with a confidence that is all the greater for being new-found and hard-won. The Englishman, however, is not confident at all. In bad faith perhaps, spitefully and captiously, still the British poet does listen to the American voice – listens to it, listens *for* it; whereas the American poet is no longer listening to any voice but his own. And for this the British have only themselves to thank. Peter Porter, for instance, an Australian poet long resident in London, has protested that 'poetry is a modest art' – a sentiment unthinkable in an American poet, or (I truly think) in any poet but a British one; and he goes on to say: 'Certainly any British poet setting out to criticise American verse had better begin by acknowledging that Americans write more audaciously and commandingly than we do, even if he's sick of being told so by the Americans themselves.' And British poets and critics have for years been selling the native product short in this way, freely though resentfully admitting that American poetry is more exciting and more ambitious and, well, just *better*. The most influential statement along these lines was by A. Alvarez in 1962, in an essay entitled 'The New Poetry, or Beyond the Gentility Principle'. This essay was Alvarez's introduction to an extraordinary anthology which he edited, called *The New Poetry*, in which eighteen British poets were mustered into line behind two Americans, John Berryman and Robert Lowell, who were pushed to the front like drill sergeants, just to show the Britishers what they ought to have been doing and so signally weren't. Anyone who reads Alvarez's essay – and it circulates widely in America, for instance in Richard Kostelanetz's symposium, *On Contemporary*

Literature – can see where Berg and Mezey got the idea that 'With a few exceptions (mainly Ted Hughes) nothing much new has happened in English poetry since Lawrence laid down his pen and died.' And yet to a British ear, unless perhaps it is Alvarez's, the mere title of Berg's and Mezey's anthology offends against that principle which Alvarez derides as 'gentility', which other Englishmen have in the past called 'a sense of proportion' or even 'a sense of humour'. *Naked Poetry:* to many Englishmen (and I am one of them) the mere strident title is good for a giggle.

And so I come back to what is the most pervasive difference between British and American poetry nowadays, the most pervasive difference and therefore the hardest to pin down. Apparently an American reviewer of Tomlinson's *American Scenes* had complained that the poet's *persona* in the poems was that of 'the considerate house guest'. Richard Tillinghast, after the predictably deferential citation of Alvarez's 'gentility principle', endorsed the earlier reviewer's supposedly weighty objection. And the British reader is bewildered. Would Tillinghast have preferred an *in*considerate house guest? (A Dylan Thomas, perhaps?) Where does it come from, this notion that good manners in a poet are a mark against him? Is the American reader never satisfied until his poet has abused him, spat in his face, beaten him over the head? The gulf that opens here is a crucial difference of *tone*: in the poetry itself, but also in the ways of talking about it, and particularly in the poets' ways of talking about themselves as poets. The British tone is too often, too cravenly, apologetic – and the American is quite right to say that this means selling out to the philistine from the start. (In Britain the philistine is usually nowadays a humanitarian; and the British poet agrees with him in this, thus offering the extraordinary spectacle of poet and philistine combined in one person.) The American poet, when he speaks about himself and his vocation, is too often gravely bardic and exalted – and the Englishman is quite right to say that this drives out any possibility of self-criticism. (Or indeed of criticising others: because all the poets are being rapt and exalted bards together, in a sublime democracy.)

My argument has been that in surprisingly many cases in British poetry in the last fifty years what is derided as 'gentility' can be glossed as 'civic sense' or 'political responsibility'; and, further, that whether a poet should be expected to display such sense and such responsibility is a real and open question – a question debated, by implication, in much British verse, but hardly ever in American. There are now on offer to the American reader anthologies of British poetry since 1945, which claim to show that British writing over this period is as 'exciting', as little 'genteel', as what was being written in America. Of the poets I have considered, it should be plain which will be represented in such an anthology, which will be excluded from it. Let Larkin stand as the example of those who will be excluded. Yet, like it or not, Larkin is the centrally representative figure. And what he represents is British poetry at the point where it has least in common with American, a poetry which consciously repudiates the assumptions, and the liberties, which American poets take for granted; a poetry in short which is, for the American reader, exceptionally challenging.

New York: Oxford, 1972.
London: Routledge & Kegan Paul, 1973.

Hardy and the Avant-Garde

In the last few years the divisions and dispositions of literary opinion in this country have been making more sense than usual. Although the book-reviews and letters to the editor may seem to be just the old infighting about who's in and who's out, quite often underneath one important issue is being debated. It's the question whether rhythmical arrangements of images can convey enough sense to stand as a mode of poetic communication. On the one hand, people maintain that the work of Eliot and Pound in particular has established that this, and no more than this, is indeed a mode of communication; certainly not the only mode that can properly be called 'poetic' (though not so long ago even this was being maintained); perhaps not even a notably efficient mode; but at least precise enough and controllable enough to be called communication of a sort. On the other hand, more and more people lately have been saying or implying that a poem which is no more than a rhythmical sequence of images can bring about only *an illusion* of communication; that for communication in anything like the normal sense the poet has to draw on other resources, of more or less explicit statement, bridging the gap between images.

The question can be complicated several ways, and usually is. For instance, the belief that a poem need be more than a sequence of images seems to have arisen in the circles of 'the modern movement', or what is now, surprisingly, coming to be called once again 'modernism'; one thinks of it as a tenet of the *avant-garde* of (in this country) the years 1910–1930. And so sometimes it seems as if the disagreement is between conservatives who believe there is nothing new under the sun, and the radicals for whom the early twentieth century saw a genuine revolution in all the arts, a revolution which our own later decades seem determined to betray. Again, this modern movement was international, or at least cosmopolitan; and so quite often the quarrel seems to be between internationalists and nationalists. And so on.

In this debate the Little Englanders quite often appeal to the poetry of Hardy, to show how an indigenous tradition – traced also through smaller poets like Auden and Graves – went on undisturbed through all the shrillness of the *avant-garde* rallying cries. And they will usually declare their conviction that Hardy's sort of poetry will wear better than Eliot's. This is to suppose, however, that Hardy never wrote poems whose meaning is all in the arrangement of their images. Remembering how conservative Hardy is in other ways, how Victorian, it's easy to think that Hardy wrote no poems of this modern sort. But is this so in fact? Now that Douglas Brown has done what so long needed doing, isolated from the unwieldy bulk of the *Collected Poems* some handfuls of pieces which show Hardy at his best, we can see that some of these are in this respect every bit as modern, as *avant-garde* even, as what Pound was writing at much the same time, from about 1912 on. There is, for instance, 'During Wind and Rain':

> They sing their dearest songs −
> He, she, all of them − yea,
> Treble and tenor and bass,
>   And one to play;
> With the candles mooning each face....
>   Ah, no; the years O!
> How the sick leaves reel down in throngs!
>
> They clear the creeping moss −
> Elders and juniors − aye,
> Making the pathways neat
>   And the garden gay;
> And they build a shady seat....
>   Ah no; the years, the years;
> See the white storm-birds wing across!
>
> They are blithely breakfasting all −
> Men and maidens − yea,
> Under the summer tree,
>   With a glimpse of the bay,
> While pet fowl come to the knee....
>   Ah, no; the years O!
> And the rotten rose is ript from the wall.
>
> They change to a high new house,
> He, she, all of them − aye,
> Clocks and carpets and chairs
>   On the lawn all day,
> And brightest things that are theirs....
>   Ah no; the years, the years;
> Down their carved names the rain-drop ploughs.

If one holds, with Graham Hough, 'that the collocation of images is not a method at all, but the negation of method', I don't know what one does with this poem. For surely a collocation of images is just what it is, that and no more. It differs from *The Waste Land* or even from a Canto by Pound, only by arranging its rhythms in an intricately repeated metrical stanza; the rhythm is still the only directing and controlling instrument offered, by which the reader can pick his way through the images. As is true of *The Waste Land* also. And the penultimate line of each stanza is pulled free of any syntactical anchorage, as happens in Eliot's poem.

In case this seems only a debating point, let's admit straightaway that the Hardy poem *feels* quite different from any *avant-garde* poem. Douglas Brown says, 'The very triviality of the scenes, curiously out of accord with the sense of loss, vouches for an integrity, a faithfulness to actual experience…' And this is true, I think; though it's not just the triviality, but also the oddity – of the quite unpredictable 'pet fowl', for instance. One goes with Brown too when he says, 'The memories… seem to come clearly and immediately upon the consciousness, containing the grief'; and, 'One feels that the memories are active of their own accord, coming back upon the poet…'. And this is true of Eliot or Pound only occasionally; more often we feel with them that the memories which get into their poems as images have been fastidiously chosen by the poet from among many others. Similarly Dr Leavis, for whom this poem is one of the half-dozen on which to rest any convincing claim to 'major status', says of this group, 'They are all records of poignant particular memories – memories poignant in themselves or by reason of the subsequent work of time'.

Well! Memories, no doubt, and poignant and particular – but not the memories of Thomas Hardy. They belonged to Emma Gifford, Hardy's first wife. This appears from a little book, as important as it is charming, lately very ably edited by Evelyn Hardy and Robert Gittings.[1] Hardy and his first wife had been estranged for many years before her death in 1912: there was a history of mental instability in Emma's family, and we had guessed already that a frightening and powerful poem called 'The Interloper', reprinted here, is about the madness which threatened Emma's last years. *Some Recollections*, which bears a date in 1911, was a manuscript found by Hardy among Emma's papers after her death; it is said there were two other manuscripts, which Hardy destroyed because they pained him too much. He seems to have pored over *Some Recollections* very attentively; not only does he speak of the manuscript and draw upon it explicitly in what is in effect his autobiography, *The Early Life of Thomas Hardy* ('by Florence Emily Hardy'), but he corrected and annotated it – and these emendations are here reproduced.

It turns out that there is hardly an image in the poem which is not lifted out of Emma Hardy's prose. Those pet fowl, for instance – Emma

1   Emma Hardy, *Some Recollections*, together with Some Relevant Poems by Thomas Hardy, edited by Evelyn Hardy and Robert Gittings (London: Oxford University Press, 1961).

records of her Plymouth childhood in a house just off the Hoe, 'At one end of our garden we had a poultry-house put up, and a choice selection of poultry was bought, for there was a mania at that time for keeping handsome fowls, and particularly Cochin-Chinas and Bramah Pouters, Speckled Hamburgs, Black Spanish and pretty Bantams... they were kept at the top of the large garden where rose trees had used to flourish named by me Rosewood.' ('And the rotten rose is ript from the wall.') The singing of the dearest songs, the word 'elders' (so oddly stilted in the poem), the shady seat, the summer tree, the view of the bay, the high new house (another Plymouth house which the Giffords moved to, later), the wind and torrential rain in which they finally left Plymouth – all these are in *Some Recollections*.

Not that any credit for the poem should go from Hardy to his wife. On the contrary, the choice of the images and the ranging of them in right sequence – this is all his; he can be seen skipping pages, pouncing on the image he wants and passing over others, collapsing two chapters of Emma's life into one, compressing a rambling narrative of a span of years into one rapid arc of feeling. And indeed this is just the point – the art is so much in masterful ellipses and abrupt juxtapositions that it looks more than ever like the art of Eliot and of Pound, from which it differs only in these respects – that Hardy draws his images from one source where they use many, and that many of theirs are drawn from literature where Hardy's are drawn from... from life, I was going to say; but wasn't *Some Recollections*, by the time Hardy came to it, literature? Just as much 'literature' as Arnaut Daniel for Pound, or *Les Fleurs du Mal* for Eliot? If that is to go too far, at least when Douglas Brown says that the memories 'seem to come clearly and immediately', we have to remark that, whatever the seeming, in fact the images came, if clearly, not immediately. For they were mediated through Emma; and only for her were they memories – for her husband they were images, which he had experienced only in the sense that reading intently and with sympathy is an experience on a par with any other.

To be sure, the seeming may be important. I am talking, not of the effect the poem makes, but of the facts about its composition. And if any reader objects to Pound and Eliot that the poet should *seem* to have experienced his images otherwise than through books, even when (like Hardy) he hasn't, there is no more to say. But this isn't how Hardy is usually distinguished from his *avant-garde* contemporaries, or preferred before them.

And of course, not many of Hardy's poems are like this one. But then, not many of them are the work of a great poet. Another one that is, is 'After a Journey', which also owes much to *Some Recollections* – not so much as 'During Wind and Rain', and yet more than appears on the surface. But to establish this would involve understanding clearly what we mean by 'image'. In particular we'd have to ask whether the simple naming of a thing in a poem can make it an image; and I think we'd have to agree that it can, the poetry then being not in any vividness of phrasing but simply in the place found for this name in a sequence of other names.

New Statesman, 20 October 1961.

II

Remembering the 'Thirties

I

Hearing one saga, we enact the next.
We please our elders when we sit enthralled;
But then they're puzzled; and at last they've vexed
To have their youth so avidly recalled.

It dawns upon the veterans after all
That what for them were agonies, for us
Are high-brow thrillers, though historical;
And all their feats quite strictly fabulous.

This novel written fifteen years ago,
Set in my boyhood and my boyhood home,
These poems about 'abandoned workings', show
Worlds more remote than Ithaca or Rome.

The Anschluss, Guernica – all the names
At which those poets thrilled or were afraid
For me mean schools and schoolmasters and games;
And in the process some-one is betrayed.

Ourselves perhaps. The Devil for a joke
Might carve his own initials on our desk,
And yet we'd miss the point because he spoke
An idiom too dated, Audenesque.

Ralegh's Guiana also killed his son.
A pretty pickle if we came to see
The tallest story really packed a gun,
The Telemachiad an Odyssey.

II

Even to them the tales were not so true
As not to be ridiculous as well;
The ironmaster met his Waterloo,
But Rider Haggard rode along the fell.

'Leave for Cape Wrath tonight!' They lounged away
On Fleming's trek or Isherwood's ascent.
England expected every man that day
To show his motives were ambivalent.

They played the fool, not to appear as fools
In time's long glass. A deprecating air
Disarmed, they thought, the jeers of later schools;
Yet irony itself is doctrinaire,

And curiously, nothing now betrays
Their type to time's derision like this coy
Insistence on the quizzical, their craze
For showing Hector was a mother's boy.

A neutral tone is nowadays preferred.
And yet it may be better, if we must,
To praise a stance impressive and absurd
Than not to see the hero for the dust.

For courage is the vegetable king,
The sprig of all ontologies, the weed
That beards the slag-heap with his hectoring,
Whose green adventure is to run to seed.

The Spectator, 26 June 1953; first collected in *Brides of Reason* (Eynsham: Fantasy Press, 1955)

The Poetic Diction of John M. Synge

It has recently been argued that the literary achievement of J.M. Synge is meretricious; that his use of Irish speech in his writing was entirely a literary manoeuvre; that, in using that speech, he betrayed his lack of sympathy with the concerns and aspirations of the Irish people; and that his concern with their speech was therefore only superficial. This is a controversy into which I need not enter. In the first place, it is a matter which can be decided only by Irishmen, in which the word of a foreigner such as myself can carry no weight. In the second place, such claims as are made for Synge as a great artist must rest upon his achievement in drama; and here I am only concerned with his volume of *Poems and Translations*, first published in 1909 and recently reprinted. No one, I think, makes any great claims for the intrinsic importance of this part of Synge's work. It is of great historical importance, as a sort of challenge and manifesto, and as such, its significance in the history of the Irish literary movement has been examined by Mr Robert Farren and others. I want to look at it in another light. For Synge's volume is a challenge not only to the Irish poets of his time, but to everyone who tries to write poetry in English at any time. This is what interests me most in his verse, and it is from this point of view that I want to consider him.

This sort of interest was invited by Synge himself. In his preface he wrote as follows:

> I have often thought that at the side of the poetic diction, which everyone condemns, modern verse contains a great deal of poetic material, using poetic in the same special sense. The poetry of exaltation will be always the highest; but when men lose their poetic feeling for ordinary life, and cannot write poetry of ordinary things, their exalted poetry is likely to lose its strength of exaltation, in the way men cease to build beautiful churches when they have lost happiness in building shops.
>
> Many of the older poets, such as Villon and Herrick and Burns, used the whole of their personal life as their material, and the verse written in this way was read by strong men, and thieves, and deacons, not by little cliques only. Then, in the town writing of the eighteenth

century, ordinary life was put into verse that was not poetry, and when poetry came back with Coleridge and Shelley, it went into verse that was not always human.

In these days poetry is usually a flower of evil or good; but it is the timber of poetry that wears most surely, and there is no timber that has not strong roots among the clay and worms.

Even if we grant that exalted poetry can be kept successful by itself, the strong things of life are needed in poetry also, to show that what is exalted or tender is not made by feeble blood. It may almost be said that before verse can be human again it must learn to be brutal.

The poems which follow were written at different times during the last sixteen or seventeen years, most of them before the views just stated, with which they have little to do, had come into my head.

I do not agree that 'in the town writing of the eighteenth century, ordinary life was put into verse that was not poetry'. That was a view common enough when Synge wrote, but discredited today. And I think that Dean Swift, for instance, wrote *poetry*, not merely verse. But that is another argument into which it would be idle to enter now. And I mention it only for this reason: that if Synge had wanted traditional authority for his views on poetry, he would have had to go back just to those eighteenth-century poets whom he condemns. For instance, the distinction which he makes, between 'the poetry of exaltation' and 'the poetry of ordinary things', between poetry which is 'exalted' and poetry which is 'tender', is just the distinction habitually made in the eighteenth century between 'the sublime' and 'the pathetic'. And the eighteenth century would have agreed with Synge that sublime poems require a different sort of diction from pathetic poems.

About this question of poetic diction we have very confused ideas. Many readers of poetry, and many poets even, still believe that poetic diction is '*a bad thing*'. They think it is the name for a poetic vice, connected with the false idea that only 'poetical' words can be used in poetry, and that ugly or common words should not be used by poets. Most people today would argue that poetry can be made out of any words, however common or ugly; and that to speak of 'poetic diction' implies that this is not the case. On the other hand the fashion for regarding 'poetic diction' in this way was set by Wordsworth; and people are beginning to realize that what Wordsworth said about this, in his famous preface to *Lyrical Ballads*, was wrong or, at any rate, incomplete. Oliver Goldsmith, for instance, believed in poetic diction. We know from his criticism, and we see from his poetry, that however many poems he wrote he would never has used certain common or ugly words, which he thought too undignified and coarse. Yet 'The Deserted Village' is a great poem, and a poem about ordinary things; and some of the pleasure we get from reading the poem derives from our sense that the language the poet uses is carefully selected, a 'choice' language. It is as if words from the English language were beating at the walls of the poem, asking to be let in, and the poet is keeping them out; we enjoy and appreciate the skill with which he does this, for by using dignified language he gives dignity to the ordinary things of life. We can see, therefore, that poetic diction is not necessarily a bad thing; for certain poets can only make the worthwhile effects they want, by using a careful selection from the language, instead of the whole of it.

If we read Synge's poems with this in mind we see, in fact, that he is using a poetic diction as much as Goldsmith is:

The Passing of the Shee

> Adieu, sweet Angus, Maeve, and Fand,
> Ye plumed yet skinny Shee,
> That poets played with hand in hand
> To learn their ecstasy.
>
> We'll stretch in Red Dan Sally's ditch,
> And drink in Tubber fair,
> Or poach with Red Dan Philly's bitch
> The badger and the hare.

This poem was written 'After looking at one of Æ's pictures'. It expresses Synge's dissatisfaction with the practice of writing poetry about the ancient mythology, and his determination of writing poetry about the real life of Ireland in his time. It means too (what amounts to the same thing) that he will avoid the poetic diction of Irish poets at that time, a diction which, as he says, is different from that condemned in eighteenth-century poetry, but no less restricted. And so he uses common or ugly words like 'skinny', 'ditch', 'poach', 'bitch'. The point I am trying to make is that, in doing this, Synge is not, as he seems to think, avoiding poetic diction altogether, but only substituting one sort of diction for another. He is still refusing to use certain words, the words of romantic glamour; he has only chosen to exclude a different set of words. He is still using a poetic diction, a selection of words; he is only making his selection on different principles.

It is true that Synge in his preface warns us against trying to trace in his poems the principles which he lays down. And it is obvious that, as he says, many of his poems were written without those principles in mind. For instance 'In Kerry':

> We heard the thrushes by the shore and sea,
> And saw the golden stars' nativity,
> Then round we went the lane by Thomas Flynn,

Across the church where bones lie out and in;
And there I asked beneath a lonely cloud
Of strange delight, with one bird singing loud,
What change you'd wrought in graveyard, rock and sea,
This new wild paradise to wake for me...
Yet knew no more than knew those merry sins
Had built this stack of thigh-bones, jaws and shins.

Here such words as 'a lonely cloud of strange delight' are just those romantically glamorous words which Synge was later determined not to use. They belong to the poetic diction which he refused. And very many of his poems are of this kind.

Now, as I pointed out, a poetic diction is used because it lends dignity to ordinary things and common human activities. Therefore, the question of what diction a poet shall use depends upon the poet's idea of what it is that gives man his dignity. What, for instance, distinguishes man from the brute? What is the noblest human faculty? Is it man's will, or the force of his emotions, or the discrimination of his senses, or his control of himself by reason? In the eighteenth century, most poets believed that what dignified man and distinguished him from the brute was his faculty of reasoning; so the poetry they wrote was reasonable and intellectual; and the diction they chose included many words for operations of the reason, such as generalization and analysis. In the nineteenth century most poets glorified man's will or his passion or his sensibility, rather than his reason; and their diction changed accordingly. Synge had the novel idea of seeing human dignity not in what distinguishes man from the brute, but in what he and the brute had in common, in a word, in man's brutality: 'It may almost be said that before verse can be human again it must learn to be brutal.'

The clearest example of this deliberate brutality is the ballad 'Danny':

One night a score of Erris men,
A score I'm told and nine,
Said, 'We'll get shut of Danny's noise
Of girls and widows dyin'.

There's not his like from Binghamstown
To Boyle and Ballycroy,
At playing hell on decent girls,
At beating man and boy.

He's left two pairs of female twins
Beyond in Killacreest,
And twice in Crossmolina fair
He's struck the parish priest.

But we'll come round him in the night
A mile beyond the Mullet;
Ten will quench his bloody eyes,
And ten will choke his gullet.'

It wasn't long till Danny came,
From Bangor making way,
And he was damning moon and stars
And whistling grand and gay.

Till in a gap of hazel glen –
And not a hare in sight –
Out lepped the nine-and-twenty lads
Along his left and right.

Then Danny smashed the nose on Byrne,
He split the lips on three,
And bit across the right hand thumb
Of one Red Shawn Magee.

But seven tripped him up behind,
And seven kicked before,
And seven squeezed around his throat,
Till Danny kicked no more.

Then some destroyed him with their heels
Some tramped him in the mud,
Some stole his purse and timber pipe,
And some washed off his blood. […]

And when you're walking out the way
From Bangor to Belmullet,
You'll see a flat cross on a stone
Where men choked Danny's gullet.

To do Synge justice, he proposes this brutality in poetry only as a
temporary expedient. He wants to shock the inhumanly exalted poetry of
his time by writing poems of all too human degradation; but only in
hopes that between the two extremes poetry may come to rest in a central
area of human interest and compassion. By thus seeing the poetic tradition in terms of action and reaction, Synge proves himself a thoroughly
modern mind. He is taking the same position as Mr T.S. Eliot who is now
recanting all his critical pronouncements of twenty years ago, because
they were made in a period when poetry had to be brought close to
colloquial English, whereas now the situation is quite different and poetry
needs to move away from the colloquial once more.

All the same one may doubt whether these changes come about quite as Synge and Mr Eliot would have us believe. I doubt whether poetry is such an independent activity that its language changes according to laws and by a rhythm of its own. After all, words have meaning. And the poets choose among words by reference to their meanings. Therefore, the words chosen by a poet, his diction, will vary according to what he believes about such questions as the nature, the dignity and the destiny of man. For poetry to be semi-permanently concerned with the pathos of common life, the language of poetry must be chosen by reference to a reasoned body of traditional belief about human nature and destiny. Such was the poetry of Goldsmith and his contemporaries, written in a diction which was part and parcel of the religious and philosophical convictions of the age. A poetic diction which acknowledges no authority outside poetry can never produce poems so assured and humane as 'The Deserted Village'. For all Synge may say, his best poems remain illustrations and examples of a critical theory about the language of poetry. Parts of his theory are questionable. But he remains one of the very few poets, writing in English since the end of the eighteenth century, who have talked sense about the question of diction in poetry.

Dublin Magazine, ns, 27: 1 (Jan–March 1952); reprinted in *The Poet in the Imaginary Museum*.

Introduction to Charles Tomlinson's
The Necklace

These poems require no introduction. From one point of view this is the most astonishing thing about them, the way they build up for themselves their own poetic universe. And if the world they inhabit is conspicuously 'their own', it is not therefore a private world. On the contrary; we are offered here no private symbolism or *ad hoc* mythology, no projection of conflicts personal to the poet. The world of these poems is a public one, open to any man who has kept clean and in order his nervous sensitivity to the impact of shape and mass and colour, odour, texture, and timbre. The poems appeal outside of themselves only to the world perpetually bodied against our senses. They improve that world. Once we have read them, it appears to us renovated and refreshed, its colours more delicate and clear, its masses more momentous, its sounds and odours sharper, more distinct. Nothing could be less literary, less amenable to discussion in terms of schools and influences.

But it is just this, perhaps, that to one sort of reader will be a difficulty. We are so used, some of us, to taking our bearings from literature that we are at a loss without them. To such readers one might offer one or two suggestions.

Like most considerable poets of the past thirty years or more, Charles Tomlinson has taken note of the experiments and achievements of French symbolism. This does not mean that he belongs to the post-symbolist 'school' or the post-symbolist 'movement', if there are such things. For my own part I find that I need to remember only one aspect of symbolism, and that an easy one, Rimbaud's 'dérèglement de tous les sens':

> The glare of brass over a restless bass
> (Red glow across olive twilight)

There is nothing recondite in this. Was it not Gustav Holst who composed a suite of musical pieces, each to render the quality of a particular colour? And we all know that a vulgar tie is 'loud', that when a woman wears a purple hat with a green coat, the colours 'shout' at each other. In many of these poems the central artifice is as simple as that; and it can be understood and accepted without knowing anything about Rimbaud at all. It is a familiar phenomenon of all human perception, and it is an artifice only in the sense that the poet takes this most natural phenomenon and refines upon it.

For of course the lines just quoted present the phenomenon only in its simplest form. The clue once given, the poet elaborates upon it. And in its subtler manifestations, it may go unnoticed unless we are prepared for it. For instance the poem called 'Nine Variations in a Chinese Winter Setting' is no piece of fashionable chinoiserie. Nor has it anything to do with translations from the Chinese by Arthur Waley or Ezra Pound. It is an exercise in rendering the perceptions of one sense by vocabulary drawn from the others:

> Pine-scent
> In snow-clearness
> Is not more exactly counterpointed
> Than the creak of trodden snow
> Against a flute.

Scent and sight and sound flow together. And I have already falsified. For it is not after all a question of describing scent or sight in terms of sound, as in the first example where 'glare of brass' equals 'red glow' (and note, even here, that it is *glare* of brass, not *blare*). Rather, what emerges from the stanza is not scent or sound or sight, but a quality that is all of these and none of them, that comes to life only when all of them, each in its own rich identity, come into perception together.

What is more, the poet can arrange the properties as he pleases. By arranging together pines, snow, walking feet, flutes, and a particular sort of light, or raffia, bow-strings, bows, bats, winds, bamboos, and flutes (his fourth variation) he creates a sound, a scent, a sight, and a peculiar atmosphere compounded of these, that 'never was on sea or land'. And this again (not that it matters) is an elaboration of the symbolist *paysage intérieur*.

The poet can go further. For there is another essential component of the 'paysage' – the observer, the apparatus that records the impacts made upon it by the senses. The sense and sounds, and the atmosphere compounded of these, will vary with the nature of the thing that responds to them. Bats hear sounds pitched too high for the ear of man, dogs smell what we cannot. The asdic transforms shape and mass into sound. Hence we can imagine a peculiar cast of mind, or a magic glass, or an apparatus of a special sort; and having imagined these, we can deduce with a sort of logic the world that this mind would perceive, or that this machine would render for our inspection. This is what happens in the difficult poem 'Dialogue', where the thing discussed may be the mind of an artist, or a sort of radar-cum-convex mirror-cum-X-ray. As we deduce the mind of a painter from his vision of the world rendered upon canvas, so we deduce the nature of this thing from the sort of world it presents for our inspection. The logic works both ways.

Again, if one requires a precedent, it can be found, in the poet who supplies an epigraph, and something more to this volume, the American poet, Wallace Stevens. Tomlinson having found an image for the sea, remarks,

> A static instance, therefore untrue,

for the world changes perpetually before our eyes, and no sooner have we recorded our momentary perceptions than they are proved false. Wallace Stevens, in his 'Sea Surface Full of Clouds', shows how the sea alters, not only with alterations in the sky above it and the sea-floor beneath it, but with changes in the climate of our mood as we perceive it. And a later poem by Stevens, 'Thirteen Ways of Looking at a Blackbird', passes, as Tomlinson does in his 'Dialogue', from observation to constructive hypothesis. The way we look at blackbirds depends on the circumstances in which they appear, circumstances which include the sort of people we are, and the sort of mood we are in. We can construct a set of circumstances; and however unlikely these are ('He rode over Connecticut / In a glass coach') we can deduce by the logic of imagination how blackbirds would appear in those circumstances.

This poem by Stevens has suggested, I think, the form employed by Tomlinson in his 'Eight Observations on the Nature of Eternity' and 'Nine Variations in a Chinese Winter Setting'. A title like 'Suggestions for the Improvement of a Sunset' similarly recalls titles used by Stevens. So it is just as well to point out that what we have here is no slavish imitation, conscious or unconscious pastiche. Stevens has been a model certainly; but he has not been allowed to dictate, to overpower the different vision of the poet who has learned from him. It would be truer to say that this poet has chosen to develop one side of Stevens, the side represented by 'Thirteen Ways of Looking at a Blackbird'.

For the effect of reading these poems is quite unlike the effect of reading a volume by Stevens. It is even more unlike the effect of such other poets as Keats and Tennyson, who are both concerned in their different ways, as this poet is, to register sense-perceptions with exquisite precision. The effect of these poems is anything but languorous or hectic or opulent. On the contrary they are taut, bare, and alert. This is largely a matter of versification. There are many kinds of free-verse: Charles Tomlinson's, I think, is designed to keep out of his poetry all effects as of surging violins and insistent drum-beats. One finds one's self compelled to use his vocabulary, to talk of one sense in terms of another, one art in terms of the other arts. His verse is musical; it is euphonious, and it sets up rhythms which are interesting and memorable. But these rhythms are curt, they stop short at just the point where they might become powerful and intoxicating. It is this that gives the effect of alertness and chastity. At its best, this poetry reminds us of what the musician means by 'phrasing'; in the blank spaces on the page, at the end of each line, after each comma or full-stop, the sound of what we have just heard goes on echoing in the mind. The poet expresses this himself in the recurrent image of the flute; for the most part he is writing an unaccompanied melody for the flute, where Stevens and Keats and Tennyson use the whole orchestra.

Diction and versification go together:

> There must be nothing
> Superfluous, nothing which is not elegant
> And nothing which is if it is merely that.

This is more than Stevens could say, and more than he would want to say. In 'Sea Surface Full of Clouds' there is a great deal that is elegant for its own sake. And this is all very well for Stevens, who declares himself a Romantic, prizing excess in human behaviour as in human language. But Tomlinson is vowed to the flute:

> The glare of brass over a restless bass
> (Red glow across olive twilight)
> Urges to a delighted excess,
> A weeping among broken gods.
>
> The flute speaks (reason's song
> Riding the ungovernable wave)
> The bound of passion
> Out of the equitable core of peace.

In 'Through Binoculars' we learn that 'Binoculars are the last phase in a romanticism', from which the poet returns with relief to 'normality'. And in 'Observation of Facts', elegance is merely 'frippery' until it incorporates 'mental fibre', like 'a rough pot or two' introduced into a too feminine room. Tomlinson's morality is sternly traditional, classical, almost Augustan. If he had not chosen to make this explicit, we could still have inferred it from the dryness and reticence of his art, its addiction to the bleak contour, to terse understatement and brief energetic rhythms. Just because he is as far as possible from a hedonist or Art-for-Art's-Saker, the pleasures of sensuous perception, as we gather them from his poems, never cloy or go stale on the tongue through over-indulgence.

I end as I began. These poems present analysis of human perception, how it works and how it ought to work, in a healthy personality. But the proof of the pudding is in the eating, the proof of the analysis is in the buoyant health of the poet's own perceptions, their crispness, the inevitability of the phrasing he finds for them:

> The scene terminates without words
> A tower collapsing upon feathers...
>
> The sea-voice
> Tearing the silence from the silence...

I have derived, and I still derive, enormous pleasure from these poems. So will others, I am sure.

Eynsham: The Fantasy Press, 1955.

See, and Believe

Charles Tomlinson, *Seeing is Believing* (New York: McDowell, Obolensky, 1958).

This is Tomlinson's third collection of poems, but the first that is both substantial and representative. His first, published quite some years ago by the Hand & Flower Press, contains, as they say, 'prentice-work', promising, intelligent and various, but now interesting chiefly because it shows the poet casting about for the style he wanted. In *The Necklace*, fifteen poems published four years ago by the Fantasy Press, the style has been achieved completely, but appears a specialized instrument for very special purposes. Special, and limited. Of course. But not at all so limited as people thought. The proof is in this collection, where what is recognizably the same style has been adapted, refined and elaborated so as to serve a much wider range of experience – as wide a range, in fact, as anyone has the right to demand of any poets except the greatest.

The word which the reviewers found for *The Necklace* was 'imagist'. But it was the wrong word, as Geoffrey Strickland pointed out in this journal; for Tomlinson had entered into his landscapes with far more of himself than an Imagist poet could ever afford to deploy. What he aimed at and achieved was a sensuous apprehension more comprehensive and more comprehending than the Imagist programme, bound to the one sense of sight and the one stance of cool observer, could allow for. Tomlinson's attitude, as distinct from his techniques, was far nearer to Lawrence's (in a poem like 'Snake') than to Pound's or Hulme's. What prompted the word 'imagist' was the one thing no one could deny, however little he might value it: the exquisitely accurate register of sense-impressions. What wasn't realized was that this scrupulous exactness wasn't there for its own sake, but as a discipline and a control; controlling an exceptionally passionate and whole-hearted response to the world, to a world that bore in, not just on the five senses, but also on a man's sentiments, a man's convictions. The American reviewers seem, some of them, to be making the same mistake with this collection.

But for heaven's sake let's not carp at the Americans. They have published, first in their magazines and now in this very elegant book, poems which (as I know) have for years been hawked in vain round the British magazines, the British anthologists and the London publishing houses. All honour to Miss Erica Marx and Mr Oscar Mellor, and to those editors who have published Tomlinson in British magazines, even if they did choose to print mostly pieces which were marginal and untypical. The blunt fact remains: that *The Necklace* was unavoidably a slight and fugitive publication, and that otherwise this most original and accomplished of all our postwar poets, profoundly English as he is in his attitudes and nowadays his landscapes, had to wait for a transatlantic critic, Hugh Kenner, to discover him; for transatlantic magazines to publish him in bulk, pay him, and award him prizes; and for a transatlantic publisher to bring him out between hard covers. Your withers, of course, remain unwrung. Am I trying to pretend that this is a national disgrace? Nothing less. But anyhow, the case is no special one: the publication of this volume gives point to desultory arguments that have gone on for some time, about whether New Provincial isn't Old Parochial, whether the glibly cosmopolitan is any worse than the aggressively insular. For Tomlinson's models are largely French and American; that is, he refuses to join the silent conspiracy which now unites all the English poets from Robert Graves down to Philip Larkin, and all the critics, editors and publishers too, the conspiracy to pretend that Eliot and Pound never happened. Tomlinson refuses to put the clock back, to pretend that after Pound and Eliot, Marianne Moore and Wallace Stevens have written in English, the English poetic tradition remains unaffected. He refuses to honour even the first rule of the club, by sheltering snugly under the skirts of 'the genius of the language'; instead he appears to believe, as Pound and Eliot did before him, that a Valéry and a Mallarmé change the landscape of poetry in languages other than their own. No wonder he doesn't appeal to our Little Englanders.

This, the debt to the French, is the subject of the elaborate tail-piece to this volume, an eight-page poem in six parts entitled 'Antecedents'. It is the only lineal descendent of Pound's *Mauberley*, and worthy of that great original, limited only as that is limited, by offending against Sidney's injunction that the poet should not confound himself with the historian. The hero is Jules Laforgue, introduced in the second section after a brilliant capsulated history of French symbolism as the logical consequence of the Romantic Movement, the whole orchestrated in terms of two arch-Romantic images, sunset and the call of a horn, conflated in a series of synaesthetic perceptions like those of the symbolists themselves ('Slow horn pouring through dusk an orange twilight'). After Byron, Tennyson, Nietzsche, Wagner, Mallarmé, Baudelaire, enter Laforgue:

> We had our laureates, they
> Their full orchestra and its various music. To that

  Enter

       On an ice-drift
       A white bear, the grand Chancellor
       From Analyse, uncertain
       Of whom he should blow to, or whether
       No one is present. It started with Byron, and
       Liszt, says Heine, bowed to the ladies. But Jules…
       Outside,

         De la musique avant toute chose
       The thin horns gone glacial
       And behind blinds, partitioning Paris
       Into the rose-stained mist,
       He bows to the looking-glass. Sunsets.

Will Tomlinson be told to bear his learning more lightly? But where do
we find a lighter touch than in the elegant fantasy (adapted from Laforgue
himself) which makes the blank white page and the blank space on the
page a polar bear on an icefloe? Mallarmé said, 'L'armature intellectuelle
du poème se dissimule et tient – a lieu – dans l'espace qui isole les stro-
phes et parmi le blanc du papier: significatif silence qu'il n'est pas moins
beau de composer que les vers.' If this is one of the most perceptive things
said about the art of poetry in the last hundred years, how can we maintain that a professional poet should not know this, or that, if he does, he
should conceal the fact? But he answers such objections himself:

                         Our innate
       Perspicacity for the moderate
       Is a national armory. 'I have not
       Read him: I have read about him':
       In usum delphini – for the use
       Of the common man. After Nietzsche
       (Downwards) Sartre, for whom
       Anouilh, dauphin's delight. And thus
       Rimbaud the incendiary,
       Gamin contemporary
       With Gosse, the gentleman
       Arrived late. He was dressed
       In the skin of a Welsh lion, or the lion
       Wore his – for the light
       Was dubious, the marsh softening
       And the company, willing to be led
       Back to the forsaken garden by a route
       Unfamiliar – yet as it wound
       Dimly among the fetishes, a bewilderment

Of reminiscence. The force
That through the green dark, drove them
Muffled dissatisfactions. Last light, low among tempests
Of restless brass. Last music
For the sable throne (She comes, she comes!)
As the horns, one by one
Extinguish under the wave
Rising into the level darkness.

Except for the strident and typically Poundian pun ('delphini'/
'dauphin's'), this is more Eliotic than Poundian, in the interlarded quotations of course, but more importantly in the Mallarméan syntax which
acts out, for instance, the anachronism of Dylan Thomas playing in 1940
the Rimbaud game for which the right time was 1870:

> And thus
> Rimbaud the incendiary,
> Gamin contemporary
> With Gosse, the gentleman
> Arrived late.

This is wit that is something better than deprecating, because this is a poet
with something better to write about than himself. Laforge had nothing
better – 'He bows to the looking-glass'; and so 'Antecedents' is, as the
title says, at once 'A homage and a valediction'. Tomlinson is a post-
symbolist poet, not a symbolist absurdly belated. And he is not going to
make the mistake he diagnoses in Thomas, of playing Laforgue as Thomas
played Rimbaud, a half-century too late.

How to utilize the symbolist disciplines and procedures while escaping
from the symbolists' solipsistic trap – this is spelled out in the last section
of 'Antecedents', as well as at other points. But Tomlinson's style (and I
don't mean the specially contrived style of 'Antecedents') does better than
spell out the answer; it exhibits it in living action. For the style which
Tomlinson discovered in *The Necklace* and has here developed so flexibly
is not just a way of writing, not at all a way of writing in any sense that is
not also a way of perceiving, a way of responding. Central to this style of
perceiving is a symbolist idea generally known to us only in the rather
special version that Eliot gave of it when he spoke of the objective correlative. It is the idea that an arrangement of objects or events in the apparently external world may so correspond to a pattern of thought and
feeling in the mind, that the latter may be expressed and defined in terms
of the former. It is against the background of this conviction that
Tomlinson can speak (as, to be sure, others have spoken) of 'a certain
mental climate', of 'the moral landscape of my poetry in general'. These
are something better than metaphors or, if they are metaphors, these

metaphors underpin everything Tomlinson writes. Now it is obvious
that the idea as just outlined permits of a two-way traffic between the
poet's mind and the world: he may proceed from himself outward,
starting with a state of feeling in himself and seeking an objective correlative for it; or he may start with perceptions of the objective world, and
move inward to find a subjective correlative for them in a state of feeling
he induces or imagines. Symbolist poetry characteristically seems to have
run the traffic all the first way, to the point indeed at which the reality of
the supposedly objective world, as anything but a phantasmal reflection of
the subjective, becomes highly questionable. Tomlinson too may run the
traffic this way, as when he answers Amis's notorious 'Nobody wants any
more poems about foreign cities', by conjuring up cities imagined so as to
correspond to states of mind:

> Not forgetting Ko–jen, that
> Musical city (it has
> Few buildings and annexes
> Space by combating silence),
> There is Fiordiligi, its sun–changes
> Against walls of transparent stone
> Unsettling all preconception – a city
> For architects (they are taught
> By casting their nets
> Into those moving shoals)

But far more characteristically (and specifically so as to escape the
symbolist vertigo about whether the objective exists), Tomlinson runs the
traffic the other way, insisting upon the irreducible Otherness of the non-
human world, its Presence in the sense of its being present, its being
bodied against the senses, as the irreplaceable first principle of all sanity
and all morality. Of many statements of this (for it is after all what gives
the book its title), I take 'Cézanne at Aix':

> And the mountain: each day
> Immobile like fruit. Unlike, also
> – Because irreducible, because
> Neither a component of the delicious
> And therefore questionable,
> Nor distracted (as the sitter)
> By his own pose and, therefore,
> Doubly to be questioned: it is not
> Posed. It is. Untaught
> Unalterable, a stone bridgehead
> To that which is tangible
> Because unfelt before. There

In its weathered weight
Its silence silences, a presence
Which does not present itself.

Some objections may here be anticipated, and a concession made at no cost (which is that, yes, there are about five unsuccessful poems here, out of thirty-five). It will be objected that the poems are inhuman, that they never deal with people, human relations, human sentiments. In fact, the great advance on *The Necklace* is precisely here, in commenting (but by implication, always by implication from arrangements of sense-perceptions) on the life of man in history, especially on his communal life as registered by his buildings, by the nature and quality of his tools, by the landscapes he has modified. Secondly, it appears that readers have difficulty with Tomlinson's metres. Like most of Eliot (and how much else?), the metre is on the uncertain borderline between *vers libre* and loose (basically four-stress) accentual verse. For my part, I am sure that to count syllables as well as stresses is to have an instrument more delicate and various. But it is disingenuous to object to Tomlinson's metre while accepting Hopkins and Eliot – he is less emphatically muscle-bound than the one, more alert and vigorous than the other. The stops and starts of syntax play over against, and tauten, the runs and pauses of rhythm; and there is a Hopkinsian (but again less emphatic, and so more flexible) richness of orchestration in internal echoes and half-echoes of consonance and assonance, lacing clauses and lines together.

When I turn from these poems to work by highly and justly commended writers, such as R.S. Thomas, say, or even Edwin Muir, what dismays me about these is a pervasive slackness – not in perception nor in seriousness (for both are commonly as honest and truthful as Tomlinson), but simply in artistic ambition. In their hands the medium is used scrupulously and well, to good and important ends; but it is *not wrought up to the highest pitch*. They do not say a thing once and for all, then move on fast to another thing. Their expressions could be, not more true, but more forcibly, more brilliantly and compactly true. What people don't realize is that in poetry there can be no question of choosing between the thing well done and the thing done consummately, conclusively. The art imposes its own laws: it demands to be pushed to the extreme, to be wrought up to the highest pitch it is capable of. There are degrees of meritorious performance, certainly, but there can be no question – not for the poet nor for the responsible reader – of preferring the less degree to the greater, as one may prefer weak tea to strong. Thus it is nonsense to say of Tomlinson, as some have said, that of course his diction and his music are choice and distinguished beyond the reach of his contemporaries, but nevertheless a coarser music may be better, a diction more vulgar may be more vigorous and so more valuable. The muse is not to be fooled, and vigour bought at that cost will soon be exhausted.

As an art, poetry cannot juggle with its own hierarchies. This is also the reason why it cannot stand still; why a poet who writes as if Pound and Mallarmé had never written may have merit, certainly, but other things being equal he can never have equal merit with a poet whose writing acknowledges the heights to which the art was wrought at those hands. This book, I am sure, is a landmark. What a pity it should mark a new peak in the obtuseness of the English to their own poets, as well as a new height gained in the long struggle back to English poetry considered by the poet as a way of spiritual knowledge.

Essays in Criticism, 9: 2 (April 1959); reprinted in *The Poet in the Imaginary Museum*.

Remembering the Movement

I've been thinking for some time that I ought to set down my recollections and impressions of the last few years, so far as they may amount to a chapter of literary history. But I've never seen myself putting this straight into print. Always it seemed that the time for that wasn't ripe, the occasion disreputable. Now that I find myself writing for print after all, I feel impatient with all the crippling embarrassment and Simon-Pure evasiveness that prevented me from doing so before, and still obstruct me now. And this wasn't peculiar to me: nothing now strikes me as so significant and so queer about 'the Movement', as the way all of us who were supposed to be 'in' it still spoke of it among ourselves inside invisible quotation-marks. We ridiculed and deprecated 'the Movement' even as we kept it going. I don't know, but I should imagine that this would have been the most baffling thing about us, to any Frenchman (say) or American, who got into company with two or three of us. For in their countries, so far as I can see, writers who set out in concert to write a chapter of literary history don't have to pretend elaborately to be doing something else. Why should they? We in the Movement did so, for the same reasons which brought the whole thing to a halt and broke it up before it was under way – out of pusillanimity; from the unforgivable literary sin of going much further than halfway to meet our readers, forestalling their objections, trying to keep in their good books. Ours was writing which apologized insistently for its own existence, which squirmed in agonies of embarrassment at being there in print on the page at all. In the interstices of our poems – in the metrical places wasted on inert gestures of social adaptiveness – 'no doubt', 'I suppose', 'of course', 'almost', 'perhaps' – you can see the same craven defensiveness which led us, when we were challenged or flattered or simply interviewed, to pretend that the Movement didn't exist, that it was an invention of journalists, that we had never noticed how Larkin and Gunn and Amis had something in common, or that, if we had noticed, it didn't interest or excite us.

Other people have said this before, have pointed out for instance how Amis's and Larkin's dislike of foreign travel and foreign languages seems meant to ingratiate them with aggressively insular philistines among their readers. But I have in mind something else. There are insular philistines among readers of the *Sunday Times*, and John Betjeman knows how to tap their prejudices to good purpose. Just as insular, just as philistine, are their political enemies, the readers of *Tribune* whom Amis seems to be wooing. But there is insularity and philistinism – the first, and therefore the second – among the readers of *Essays in Criticism* and the ex-readers of *Scrutiny*; among, in fact, just the self-conscious élite which is first to leap on 'the Movement' for selling out to the middlebrows. The longer I look at it, the more it seems to me that it was the selling out to *this* public, the attempts to placate in advance *these* readers, which crippled 'the Movement' from the start. What did for us was conceding too much, not to the insularity which orders baked beans on toast in Pavia and thinks all foreigners are dirty, but to the insularity which has ready its well-documented and conclusive sneer at Colette and Marianne Moore, Cocteau and Gide and Hart Crane. This is probably the time to speak only for myself, and to admit that while I hadn't hope of many readers from *Tribune* or the *Sunday Times*, I had hopes of readers from among this highbrow élite; and now when I reread my poems of those years it seems all too obvious how far I was ready to go to woo and placate these bodies of feeling and opinion.

This isn't just to concede everything to the gibe which was flung at us from the beginning, that we were 'academic'. Academic is no bad thing to be, and in any case becomes inescapable, as the philistinism of Anglo-American society forces all artists – not just writers – back into the campus as a last stronghold. It is a question whether the universities can rise to this emergency. But it has been normal at every period for the poet to be a learned man; and if universities exist for or provide for the pursuit of learning, it is proper and natural that the poets should cluster round the campuses. In any case, in so far as academicism is a besetting danger for the poet, the most full-blooded and best-informed campaigns against that academicism have always come from inside the academic body. I foresaw and intended that some of the dons I knew would be affronted and offended by what I wrote, and many more would ignore it. I addressed myself hopefully not to the academic profession but to a group within the profession, very consciously at odds with the rest and more or less committed, appropriately enough, to the idea of 'a minority culture'. In so far as the others shared my hopes of these readers (and I think they did, up to a point), we were all disillusioned. The radicals of yesteryear were now the guardians of the law; and those who had once fought to get Eliot and Lawrence on students' reading-lists were now the most determined that no later writer should figure there, the most careful not to risk a good opinion of a contemporary.

Meanwhile all of us in the Movement had read the articles in *Scrutiny* about how the reputations of Auden and Spender and Day Lewis were

made by skilful promotion and publicity; and it was to placate *Scrutiny*
readers that we pretended (and sometimes deceived ourselves as well as
others) that the Movement was not being 'sold' to the public in the same
way; that John Wain on the BBC, and later Bob Conquest with his
anthology *New Lines* weren't just touching the pitch with which we
others wouldn't be defiled. Again I limit myself to my own case: I
remember nothing so distastefully as the maidenly shudders with which I
wished to know nothing of the machinery of publicity, even as I liked
publicity and profited by it. Of course, once the machinery was set going,
there was no controlling it; and Wain, Gunn and Larkin figured in a series
of 'profiles' in *The Times Educational Supplement*, lately almost duplicated
in the *Sunday Times*, from which I can in all honesty rejoice to have been
excluded. And of course there is a quite drastic coarsening and simplifica-
tion that goes on even at the hands of a sophisticated publicity-agent like
G.S. Fraser. But for heaven's sake publicity is what in some degree we all
want, quite legitimately; and the prissiness which won't pay any of the
price, won't use any of the channels which it knows are available, only
brings about the sort of half-hearted falling between two stools which
made the Movement abortive. The writer's job, I now think, is to make
sure that the wares are good; and then to be as cynical and ingenious as
possible in marketing them by the only channels that are open.

There's a lot more than this to be said about publicity. Too much of
it, for instance, is certainly worse than too little. Kingsley Amis suffered
from this far more than the rest of us; and his staying in his academic job
in the provinces, as well as his refusal to contribute to some of the Angry
Young Man book-making, were brave and level-headed attempts to resist
the publicity that came to him. These were acts of integrity and of a very
just perception of where publicity begins to do too much damage – to the
writer, and to his relations with the public.

But it's just there – in the relations with the public (not with this
public or that one, but with 'the reader' in general, however conceived
of) – that the Movement seems to me to be most instructive. I come back
to my first point – it wasn't so much that we addressed the wrong set of
readers, as that we addressed *any* reader too humbly. We were deprecating, ingratiating. What we all shared to begin with was a hatred for
writing considered as self-expression; but all we put in its place was
writing as self-adjustment, a getting on the right terms with our reader
(that is, with our society), a hitting on the right tone and attitude towards
him. And in fact, this was the only alternative to exhibitionism, to 'self-
expression', which our education and the climate of ideas presented us
with. It's still true that literary criticism in Britain cannot conceive of
anything else. Just consider how much of an okay word 'tone' is, and has
been ever since I.A. Richards put it into general currency; and how difficult we find it to conceive of or approve any 'tone' that isn't ironical, and

ironical in a limited way, defensive and deprecating, a way of looking at ourselves and our pretensions, not a way of looking at the world. Hardly ever did we seem to write our poems out of an idea of poetry as a way of knowing the world we were in, apprehending it, learning it; instead we conceived of it as an act of private and public therapy, the poet resolving his conflicts by expressing them and proffering them to the reader so that vicariously he should do the same. The most obvious register of this is the striking absence from 'Movement' poetry of outward and non-human things apprehended crisply for their own sakes. I'm not asking for 'nature poetry', but simply for an end to attitudinizing. In 'Movement' poetry the poet is never so surrendered to his experience, never so far gone out of himself in his response, as not to be aware of the attitudes he is taking up. It is as if experience, as if the world, could be permitted to impinge on the poet only if he had first defined the terms in which it may present itself; as if the world never imposes its own conditions, but must wait cap-in-hand until the writer is prepared to entertain it (with the lighting and the angles previously arranged). This imperiousness towards the non-human goes along with the excessive humility towards the human, represented by the reader; you can be as arrogant as this towards the natural only if you assume (as I think we all assumed) that the sole function of the natural is to provide a vocabulary of terms – 'symbols', 'images' – by which people, poet and reader, can get in touch with each other.

Instead of now trying to find good things to say of the Movement (I could say plenty) or finding creditable exceptions among Movement writers, I prefer to point out that what I've just said against it applies equally well to most English and a great deal of American poetry in the present century and at the present day. Auden and Empson woo their readers as blatantly as Movement poets do; the manipulation of 'tone' plays as big a part in their poems as in Amis and Larkin. Yeats has as little interest in alien modes of being, as imperiously makes of a swan or a tree only a symbol for something in himself, as Thom Gunn does. The younger Eliot, manipulating the defensive ironies of Laforgue and reducing the various liveliness of the natural world to a repertoire of objective correlatives for states of mind, is just as little interested in poetry as a way of knowing that world in its multifarious otherness. As for the Americans – certainly it is harder for them, faced with the impersonal plenitude of landscapes in Utah, Nevada, California, to relegate the world to a mere vocabulary of communication. Yet William Carlos Williams, for instance, honoured father-figure of avant-garde Americans on the West Coast and elsewhere, who has tried to keep his eye on the subject instead of on the reader, seems to have failed most of the time: his 'tone', his way of playing for the reader's attention and getting the reader on his side, is very obvious indeed – it is the excruciating tone of the *faux-naïf*, and it survives into most of the poems of his followers, just as distractingly as the tone of ironical urbanity in us or in the Americans from the Eastern campuses.

Postscript: The occasion for this piece determined its tone. The anger – with myself, as well as with others – is designedly unbuttoned and topical. But it is not for that reason to be dismissed as 'dated', as of 'only historical interest'.

Prospect (Summer 1959); reprinted with postscript in *The Poet in the Imaginary Museum*.

To a Brother in the Mystery

Circa 1290

The world of God has turned its two stone faces
One my way, one yours. Yet we change places
A little, slowly. After we had halved
The work between us, these grotesques I carved
There in the first bays clockwise from the door,
That was such work as I got credit for
At York and Beverley: thorn-leaves twined and bent
To frame some small and human incident
Domestic or of venery. Each time I crossed
Since then, however, underneath the vast
Span of our Mansfield limestone, to appraise
How you cut stone, my emulous hard gaze
Has got to know you as I know the stone
Where none but chisels talk for us. I have grown
Of my own way of thinking yet of yours,
Seeing your leafage burgeon there by the doors
With a light that, flickering, trenches the voussoir's line;
Learning your pre-harmonies, design
Nourished by exuberance, and fine-drawn
Severity that is tenderness, I have thought,
Looking at these last stalls that I have wrought
This side of the chapter's octagon, I find
No hand but mine at work, yet mine refined
By yours, and all the difference: my motif
Of foliate form, your godliness in leaf.
       And your last spandrel proves the debt incurred
Not all on the one side. There I see a bird
Pecks at your grapes, and after him a fowler,
A boy with a bow. Elsewhere, your leaves discover
Of late blank mask-like faces. We infect
Each other then, doubtless to good effect...
And yet, take care: this cordial knack bereaves
The mind of all its sympathy with leaves,

Even with stone. I would not take away
From your peculiar mastery, if I say
A sort of coldness is the core of it,
A sort of cruelty; that prerequisite
Perhaps I rob you of, and in exchange give
What? vulgarity's prerogative,
Indulgence towards the frailties it indulges,
Humour called 'wryness' that acknowledges
Its own complicity. I can keep in mind
So much at all events, can always find
Fallen humanity enough, in stone,
Yes, in the medium; where we cannot own
Crispness, compactness, elegance, but the feature
Seals it and signs it work of human nature
And fallen though redeemable. You, I fear,
Will find you bought humanity too dear
At the price of some light leaves, if you begin
To find your handling of them growing thin,
Insensitive, brittle. For the common touch,
Though it warms, coarsens. Never care so much
For leaves or people, but you care for stone
A little more. The medium is its own
Thing, and not all a medium, but the stuff
Of mountains; cruel, obdurate, and rough.

Encounter, 14: 6 (June 1960); first collected in *New and Selected Poems* (Middletown, Connecticut: Wesleyan University Press, 1961).

Impersonal and Emblematic

After reading through Robert Graves's *Collected Poems* (not the first Graves 'Collected', nor perhaps the last), I am confirmed in my sense of where his surest achievement lies, though my sense of it is enriched by examples I hadn't noticed. His natural and characteristic form is the epigram. I think of such poems as 'Love without Hope', 'Flying Crooked', 'On Portents', 'Woman and Tree' and (a new one to me) 'New Legends'; it seems that this sort of achievement has been possible for Graves at every stage of his career. And it would be easy to elaborate this into a view of Graves as the Landor of his age. Not only the addiction to epigram (in the fullest Greek-Anthology sense, with a special place for the sumptuous love-compliment in this form), but also the self-imposed long exile by the Mediterranean, and the face turned to the public at large (irascible, scornful, selfconsciously independent) are things that Graves and Landor have in common. What's more, the difficulty we have in making Landor fit (into his age, that is, with Wordsworth and Coleridge, Shelley and Keats) is just the difficulty we have seeing where Graves fits in with Eliot and Pound and Yeats, Auden and Thomas. As historians forget about Landor, so, I suspect, they will try to forget Graves. Each poet seems to be the exception that proves the rule about his time, the case which belies the generalization but cannot disprove it because the case is so clearly a special one. Yet this last limitation (for that's what it is) is not at all so clear in Graves's case as in Landor's; and that's why the comparison shouldn't be pressed – not because it is 'academic' but because it prejudges the issue.

To begin with, the epigrams are only a small part of Landor's work as a whole, from which moreover they stand apart in a category of their own. And this isn't true of Graves: it is recognizably the virtues of the epigram which inform much work by Graves that is ampler and more relaxed than the epigram proper. And this means that to do him justice we have either to extend the term 'epigram' to a point where it's meaningless or else find a term more comprehensive. I believe the right term is 'emblem'. This can be applied to a poem like 'Vain and Careless', which develops in very leisurely fashion indeed (such as the strict epigram can never afford) through six quatrains which nevertheless stand to the moral discovery in the final quatrain – 'Water will not mix with oil, / Nor vain with careless heart' – in precisely the same relation as the body of an epigram to its pay-off line. The story of the lady so careless she mislaid her child and the man so vain he walked on stilts is an emblematic fable, as 'The Glutton' is an emblematic image:

> Beyond the Atlas roams a glutton
> Lusty and sleek, a shameless robber,
> Sacred to Aethiopian Aphrodite;
> The aborigines harry it with darts,
> And its flesh is esteemed, though of a fishy tang
> Tainting the eater's mouth and lips.
>
> Ourselves once, wandering in mid-wilderness
> And by despair drawn to this diet,
> Before the meal was over sat apart
> Loathing each other's carrion company.

This is the emblem in the form of riddle. (The answer to the riddle seems to be 'Lust'.) Graves has been much interested in poetic riddles, and in those bodies of literature (e.g. Celtic poetry, and English and Irish folk-lore) which are especially rich in them. Not many of his own riddles are so easy to solve as 'The Glutton'; one of the finest and most extended is also one of the hardest, 'Warning to Children', which I now take to be just about the most ambitious poem Graves has ever written.

It is common, and reasonable, to define 'emblem' by distinguishing it from 'symbol'. And part of the difficulty we have with Graves has to do with his being an emblematic poet in an age when symbol has been most practised and most highly esteemed. It seems important to insist that the one is not an inferior version of the other; every image in George Herbert, for instance, is an emblem. One can define the difference by saying that the symbol casts a shadow, where the emblem doesn't; the symbol aims to be suggestive, the emblem to be, even in its guise as riddle, ultimately explicit. Another difference might be that the emblem is made, fabricated, where the symbol is *found*; or rather, since it seems plain that both 'making' and 'finding' are involved in any act of imagination, let us say that the symbol aims to give the effect of having been discovered, where the emblem aims at the effect of having been constructed. This is an important distinction, for it means that part of the impressiveness of the good symbol lies in the place and circumstances of its finding, whereas with the emblem this isn't true. We think the better of Eliot and Baudelaire for finding their symbols in the unexpected because largely unexplored life of the industrial metropolis; but this is no warrant for thinking worse of Graves because he finds his emblems most often in a rural and agrarian England which has vanished. (It's not here that the label 'Georgian' can be made to stick, but rather on an occasional ponderous whimsy, like 'The General Elliott'.) Who can doubt that the rustic image of 'Love without Hope' was specifically constructed (perhaps out of memory, but perhaps not) to stand as full and explicit counterpart to the abstractions of its title?

> Love without hope, as when the young bird-catcher
> Swept off his tall hat to the Squire's own daughter,
> So let the imprisoned larks escape and fly
> Singing about her head, as she rode by.

The fullness and explicitness, the dry sharp unshadowed silhouette, the lack of resonance and overtone – these are the virtues of this emblematic writing; and the air of fabrication, even of contrivance (but not laboured contrivance), the evidence of forethought, plan and design – these will displease only the reader who comes to this verse for what it never offered to supply.

Sometimes, it's true, Graves seems not to understand the nature of his own gift. We have implied that the emblem is fitted to deal with those experiences which can be made explicit, whereas the symbol exists to deal with just those experiences which cannot be grasped, which can only be hinted at, seen askance out of the corner of the eye, part of the penumbra which in our mental life hangs densely about the cleared area of experience which we can formulate. When Graves tries, as he does quite often, to render experiences of nightmare obsession and anxiety, of self-disgust or the fear of madness, his dry and definite technique fails him; and we get the disconcerting effect of a nicely adjusted and chiselled frame about a vaporous centre. The much admired 'Nature's Lineaments' seems a case of this, and 'Welsh Incident' virtually admits as much. Another example, and an instructive one, is 'The Pier-Glass', a piece which could certainly be spared, bearing as it does every evidence of being very early work. This is almost entirely parasitical on early Tennyson ('Mariana' and 'The Lady of Shalott'), and it is interesting chiefly for being so much less 'modern' and 'symbolist', so much more explicit (on a theme which defies explicitness) than Tennyson was in the last century.

One great advantage of emblematic writing is its impersonality. A poet who deals with symbols, a Mallarmé or an Eliot, has to struggle much harder to cut the umbilical cord between poet and poem, so that the poem wills stand free and independent. Of course there are those, like Yeats and his admirers, to whom impersonality seems not worth striving for. They find nothing attractive or valuable in the illusion which other poets seek to create, by which the poem shall seem to be a product of the language, and the poet merely a medium through which the language becomes articulate. For them poetry-making is inevitably a histrionic faculty, and they are quite happy to see poetry as the vehicle of personality. It's worth making this point because of a curious passage in Graves's

Foreword where, after pointing out that he has lived and written in many countries, he remarks, 'But somehow these poems have never adopted a foreign accent or colouring; they remain true to the Anglo-Irish poetic tradition into which I was born.' What is the Anglo-Irish tradition? It's true we may think of Father Prout and 'The Groves of Blarney', the Irish tradition of comic and macaronic verse, when Graves turns the delicious joke of a poem written in the pidgin idiom of a Mallorcan pamphlet for English-speaking tourists. But there isn't enough of this sort of thing for Graves to have had it principally in mind. In view of what we know to be his opinion of Yeats, he can hardly mean that either. And yet, to the English reader (rightly or wrongly) the Anglo-Irish poetic tradition means Yeats first and the rest nowhere. Is there any point in comparing Graves with Yeats?

The comparison could be sustained about as far as the comparison with Landor (*The White Goddess*, for instance is a parallel case to Yeats's source-book, *A Vision*), but in the end it is no more fruitful. Yet the word 'histrionic', as it comes to mind in relation to Yeats particularly and the Anglo-Irish in general, is worth pondering. Graves has shown himself thoroughly at home in the world of the TV screen and the news-reel cameraman; he is not at all reluctant or maladroit in projecting a public image of himself. And this goes along with a self-regarding element in his own poetry, as in poems about his own name or about his own face in a mirror. This is very Yeatsian. Yet in general it's true that Graves uses other media than poetry in which to project his public image. The poems are impersonal in effect, even when they are on very personal themes. And it is the emblematic style which brings this about, whether the poet intended it or not. The histrionic attitude shows through in some of the early poems, notably the much-anthologized 'Rocky Acres', which I was sorry to see had been chosen by George Hartley for his long-playing disc of Graves reading:

> Yet this is my country, beloved by me best,
> The first land that rose from Chaos and the Flood,
> Nursing no valleys for comfort or rest,
> Trampled by no shod hooves, bought with no blood.
> Sempiternal country whose barrows have stood
> Stronghold for demigods when on earth they go,
> Terror for fat burghers on far plains below.

What can the last lines mean except that the poet is himself one of the demigods, poised at the verge of his harsh and craggy kingdom, prepared to harry and pillage bourgeois society? And is this not indeed very like the talk and boastful rant of Yeats in many poems, and of the professional Irishman everywhere? And if Yeats is frequently superior to this, isn't it in so piling on the extravagance as to show that he's not taken in by his own performance, but can ironically recognize blarney even when he speaks it himself? It will be interesting to hear how Graves reads this poem, for his very idiosyncratic reading manner, flat and casual, seems designed specifically to avoid rant of any kind.

The precautions he takes against rant aren't characteristically ironical; one sees them almost at once when, a few pages after 'Rocky Acres', that poem is as it were rewritten in a much terser mode, as 'Angry Samson':

> Are they blind, the lords of Gaza
> In their strong towers,
> Who declare Samson pillow-smothered
> And stripped of his powers?
>
> O stolid Philistines
> Stare now in amaze
> At my foxes running in your cornfields
> With their tails ablaze,
>
> At swung jaw-bone, at bees swarming
> In the stark lion's hide,
> At these, the gates of well-walled Gaza
> A-clank to my stride.

This isn't an important poem, but it has all the impersonality of the emblem, of a medallion; and it seems that not the poet but the English language wrote it, out of the range of meanings that, for instance, 'Philistine' has taken on between the Authorized Version and Matthew Arnold. A good way to see the de-personalizing virtue of the emblem is to compare 'The Reader over My Shoulder' (direct and personal, with accordingly a disastrous thumping of the chest in the last lines) with 'The Legs', which stands beside it and treats the same subject – the poet's attitude to his readers, his public, i.e. his society at large – with completely assured and telling control, only possible after he had objectified it fully, in a contrived fable. Hereabouts in the collection – in sections II and III – the fine poems come thick and fast: 'Full Moon', 'Pure Death', the incomparable 'Sick Love', 'Saint', 'Gardener', 'In Broken Images', 'Flying Crooked' – nearly all of these are emblems. 'Flying Crooked' is one such, in which the poet distinguishes himself from other sorts of thinkers, such as logicians; 'In Broken Images', constructed in propositions in couplets, has the same theme, and thus mimics very effectively that very discourse, the logician's, from which it distinguishes itself – and this neatness attained by other means has just the distancing de-personalizing effect of the emblems.

In section IV there are abundant signs of enormous bitterness, seldom defined and as seldom mastered: such emblems as 'Hell', or 'Nature's Lineaments' or 'Ogres and Pygmies' are off-centre, registering an experience they cannot comprehend. This shows up in minutiae like the word 'raffish' in the penultimate line of 'Nature's Lineaments', which would certainly have been another word if the poet hadn't wanted a rhyme for 'fish'. The effect of thin shallowness in these pieces seems the product not of writing that is superficial, insufficiently engaged, but of writing that is engaged in the wrong way, produced out of the jangle of raw nerves not from perturbation of imagination. In 'With Her Lips Only', the shallowness shows up in another way, as knowledgeable glibness. In different ways two poems do establish imaginative control over the screaming nerves: they are 'Down, Wanton, Down!' and the admirable 'Certain Mercies', and George Hartley takes them both for the disc. He's to be complimented also on choosing 'To Evoke Posterity', a less familiar poem which provides a text to hang in the study of every poet and still more of every poetry-reader.

> To evoke Posterity
> Is to weep on your own grave,
> Ventriloquizing for the unborn.

Another body of work that hangs together usefully is section VII, where Graves seems to have herded together most of his poems that can be described as marginalia, witty but trivial pieces like 'The Persian Version', 'Apollo of the Physiologists' and '1805'. These are the graceful trivia with which he now appears every few weeks or so, in the weekly magazines; one wishes one could be sure that editors and readers are as aware as their author is, of how marginal such pieces are to his and poetry's central and exacting concerns.

Listen, 3: 3–4 (Spring 1960); reprinted in *The Poet in the Imaginary Museum*.

A'e Gowden Lyric

'Better a'e gowden lyric / Than a social problem solved', wrote Hugh MacDiarmid thirty years ago; and again – 'Better a'e gowden lyric / Than onything else ava!' So too, in his 'Second Hymn to Lenin':

> Sae here, twixt poetry and politics,
> There's nae doot in the en'.
> Poetry includes that and s'ud be
> The greatest poo'er amang men.
>
> – It's the greatest, *in posse* at least,
> That men ha'e discovered yet
> Tho' nae doot they're unconscious still
> O' ithers faur greater than it.

MacDiarmid alone among British socialist writers has kept the priorities thus clear. It's a great thing to have done.

On the other hand we look in vain for any reason why lyric poetry is such a tall order. We are no wiser at the end of 'One Golden Lyric' about what makes a lyric golden, what golden-ness is. Perhaps this is the critic's job, not the poet's; but the trouble is that the calling of lyrics 'golden', with no questions asked, is precisely the language of bad critics – and spelling it 'gowden' doesn't make it any better.

Still, the young MacDiarmid had better things to do. Instead of arguing the case, he proved it – by exemplifying, in one lyric after another, the golden-ness we can recognize before we can define it. 'The Frightened Bride', 'Farmer's Death', 'Wild Roses', and the Hardyesque 'Sea-Serpent'; the equally Hardyesque trio, 'God Takes a Rest', 'In the Pantry' and 'The Innumerable Christ'; 'Crowdieknowe' and 'Whip-the-World'; 'Trompe L'Oeil', 'Scunner', 'On the Threshold', 'Supper to God', 'The Quest', 'Empty Vessel' – what a harvest!

There may indeed be others, for reading Lallans with the usual maddeningly inadequate glossary, an English reader finds many that remain locked in their foreign language. Is it the foreign language that has kept these poems almost unknown outside Scotland? I should like to think so. But I'd blame instead chiefly our squeamishness about eroticism, in particular the notion that in love tenderness and heated solemnity go together; that, and the distrustful philistinism which thinks a poem of eight lines necessarily more 'slender' than one of eighty.

What is especially astonishing is that all the poems I've listed come from the two collections, *Sangschaw* (1925) and *Penny Wheep* (1926). However, if this is the glory, it is also the sadness of MacDiarmid's *Collected Poems* (Oliver & Boyd, 1962). For where in his later work do we find poems to set by these? In *A Drunk Man Looks at the Thistle*, there is one that surpasses them all, the justly famous 'O Wha's the Bride?' And in *Stony Limits* (1934) there are the nine Shetland Lyrics, which include for instance 'Gruney'. Otherwise there is terribly much of this:

> The sin against the Holy Ghost is to fetter or clog
> The free impulse of life – to weaken or cloud
> The glad wells of being – to apply other tests,
> To say that these pure founts must be hampered, controlled,
> Denied, adulterated, diluted, cowed,
> The wave of omnipotence made recede, and all these lives, these
>   lovers,
> Lapse into cannon-fodder, sub-humanity, the despised slum-crowd.

And at once we know what the lyric golden-ness is; it is language on the gold standard, each word ringing true and worth its weight, not needing to be supplemented, eked out, overlapped. It is 'vigil's pin-point motion': it assuredly is *not* 'to weaken *or cloud*', 'to fetter *or clog*'.

This comes from a poem, 'In the Slums of Glasgow', which neither MacDiarmid nor anyone else would describe as a lyric. But then golden-ness of this sort is what nowadays we demand of all poetry, lyrical or not. MacDiarmid however might not agree. For this demand we make, for a lyrical cleanness in the language of all poetry whatever, is almost entirely a distinctively modern thing. And MacDiarmid, though he is the least insular of British poets, is also among the most old-fashioned; at least as old-fashioned as Hardy. More indeed; for the poems of his which recall Hardy recall not the greatest Hardy but the dated and quaint, though sturdily impressive Hardy who is ironical about the cosmos. Similarly, when MacDiarmid wanted to extend his range from the lyric as traditionally conceived, the best he could do was, like Hardy, to contrive what used to be called 'a dramatic framework'. In *A Drunk Man Looks at the Thistle* this is less cumbrous than in *The Dynasts* because it is less ambitious. Instead the poetry remains in that awkward half-way house to drama, the Browningesque dramatic monologue.

> Eneuch? Then here you are. Here's the haill story.
> Life's connached shapes too'er up in crowns o' glory,
> Perpetuatin', natheless, in their gory

Colour the endless sacrifice and pain
That to their makin's gane.

The ugliness of this writing is not the sometimes functional ugliness of modernism: it is something inseparable from the dramatic monologue, which fakes up by such uncouth gambols the liveliness of those dramatic exchanges it cannot provide. The speaker gets more and more embarrassed by his own garrulity, and the ugliness is how his embarrassment shows up.

A Drunk Man Looks at the Thistle is the turning-point in MacDiarmid's career. (Its date remarkably is 1926, the same as *Penny Wheep* – MacDiarmid in the twenties was very prolific.) One sees why it was necessary and even admirable for MacDiarmid to write this book, and there are fine things in it; but it makes tedious reading as a whole. The form he found for it was too much of a makeshift, and discredited before he chose it; as a result even the fine things are jammed in with poor stuff. (compare, in 'The Light of Life', the first three stanzas with the last two.)

It would be wrong to think, though, that MacDiarmid's talent never recovered from the violence he did to it in order to write *A Drunk Man*. True, there are no more lyrics like 'The Frightened Bride' and 'Wild Roses'. But their disappearance was probably inevitable anyway. Even as one turns from *Sangschaw* to *Penny Wheep* one sees the stance growing oblique, quizzical, even knowing; and 'Scunner', for instance, is a coarsening of 'The Frightened Bride'. There would be something wrong and retarded, or too complacent, about a poet nowadays who stayed lyrical all through.

In any case the more relaxed and expansive writing that MacDiarmid has mostly done over the last thirty years is not all like 'In the Slums of Glasgow'. A poem must be permitted to set its own pace; and to ask for language to be golden all through a poem is not to demand that every word be a full sovereign, nothing of smaller denominations. There must always be room for the small change. This is seldom understood; and a poem such as 'Direadh III' has been grossly underrated already, and will be again. It moves from a delighted but leisurely description of a particular scene 'near the summit of Sgurr Alasdair', through an extended Ruskinian simile between 'water-crowfoot leafage' and 'the Gaelic genius', into a brief sad diatribe against the modern world; then a description of a rock-pigeon recalls a line from Euripides and sparks off a comparison between the Greek spirit and the Scottish (the Chinese too – but this is gratuitous), and between MacDiarmid's service to Scotland and the Greek-inspired Hölderlin's to Germany; so back to the Gaelic genius compared now with 'quake grass'; and the poem concludes by identifying the poet's feeling for Scotland with his feeling for a loved woman. Here again it's easy to go wrong. Seeing the wayward progression, the abrupt transitions, the lines occasionally interlarded in Greek and German, the chopped-up prose of citations from academic authorities, one begins to think that this is a modernist poem like one of Pound's *Cantos*. And certainly there are things in common – MacDiarmid's political affiliations have become as ruinous to him as Pound's were to Pound, and they produce a more-than-Poundian silliness. But this is not really a 'modern' poem at all. The models for it are not in Pound, not even the Pound of the Pisan sequence. The poem is a meditation. To object to it that it 'rambles' is to miss the point entirely. In the rambling is all the beauty and the truth.

The precedents are in Romantic poetry. I think particularly of Wordsworth's lines, 'When to the Attractions of the Busy World', where not only is there the same pleasure in thinking 'Wherever will he go to next?' but also in Wordsworth's blank verse, as in the free verse of 'Direadh III', the full sum is made up entirely of coins of small denominations, very prosaic language. 'Direadh III' is prosaic where 'In the Slums of Glasgow' is prosy; there is all the difference in the world.

A poem like this, in fact, answers exactly (though on a small scale compared with the gigantic structures that MacDiarmid now envisages) to what the poet himself seems to be asking for in 'The Kind of Poetry I Want'. According to Edwin Morgan, writing very persuasively in *Hugh MacDiarmid: a Festschrift* (edited by K.R. Duval and Sydney Goodsir Smith), what MacDiarmid is demanding

> is a poetry which is highly organized in parts, but not prescriptively with regard to the whole. It is not so much an organism as a colony, a living and in one sense formless association of organisms which share a common experience. Shape and architectonics are not so important as the quick movements of the thought... As zoologists may argue whether a colony is an organism, critics may hesitate to say that the kind of *poetry* MacDiarmid wants is a kind of *poem*.

Perhaps Morgan would agree that such hesitation among critics is rather pointless, since for a hundred and fifty years they've been hesitating on just these grounds about some of the open-ended poems of Wordsworth, and indeed of other Romantics.

The happiest sort of Collected Poems is the volume which makes us feel how each new phase of the poet's life, though it may be less fruitful than what went before it, yet grows out of that earlier one as if inevitably, in a living rhythm which is apparent to hindsight though never predictable. None of the fifteen contributors to the *Festschrift* find that sort of organic inevitability in MacDiarmid's career. (Do we find it for that matter in Wordsworth's?) And in fact the *Festschrift* is good just because nearly every admiring essayist has to disentangle what he admires in MacDiarmid from much that he doesn't. Though he sometimes seems to boast, MacDiarmid has never spared himself, never stopped being restless. This is why the *Collected Poems* show an account that is still open. The crown may not yet be set on this life's work. If energy and seriousness could earn it, it has been earned already, many times over.

Postscript: Most admirers of MacDiarmid think better than I do, of *A Drunk Man Looks at the Thistle*. If I were to write on MacDiarmid now, I should want to dwell admiringly on a relatively late non-lyrical poem like 'On a Raised Beach'. I recall reading for this article, and composing it in my head, in a pavement café in Leghorn – the deliciousness of such aromas!

New Statesman, 10 August, 1962; reprinted with postscript in *The Poet in the Imaginary Museum*.

The Letters of MacDiarmid and Graves

The Letters of Hugh MacDiarmid, edited by Alan Bold (London: Hamish Hamilton, 1984).

Between Moon and Moon: Selected Letters of Robert Graves 1946–1972, edited by Paul O'Prey (London: Hutchinson, 1984).

For the rather few people nowadays who still believe that modernism was something that really happened to or in our poetry, something of which the energies are not yet spent, three names are commonly brought up to show that the modernist impetus survived in the generation after Pound: David Jones, Anglo-Welshman; Basil Bunting, Northumbrian Englishman; and Hugh MacDiarmid, Lowland Scot. The claim for Jones seems the weakest: it is advanced by Jones's admirers, not by the poet himself, who took no interest in the question, having other fish to fry; and unlike most modernists, Jones had no patience with prosody. The claim for Bunting is not contested, and seems incontestable. As for MacDiarmid, he certainly made the claim for himself, loudly. But as in other matters on which he declared himself, the loudness is itself suspect: he goes through some modernist motions, and contrives modernist surfaces, but in ways that can seem mechanical and programmatic, asking us to take the will for the deed. And he had not much more interest in prosody than David Jones.

Harvey Oxenhorn, in an admirably patient and respectful study,[1] points out MacDiarmid's 'need to provoke and convince', and remarks: 'As readers we are not much attuned these days to a verse of exhortation and overt opinion; where MacDiarmid's writing offers this it is closer in feeling to Victorian than to modern poetry.' One sees what he means; and certainly in its *symboliste* and immediately post-*symboliste* phases, modernism was at pains to purge poetry of Arnoldian or Browningesque exhortations. But by the time moderism threw up Pound's *Cantos* 'exhortation and overt opinion' were back with a vengeance; and most readers of the later Yeats will think that many of that poet's opinions are overt enough, and pressed upon us with sometimes strident emphasis. So

---

1 *Elemental Things: The Poetry of Hugh MacDiarmid* (Edinburgh, 1983).

I wouldn't agree that MacDiarmid's hectoring of his readers puts him out of the modernist camp. Indeed it now seems clear that, much as the modernists disliked being exhorted to have noble sentiments, they disliked as much or even more that other Victorian bequest, epitomised by Palgrave's Golden Treasury: the shrinking of all the poetic kinds into one exclusive or pre-eminent kind, the *lyric*. (Even now, or rather once again now, most readers seem to thing that 'poem' and 'lyric' mean the same thing.) Down this perspective MacDiarmid's career seems almost exemplary. I used to think, with many others, that two early collections of Lallans lyrics were the crown of MacDiarmid's poetry, from which everything that followed was a falling-off. Certainly that earliest work had a purity and a succinctness that the poet would never recover. But reading these letters, one cannot fail to be impressed by the firmness and clearsightedness with which he changed direction, the consistency with which MacDiarmid refused to remain a purely lyrical poet, and for reasons that followed the logic of modernism. One sees the same development not only in Pound but in Pasternak and in a later modernist like Czeslaw Milosz (who incidentally shares MacDiarmid's veneration for Leo Shestov). The development is inevitable for any poet who thinks that his calling imposes on him some social responsibility. The lyrist does not recognise that, and is glad not to have the burden of it; and his admirers are likely to think that poets less disarmingly winsome are taking too much on themselves.

We must all think so at times, of a polemicist so unflaggingly cocky and vehement as MacDiarmid. In public debate his manners and also his tactics were very rough indeed and not always candid, as this volume shows very clearly. As Harvey Oxenhorn says memorably, reminding us that MacDiarmid was both a Stalinist and a plagiarist, 'consistency may be the hobgoblin of small minds, but accountability is still the hallmark of complete ones.' And too often MacDiarmid did not hold himself accountable. Accordingly the case for the prosecution – as it has been presented with some heat by earlier reviewers, especially the Anglicised Scots among them – is up to a point irrefutable. On the other hand, it's surely true that a more civil writer could not have made equal impact on the public life of Scotland.

Another respect in which MacDiarmid was intransigently a modernist was his élitism. Nothing will more surprise readers who dip into this hefty volume of nine hundred pages, after little previous acquaintance with its author. And of course this is particularly piquant, and worth thinking about, coming from a position on the far Left, where genuflections to the masses, to the folk, to the common man are normally the order of the day. MacDiarmid as an impenitent Leninist will have none of that:

Homer, Plato, Plotinus, Catullus, Horace, and scores of others of whom 'the ordinary people' know nothing are nevertheless immortal.

'The ordinary people' do learn a little about some of the great figures in literature during their school years, but they do not read them afterwards. What they do read is for the most part beneath contempt...

All the great things in the arts and in the sciences have been the creation, very often 'against the current' (i.e. in the teeth not only of unutterable ignorance and indifference, but even of active hostility on the part of the hoi polloi), of a very small minority of people – a minority that is practically constant throughout the whole of history. It is that minority with which I am concerned. The opinions of the others do not matter a rap to me.

There speaks a man who had no formal education beyond secondary school, who survived into the age of the computer when school-children are lucky to learn even a little about any of 'the great figures in literature'. No modern British writer was less of an egalitarian; and often when MacDiarmid's contemporaries and juniors take issue with him on more defensible grounds, one suspects that what incurably rankles with them, underneath the plausible pretext, is the insistence on inequalities that cannot be argued away. This carries over into his literary judgements, and means that if you scratched his back, he was under no obligation to scratch yours; Edwin Morgan, Robert Garioch and Ian Hamilton Finlay are three Scottish poets whose work he dismisses where he might have been expected, if only for tactical reasons, to approve it. It is the same with Scottish literature of the past. MacDiarmid is almost alone among its formal and informal historians in never forgetting that, however purely and nobly patriotic an author, however scrupulously 'correct' in his choice of linguistic medium, nevertheless, as MacDiarmid asked with unwonted plaintiveness as early as 1921, 'Is not, in fact, the only criterion literary merit?' That some writing is meritorious *as literature*, and some other writing isn't, and that there are degrees of meritoriousness, is the one tenet of modernism which more than any other has made it imperative, in recent years, to declare that modernism is over and done with. Unfortunately, in this as in other areas, MacDiarmid's right principles are not backed up by, in Poundian phrase, 'a sufficient phalanx of particulars'. He had not read enough, never found enough time or patience, to check his intuitions against the evidence. Thus, whereas he rightly recognised in Norman MacCaig a Scottish poet who wrote better in English than others had done in braid Scots or Lallans, he could still in 1950 endorse Herbert Read's foolish and sweeping judgement: 'There is no great English poetry written by a Scotsman.' Had neither he nor Read ever looked into James Thomson's *Seasons*?

For much of MacDiarmid's life – certainly up to 1945, when he was already 53 – time and patience were just not available to him; in the starkest financial terms, they were what he could not afford. After that date one comes to think that they were not what he wanted anyway, that he would not have known what to do with them. In the hurly-burly of committees and political organisations and speaking engagements, it is clear that he left himself next to no time, not just for writing and revising, but for the mere preservation of what he had written already, even what he had published. He brags of how much he is in demand, not least in the Communist countries where he was trotted out as a Stalinist token-figure – in Cuba, China, Prague, East Berlin. We need look no further to understand, not only why his literary judgements were sound in principle but wrong in detail, but also why even the best of his later poems, though strongly and originally conceived, are deplorably and sometimes risibly rough-edged in the execution.

There is no doubt about Robert Graves: no modernist, he. And a lyrist almost exclusively, recognising in his capacity as poet no responsibility to society at all – at any rate, not in the years covered by this selection of letters. (The earlier ones came out as *In Broken Images* in 1982.) Alan Bold's index to the MacDiarmid volume has no entry for Graves, any more than Paul O'Prey's has for MacDiarmid. The two poets, though contemporaries, might have been inhabiting different planets. And yet the impression one gets from the two books is not dissimilar: both men were indefatigably productive; both were male chauvinists; both were naïvely – perhaps the word is 'touchingly' – gleeful at receiving international acclaim in their later years without much fastidiousness about where the acclaim came from, or at what price; and – surely the most telling resemblance – each of them, while declaring himself poet and claiming many privileges on that score, writes in his letters about anything rather than poetry. This is not quite fair to Graves, from whom we get two untypical letters – one to Alan Sillitoe, the other to Ruth Fainlight – of the sort that we might expect from a master instructing neophytes. To Sillitoe for example, in 1954:

> Your poem sounds good, holds together well, but the language has been taken a stage beyond common sense, and that I always regret. A poem should always be able to stand with a dictionary in its hand and swear: 'This is not anything else but this; see pages so and so.'
>
> Once you do violence to common sense there is a danger of ridicule: e.g. pillows raped beyond repair, sounds like the work of a big pimpled boy at a Reform School. And 'green' does not explain itself with music. 'Green' may mean frightening: as in Greek 'green fear'. Or it may mean 'fresh'; or it may mean *verde*, erotic.

This is neither modernist doctrine, nor anti-modernist; it concerns itself simply with the nuts and bolts of writing, whether in verse or prose, whether modernist or not. Lamentably, Graves always belittled this command and grasp that he had, though it is what saves his poetry even when the overt theme of that poetry will not stand up to rational scrutiny. Thus in 1964 he writes that he is 'talking at Oxford on verse craft as opposed to poetry'; and, more dismayingly: 'my view is that one can achieve a command of one's language by continually thinking about it at all historical levels and in all social gradations. But to write poetry one must *love* and keep one's spiritual integrity; and the miracle is beyond comment or explanation.'

Whatever one's reservations about deconstructionist or post-structuralist theorists, one must be grateful for their insistence that 'command of one's language', the weave of the verbal fabric, is all that is overtly *there* in any writer's work, as that on which to judge him. What the energies were which set him to writing in the first place – this cannot be determined, and for criticism it is an irrelevance. The energies may be fuelled by something as outlandish and rationally insupportable as Graves's notion of 'the Muse' (who for Graves in the period of these letters was successively embodied in four unbalanced or bewildered young women called respectively Margot, Laura, Cindy and Juli), or else as MacDiarmid's bizarre notion of 'the Gaelic genius, from its origin in Georgia to its modern expression in Scotland, Ireland, Wales, Cornwall, Galicia and the Pays Basque'. The self-evident rottenness of the timber that stokes the fire is beside the point: what matters is the fire, the heat of it and the light it throws. (Which is not to deny that in the case of poets better than either MacDiarmid or Graves we respect the soundness of the timber that is consumed to fire them.)

A name that crops up in both sets of letters is that of John Wain. Wain in 1962 wrote to the *Guardian* about MacDiarmid: 'He is simultaneously truculent (to Whitehall) and fawning (to Moscow). He simultaneously praises some hog-wash written by a Government hack in Budapest and thumbs his nose at the Americans who print his work. Simultaneously the bold border-reiver and the flunkey of international communism.' And in 1960 Wain, while professing great admiration for Graves's poetry, found his criticism 'aggressive and unbalanced, often showing a repulsive ungenerosity about poets he happens not to enjoy'. In response, whereas MacDiarmid could only bluster, Graves both in public and private was suave, yet pointed and probing. But Wain was surely right in both cases. Graves's criticism has been mischievous, in a way that is quite unappealing. Rather than cite his outrageous treatment of Yeats and Pound in his Cambridge lectures, or of Virgil in his lectures at Oxford, one thinks rather of a send-up of Wordsworth's 'The Solitary Reaper' in the volume called *Steps*. This was first an address to a women's college in America, and as one reads it one sees all too clearly how rapturously the co-eds must have responded to one cheap shot after another; whatever else it was, the occasion was plainly not educational. Similarly with MacDiarmid... the fact that he rejoined the Communist Party in 1956 when hundreds were leaving it because of the suppression of the Hungarians is not necessarily the first thing one thinks of when the poet is named, certainly not the first and last thing, but it's something to be remembered all the same. And it's not enough to object to Wain's language that it is intemperate and vulgarly self-righteous; in both cases the charge is just, and it sticks or it ought to stick. What neither of the older poets seem to have recognised was that Wain's was, if not the voice of posterity, the voice of the immediate future – a future that would hold poets accountable, would deny them that privileged irresponsibility which in their different ways both Graves and MacDiarmid took for granted and indulged, as if it were a right that could not be denied them once they had declared their vocation.

In the Pity

When Yeats in 1936 excluded Wilfred Owen from the *Oxford Book of Modern Verse*, there was a storm of protest. Now when a Professor from West Virginia painstakingly and at length endorses Yeats's verdict, no one complains.[1] I find this depressing. 'The poetry is in the pity,' said Owen. And Yeats was right: that is not the place for poetry to be, or not so exclusively. Owen was too categorical, and British poetry since has suffered for it. It has been, and it is still, too humanitarian to be altogether human. But failure on these terms is almost more honourable than success; it was certainly more honourable for Owen, writing as and when he did. Professor Johnston's sub-title, 'A Study in the Evolution of Lyric and Narrative Form', from this point of view seems comically irrelevant, even to those of us who are professional students of literature, at least if we are British. There were war-poets writing in German, in French, in Italian, in Russian; and it would have done no harm for Professor Johnston to remind himself of this. And there are Canadian and American poets in Brian Gardner's new anthology,[2] as well as Yeats himself, with 'An Irish Airman Foresees his Death'. But among English-speakers the experience of the Flanders trenches was overwhelmingly a British experience, and was felt to be so at the time. In fact, the poems themselves characteristically appeal to 'England' and 'the English', and it's not clear in every case that England means Britain, and English British. At any rate, this writing which Johnston deals with as a case in the evolution of *genre* can be seen, and I think must be seen by the British reader, as documenting a crisis in the life of this nation. The British imagination, it may be, has never to this day recovered from the shock of Passchendaele; and the damage done to it there puts the British writer out of step with the American, not just Graves out of step with Eliot, but at the present day Larkin and Hughes out of step with Charles Olson and William Stafford.

Yeats the Irishman did not think like this, nor does the American Johnston. Johnston would have to deny the thesis in any case, because he believes there is one work in which a British imagination comprehended

---

1   John H. Johnston, *English Poetry of the First World War* (Princeton: Princeton University Press, 1964).
2   *Up to the Line of Death*, edited by Brian Gardner (London: Methuen, 1964).

and mastered the Flanders experience, and this is David Jones's *In Parenthesis*, written in 1937, which draws on the precedent of *The Waste Land* and so heals the breach between British and American. It was high time that such claims were made for *In Parenthesis*, but even so Jones's book may still be the exception which proves the rule – the rule that since 1917 the British imagination has been as if were cauterised, numbed to large sectors of experience.

These are the sectors which Johnston would label epic and tragic. For his argument is that trench-warfare demanded, if it was to be comprehended in poetry, some form other than lyric, though lyric was all that the poets of the trenches could command. This means that Johnston is not after all of one mind with Yeats. For Yeats's objection to Owen was quite bluntly that Owen wrote badly. He said he considered him 'unworthy of the poets' corner of a country newspaper'. And he exhorted Dorothy Wellesley to 'look at the selection in Faber's Anthology – he calls poets "bards", a girl a "maid" and talks about "Titanic wars".' Yeats is simple-minded here, because there are surely contexts in which 'bard' for 'poet', and 'maid' for 'girl', are perfectly acceptable expressions and in fact better than any others. One of the best things in Johnston's book is the persuasive case he makes for the war-poems of Blunden, whose diction is characteristically very choice and elaborate and 'poetical'. This doesn't help Owen, however. Blunden maintains decorum and is consistent within his often stilted conventions, as Owen is not. Owen *does* write badly, he just is not skilful nor resourceful enough to do justice to his own conceptions:

> Kindness of wooed and wooer
> Seems shame to their love pure.
> O love, your eyes lose lure
>   When I behold eyes blinded in my stead!

That sequence of rhymes – *wooer, pyeur, luer* – is excruciating. And if this is true of Owen, what shall we say of Rosenberg? Even Johnston, who seldom stoops to notice these niceties and nastinesses of wording, is worried about whether Rosenberg's 'Dead Man's Dump' is not just a sheet of memoranda for a poem that never got written.

But even if Yeats is thus proved right, what follows? That 'Dead Man's Dump', and Owen's 'Greater Love', ought to be forgotten? They will not be. If we are moved when we read them, far more moved (this is certainly my own case) than by Yeats's 'Irish Airman', ought we to be ashamed? Certainly as a poem in any strict sense 'Dead Man's Dump' is indefensible. But the truth is surely that for the British reader these pieces by Rosenberg and Owen are not poems at all, but something less than that and more; they are first-hand and faithful witnesses to a moment in the national destiny. Or if that sounds chauvinistic, think of them as high-water marks in the national psychology. In Owen's 'Anthem for Doomed Youth' an Englishman is brought to the point where, like Ivan Karamazov, he 'returns God the ticket'. The nightmare perspectives of Dostoievskyan psychology, which in 1880 had seemed outside the range of British experience, by 1917 are being verified in that experience. And these gulfs and vistas are experienced not vicariously, not in the imagination of a novelist, but directly: it is as if the poems were written by Ivan Karamazov, and no wonder if Karamazov is not so good a novelist as Dostoievsky. It is part of the pathos and the meaning of Owen and Rosenberg that they should be amateurs – amateur soldiers but amateur poets too, and amateurs not as Robert Gregory was ('our Sidney and our perfect man,' said Yeats of that Irish airman), but in a sense that has everything to do with the amateurish.

So too with Sassoon:

> The House is crammed: tier beyond tier they grin
> And cackle at the Show, while prancing ranks
> Of harlots shrill the chorus, drunk with din;
> 'We're sure the Kaiser loves our dear old Tanks!'
>
> I'd like to see a Tank come down the stalls,
> Lurching to rag-time tunes, or 'Home, sweet Home',
> And there'd be no more jokes in Music-halls
> To mock the riddled corpses round Bapaume.

Any beginner can see that calling chorus-girls 'harlots' loses all the actuality of them as girls and gets nothing in return except the scandalized huffing and puffing of some Mrs Grundy alderman; and he can see that having the line-break between 'grin' and 'cackle' only shows up how little 'cackle' has to add. But for heaven's sake, what does it matter? Sassoon's eight lines are amateurish writing – who ever thought otherwise? The value of the eight lines, for a British reader, has really nothing to do with their very dubious status as poetic art.

The professional of that generation was Blunden. Earlier it had been Brooke. And if Brooke had not existed, it would have been necessary to invent him. For without Rupert Brooke as their foil, both Owen and Sassoon would shrink; to the poetry of the trenches considered as recording a moment in the national destiny, Brooke's 'If I should die' weighs equal with 'Strange Meeting'. Grenfell's 'Into Battle' will not do instead of Brooke's sonnet, nor will Sorley's 'All the hills and vales along', which alone among the poems of the early years can bear up under our hindsight. For Grenfell and Sorley are both amateurish beside Brooke; and just as Sassoon and Owen need to be amateurish if they are to keep their legendary pathos, so Brooke on the other hand has to be, in every corrupted suavity of style as well as in all we know of his biography, the professional master of language, the expensively schooled rhetorician equipped as it must have seemed completely against all eventualities that Edwardian England could conceive of.

The myth must be symmetrical. It must be a golden boy who fails. So it is as wide of the mark to see Brooke as a bad, a hollow and dishonest and heartless poet, as it is to pretend that Owen, because he rhymed badly and knew it and took the sensible precaution of allowing himself half-rhyme, was by that token an artistic innovator who transformed and renewed the medium for himself and others. 'Above all,' said Owen, 'I am not concerned with Poetry.' And Johnston does not convince me that the poetry which Owen here disowned was 'the thoughtless pursuit of beauty', or else that Brookean poetry which he had begun by writing himself. Owen means, surely, that if he is to be set up against Rupert Brooke, it is not as one kind of poet against another kind (as it might be, the clumsily honest against the brilliantly hollow), but as the English soldier of 1917 against his own still illusioned self, the English soldier of 1914. It is a quarrel with history, or with God, but it is a very private quarrel, having to do with one generation in one nation at one very precisely specified time.

Johnston does not see the trenches poets in this way, and there is no reason why he should. For us as British readers it is salutary to be made to realize what a specially insular and self-regarding attitude we have to these poets, and how impossible it is for others to share our assumptions. In particular we need to have it brought home to us how, so long as the poetry is in the pity, it cannot be tragic poetry. But in fact Professor Johnston has rather little to say of tragedy: what he misses in the trenches poets is less the tragic note than the note of epic. *The Battle of Maldon* is his example of what he means by an epic poem. And it is just as well that we have this example, otherwise we might be thinking rather of something like 'Sohrab and Rustum'. For there is a distinctly high-Victorian ring, an inflection of Arnold or Pater, about the terms in which the epic is commended to us: its breadth and harmony, its proportion and repose-fulness or at least its composure – these are the qualities which Johnston looks for in vain until he gets to David Jones.

In Parenthesis, he suggests, is modern epic; and therefore necessarily superior to the poems written between 1914 and 1918, all lyrics of various kinds. The trouble is that we get no definition of modern epic. It seems that it will be narrative; and yet one of the few modern poems which explicitly offers itself as epic, Pound's *Cantos*, is not narrative at all. Nor is *Y Gododdin*, the ancient Welsh poem which stands behind *In Parenthesis*. Johnston concedes that *Y Gododdin* 'may not be epic poetry in the formal sense' (what other sense can the word have?) 'but it communicates the heroic spirit nearly as well as any epic narrative'. It is that 'heroic spirit' that gives the game away. The truth is that Professor

Johnston just wants to like war and warfare more than Owen and Sassoon will permit. There is nothing more subtle than that at stake when he deplores in them the lack of the heroic spirit. There could be no better testimony to the continuing sharpness and relevance of these poems, Sassoon's in particular, than the signs of how they have needled one reader into 350 pages of muffled expostulation, so as to argue himself out of accepting what they incontrovertibly assert.

New Statesman, 28 August 1964.

David Jones in his Letters

1

Dai Greatcoat: A Self-Portrait of David Jones in his Letters, edited by René Hague (London: Faber and Faber, 1980).
Introducing David Jones: A Selection of his Writings, edited by John Matthias (London: Faber and Faber, 1980).

In 1934 David Jones, suffering from his first 'nervous breakdown', was carried off on a sea-voyage to Egypt by his friend Tom Burns. The cure worked; even the cautiously hypochondriac Jones would admit later that the trip 'had done me a great deal of good', though (he was in a hurry to say) he was 'still not up to much'. From Cairo Jones went by air to Lydda and by car to Jerusalem, where his old friend and mentor Eric Gill was at work on commissioned sculptures. Gill 'was greatly annoyed that David should stay indoors reading *Barchester Towers*'. More than thirty years later, in a letter to Saunders Lewis, Jones agreed that 'I hardly moved out of the Holy City, but used to watch from my window which faced south…' In the same letter this famous poet of Roman Christendom confessed, 'I should never have gone to Palestine off my own bat, for I hate what our American friends call "going places".' More to the point than the dated and nervous reference to 'our American friends' is what Jones did vividly recall from that Jerusalem visit:

> But occasionally I saw either from my window or in mooching around, a squad of these figures that seen singly evoked comparisons of twenty years back, in the Nord or the Pas de Calais or the Somme. But now in their full parade rig, the light khaki drill shirts, the bronzed arms bare from above the elbow to the wrist and pale khaki shorts leaving equally bronzed legs bare from above the knee to the brief ankle socks, the feet in heavy field-service hob-nailed boots, but above all the riot shields aligned to cover the left side and in each right fist the haft-grip of a stout baton, evoked not the familiar things of less than two decades back, but rather of two millennia close on, and the ring of the hob-nailed service boots on the stone sets and the sharp commands – so they were a section from the Antonia, up for duties in

Hierosolyma after all!

And as the days and weeks passed this analogy I would say increased, but became established – there was a good deal else to think on. I did go to Bethlehem, which is, or *then was*, very beautiful.

The contrast between Bethlehem ('very beautiful') and the squad of British soldiers ('...the shirts... the bronzed arms... the brief ankle socks, the feet... the left side... each right fist...') can leave us in little doubt which spectacle had registered on Jones more compellingly. And now that hardly any veterans of the Western Front survive, what is one to say to the not excessively tender-minded reader who should protest indignantly that he doesn't know which alarms him more – the insularity, or the militarism? All one can tell him surely is to read *In Parenthesis*.

Or rather, since after more than forty years Jones's procedures in that book are still caviare to the general (not that there's much excuse for that), the new reader should start with the three extended and excellently chosen passages in John Matthias's selection – Part 3 and excerpts from Parts 4 and 7. If after reading the last of these in particular he does not understand the quality of Jones's loyalty to the infantrymen who died beside him in Mametz Wood in 1916, and his admiration for the real and time-honoured *culture* which bound them together in the trenches, the reader can only be abandoned to an arid future among 'isms' – colonialism, nationalism, militarism. *In Parenthesis* is more moving, at once harrowing and inspiring, on each new reading; and the artistry of it – in particular the welding together of astonishingly vivid recollection with daring but never irresponsible invention – is each time more impressive. (We are not called on to decide whether it is or is not a poem; it is at any rate a magnificent feat of language.)

Thus all we need is a modicum of historical imagination to distinguish Jones's ardour about British soldiers in Jerusalem from something like Max Beerbohm's living forty-five years in Italy without learning Italian. ('One may be amused,' said W.H. Auden, 'but not very.')

Still, without that act of imagination there may seem to be common ground, as also between either of these cases and Union Jacks painted on the faces of football fans in Turin who have to be dispersed by tear-gas when England's opponents score an equalizing goal. And that is something so very ugly that Jones must be cleared of any association with it, more particularly because he told Saunders Lewis that from this unsought-for visit to the Holy Land he derived not only *The Anathemata* but also the best part of 'The Tribune's Visitation' and 'The Tutelar of the Place' (both in John Matthias's selection), and such other late pieces as 'The Wall', 'The Fatigue' and 'The Dream of Private Clitus'. All of these have as much in common with *In Parenthesis* as with *The Anathemata* or with each other: and insularity (though not nationalism) is unashamedly the burden of all of them, in a way not lessened but in fact intensified by the identification of British soldiers with Roman legionaries.

There is a special reason why this must be insisted on. Because in all or most of these pieces he juxtaposed Latin and Welsh with English (being conversant, as he admitted frankly, with neither of these foreign languages, nor with any other), David Jones has been marshalled into the ranks of an allegedly cosmopolitan or 'international' tradition in English writing, supposedly at odds with a 'native' or insular tradition – whereas it makes more sense to say that on the contrary he was insular to a degree unequalled in his own generation or since. Indeed his insularity is so extreme, so literal (*insula* – 'this island', as he says many times), and adhered to so passionately, that it takes on an authentic grandeur. It was at all events quite unforced and unaffected, and carried through into his epistolary vocabulary which is, I suppose we must think, always the vocabulary of the regimental lines: 'I can't work: it's a fair sod: the whole thing's a monumental bollux, a first-class buggeration.' The contrast between this and the very special but effective terminology which Jones laboured into printed prose (as in the Preface to *The Anathemata*, given almost in full by Matthias), or more strikingly between 'bollux' and the diaphanous delicacy of his loveliest pictures, is piquant.

And this piquancy is everywhere in René Hague's affectionate and exceptionally honest memoir. With such friends, who needs enemies? No, the overworked catch-phrase doesn't fit. For precisely by seeing and saying in advance what the unsympathetic reader might come up with on his own (for instance, 'it would be unkind, maybe, to say that he was lazy and spoilt – let us say, "constructively inactive" and "joyfully served"'), René Hague persuades us, as a more circumspect biographer couldn't, that his subject was a genuine 'original'. The question that arises, which he understandably doesn't envisage or answer, is whether the unstinted assistance that he and Tom Burns and Harman Grisewood and others gave to this original wasn't such as to push him into ever more damaging and constricting idiosyncrasy. To raise that question would be to open up a vast and long overdue enquiry into patronage of the arts and of artists, and into that persisting sub-Romantic image of the artist as 'ineffectual angel' on which all such patronage, whether private or public and astonishingly generous as it often is, nowadays seems to be based. It's a harsh thing to suggest; but it's at least possible that David Jones would have been a better artist, at all events a better *writer*, if his self-denying patrons had not exerted themselves so consistently to cushion him from the economic and ideological realities of the world he was living in.

Jones himself, unlike many artists of equal or greater stature, did have an ideology, and one that was no worse for being home-made. Indeed, in the perspective of millennia to which his imagination had habituated itself by 1940, Jones's ideology or 'philosophy of history' is bleakly impressive, even persuasive; and one fears that in certain classrooms up and down the English-speaking world students are at this moment deciphering *The Anathemata* so as to carry away from it, as its 'real meaning', Jones's philosophy. But as in so many similar cases, romping up and down the millennia did not yield any or much understanding of what was happening year by year; and even René Hague is constrained to withhold some of the documents that show how widely Jones's understanding of 1938 and 1939 diverged from what currently received wisdom holds to be the truth about those years.

If we do not read *The Anathemata* for its message, what can we say of it? One thing that is seldom or never said is that much of it is brutally cacophonous. Did any one ever want to read aloud any page of it? Because Jones has been misread as an 'internationalist' (at one time *The Anathemata* was thought to be like Pound's *Cantos*, which Jones had never read), some have been led to compare him with Basil Bunting. And indeed Bunting and Jones have something in common: outside of their writing both seem to have trusted demotic English to say things that it is not capable of saying with any nicety. But whatever else may be wrong with Bunting's poetry, his ear has always been true; and those who hear his verse as cacophonous are doubtless, as he has always maintained, hearing his Northumbrian English with a Southron ear. Nothing like this can be claimed for Jones: his was a Home Counties ear, and his experiments in Cockney or Anglo-Welsh speech are to be understood as divagations from that norm.

Reading *The Anathemata* in that way, one has to say that its cadences are at best uninteresting, at their frequent worst (usually with interlardings of Latin and Welsh) they are jaw-breaking. Nothing is more instructive in this respect than a 1945 report to Harman Grisewood on a dinner with W.F. Jackson Knight:

> These chaps are awfully interested in the metre thing, aren't they? – and on what you contrive with vowels and consonants and all that (things you don't know you've done except that it seemed the only way to do it to make it tolerable and to say what you meant).

'Awfully interested in the metre thing' was what David Jones most awfully wasn't; and that's all right so long as your ear is good enough. But his ear, we must conclude, wasn't:

At these Nocturns the hebdomadary
is apt to be invested for five hundred thousand weeks.
Intunes the dog:
> *Benedicite ignis…*
Cantor Notus and Favonius with all their south-aisled numina:

> *con flora cálida*

> *mit warmer Fauna*
> The Respond is with the Bear:
> > *Benedicite frigus…*
> Super-pellissed, stalled in crystallos, from the gospel-side, choir all
> the boreal schola
> > *mit kalter Flora*
> > *con fauna fría*

Never mind what it means: what does it sound like? Surely it sounds like
bedlam. 'Cantor Notus and Favonius with all their south-aisled numina'
– to incorporate a line like that in a meaningful melodic progression is not
impossible, but would require an exceptionally well-schooled and sensitive ear. What Jones does with it, or fails to do, seems to show not just
that he hasn't such an ear, but that he has failed even to realize how such
a faculty is possible, or why it is necessary. Geoffrey Hill's unmetred
Mercian Hymns, we may well think, have since taken over what is viable
in this style of *The Anathemata*, and made sense of it for the ear as well as
the intelligence. And yet Jones insisted that *the Anathemata* was to be read
aloud:

> I intend what I have written to be said. While marks of punctuation,
> breaks of line, lengths of line, grouping of words or sentences and vari-
> ations of spacing are visual contrivances, they have here an aural and
> oral intention. You can't get the intended meaning unless you hear the
> sound and you can't get the sound unless you observe the score: and
> pause-marks on a score are of particular importance.

The only possible response to this is: Well of course! And although it is
sadly true, now as when *The Anathemata* was first published, that readers
need to be instructed in such rudiments as these, one cannot escape the
suspicion that the author's own understanding of these matters was not
much less rudimentary. How far the subtleties, not just of skilled metrical
writing, but of accomplished free verse also, go beyond this rough-and-
ready delimitation of cadences between 'pausemarks'! And 'rough-and-
ready' seems apt enough for the melodic quality of many pages of *The
Anathemata* and of others of the later works:

> Plotting his course by the North Drift route that streams him
> warm to Hordaland
> > to Noroway o'er his faem
> over the gurly brim in his mere-hengest
> > (he's stepped the Yggdrasil for mast!)
> To the Horder's moot in Norvegia
> > over the darkening mere-flood
> on a Gwener-Frigdaeg noon.

(To add a bit *more*

to his old *mabinogion?*

Will he Latin that *too*

to get some Passion into his Infancy?

By the Mabon!! he will

when he runes the Croglith,

in all the white bangors

of the islands of the sea

where there is salt

on the Stone within the *pared*.)

When we have studied how to get our tongues around 'Gwener-Frigdaeg' and 'the Mabon' and 'the *pared*', what does it profit us? Surely the excitably over-emphatic signals that Jones makes to us – italics, single and double exclamation marks – in effect concede his inability to direct intonation and tone by any more refined means. John Matthias in his introduction gives from 'The Wall' an example of what he calls 'embroidery of sound'; and certainly in the lines he quotes there is some contriving of 'vowels and consonants and all that'. But even here the syntax, so invaluable an aid to melody in the hands of a master, is simply and monotonously that of the rhetorical question, which Jones in general falls back upon very often.

It is the more refreshing to turn, among the late pieces, to 'The Tutelar of the Place', where the speaker no longer exclaims and nudges but is declarative, oracular. Here Jones once again speaks with unflurried authority of the survivor, the 'one who was there'. Perhaps because of this, and of the more driving declarative syntax which it makes possible (the piece itself speaks of those 'who seek hidden grammar to give back anathema its first benignity') *The Tutelar of the Place*, like *In Parenthesis*, is rewarding to read aloud. And it announces at the very start, with great conviction, Jones's central theme, insularity.

Tellus of the myriad names answers to but one name: From this tump she answers Jac o' the Tump only if he call Great-Jill-of-the-tump-that-bare-me, not if he cry by some new fangle moder of far gentes over the flud, fer-goddes, name from anaphora of far folk wont woo her; she's a rare one for locality.

If on the one hand this is the voice of an insular sensibility that preferred Langland to Dante, on the other hand this insularity, recognizing Church-Latin and Brythonic Welsh as tongues of the *insula* along with middle-English, is more notable for what it disconcertingly invites in than what it comfortably shuts out.

Times Literary Supplement, 22 August 1980.

2

Among the several better than topical things that we were able to secure for *PN Review* 22 were John Matthias's transcriptions of letters from David Jones to Jim Ede of Kettle's Yard, Cambridge. The materials that Matthias excerpted for us undoubtedly and very valuably fill out and qualify the skilfully tailored versions of Jones that the late René Hague presented in his *Dai Greatcoat*, which was approvingly reviewed by Matthias in the same issue. Particularly significant from one point of view is what Jones wrote to Ede some time in 1933:

> ... The Engl. Bible, Milton, the Puritan Revolution, the Jacobeans, Pope – anything you like– 'Ann' civilization, the whole 18th Cent business, God knows are England enough – but a great foreign influence seems to have all but strangled the particular quality we seem to all recognize electric from the remote past – Celtic-Anglo-Saxon – to make you weep in the early middle age...

All of which – inchoate punctuation and all (indeed, the inability or reluctance to punctuate is very significant) – chimes in, so some of us will think, with Jones's response, nine years later to Henry Moore's drawings of sleepers in the underground air-raid shelters: 'the *best* things he's ever done. God be praised! They are somehow "romantic" in the true sense. English artists are "Romantic" or nothing – I'm sure of that...'. 'Romantic', first without capital R but then with it, in both cases put between quotation-marks and qualified by the all-purpose disclaimers, 'somehow' and 'in the true sense' – this is all of a piece with, in the earlier letter, 'anything you like' and 'the whole 18th Cent business', and with the punctuation. There is no way for anyone to engage, for the purpose of serious consideration, with concepts and perspectives defined so cloudily, and no sooner advanced than they are backed away from. To make doubly sure that he can never be brought to account for the highly tendentious and implausible and unsupported view of the English tradition that none the less he is proposing, Jones hurries to allow in the letter of 1933 that all he writes of the English Bible, Milton and eighteenth-century English art is 'ill-put, open to every wrong interpretation... & not to be taken at all literally'. If H.S. Ede was not to take these remarks 'literally', then how was he to take them? And how are *we* to take them, now that they have become public property?

Jones's position is as impregnable, now when he posthumously addresses us all, as it was in life when he addressed Jim Ede. We can take his remarks *either* as the oracular and thus unchallengeable pronouncements of eccentric genius, *or else* as the endearingly muddle-headed bumblings of a lonely naïf unable to cope on level terms with 'you clever chaps'. In the one way or the other Jones can always slip out from whatever net we try to cast over him. Any question we might put to him would have to begin: 'Do you *really* mean to say that...' (for instance that the King James Bible is less 'English' than the Vulgate)? And the situation has been rigged so that anyone who puts such a question is a pernickety pedant, or an obtuse philistine, or both of those unlovely characters rolled into one.

René Hague's portrait, though it was meant to be (and is) a tribute, consistently shows Jones, certainly in his life and often in his art, getting mileage out of this notion that the artist has the right to be muddle-headed, muzzy and ineffectual so long as he is strenuously well-intentioned. And yet David Jones was not a charlatan. Moreover his neurasthenia, though it remains mysterious, was undoubtedly real: and it explains or excuses a great deal. So it seems more charitable to take him as a representative rather than extreme case of how the British artist responds to what the British public expects of him; in particular what it expects of him *intellectually*. That public does not expect of him, indeed it is positively affronted when it finds in him, any capacity for systematic or rigorous thought about what he is doing, and how it relates to what has been done along the same lines in the past. The puerility of Jones the poet's reflections about metre (they can be found in *Dai Greatcoat*) is only one instance out of many. In common talk about the arts, the frequently expressed hostility to 'the academic' is in many ways and on many grounds justified; but too often it masks this at once protective and condescending conviction that the true artist is, when it comes to intellectual formulation and explanation, a more or less winsome *child*. It was not a child who wrote 'The Tutelar of the Place' or *Epoch and Artist*. But there ought to be a way of recognizing these as moving and tough-minded achievements while yet acknowledging that the man who wrote them also wrote things that are silly and irresponsible. Discrimination – between the places where an artist lives up to his capacities, and those where he doesn't – is a duty laid on all of us, which few of us measure up to. But in the case of writers like David Jones we have to acknowledge the more dispiriting possibility that a poetic writer may live up to his responsibilities as a writer even as he falls short of his responsibilities as a man of letters.

Editorial, *PN Review* 24, 8: 4 (Autumn 1981).

Ivor Gurney's Letters

Ivor Gurney, *Collected Letters*, edited by R.K.R. Thornton (Manchester: MidNAG and Carcanet, 1991).

In 1983 R.K.R. Thornton published a selection of what he called *Gurney's War Letters*; there were 150 of them. Now in the *Collected Letters* ('Collected', be it noted, but not yet nor perhaps ever 'Complete'), he gives us 470. And what a difference it makes!

The earlier collection was poignant and touching, but a lot of the poignancy had to do with our sense that Gurney, however appealing, could never be more than a marginal case, an offbeat enthusiasm for a few people. But it looks as if Thornton and his risk-taking provincial publishers have been heartened, as well they might be, by the devoted and widespread following that has rallied to Gurney in the past few years. If so, *War Letters* was a trial balloon for what we now have: a body of letters that challenges comparison with those of John Keats, surely the supreme example in English of letters written not by a writer but specifically, even remorselessly, by a poet. (A musician, too, of course, but that's another story.)

This is an audacious claim to make, but Gurney even *sounds* like Keats:

> In winter when the trees are naked, and frost binds all moist things with iron, and breath goes strangely up in vapour – then who goes out from the warm neighbourly comforting firelight and stands in mere starlight and earthy gloom, what a continual surprise, what a revelation of unknown purpose is his who turns his eyes upwards and sees that majestical roof fretted with golden fire! It is a strong assurance to man, that his mind, confronted with the sight of all those worlds, some of them thought to be dead, many dying, as even this our own; that his mind, I say, though humble before these unintelligible mysteries is exalted with an uprushing or fierce and tender joy, and strangely, of a pride in God's Handiwork, as if a private should view his Chief Commander's handiwork or a molecule take pleasure in the soft fantastic imagery on English autumn trees.

Such eloquence, so shamelessly striking the Shakespearian note, is for us highly suspect; and we are relieved when Gurney, in this too like

Keats, appends a humorously deflating parenthesis: ('Copyright in USA'). Even so, remembering that this was written in 1915 by an infantryman in training, we can be forgiven for recalling Philip Larkin's poem about the year 1914: 'Never such innocence, / Never before or since, / ...Never such innocence again'. For it is true that such a passage seems nearer to 1820 than to anything we might find, or would tolerate, in 1991.

But Larkin's poem, though it articulates a sentiment we all must feel and need not be ashamed of, rests on an assumption that is really very dubious. The formula 'Never again would...' is not borne out by unprejudiced experience, nor by scrutiny of the historical record. Like it or not (and one may deplore it quite indignantly), structures of thought and feeling are seldom if ever conclusively exploded by historical events. The Keatsian, or for that matter the Shelleyan, approaches to experience perhaps ought to have been ruled out by the experience of the Flanders trenches; but the eager response to Gurney in recent years is only one piece of evidence that the Keatsian eloquence, in verse and prose, is still acceptable to people who have not wholly disregarded the history of the past eighty years. The tone and substance of current dispatches from the Gulf war may prompt the reflection 'We never learn'; but also, with a different inflection, 'Things never change'.

Gurney's poems and letters are not centrally concerned with these matters. A patriot sure enough, though an obsessively *local* one, as a Gloucester man serving with the Gloucesters, Gurney's enlistment for what turned out to be a long and atrocious spell on the Western Front was for him, as these letters make clearer than ever before, part of a private bargain: he would endure what the Army and the enemy's army could throw at him, to cure by those drastic means the physical and mental debilities that otherwise, he rightly judged, would prevent his achieving in poetry and music what he had in him to achieve. The pity is that, though he manfully kept his side of the bargain, the other party did not: when the war was over, his afflictions returned to visit him more grievously than ever. Though Gurney's best poems were written after he was demobbed, the eighty pages that Thornton gives to the years 1919–1922 are, towards the end, quite horrifying; one is thankful to be spared the letters from the asylum through fifteen years thereafter. Michael Hurd's *Ordeal of Ivor Gurney* (1978) gives examples of those.

Thus, what did for Gurney wasn't Kaiser Bill, nor Kitchener nor Earl Haig. Nor was it the English class system, that sent him into the world (as it had sent Keats a century before) from near the bottom of the social pile. We try in vain to convict history. Like Keats's tuberculosis, Gurney's complicated disability – it still resists diagnosis, apparently – was a fate visited on him from outside history. He was doomed, as characters in Hardy are doomed.

And yet Gurney resisted Hardy's bleakness, acknowledged his greatness only reluctantly. This can be seen by checking the entry for Hardy in Thornton's index, which is as careful and reliable as the rest of his never excessive editorial apparatus. The entries under Milton and Wordsworth tell the same story: Gurney was determined to be sanguine and affirmative. To his correspondents, even when he shares with them only the memory of modest domestic vivacities, he is always heartening, always *perky*. When his circumstances, even his temperament, prompt him to less sunny sentiments, he will not listen to such promptings. A really merciless diagnosis of his case might say it was this that broke him: his determination always to look on the bright side, in the face of the accumulating evidence to the contrary.

Not many readers will want to read this volume through from first to last. Dip into it where you will, and read on for a few pages, you experience tragedy and tragic heroism – not on the classic or Shakespearian pattern, but authentic and disorienting. This is a document that only the heartless can ignore.

Independent on Sunday, 17 February 1991.

As Deep as England

Ted Hughes, *Woduo* (London: Faber and Faber, 1967).

In his 'Mayday on Holderness' Ted Hughes wrote of the North Sea:

> Beneath it
> Smoulder the wars: to heart-beats, bomb, bayonet.
> 'Mother, Mother!' cries the pierced helmet.
> Cordite oozings of Gallipoli,
>
> Curded to beastings, broached my palate,
> The expressionless gaze of the leopard,
> The coils of the sleeping anaconda,
> The nightlong frenzy of shrews.

'Beastings' – the NED knows no such word. But it knows of 'beastlings', a variant of 'beestings'. And 'beestings' or 'beest' is 'the first milk drawn from a mammal, especially a cow, after parturition'. 'Beestings' means also a disease caused by imbibing beest. Hughes's word draws on all these meanings, and adds another he has made for himself – the bestiary habit of his imagination, which makes poem after poem about wolves, otters, pigs, horses, pike, crabs, rats.

It is alarming to find a poet who knows so exactly what he is up to. And some of the poems are too deliberate, Parnassian. They smack of Leconte de Lisle. And very splendid too, parnassianism at that level: if we're going to have anthologies, let the anthology pieces be sumptuous. But in others the whiff of cordite comes through. In 'Pike', for instance:

> A pond I fished, fifty yards across,
> Whose lilies and muscular tench
> Had outlasted every visible stone
> Of the monastery that planted them –
>
> Stilled legendary depth:
> It was as deep as England.

England expects – what? An efficient cruelty equal to the pike's? It was what she expected at Gallipoli. It's clear that Hughes's pike and horses are not in the poems for their own sake, but as 'stand-ins' for something psychological. What's not noticed is that the psychology is not just personal, but national.

And so the generous appreciation of Hughes by A.E. Dyson as early as 1959 (in the *Critical Quarterly*, when Dyson had before him only the first collection, *The Hawk in the Rain*) went far astray when it suggested that Hughes wrote of the First World War rather than the Second only because trench warfare belongs to 'the pre-hydrogen age, when personal heroism was still of merit in the scheme of things'. And Dyson was wrong again when he remarked in Hughes's work 'the absence of compassion, anger, humility, nostalgia, disgust, and the other attitudes belonging to the perspectives of time'. All of these attitudes, even nostalgia (notably in 'The Retired Colonel' and the admirable 'Dick Straightup' – both from *Lupercal*), have appeared in Hughes's later work, sometimes to momentous effect. And in *Wodwo*, which includes stories and a play as well as poems, compassion towards beasts appears in a way to gladden the RSPCA.

In *Wodwo*, the point about 'beastings' is made all over again. In the very fine first poem, 'Thistles', the thistles are said to be

> Every one a revengeful burst
> Of resurrection, a grasped fistful
> Of splintered weapons and Icelandic frost thrust up

> From the underground stain of a decayed Viking.

And in 'Ghost Crabs', the apparitions which emerge from the sea at nightfall are

> Giant crabs, under flat skulls, staring inland
> Like a packed trench of helmets.

That seemingly gratuitous image of Flanders is picked up in the play, *The Wound*, and again, memorably, in one of a second batch of poems which completes the book:

> My father sat in his chair recovering
> From the four-year mastication of gunfire and mud.

The Viking is taken up in another of the second batch of poems, 'The Warriors of the North'. For, true to that historical vision which A.E. Dyson denied him, Hughes evokes the historical continuity of his England, which is Pennine England (experienced too intimately to be offered as attractive, as anything but powerful), in images of the Norsemen. But the centrally illuminating piece of *Wodwo* is a story, clumsily but honestly written, about a north-country grotesque who earns his beer by catching and killing rats in his mouth. This is obviously related to a remarkable poem, 'Song of a Rat'. And here too Gallipoli sends its whiff of cordite:

Harry Rutley, pale, slow, round, weighed his jack. He had lost the tip of an ear at the Dardanelles and carried a fragment of his fifth rib on the end of his watch-chain.

The wolves which hunt through the boy narrator's mind, the rats, the hawks, the otters and crabs – all the predatory and preyed-upon beasts which figure in the other poems – are projections of the predatory violence which is the only guise through which the English tradition is mediated to the poet through his war-shattered father. The violence for which Hughes is extolled, which enters into and informs at the same time as it constricts his style – this, which is applauded by his jaded admirers for the kicks it gives them, in fact is his burden which he continually tries to cast off and to see behind.

That connoisseur of literary violence, A. Alvarez, has lately instructed us in the *TLS* about the modern artist:

> He lacks altogether the four traditional supports upon which every previous generation has been able, in one degree or another, to rely: religion, politics, national cultural tradition, reason.[1]

On this showing Hughes will never be a modern artist, for he has not broken free from the English cultural tradition, with which he grapples constantly. It is entirely and historically appropriate that in a late poem like 'Skylarks', his style has been rejuvenated out of the poems of D.H. Lawrence, that other English genius who spent himself trying to discover if anything of the English tradition had survived 1918, apart from naked and stoical violence.

---

1   'Beyond All This Fiddle', *Times Literary Supplement,* 23 March 1967, pp. 229–232. Reprinted in A. Alvarez, *Beyond All This Fiddle* (London: Allen Lane, 1968). Davie responded to Alvarez's article in 'Beyond All This Fiddle: A Rejoinder to A. Alvarez', *Times Literary Supplement,* 25 May 1967, p. 472. [Ed.]

The Industrial Landscape in British Literature

By 1850 in Britain, as in other countries, what historians of all the arts recognize as 'the Romantic Movement' had overcome early opposition and derision and had established itself as a reigning orthodoxy. There would be still, through many decades to come, pockets of resistance; and in those pockets there would be articulate people of real distinction. But their anti-Romanticism, whether well or ill conceived, would be a minority opinion.

When we consider how any of the arts treated landscape, one feature of the Romantic Movement must surely bulk larger than any other: the displacement of the aesthetic category of 'the beautiful' by that of 'the sublime'. Edmund Burke's *Philosophical Inquiry into the Origin of Our Ideas of the Sublime and Beautiful* had appeared as long ago as 1756; but its coming so soon, and anticipating so much, only shows Burke's genius. Already in this seminal treatise 'the beautiful' is continually in danger of being demoted to the merely pretty, and it is plain that Burke was far more excited by 'the sublime', alike in nature and in art. Of the sublime, as Burke expounded it, two related characteristics are particularly important for students of the way in which modern art has rendered landscape: first, the sublime has to do characteristically with objects and scenes of a physical magnitude beyond that which the beautiful could sustain; secondly, and largely as a result, sublime art and sublime nature make us *frightened* – with a fright that, oddly enough, we take pleasure in.

In *The Old Curiosity Shop* (1840–41) Charles Dickens described a landscape which, both in magnitude and frightfulness, answered to Burke's criteria for the sublime, though it was landscape of a kind that Burke could not have known. It was the recently but comprehensively industrialized landscape between Birmingham and Wolverhampton:

> a long, flat, straggling suburb passed, they came by slow degrees upon a cheerless region, where not a blade of grass was seen to grow; where not a bud put forth its promise in the spring; where nothing green could live but on the surface of the stagnant pools, which here and there lay idly sweltering by the black roadside.

This passage is quoted by Margaret Drabble, to whose *A Writer's Britain, Landscape in Literature* (1979), we must be indebted for a demonstration of how, consistently and from early on, industrialized landscapes satisfied the criteria of sublimity as well as, or better than, any non-industrialized landscapes could.

This put the Victorian artist in a quandary. For the passage from *The Old Curiosity Shop* makes it quite clear that for Dickens the blasted sublimity of the Birmingham/Wolverhampton landscape was bought at an altogether exorbitant cost, humanly, socially, even aesthetically. Accordingly the entire category of the sublime, as equal or superior to the beautiful, was called into question. Ian Jeffrey for one has noticed how frequently in the 1850s (Dickens himself as a prime example) there is a nostalgic appeal back to the eighteenth-century England of 'the old Squire' – that is to say, to an English landscape where the modest scale of 'the beautiful' (cornfields and spinneys, dells and dingles) is preferred to the more vaunting scale of 'the sublime'. Moreover it is not a simple matter of preferring agrarian to industrial scenes; for agrarian landscapes had themselves been industrialized, in the sense that in some areas, particularly in the North of England, agriculture had been rationalized by landowners intent on maximum profits, who had therefore merged many small holdings into one vast sweep of cornfields, of which the extent, the sheer magnitude, dismayed may visitors from the south, as once again Ian Jeffrey has noticed. Accordingly, when Victorian sages like Thomas Carlyle (*Past and Present*, 1843), George Eliot (*Felix Holt*, 1866), Matthew Arnold (*Culture and Anarchy*, 1869) or John Ruskin (*Unto This Last*, 1860) regarded the growth of industry with at least dismay and apprehension, and often enough with anger and indignation, their protests cannot be set aside as the ultimately frivolous petulance of privileged aesthetes. Their horror at what industry was doing to the landscapes of Britain came not from the eradication of many scenic prospects that they could have taken pleasure in, nor did any of them for long imagine that they could put the clock back. They were concerned with landscapes as arenas in which lives are lived, even as images of how private and communal life could be conducted either satisfyingly and with decency or else brutally. The point was that people lived, and would continue to live, between Birmingham and Wolverhampton; that the landscape there, precisely by its sublimity (for the sublime was by definition on a more than human scale), seemed to threaten that the lives lived there could not be satisfyingly human. Thus the sense of affront, of outrage, conveyed by Ruskin in particular is, it may well be thought, something we cannot afford to leave behind; for it derives from considerations that are humane and civic rather than, in any narrow sense, aesthetic.

All the same, by 1870, if what you wanted of English landscapes was 'the sublime', there seemed no doubt that industrial landscapes supplied it, or would soon supply it, better than agrarian or pastoral landscapes. Though the mountains of Wales and Scotland, not to speak of Ireland, were still grander and more awesome than any industrialized areas of those countries, in England that was not the case. For the man-made or man-devastated landscapes of Manchester and Salford already rivalled in sublimity the nature-made landscapes of Wordsworth's (or Ruskin's) Lake District. Very curious in this perspective is R.D. Blackmore's description of the Doone Valley in chapter 4 of his *Lorna Doone* (1869):

> ...she stood at the head of a deep green valley, carved from out the mountains in a perfect oval, with a fence of sheer rock standing round it, eighty feet or a hundred high; from whose brink black wooded hills swept up to the sky-line. By her side a little river glided out from underground with a soft dark babble, unawares of daylight; then growing brighter, lapsed away, and fell into the valley. There, as it ran down the meadow, alders stood on either marge, and grass was blading out upon it, and yellow tufts of rushes gathered, looking at the hurry. But further down, on either bank, were covered houses, built of stone, square and roughly cornered, set as if the brook were meant to be the street between them. Only one room high they were, and not placed opposite each other, but in and out as skittles are; only that the first of all, which proved to be the captain's, was a sort of double house, or rather two houses joined together by a plank-bridge over the river. Fourteen cots my mother counted, all very much of a pattern, and nothing to choose between them, unless it were the captain's. Deep in the quiet valley there, away from noise, and violence, and brawl, save that of the rivulet, any man would have deemed them homes of simple mind and innocence. Yet not a single house stood there but was the home of murder.

This is composed with admirable craft, particularly in the ways the sublimity of the moor around ('fence of sheer rock'... 'black wooded hills swept up to the skyline') is evoked to surround 'the beautiful' in the isolated settlement, with its 'cots' and 'rivulets'. There is no wonder that *Lorna Doone* reads as seductively now as it did a hundred years ago. Yet now, when we can visit the Doone valley by motor-coach, the gestures towards the sublime seem unconvincing, almost comically so. In the age of the motor-car Exmoor itself has shrunk for the imagination; it is hard to attach such words as 'wild' or 'remote' to a terrain that one may cross in a half-hour at most. This drastic contraction of distances, the consequence of rapid transport, stands between us and the landscapes of many late Victorian writers. Richard Jefferies for instance often tries to convey a sense of remoteness and loneliness in describing landscapes of southern England that we have good reason to think of, from our own experience, as thoroughly cosy and densely peopled. And although in Jefferies' case Jeremy Hooker may be right to see this as the projection on to landscape of psychological loneliness and alienation in Jefferies himself, the same cannot be said of Thomas Hardy, though there are occasions in *Jude the Obscure* or *The Return of the Native* when Hardy attributes to various Wiltshire or Dorsetshire uplands qualities of sublimity which, if we have motored thereabouts, we may find it hard to accord to them. Hardy himself was aware of this change of scale in our perception of landscape, and there is a very astute passage in *Jude the Obscure* about the coming of the railway which, at the same time as it made accessible places previously remote, made *more* remote other places that had been on the stage-coach routes but were now bypassed by the railway. For that matter Blackmore was already writing in the Railway Age, and he was able to endow Exmoor with sublimity chiefly by telling his story through the eyes of the seventeenth-century yeoman John Tidd. His style, in the passage quoted and throughout the story, moves very adroitly and with marvellous resourcefulness between normal Victorian English and a pastiche of what we can imagine as provincial seventeenth-century speech. Some Edwardian authors who wrote about what was by then called 'the countryside' fabricated and used, much more heavy-handedly and with far less logic, a self-consciously archaic English which is sometimes used even now, for instance in brochures for the tourist trade. Meanwhile other originally Edwardian writers, as different as Arnold Bennett and D.H. Lawrence, were attempting the surely more honourable task of showing that in thoroughly industrialized landscapes, despite the privations that they imposed on their inhabitants, lives of decency and crippled dignity could be lived.

We may set beside Dickens in the 1840s between Birmingham and Wolverhampton George Orwell in the 1930s outside Wigan:

> I remember a winter afternoon in the dreadful environs of Wigan. All round was the lunar landscape of slag heaps, and to the north, through the passes, as it were, between the mountains of slag, you could see factory chimneys sending out their plumes of smoke. The canal path was a mixture of cinders and frozen mud, criss-crossed by the imprints of innumerable clogs, and all around, as far as the slag heaps in the distances, stretched the 'flashes' – pools of stagnant water that had seeped into the hollows caused by the subsidence of ancient pits. It was horribly cold. The 'flashes' were covered with ice the colour of raw umber, the bargemen were muffled to the eyes in sacks, the lock gates wore tears of ice. It seemed a world from which vegetation had been banished: nothing existed except smoke, shale, ice, mud, ashes, and foul water.

The coincidence over more than a century between Dickens and Orwell is surely extraordinary; not only the tone but many of the images – the stagnant water, for instance – are identical. The English imagination, one is tempted to say, had over a century made no progress in accommodating, in *humanizing*, industrial landscapes. John Berger, in an essay on the painter L.S. Lowry ('Lowry and the Industrial North', 1966, in *About Looking*, 1980) has harshly but justly complained of 'the submerged patronage found in nearly all critical comment on Lowry's work'. Lowry's landscapes of industrial Lancashire are treated, says Berger, 'as though they dealt with the view out of the window of a Pullman train on its non-stop journey to London, where everything is believed to be different'. It would be intolerable to call Orwell's appalled compassion for the unemployed of Wigan 'submerged patronage', but it is true that his description of the environs of Wigan, if it is not quite the view through the window of a Pullman train, is still, like Dickens's view of Wolverhampton, the view of an outsider, a tourist. Lowry's view on the other hand, like Arnold Bennett's view of the Potteries or Lawrence's of industrial Nottinghamshire, is the view of an insider, for whom the landscape that Orwell describes is the landscape of the native habitat. 'Dreadful', Orwell's epithet, is not what would come to the lips of one who had grown up in such scenes. And the point is important. Berger, quoting this Orwell passage (from *The Road to Wigan Pier*) declares that it 'is virtually describing a painting by Lowry'. We need not quarrel with that. But to give a virtual description of a painting is different from giving an *equivalent* of that painting in the alternative medium of words. It is not in Orwell's prose but only in Lowry's paint that we find what Berger finely identifies as the content of Lowry's paintings: 'The notion of progress – however it is applied – is foreign to them. Their virtues are stoic; their logic is one of decline.' About progress or decline, as about stoicism, Orwell's honourably shocked prose has nothing to say, one way or the other.

It is worth noticing two points at which Orwell's English could have risen above itself, to something artistic, more than documentary. One is at the expression 'to the north through the passes', where a more artistic writer would have exploited the possibility of an allusion, melancholy or sardonic, to those romantically sublime landscapes which the Wigan landscape parodies – if only, it may be thought, by carrying them to their historically logical conclusion. And the other comes with the word 'flashes'. Does this local usage derive from something like the American expression, 'flash-floods'? Or does it not, more affectingly, register how the sheets of standing water take the light, the sky, and render it back to the observer as an illumination, an enlightenment? Orwell passes over the word without dwelling on it – he is using language as an instrument, not as an artistic medium.

Those pools of standing water in industrially ravaged scenes, which move Dickens and Orwell to the aversion registered by 'stagnant' and 'foul', can appear quite differently to the eye of an insider like Lowry or the poet Charles Tomlinson, native of industrial Staffordshire:

> It was a language of water, light and air
>> I sought – to speak myself free of a world
> Whose stoic lethargy seemed the one reply
>> To horizons and to streets that blocked them back
> In a monotone fume, a bloom of grey.
>> I found my speech. The years return me
> To tell of all that seasoned and imprisoned:
>> I breathe familiar, sedimented air
> From a landscape of disembowellings, underworlds
>> Unearthed among the clay. Digging
> The marl, they dug a second nature
>> And water, seeping up to fill their pits,
> Sheeted them to lakes that wink and shine
>> Between tips and steeples, streets and waste
> In slow reclaimings, shimmers, balancings,
>> As if kindling Eden rescinded its own loss
> And words and water came of the same source.
>> ('The Marl Pits', from *The Way In*, 1974)

Berger's perception of stoicism as the implicit moral content of Lowry's pictures is endorsed by Tomlinson in the phrase 'stoic lethargy'. But by Tomlinson this condition is named only so as to be transcended. And it is transcended not by moving away, in fact or in imagination, to a place where water is purer, air cleaner, but on the contrary by dwelling ever more intently on the local fact to the point where water, however fouled, can still be identified as the element, water, and air, however smoky, can still be welcomed as the element, air – to the point indeed where Burslem or Hanley can be retrieved as 'Eden'. To achieve this, or to prove the achievement, all the energies of words must be released, down to what is as raw material no more than a rhyming jingle – of 'kindling' for instance with 'rescinded'.

To those with a strong humanitarian and/or political concern about injustice, anxious to ameliorate the privations of the labouring or unemployed poor imprisoned in the blighted landscapes of old and declining industry, such a transcendence as Tomlinson's poem proclaims and proves is far from welcome. For they will argue, from their standpoint quite justly, that every testimony to how a deprived lot can be transcended saps the will of the deprived to change their lot by political, perhaps revolutionary, action. And this, we may suspect, is John Berger's way of thinking. For he says of Lowry's art: 'It does not belong in the mainstream of twentieth-century art, which is concerned in one way or

another with interpreting new relationships between man and nature.'
And in another essay in *About Looking* ('Romaine Lorquet', 1974), he
explains what he has in mind:

> All art, which is based on a close observation of nature, eventually
> changes the way nature is seen. Either it confirms more strongly an
> already established way of seeing nature or it proposes a new way.
> Until recently a whole cultural process was involved; the artist
> observed nature: his work had a place in the culture of his time and
> that culture mediated between man and nature. In post-industrial soci-
> eties this no longer happens. Their culture runs parallel to nature and
> is completely insulated from it. Anything which enters that culture has
> to sever its connections with nature. Even natural sights (views) have
> been reduced in consumption to commodities.
>
> The sense of continuity once supplied by nature is now supplied by
> the means of communication and exchange – publicity, TV, newspa-
> pers, records, shop-windows, auto-routes, package holidays, curren-
> cies, etc. These, barring catastrophes – either personal or global – form
> a mindless stream in which any material can be transmitted and made
> homogeneous – including art.

Those of us who, while recognizing in Berger's account some of the
indeed dismal features of our present situation, yet feel that his condemnation is too sweeping, may take heart by looking again at Tomlinson's
poem. For does Tomlinson's art there propose 'a new way' of seeing
nature? Clearly it does not; it applies itself strenuously to recovering an
old way, long lost – which is, of course, quite different from confirming
'an already established way'. Thus John Berger's either/or – *either* change
the way nature is seen *or else* confirm an already established way – is false.
These are false alternatives. For it may be argued that the best British
writing through the past hundred years and for longer has concerned
itself, as Charles Tomlinson's poem does, with a third way that John
Berger either fails to see or refuses to acknowledge. This third way is a
way of recovery – recovery of ways of seeing long lost but still available
to us if we will take the trouble to look for them. To find them we need
to look in ourselves as well as in landscapes; for they are to be found, in
fact, in the transaction between ourselves and the landscapes that we
inhabit and move among and (too seldom) pause to contemplate.

Meanwhile, however, we may suspect, taking note of the poems as well
as the paintings most popular among us, that 'landscape' as most of us
understand it tacitly excludes the industrial landscapes we have been
talking of. How do we explain this persistently greater popularity of
pastoral and rural landscapes? Margaret Drabble's explanation seems to be,
very gently and obliquely, that this is infantile; that in reverting from the

sublime to the beautiful, we have demoted the beautiful not to the pretty but to the *cosy*; that in opting for the smaller scale of the beautiful we have in fact sought, if not the womb, at least the cradle. Undoubtedly for the most industrialized and urban of nations to seek so persistently in its art for the pastoral, the pre-industrial, can hardly be a sign of health. If so, there is still point to the gibe at the self-styled 'Georgian' poets of the time of the First World War that the rural landscapes in their poems were word-painted by week-enders from London or some other city. (It is perhaps significant that this gibe was more commonly heard forty years ago than today.) Undoubtedly, however, this charge can be levelled too unthinkingly. On the one hand, the idyll has been from ancient times, in painting and in literature alike, an art-form which, by presenting what ideally ought to be and perhaps once was, by implication criticizes caustically what has in fact come to pass – in landscapes and in the societies that those landscapes image or imply. Thus, a work of art which paints a picture of a Britain that once was, or once may have been, may be commenting sharply on the very different Britain that we inhabit. And on the other hand, Richard Jefferies was not the first or the last English artist to practise what the French call *paysage intérieur* – that is to say, while offering to present a landscape exterior to himself, in fact he expressed and communicated a landscape in his head or in his heart. The loneliness of Edward Thomas, like the loneliness of Jefferies, is projected on to the outside world but is really a psychological state which cannot find expression in any other way. The clue to this is that both Jefferies and Thomas see something deadly in the non-human Nature that they celebrate. And if this seems a devious way of expressing one's self, it is borne out by common usage. For how strange it is, after all, that we can and do speak of 'a lonely place' as of 'a lonely person'. Indeed if it should be true, as some psychologists tell us, that loneliness (alienation) is the besetting malady of the industrially urbanized man and woman, then – paradoxically – we can expect to meet more lonely and unpeopled landscapes in poems and paintings, even as such landscapes become harder to find in actuality.

Finally, we may pause on a word that John Berger uses: 'post industrial'. In trying to understand what this might mean, we may perhaps think first of electronic or 'clean' industries. Certainly the industrial presence in our lives is no longer, for most of us, signalled by reeking smoke or by burning flares in the night from chemical factories or from foundries. A new sort of industrialized landscape was heralded by the development, fifty or more years ago, of the Great West Road's approach to London: 'glittering white factories with green lawns and beds of tulips'. Interestingly, Orwell objected to this vehemently, declaring, 'A dark Satanic mill should be like a dark satanic mill.' Margaret Drabble sees Orwell here as 'tempted by the "sublimity" argument'. Of course we see what she means. But by now we have 'industrial archaeology'; probably' as many coaches visit the long abandoned factories in Coalbrookdale as cruise into the Doone valley. John Betjeman's poem 'A Shropshire Lad' (in *Old Lights for New Chancels*, 1940) was already wringing pathos out of once-industrial Shropshire, since reverted to pastoralism; as at the same time was W.H. Auden out of the abandoned mine-workings of his native Craven in Yorkshire. It is from a standpoint of sympathy with industry in its pioneering and massively grim Victorian embodiment that we can dislike hygienic factories among beds of tulips as, in John Berger's words, part of the 'mindless stream' constituted by 'the means of communication and exchange'. Certainly, if we see industry in the image of the credit-card and the TV set, we image it quite differently from Dickens and Orwell and Tomlinson, with their pools of standing water among spoiled earth. From this point of view, we might maintain that the great achievement of English landscape art over the past 130 years has been the assimilation and humanizing of the first Industrial Revolution; and the challenge which confronts it now is the assimilation of the Second (Computerized) Industrial Revolution, so much more suave and twinkling, with no longer any visible claim to sublimity. And doubtless, in the hands of a few earnest and dedicated masters the rural idyll will stand as stern a reproach to the Second Industrial Revolution as to the First.

Landscape in Britain, 1850–1950 (London: Arts Council/Hayward Gallery, 1983).

The Poetry of Elizabeth Daryush

When an unprejudiced literary history of our century comes to be written, our failure to recognize Elizabeth Daryush will be one of the most telling and lamentable charges that can be laid at our door. The cold silence that has prevailed about her work, through one decade after another, is so total that there can be no question of fixing the blame here or there, finding scapegoats. We are *all* at fault, in a way which points therefore to some really deep-seated frivolity, superficiality, cynicism through several generations of readers of English poetry.

Certainly, I cannot absolve myself. For it so happens that I had the good fortune to stumble, while I was still young, on the writings of the one critic who *did* recognize the achievement of this poet, who tried not once but many times to force his contemporaries to confront the challenge of her work. I mean, the late Yvor Winters. And why, I now angrily ask myself, did I, who knew that I had been instructed by Winters time and again about the poetry of our time and the past, flinch from the responsibility that his championing of Mrs Daryush laid upon me as upon others who listened to him – some of whom, incidentally, rose to the occasion as I didn't? I have given the answer: mere frivolousness, an anxiety not to be too far out of the fashion, above all a demand for quick returns upon a very small investment of time and attention. There can be no excuse.

In his *Primitivism and Decadence* (1937) Winters printed the poem, 'Still-Life', from Mrs Daryush's *The Last Man & Other Verses* (1936):

> Through the open French window the warm sun
> lights up the polished breakfast-table, laid
> round a bowl of crimson roses, for one –
> a service of Worcester porcelain, arrayed
> near it a melon, peaches, figs, small hot
> rolls in a napkin, fairy rack of toast,
> butter in ice, high silver coffee-pot,
> and, heaped on a salver, the morning's post.
>
> She comes over the lawn, the young heiress,
> from her early walk in her garden-wood,
> feeling that life's a table set to bless

> her delicate desires with all that's good,
>
> that even the unopened future lies
> like a love-letter, full of sweet surprise.

When Winters included *Primitivism and Decadence* as part of his *In Defense of Reason* (1947), there was the Daryush poem again. It was there that I read it first, and I kick myself for not having been incited by it, by something so wholly unlike any other English poem of our time up to that date. (Since then, Thom Gunn's 'Autumn Chapter in a Novel', a poem which may owe something to 'Still-Life', may be set beside it.) My excuse, a poor one, must be that Winters cited and discussed the poem exclusively in relation to its metre, as a fine example of what can be achieved in English in a strictly *syllabic* metre, as distinct from the more orthodox accentual-syllabic. A far more generally illuminating discussion of the poem is in Winters's essay, 'Robert Bridges and Elizabeth Daryush' (in the *American Review* for 1936–37). In this essay, which only the devoted enterprise of Francis Murphy has made generally available,[1] Winters wrote:

> If we regard the subject-matter of this poem, we find something rather curious: the matter explicitly described implies, largely through the ominous and melancholy tone, a social context which is nowhere mentioned, yet from which the poem draws its power, a power which is not only real but great. This implication probably reaches its most intense impression in the two lines, unforgettable in the melancholy of the cadence, which open the sestet; but was never absent.

And he goes on to relate this to a new element in what were in 1937 'the last two books' by Mrs Daryush; that is to say, *Verses, Fourth Book* (1934), and *The Last Man & Other Verses* (1936). That new element Winters defines by saying: 'she appears to be increasingly conscious... of social injustice, of the mass of human suffering'. And this brings to our attention a matter of the first importance: Elizabeth Daryush, unlike her father Robert Bridges and unlike a greater poet of whom she sometimes reminds us, Thomas Hardy, is a poet in whom we can discern a development, not merely technical but thematic also, a deepening and changing attitude to the world she lives in. Quite simply, she has not lived through the first three quarters of the twentieth century in England without registering and responding to the profound changes that have transformed the world of the English gentry which, as the daughter of Robert Bridges, she was born to. No one is yet in a position to trace this development, and for the merest bare bones of it we are once again indebted to the one serious

---

1   Yvor Winters: *Uncollected Essays and Reviews*, edited and introduced by Francis Murphy, (Chicago, 1973), pp. 271–83.

reader she had, Yvor Winters, who read her in California and never once in his life visited England: 'Mrs Daryush has disowned her first three books, published in 1911, 1916, and 1921 and wishes them destroyed. ...Her mature career may be said to have begun with *Verses*, published in 1930, to have reached its most perfect achievement in *Verses, Third Book*, published in 1933, to have reached a crisis and collapse of form in *Verses, Fourth Book*, published in 1934, as a result, it would seem, of the discovery of new matter to which she found her style ill-adapted, and to have begun the mastery of this new matter, or of a few aspects of it, in *The Last Man & Other Verses*, published in 1936.' It would be odd if the nearly forty years that have supervened since Winters wrote thus – years that have seen Mrs Daryush continue writing up to *Verses: Seventh Book* (Carcanet Press, 1971) – do not cause us to revise, as well as extend, this account of her development. Meanwhile, however, Winters's comment is very much to the point: 'Her talent, then, although it was obviously formed by her father's influence, appears to have borne fruit only after his death, and to have developed very rapidly within a very short period, after a long period of stagnation.' And this is a good point at which to take note of the poem, 'Fresh Spring, in whose deep woods I sought', from *Verses, Third Book*, one of the Daryush poems which Winters most esteemed, which he learned with dismay that the author intended to suppress. I give it as my hesitant opinion that she was more nearly right about this, than he was.

For understandable reasons, not only Yvor Winters's account of Elizabeth Daryush but also the more belated and yet more momentous account of her by Roy Fuller, when he was Professor of Poetry at Oxford, gave disproportionate emphasis to her experiments with syllabics. If on the contrary we attend to the substance of 'Still-Life', to what it is saying, we shall find its companion-piece in 'Children of Wealth' which, originally in *Verses, Sixth Book*, appears only one poem away from 'Still-Life' in the *Selected Poems* which Elizabeth Daryush arranged for Carcanet Press in 1972. And 'Children of Wealth' is a sonnet in orthodox accentual-syllabics:

> Children of wealth in your warm nursery,
> Set in the cushioned window-seat to watch
> The volleying snow, guarded invisibly
> By the clear double pane through which no touch
> Untimely penetrates, you cannot tell
> What winter means; its cruel truths to you
> Are only sound and sight; your citadel
> Is safe from feeling, and from knowledge too.
>
> Go down, go out to elemental wrong,
> Waste your too round limbs, tan your skin too white;
> The glass of comfort, ignorance, seems strong

> Today, and yet perhaps this very night
>
> You'll wake to horror's wrecking fire – your home
> Is wired within for this, in every room.

Each reader must decide for himself which of the metres – syllabic, or accentual-syllabic – supplies him with the more haunting, more memorably poignant, cadence. What cannot be doubted is that the two poems support each other, to show that the poet in the late 1930s came quite suddenly to the perception of what her relatively privileged birth committed her to, or excluded her from: the double pane of glass which that privilege of birth erected between her and the mass of suffering humankind. The perhaps excessive, certainly very violent, pressures that disturb the pentameter in line 10 – 'Waste your too round limbs, tan your skin too white' – indicate the desperation, barely under control, with which the poet thus recognized and diagnosed her plight. And as for the syllabics of 'Still-Life', since in most reader's ears they are indistinguishable from free verse, the gauntlet that Yvor Winters threw down in 1937 still lies where he cast it: 'One imagines that the medium could not be used with greater beauty than in this poem; there is certainly nothing in the work of the American masters of free verse to surpass it, and there is little to equal it.' As much might be claimed, I'd say, for 'Forbidden Love' from *Verses, Fourth Book*, which is remarkable as perhaps the last thoroughly accomplished poem in English to invoke, with pride and without qualification, the chivalric code for the ordering of sexual relations. (Its language is accordingly, and quite properly, stilted.)

But it is more important to recognize that the poet's experiments with syllabics never stopped her from writing in more orthodox metres, nor is she manifestly better in the one sort of metre than the other. We've seen this already with the companion-pieces, 'Still-Life' and 'Children of Wealth'. A similar set of twins is 'Winter Larches', from *The Last Man*, and 'Here, where the larks sing, and the sun's so warm', from *Verses, Fourth Book*. Because these are what used to be called 'nature-poems', they are of course less intense than the poems we've looked at first. But as Wordsworth said, 'The human mind is capable of being excited without the application of gross and violent stimulants.' It's a saying which is relevant to many poems by Elizabeth Daryush, and not just to her 'nature-poems', numerous and lovely as those are.

In his own way Winters too asked for *intensity*. And that explains the praise that he heaped on 'Anger lay by me', from *The Last Man*:

> Anger lay by me all night long,
>   His breath was hot upon my brow,
> He told me of my burning wrong,
>   All night he talked and would not go.

He stood by me all through the day,
    Struck from my hand the book, the pen;
He said: 'Hear first what *I've* to say,
    And sing, if you've the heart to, *then.*'

And can I cast him from my couch?
    And can I lock him from my room?
Ah no, his honest words are such
    That's he's my true-lord, and my doom.

Winters says of this, 'Such work represents, I believe, and in spite of the italics, which could easily... be dispensed with, the perfection of English poetic style...'; and also, 'There is much other great poetry in English, but poetry of this type, at is best, is probably the greatest, and in its purity of style and richness of meaning it defines the norm, the more or less clear consciousness of which probably gives much of their identity to the variant types'. To understand this, one needs to study Winters's criticism as a whole, and also his own poems; for it was his single-minded purpose through more than thirty years to restore poetry of this kind to the central place from which nineteenth-century and twentieth-century opinion had dislodged it, with (as Winters saw the matter) disastrous results. Readers who have not had the benefit of Winters's instruction will almost certainly be baffled by the high claims that he makes for a poem like this, so bare and seemingly so rigid. Such writing flies so directly in the face of current preconceptions about poetry that one does not come to love and admire it at all soon, or at all easily. A useful starting-point is Winters's confession: 'The quality which I personally admire most profoundly... is the ability to imbue a simple expository statement of a complex theme with a rich association of feeling, yet with an utterly pure and unmannered style.' Serviceable short cuts to what Winters is getting at might be afforded by some of the early poems of William Blake, and by (in Blake's background) the best of the congregational hymns of the English eighteenth century – by Isaac Watts, Charles Wesley, and Cowper. And another way to get at the austere virtues of this style is to see them tightened into the fierce hostility of the epigram, as in this poem from *Verses, Fourth Book*:

It is pleasant to hang out
this sign at your open gate:
'Succour for the desolate' –
your neighbours praise you, no doubt;

but woe to whoe'er in need
at the inner door has knocked,
found the snug room barred and locked
where alone you fatly feed.

And we may well think that this caustic image of the professional do-gooder brings us back to the social consciousness of 'Still-Life' and 'Children of Wealth'.

* * *

To have the Poet Laureate for one's father is a grievous disadvantage for any poet to labour under. And there can be no doubt that the shadow which has eclipsed Elizabeth Daryush is the shadow of Robert Bridges. This is complicated by the fact that for the most part we have an inadequate and distorted idea of Robert Bridges, remembering him above all as the author of the unreadable *Testament of Beauty* and as the man who withheld from us, for longer than we think necessary, the poems of Gerard Manley Hopkins. We do not remember for instance that Bridges esteemed Ezra Pound, and was esteemed by him. And it should go without saying that Bridges, the author of 'Low Barometer' and 'A Passer-by', is now and has been for many years a poet grotesquely under-rated. But what has brought this about (in so far as it isn't merely the lax and heartless turn of fashion) is something that it's quite easy to put our finger on; it is Bridges's *diction*, his choice of vocabulary. Pound put his finger on it, in the Pisan Canto 80:

> 'forloyn' said Mr Bridges (Robert)
> 'we'll get 'em all back'
> meaning archaic words...

Diction is what puts us off in reading Bridges, and it is also, though not to the same degree, the great difficulty that we are likely to have with Elizabeth Daryush. Here, Winters will not help us. For diction was one dimension of poetry which Winters, so splendidly alert to other dimensions – above all metre and cadence – was rather consistently deaf to, and obtuse about. For instance, in his essay on Bridges and Daryush, he quotes, as an example of Bridges at his best, 'The Affliction of Richard', which contains the lines:

> But what the heavenly key,
> What marvel in me wrought
> Shall quite exculpate thee,
> I have no shadow of thought.

And Winters is quite unperturbed by – does not even notice – the utterly slack, unrealized and unrealizable metaphor in '*shadow* of thought'. To say that the language of these lines is what neither Bridges himself nor any one else would in any conceivable circumstances ever *say* – this is a criticism of another sort, and one which, if pushed at all far, lands us in absurdities. Nevertheless, it undoubtedly has its force. And we may as well concede that a diligent inquisition of Mrs Daryush's poems would come up with passages against which these charges lie just as heavily as against these verses by her father.

On the other hand, if Winters pays too little attention to diction, other readers of our time – especially British ones – have concentrated on it to the virtual exclusion of all else. And this is probably a worse fault. One may make the admittedly hazardous suggestion that in all poetry except the greatest there has to be a sort of 'trade off' – of cadence as against diction, of diction as against cadence. And in that case what needs to be said is that, whereas with other poets we agree to buy a racy or pungent turn of speech at the cost of an ugly cadence (a bargain we are disconcertingly too ready to strike), in the case of Mrs Daryush the trade-off is usually the other way round: we are required to tolerate a 'timeless' or archaic or improperly marmoreal expression for the sake of the beautiful and meaningful cadence which it makes possible. (This is not to deny that there are places where the game is not worth the candle, where the proffered bargain must be refused.)

But there is a stronger and a better case that can be made for the use of such 'poetical' diction as is customary with Mrs Daryush. And this rests on linking her, not with Bridges, but with the greater poet, Thomas Hardy. In the unwontedly elaborate and ode-like poem, 'The Waterfall', from *Verses, Sixth Book* (1938; it will be noted that her austerity extends to the titling of her books as well as the writing of them), we read:

> A thousand feet of torn stream falling sheer
> In fog and thunder... Like a theatre
> The rocks had taken curve as, year by year,
> The torrent wore at its hard doom-way, inch by inch...
> Imagination flew up, then would flinch
> From looking down – hung dizzied, even here...

And who, that has read in the poetry of Thomas Hardy, would deny the epithet 'Hardyesque' to 'its hard doom-way'? Can we imagine Hardy ever *saying* those words, in conversation? And if we cannot, what does it matter? They are entirely in keeping with what we recognize as Hardy's characteristic idiom. And however bizarre we find that idiom when we first encounter it, however heterogeneous and unaccountable, we recognize it – as we go on reading Hardy's poems – as a universe of language which is self-consistent within its own self-chosen boundaries, allowing certain liberties and denying itself others. It is in this sense that every poet – except, once again, the very greatest – creates his own language within the language that we share with him, a distinctive language which is private only in the first place, which becomes steadily more public and available to us, the more we familiarize ourselves with it. To speak for myself, that process for good or ill works itself out in reading Elizabeth Daryush's poems as in reading Hardy's. And this, it will be observed, is an argument for not picking out the plums from the cake but on the contrary for presenting this poet's work in bulk and *in toto*.

Poetry Nation 5 (1975), reprinted as Introduction to Elizabeth Daryush, *Collected Poems* (Manchester: Carcanet Press, 1976).

Fallen Language

Geoffrey Hill, *The Lords of Limit: Essays on Literature and Ideas* (London: André Deutsch, 1984).

If, when we rhyme 'tomb' with 'womb', we conceive that we are making a connection never before thought of, we are innocent indeed; and our innocence will rightly be derided – as a callowness in ourselves which the language that we use, British English, has long ago grown out of. We have shown ourselves to be less grown-up than the language that we attempt to bend to our immature purposes – an attempt that the language itself frustrates by appealing, implicitly and inevitably, to English-language-users more worldly-wise than we are. If this is true (it is a matter seldom canvassed), out of many possibilities that spring to mind two should be noticed: first, we may conceive of a language – as it might be Russian, or even American English – that is less worldly-wise than British-English; and secondly we may conceive of, and even think that we register around us, a linguistic community – users of British English – which by wilful or enforced ignorance of past usages may force their experienced language back into inexperience, to a point where rhyming 'tomb' with 'womb' may once again seem to be innocent, a thunderclap of unheralded revelation.

These reflections are prompted by Geoffrey Hill's formidably erudite and compacted essay, 'Our Word is Our Bond', which reappears now in *The Lords of Limit*, a volume which, it must be said, in everything from format to price does very great credit to the publishers. This particular essay has provoked in another attentive reader, John Lucas (*LRB*, Vol. 5, No 20), the reflection that 'language cannot be innocent'. But surely it needs to be remarked that whereas indeed the British English that Hill and Lucas share cannot be in this sense 'innocent', that doesn't necessarily hold true of other languages (Russian, Mexican Spanish, American English, and so on) – a possibility which at once raises perhaps insoluble problems for translators from those languages into British English. However that may be, we can with only a little rhetorical over-emphasis declare that British English is 'fallen', is 'depraved'. And such theological terminology is very much in Geoffrey Hill's line. The problem for a British poet like Hill is precisely that his medium, British English, is much more *knowing* than he can hope to be, or perhaps would want to be.

However, recognising that British English is unavoidably depraved, let us be continually aware, and make our readers aware, of how duplicitous it is – that is at all events one way forward, and the way that Hill has taken in his *Mystery of the Charity of Charles Péguy*, and in other poems also. John Lucas, once he has admitted that British English has lost its innocence, seems to have no firm footing for distinguishing, as he tries to do, acceptable from unacceptable depravities (decadent refinements) that British English, at Hill's hands, indulges in. Many of Geoffrey Hill's most devoted admirers applaud the opalescent sonorities that from time to time he contrives for them, while refusing to pay the price that he scrupulously demands – of recognising that such gratifying resonances are part and parcel of a way with language that he will expose, at other points, as heartlessly casuistical or sportive.

An important essay by Hill that he has unaccountably excluded from *The Lords of Limit* is called 'The Conscious Mind's Intelligible Structure: A Debate' (*Agenda*, Autumn-Winter 1971/2). Here Hill says of Yeats's Easter 1916': 'One is moved by... the tune of a mind distrustful yet envious, mistrusting the abstraction, mistrusting its own mistrust, drawn half against its will into the chanting refrain that is both paean and threnos, yet, once drawn, committed utterly to the melody of the refrain.' Except that Hill's poem doesn't have any one refrain to parallel Yeats's 'A terrible beauty is born', this seems to define exactly what Hill has attempted and perhaps accomplished in his poem about and for Péguy. And if Hill's poem goes much further than Yeats's in indulging clenches and word-play of the sort that moves John Lucas at times to exasperation ('the game seems solipsistic, arbitrary and tiresome'), might we not plausibly argue that Hill's British English in 1980 is unavoidably more 'depraved', more experienced, than Yeats's Anglo-Irish was in 1917? And that Hill's word-play is his way of acknowledging this? It's striking, however, that Hill doesn't exculpate himself in this way. He enters no such pleas. For his focus in his essays is nearly always philosophical or theological, hardly ever historical. In 'Our Word is Our Bond', for instance, he assumes – implausibly, surely – that the issue as between plain and figurative English was the same for Spenser and Greville and Sidney, for Hobbes and Cudworth, for Locke and Berkeley, as for J.L. Austin and Iris Murdoch and himself. Similarly he assumes that Americans like Santayana and John Crowe Ransom and Kenneth Burke, when they speak of language, have in their sights and in their ears the same language as the one that he and Austin and Iris Murdoch speak. Yet both assumptions are surely, to say the least, questionable; and they minister to the unthinking insularity which leads Austin and other British philosophers to suppose that what they can observe about the behaviour of British English today is true of all languages anywhere and at any time.

John Lucas seems to agree with them, as when in one specific and revealing instance he objects to Hill's lines:

'Encore plus douloureux et doux'.
Note how sweetness devours sorrow, renders it again.

Of this Lucas remarks, in a way that he plainly considers conclusive: 'I cannot note how sweetness devours sorrow in English, because it doesn't.' But this is to assume that English, in *that* sense, is the language that Hill's poem is written in. There is so much French in the poem that this is surely a very hazardous assumption. Lucas, we may suppose, is too sophisticated to think, with Alan Massey writing in *PN Review*, that words like 'porte-cochère' comfortably remove Hill's poem from any applicability to the England where it was written and published: 'The scene is France: the time is Péguy's time, 1873–1914...' But if that is not the function of the generously interlarded French, then what is its function? It is related surely to what Hill in 'Our Word is Our Bond' excellently defines as the effect of the quotation-marks in Pound's *Homage to Sextus Propertius* and *Hugh Selwyn Mauberley*: 'the effect is not that of avoiding the rap but rather of recording the rapping noise made by those things which the world throws at us in the form of prejudice and opinion...' (The playing around with the idiom, 'taking the rap', is of course just what we are talking about: the *knowingness* of our language.) The effect of the French words and phrases in Hill's poem – sometimes within quotation-marks, sometimes not – is surely in some measure that of the time-honoured style that was once called 'macaronic'; it announces and acknowledges, and to that extent it deflects, the criticism that the idiom the poem is otherwise written in is *infected*, perhaps incurably. A British English that so often lapses into French declares, by that token, its awareness of its own loss of innocence. As Hill finely says in his essay, '"inverted commas" are a way of bringing pressure to bear and are also a form of "ironic and bitter" intonation acknowledging that pressure is being brought.' The French interlardings in *The Mystery of the Charity of Charles Péguy* are thus crucial to Hill's intention that the poem should enact, in his own words, 'mistrusting the abstraction, mistrusting its own mistrust, drawn half against its will...'

Lucas suggests harshly but plausibly that it was the foredoomed attempt to find or recover an innocent language that destroyed Matthew Arnold as a poet. However that may be, the impossible enterprise did not end with Arnold, and it has not ended yet. On the contrary, the poetic scene is full of people who believe that by writing like Edward Thomas, on the one hand, or William Carlos Williams, on the other, they can recover or reconstitute innocence in their medium. And even a senior poet like Norman MacCaig, who is too old a hand to chase such a will of the wisp, has nevertheless over the last twenty years moved perceptibly nearer to such seemingly limpid, seemingly artless styles. Indeed, such accommodations have become so much the rule since 1960 that Hill's refusal of them takes on the character of a dogged or haughty recalcitrance. 'Post-modern' is a cant term; but if we risk it, we may say that Hill in a post-modern period has stood out as on the contrary a late, a belated, Modernist. He wants us to see his poetry (and so we can) as continuous with that of Yeats, of Eliot, and of the Pound who wrote *Homage to Sextus Propertius* if not the Pound of *The Cantos*. In its abstruse and courtly way his essay, 'Our Word is Our Bond', seeks to persuade us that any alternatives we seem to find are false: that, differentiate as we may between American English and British English and Irish English, what Eliot and Yeats and Pound demonstrated sixty years ago – the depravity of the language we have to work with – can only have been aggravated, not ameliorated, by the passage of time between their day and ours.

Yet even if we grant this, does it mean that when one of our contemporaries lightens and loosens his forms we should see in this only a canny or craven acquiescence in a shift of fashion? (Not that Hill anywhere says this, but it seems a necessary implication of his argument.) Surely not, unless we were wrong to recognise as only *one* way forward that way which Hill has taken: 'Let the depravities be seen for what they are.' Another way would be, while knowing that the depravities cannot be expunged, still so far as possible to minimise the damage that they can do. One way of doing this would be to concern ourselves much more than we usually do with genre; for overt word-play is much more in keeping with some poetic genres than with others. And another way might be to ventilate our poetic structures, to let air into them – the air that we use when we speak, as we do not use it, except minimally and notionally, when we write. This Hill has never done: his diction has never been colloquial, nor even conversational. It cannot afford to be, because the laxer structures and rhythms of speech do not permit double-meanings, submerged puns, the duplicities of British English, to grind against each other (and thus highlight each other) in the way that Hill thinks necessary and honourably required of him. It is the relaxation of rhythm (not necessarily all the way to *vers libre*) which permits of 'ventilation'. And metrically Hill has been, as he still is, very conservative – one of the least noticed accomplishments of *The Mystery of the Charity of Charles Péguy* is that it consists of 400 lines of iambic pentameter, handled very inventively so as to avoid monotony. The Marlovian 'mighty line', the drumming decasyllable, is in the background throughout, as paradigm and promise. And sure enough, at times the promise is honoured:

How the mood swells to greet the gathering storm!
The chestnut trees begin to thresh and cast

huge canisters of blossom at each gust.
Coup de tonnerre! Bismarck is in the room!

One of the things that a more ventilated poetry must deny itself is the chance of producing lines as memorable and quotable as these. Another way of saying this, or perhaps only a related reflection, is that art, to be good or even great, does not have to be monumental: whereas Hill seems always to have wanted to create a monumental art – in this following one of his American masters, Allen Tate, and disregarding another, John Crowe Ransom, who eschewed the monumental as consistently as Tate strained after it. (In *The Lords of Limit* there is an essay on Ransom which argues in the end – in the end only, for the drift is hard to discern and hold onto – that Ransom betrayed himself and his vocation.)

If British English has thus become, for us who inherit it as a literary medium, depraved and duplicitous, does it not follow that we must be cagey about it in our prose as well as our verse? Hill nowadays does not refuse the inference; and this means, I'm afraid, that for most readers most of the time his recent essays are unreadable. 'The confines of a determined world "give" so as not to give; tropes are predestined to free election; the larger determinism allows for the smaller voluntarism.' Thus to turn on a sixpence three times in one sentence might be just about tolerable if the sentence were helped out by the melody that could come of its being strung across verse-lines; without that easement it is irreparably crabbed and indigestible. And yet some of these essays in *The Lords of Limit* were originally given as lectures – if they are hard to read, what must they have been like to listen to! Hill, however, won't compromise. In one essay here he excuses, he almost applauds, the Victorian philosopher T.H. Green for being, as a lecturer, perplexed and perplexing. And in another, which doesn't persuade me at all, he goes so far as to declare 'decadent' John Stuart Mill's surely commonsensical observation that 'a certain laxity in the use of language must be borne with, if a writer makes himself understood.' Not for Hill such laxities! Instead he commends, as nineteenth-century models, Hopkins's prose and Coleridge's, and that often enough as found in their private journals and personal letters. But this is surely foolish: their prose-styles, admirable though they are in ways that Hill brings out, just are not serviceable for any of the public occasions (a newspaper review, an inaugural lecture) when prose has to serve us. Hill's wariness about our slippery language is honourable: but when it leads him to such impractical stringencies, it is self-defeating. Moreover, what we call 'stringencies' may well be called, if we shift the focus only a little, 'self-indulgences'.

In some of the earlier and less strenuous essays here, he shows he can recognise with sympathy the constraints which such public poets as Ben Jonson and Swift agreed to observe, even as they reserved the right to transgress them on occasion. More strikingly, as late as 1979, in an important lecture here printed for the first time, Hill could tease out with daunting erudition and sympathy the similar though special constraints that the recusant poet Robert Southwell likewise bowed to. When he agrees that Southwell's 'Burning Babe', with its deliberate naïvety, should be read as a sophisticated variation on the medieval nativity-ballad, he is surely near to acknowledging that we can guard against the duplicities of British English in other ways than by forcing those duplicities onto the surface and into the open. Southwell's stanzas, it might even be said, are *ventilated*. It is when Hill gets to nineteenth-century writers that suddenly this option is closed, even for a recusant writer like Hopkins. And we are invited to suppose that for us, a century after Hopkins, such an option is even less available. But we don't have to agree; and I don't think we should.

A Various Art

A Various Art, edited by Andrew Crozier and Tim Longville (Manchester: Carcanet Press, 1989).[1]

When Andrew Crozier says that the British poetry generally on offer 'furnishes the pleasures of either a happy nostalgia or a frisson of daring and disgust', he says surely no more than the truth. If these are the pleasures that you look for in poetry (or in TV programmes for that matter, and up-market newspapers), you know where to look – not very far. And you will know not to look in the bulky anthology that Crozier has edited with Tim Longville. The poetry that Crozier and Longville present has not been 'generally on offer', and surprisingly has never tried to be. The seventeen poets represented have published with Longville's Grosseteste Press or Crozier's Ferry Press, or with kindred shoe-string enterprises like Ric Caddel's Pig Press – not because they couldn't break into the ring of the big metropolitan publishers, but because they chose not to try, distrusting the big houses' media-hype and show-casing of personalities. And yet they represent neither an 'underground' nor a 'counterculture' (those cherished notions of the 1960s, when most of them began publishing). Accordingly, their coming to terms with a mainstream publisher like Carcanet is, or ought to be, a notable event. As we might expect, however, Crozier and Longville are much more austere than most anthologists: no photographs here, no biographical information, not even dates of birth. At least two of their poets are dead, but there is no way to notice this except by noticing poems in memoriam one of them, John Riley. Longville and Crozier are trying to get attention for the poetry, not the poets. And this is surely admirable, for it means offering poetry not as an alternative or supplement to other media but as a medium unique in what it aspires to and sometimes achieves. Aspiration indeed is very much the key-note, and so this poetry will seem to many readers strikingly unworldly. Douglas Oliver, a poet hard to anthologize because his *forte* is inventing non-lyrical structures for long poems, hears an oracle tell him: 'normally you would censor soft backgrounds: beware

---

1   Originally commissioned by the *Sunday Telegraph*, the review was not run; Donald Davie has expanded on his comments for *PN Review*. – Ed., *PN Review*

that because it does not only censor that softness, it also censors the mean hardness you are supposedly countering'. The 'soft backgrounds' that Oliver is here enjoined to indulge consist of an unabashed clustering of expressions like 'I am so happy'... 'a calm voice speaking from far away'... 'in the near heart of me'... 'I bless you'... 'the worth of my love'. It is easy to find this cloying, and I find it so in the late John Riley but the aspiration to cleanse such crucial though tainted words is surely admirable, perhaps heroic. No one does this better, to my mind and ear, than Tim Longville, chiefly because he, more than most, meets the requirement that his co-editor Crozier enjoins: 'the verse line should... by the pressure its energy or shape might exert on syntax, intervene in meaning.'

★   ★   ★

In *PN Review* 68 Grevel Lindop, reviewing poems by the best-selling novelist and biographer Peter Ackroyd, was driven, in order to explain their insufficiency, to some detective work: 'Noting Ackroyd's Cambridge background and various acknowledgements to the Ferry Press, one recognizes the baleful heritage of J.H. Prynne. Prynne himself is one of the very few poets who have succeeded in making something genuinely interesting out of decentred self-referential verse... but Prynne seems to infect his disciples with a pretentiousness of the most dreary kind.' At much the same time Carl Rakosi, last surviving veteran of the Objectivists, was telling Australian readers (*Scripsi* 5: 3): 'Before going to Budapest I gave a reading at Cambridge and visited my friend Jeremy Prynne, most rigorous and intellectual of British poets. When he heard I was going to Budapest he gave me the name of a young man there he thought I would find interesting, Dr Mihály Szegedy-Maszák... Years ago he [Szegedy-Maszák] had spent a year at Cambridge studying American poetry with Prynne. Prynne, who had been introduced to my work by Andrew Crozier, a former student of his, and had come to have a high regard for it, introduced his Hungarian student to *Amulet*, an early book of mine...' Such citations, which could easily be augmented from the largely unbidden publications that thud through my letter-box from places as far apart as Boulder, Colorado, and Kyoto, Japan, show that J.H. Prynne has achieved what the French (and we also) call *succès d'estime*. Such may well be the only sort of success that nowadays a self-respecting poet can hope for, or aim at. Jeremy Prynne has achieved it by consistently (it has been a long haul) following the Duke of Wellington's advice: 'Never apologize, never explain.' And it's true that, as I can ruefully testify, offers to apologize and explain don't have a significant effect on numbers of copies sold. As one who first knew Jeremy as a Jesus College undergraduate, subsequently as his colleague among the Fellows of Caius, who have never experienced from him anything but considerate courtesy, I've no wish to do anything but congratulate him on his curious success. Did you ever wonder who is the 'most rigorous and intellectual of British poets'? Now you know, on the weighty testimony of the very intelligent and honourable poet, Carl Rakosi. And did you ever wonder if there was a court of appeal beyond that of *TLS* and *LRB* reviewers, awarders of poetry prizes, contrivers of *hype* for Faber and Chatto, and voters for the Professorship of Poetry at Oxford? Now you know that there is, and may begin to understand how the hierarchy that that court of appeal underwrites bears no relation at all to the prices at which poetic favourites are quoted on the international exchange.

All the same, if Prynne won't apologize nor explain, neither will I on his behalf. Fortunately or not, many of his companions in *A Various Art* are very ready to both apologize and explain in the very body of their poems. Indeed the point of establishing Prynne as the master of a school is to forestall any pretence that this anthology features him flanked by his acolytes and protégés. Not so. The book lives up to its title. And for instance few of the poems it includes answer to Grevel Lindop's epithet, 'decentred'. (For the valuable exactness of this, consult Lindop's outstandingly sensible article.) No, the poets here may or may not admire Prynne for the consistency with which he has opted out of the poetry market; but beyond that few of them have much in common with him. Consider Douglas Oliver in his 'Bonis Avibus' ('With favourable auspices'), written in memory of John Riley, author of 'Czargrad':

> A blight from England's present-day
> covers me. I can hardly move my mind.
> Is that any way to speak? Why
> do we let these bladder tonsils swell and gag
> above the hardly-heaving tongue? Is it respectful
> to our ancestors? All outside us so encrusted
> by the soft internal harms. Like lichen
> the self tears dry from crooked eyes; values
> within us beat: 'keep pure', 'keep pure',
> as blood courses along with dust on it.
> I don't understand it: the inaction of our good.
> A gliding, smooth and polished action
> is possible – a man sidles out
> of a pew in a church of another language, touches
> the lovely kiss onto a flat piece of wood.
> It is an ending: but a life of glad anyhow,
> of steady purgation of poisons in the suburbs,
> or bless this nation, even... that whole life
> settles like a bird on the gleaming lid

      avis beyond species and out of Czargrad.
              A poem. A bird. Where the head
    rests. Are scarcely symbolic but are Robert Grosseteste's
    version of 'truths in contemplation' – all
    I believe in. The censer drifts in its chains.
    The wood reflects a dream of purified ancestral red.

There are fussy and clever-clever touches here, like the uncertainty in line eight whether 'tears' is a verb or a noun, or even (for those who haven't read Pound) who Robert Grosseteste is or was. But the new thing is such a line as 'I don't understand it: the inaction of our good.' When did we last hear bewildered frustration at the state of England so blankly expressed, without modulating at once into partisan indignation and self-righteousness? Or when in a poem did we last hear 'Bless this nation' invoked, except with a snarl? Such sentiments just about *could* be expressed in a 'decentred' discourse, with equal boldness; but the context would qualify and *dis*qualify them, the boldness would have to be shown up as illusory and hollow. This discourse is *centred*; the 'I' that speaks it is for real, and will stand by what it has uttered.

In such a case, it may be said, we see a dribbling out of the poet's authority, from simply standing over the words that he has written, to an appeal to readers to eke out those words by what can be evoked from them by way of generous sympathy. If so, such writing is – so far as I can see – at the opposite pole from Prynne's non-communicating severity. Yet such poetry can call on precedents – notably in Wordsworth who similarly, time and again, calls on his readers to 'help him out'. One thinks of 'Milton, thou shouldst be living at this hour'. It may seem to be – perhaps it seems to Prynne – an undignified expedient. Yet just as Wordsworth was compelled to it, as a cry for help directed towards the otherwise complacent obtuseness of his fellow citizens, so our own poets (Douglas Oliver, for one) may be compelled to it, forced to undergo the indignity by their wretched recognition that after all and otherwise no one is listening, except half-heartedly.

It is not for nothing that I find myself invoking Wordsworth. Leaving aside a few ambiguous cases like Prynne and David Chaloner and Nick Totton (the strategies of these last explained by John Kerrigan in *Poetry Durham*, 17), the poetry of *A Various Art* is a thoroughly *romantic* poetry, not in the reach-me-down sense that equates unmetred verse with 'freedom' and metred verse with oppression, but rather in the agonized recognition that poetry which should speak to all men at present speaks to few. In order to speak to more, this poetry will make any sacrifices, the consequence of these sacrifices being (ironically) that in the short term it gets through to even fewer. Wordsworth experienced that also. This is a poetry that envisages and addresses a public that does not yet exist, which by its exertions it intends to call into being. A saturnine classicist who has no faith in the endeavour (thinking that the regeneration looked for has to start *behind* poetry, perhaps in religion) can yet salute the generosity and the self-discipline of the enterprise.

Marjorie Perloff, a distinguished and attentive American reader, has told Australians (*Scripsi* 5: 2) to look to *A Various Art* for one sign that English literary culture is drunkenly and uncertainly climbing out of the abyss of self-regarding and cynical frivolity which Hugh Kenner diagnosed as its condition in his *A Sinking Island*. Neither Kenner's diagnosis, nor Perloff's endorsement of it, should go unchallenged. Whatever our malaise, it is not something that a single anthology can signal the end of. And we may justly observe that the American and the Australian scenes seem to be infected differently indeed but not less grievously. *A Various Art*, not content with diagnosing the disease, concocts a sort of antidote. In the poems of Tim Longville and Douglas Oliver (to single them out) the antidote seems to be powerful and effective – if only we can persuade ourselves to take the dose.

PN Review 70, 16: 2 (1989).

Scottish Poetry in the Twentieth Century

Robert Crawford, *Devolving English Literature* (Oxford: Clarendon Press, 1992).

The Faber Book of 20th-Century Scottish Poetry, edited by Douglas Dunn (London: Faber and Faber 1992).

In books that go on about how the English have imposed their language and their manners on other English-speaking nations (Australian, Canadian, Scottish and Welsh and Irish, others), what is striking is how that Anglocentrism, allegedly located in London and Oxbridge mostly, is supposed to be deeply satisfying to the English themselves. Robert Crawford, who pursues the argument on behalf of the Scots, avoids this mistake, detecting in a provincial Englishman like Tony Harrison a fury and resentment not surpassed by any Scot. But this is hardly a novel perception, for Harrison has achieved fame on the strength of it. In fact, it's hard to find any English writer who isn't provincial in origin: I'm as much a West Riding product as Tony Harrison, though I haven't traded on it much. The outcome is obvious and ridiculous: if I have as much right to wear a chip on my shoulder as any Australian or Aberdonian, then who is left to man the supposedly overbearing metropolis, unless it is Kingsley Amis and John Betjeman? The ramparts so frailly manned should have given way long ago to the armies massed against them. What Crawford doesn't realise is that this indeed has happened; he is sounding the bugle for an assault on a fortress that surrendered years ago.

The nature of surrender, and the consequences of it, are what we might reasonably ponder. Such a pondering – ill-tempered as it happens, and brilliantly unfair – was *A Sinking Island* (1987) by another chip-shouldering ex-colonial, the Canadian Hugh Kenner. Crawford doesn't like Kenner's book: naturally not, since Kenner, convicting the whole *insula* of insularity, conspicuously doesn't exonerate any Scots from the indictment (though unkindest cut – he does exonerate one Welshman, David Jones). Worse still for Crawford, Kenner announces, 'There's no longer an English literature': by which he means that, whereas 'talent has not been lacking' – on the contrary, 'good poets are dispersed round the land'

and each has a personal following – yet 'no talk, however extensive, about any of them need cause you to mention another'. Talk of 'devolving English literature'! Can devolution go further than it has gone already inside England, where no talk of any one poet need cause you to mention another? But Robert Crawford can't have this, for he needs English literature to exist, so that Scottish literature can be defined against it. So, when he looks at English poets, he stays with those he can persuade himself are mavericks, like Tony Harrison and (very implausibly) the Larkin who befriended Douglas Dunn, once his Scottish neighbour in Hull. He ignores the pair (both provincials, of course) whom Kenner singled out as the most honourable exceptions: Charles Tomlinson, who applauded William Soutar, and Basil Bunting, who befriended MacDiarmid. Yet Tomlinson and Bunting are the true mavericks, as Kenner recognized. They are mavericks because, while acknowledging class-based and region-based resentment, in themselves as in others, they refused to be hypnotized by those concerns so as to neglect poetry's more important duties. I'm not sure that Crawford, down his nationalist perspective, recognizes any duty more important than resentment.

This makes him unfair not just to English poets, but to Scottish ones too. Nowhere does he mention (nor did Kenner) W.S. (Sydney) Graham, who took, perhaps at greater cost, the same decision that Tomlinson and Bunting made. Douglas Dunn, whose anthology is blessedly free of the prejudices that constrict Crawford, allows Graham twenty pages (as against thirty-five for MacDiarmid, twenty-two for Robert Garioch, twenty-one for Iain Crichton Smith), and in his fair-minded Introduction Dunn painfully acknowledges why Graham is little honoured in Scotland: 'he lived furth of Scotland for most of his adult life, and loved Cornwall. His relative neglect is due to more than the quirk of having been not-quite-obviously-Scottish-enough; he had the cheek to live somewhere else. Andrew Young, Edwin Muir, and several others, have been treated to petty discriminations of a similar kind.' I suspect that Dunn himself is among those 'several others'.

Graham, it seems, was a drunk; and not a convivial drunk, but sour and contumacious. And he was a sponger and skiver. Not an attractive character. But from the time of *The Nightfishing* (1955), with ever more authority through *Malcolm Mooney's Land* (1970) and *Implements in their Places* (1977), this Clydeside proletarian reflected on language, on how one may utter words not to encompass known experience but to summon up experience not yet known and perhaps in the end unknowable. When in *Malcolm Mooney's Land* he draws on Fridtjof Nansen's diaries, he is building on Mallarmé, who was before him in seeing the white and virgin unwritten page as a snowfield. But he goes beyond the Frenchman, for in Graham's snowfield there are crevasses.

A writer's language has its way with him. A lot turns on how he reacts to this condition, once it is brought home to him. Graham's attitude is light years away from those who, having discovered duplicities in language, are determined to root them out; or those others who, having discovered the duplicitousness, delightedly aggravate it. The better alternative, Graham profoundly says, is to reconstruct those silences, those realms of the heretofore unsayable, which a poetic kind of saying necessarily encroaches on. And his tone is surprising; often it makes for rueful comedy, as in titles like 'What is the language using us for?' or (delightfully) 'Language ah now you have me.' Dunn's selection from Graham is full and various, but he perhaps prudently spares the common reader the undoubtedly rarefied air that the mature Graham's astonishingly plain yet singing diction makes us breathe. He has touching poems that move at less exacting altitudes, concerned with human relations. Yet it's the poems about language that put him on a peak by himself. No poet Scottish or English, not even Bunting, recognised so clearly how language commands those who most seek and seem to command it. The one and only book on Graham (by Tony Lopez, 1989) is thoroughly workmanlike and useful.

What commands the writer, according to Graham, is not this language or that, but language as such. So he soars far above disputes about Lallans or Gaelic or standard English being the right vehicle for Scottish experience. Each language is a system which ultimately subjugates to itself every user of that language. Lallans or synthetic Scots, apparently created *ad hoc* and opportunistically by the young MacDiarmid, seems to be an exception, but is not – except conceivably for MacDiarmid himself, in the first flush of his audacity. The utopian notion that there is an unobstructed avenue from experience to utterance is blocked by this language as much as by any other. MacDiarmid's mid-career switch to standard English may be thought to acknowledge this. Certainly it was recognized by later Lallans writers like Robert Garioch, for whom Dunn makes large claims that should be taken seriously. Of course Lallans was never designed to be, nor was it ever, a transcript of Scottish demotic speech. Dunn is clear about this; I'm not sure it is so clear to all the young turks who are given an airing in the last pages of his anthology.

Dunn's Introduction – in fact, a brave and searching essay called 'Language and Liberty' – is not just fair-minded. It is learned, surprising and informative. And its playing fair with us is very far from the easy even-handedness of the 'Nor should we forget' variety, that we are used to from anthologists introducing their anthologies. Douglas Dunn has thought seriously about what and where Scottish poetry has got to – as witness particularly a quotation of several hundred words from Edwin Muir's *Scott and Scotland* (1936), a text that many nationalists have thought the definitive sell-out to the occupying power. (I think Muir's text is more dated than he allows for, but it was brave of him to reprint it.) As for Dunn's even-handedness, consider his verdict on a disagreement between two Gaelic poets of our time, Sorley MacLean and Iain Crichton Smith, about a Gaelic poet of long ago, Rob Dunn (d. 1778). Judging from the poems in the anthology translated by themselves, I will trust MacLean's opinion over Smith's. But that isn't the point. For the two of them to disagree publicly about the merits of one of their own poetic forbears is in itself proof of one of Dunn's most surprising contentions: that Scots Gaelic poetry, despite its small constituency, has experienced a revival. For quarrels about the canon, rather than grateful obeisance before it, are undoubtedly a sign of life. And then look at Dunn's comment on this divergence of opinion: 'That it should exist... suggests that Gaelic poetry's struggle with modernity is one in which traditional expectations could be resistant to ideas of "good poetry" when these have been taken in some measure from languages other than Gaelic itself.' What could be more poised, more carefully nuanced, and yet more deflating? Dunn's essay will annoy Gaelic-speaking Scots as well as other sorts; and his braving them is what assures his credibility with us outlanders.

I was sorry that he didn't give us Sorley MacLean's poem about the vanished woods of Raasay. But I quite take the point that to a demotic Glaswegian like Tom Leonard (b. 1944), that scene is as foreign as to any of us English suburbanites. In which case the question re-arises: what identity does Scottish poetry have, except as that which is not-English? Douglas Dunn tries to address this question, but his answer to it is vacuous. Given the capitulation of the English half of this equation, Scots have to ask themselves whether the distinction between the two ancient kingdoms doesn't resolve itself into the fact, interesting to psephologists but to no one else, that Scotland mostly votes Labour whereas most of England doesn't.

It would be intolerably complacent, however, to assert that a Scot loses nothing when he opts to speak and write metropolitan English. There are impressive instances which seem to affirm this – notably in the eighteenth-century James Thomson, author of *The Seasons*, whom Robert Crawford treats with proper and welcome respect. Does any one seriously maintain that Thomson, a great poet, would have been greater if he had written in 'the Doric'? In the present century, however, I number among my friends several Anglicized Scots, who, I judge, were disabled by the stress of that divided inheritance. Their emblematic and exemplary representative is surely John Buchan, Lord Tweedsmuir, biographer of Montrose, who contributed to MacDiarmid's *Scottish Chapbook*, compiled in 1924, an anthology of Scots vernacular writing, and wrote a flattering preface to MacDiarmid's *Sangschaw*. In this anthology their very muted spokesman seems to be Norman Cameron:

I bought (I was too wealthy for my age)
A passage to the dead ones' habitat,
And learnt, under their tutelage,
To twitter like a bat

In imitation of their dialect.
Crudely I aped their subtle practices;
By instinct knew how to respect
Their strict observances.

The regions of the dead are small and pent,
Their movements faint, sparing of energy...

Cameron was dead at 48, and who knows what he might have gone on to do, had he lived longer? So he isn't a clinching witness. But the combination in his poems generally of extreme and witty delicacy in expression with paucity of energy, and indeed of subject-matter, does seem symptomatic. His poem is called 'A Visit to the Dead'; and it doesn't seem excessive to suppose that the English enunciation he learned at Fettes was indeed, for him, a voice of the dead. The case of Buchan shows that the Anglicized Scot certainly isn't disabled from succeeding in public life: but it may be that he's somehow maimed in his imagination.

English and American in Briggflatts

Anglo-American poetry… if we need such a category at all, and whatever we might mean by it, Basil Bunting's poetry seems to belong there. His sensibility is profoundly English – not British, but *English*, and Northumbrian English at that; and yet his techniques, his acknowledged masters and peers in the present century, are all of them American. This makes him a difficult poet. For the American reader he is difficult because the voice that speaks in his poems (and in his case 'voice' must be understood very literally), no less than the range of his allusions, especially topographical ones (and in *Briggflatts* topography is crucial), utter insistently an alien, a non-American, experience and attitude. For the English reader he is difficult because, line by line and page by page, his words come at us according to a system of juxtapositions and disjunctions which, because we can find no precedent for it among English poets, strikes us as not systematic at all but random and arbitrary. But plainly, on this showing, the English reader is better placed than the American: whereas one hardly knows where to tell an American reader to start in order to come to terms with Bunting, the English reader has only to acquaint himself with the body of arguments and assumptions about poetry that Bunting in his youth worked out in alliance with certain American contemporaries. We study his American associations only so that we may subsequently discount them. And we may well think that in the future we shall have to do the same with other English poets besides Bunting. *Technically*, surely, Anglo-American is what our poetry will be henceforth, but at levels more profound than technique – to which however only technique gives us access – the English poet will remain as English as ever, the American as American.

In 1966 the American poet and declared 'Objectivist', George Oppen, was explaining himself to his French translator: 'Several dozen commentators and reviewers have by now written on the assumption that the word "Objectivist" indicated the contributors' objective attitude to reality. It meant, of course, the poets' recognition of the necessity of form, the objectification of the poem.'[1] With that 'of course' Oppen is

---

1   See Serge Faucherau, 'Three Oppen Letters with a Note', *Ironwood* 5, Tucson, Arizona (1975), pp. 78–85.

too sanguine, as he is again when he goes on to say: 'The point may seem rather obvious today…' The point is so far from obvious that what is meant, or might be meant, by 'the objectification of the poem' is a question not even debated, let alone resolved. As Hugh Kenner has said, '*That* history is still unwritten.'[2] History in the first place, not theory… For Oppen in 1966 was a veteran harking back nearly forty years to the initial formulation of a conviction that had governed his writing over the years since. Thus when he speaks of 'the contributors', he means the contributors to *An Objectivists' Anthology*, which appeared in 1932, edited by Louis Zukofsky and published by Oppen and his wife on a small press of their own in a French provincial town. The anthology is dedicated to Ezra Pound, and it includes two poems by Pound, but the contributors that Oppen has in mind are Basil Bunting, Robert McAlmon, Carl Rakosi, Kenneth Rexroth, Charles Reznikoff, William Carlos Williams, Louis Zukofsky. This group had good reason to be grateful to Pound because a year before he had donated to them space allotted to him in the magazine *Poetry* (Chicago). And the interesting and affecting thing is that in 1966 Oppen still aligns himself with these men: '…it remains my opinion that Reznikoff, Rakosi, Zukofsky, Bunting of Briggflats [*sic*] are the most considerable poets of my own generation.' How wide of the truth it is, to say that the point these poets were making 'may seem rather obvious today', is apparent in the fact that most of these names are still unknown or go largely unregarded – the most flagrant case being that of Zukofsky, originally the spokesman and theorist for the entire group.

For our purposes, the intriguing feature is that all these names are American, save one – Basil Bunting, a name that figures along with Zukofsky's and Oppen's in Pound's own *Active Anthology* of 1933. But in the first place it's precisely Pound's patronage of this group that may cause misunderstandings. There is a general notion abroad that as it were the Poundian scriptures were promulgated, the tablets of the Poundian law were handed down, once and for all in the period of Imagism and Vorticism, and that thereafter Pound would patronize only poets who hewed very close to the line thus laid down. This is quite untrue. Some years before 1930, in his ill-advised campaign on behalf of Ralph Cheever Dunning, Pound had irritably exclaimed against those who took statements appropriate to the particular circumstances of 1914 as if they were injunctions binding upon all poets at all times; and in a few years time he was to be forced to the same exasperated protest when he wanted to applaud Binyon's translation of Dante. And so it should come as less of a surprise, to find Oppen beginning his case for Objectivism by attacking a central Imagist document:

2   Hugh Kenner, *The Pound Era* (Berkeley, 1971), p. 406.

We could say – surely *I* would say –: The image for the sake of the poet, not for the sake of the reader. The image as a test of sincerity, as against (tho I may quote inaccurately here): 'The sun rose like a red-faced farmer leaning over a fence', which last is a 'picture' intended for the delectation of the reader who may be imagined to admire the quaintness and ingenuity of the poet, but can scarcely have been part of the poet's attempt to find himself in the world – unless perhaps to find himself as a charming conversationalist.

Of course Oppen *does* misquote. What he has in mind is T.E. Hulme's 'Autumn', the first of five poems which Pound printed provocatively (as 'The Complete Poetical Works of T.E. Hulme') at the end of his *Ripostes* in 1912:

> A touch of cold in the Autumn night –
> I walked abroad,
> And saw the ruddy moon lean over a hedge
> Like a red-faced farmer.
> I did not stop to speak, but nodded,
> And round about were the wistful stars
> With white faces like town children.

Yet Oppen's misremembering does not destroy the point he is making. For it is surely quite true that in Hulme's piece there is indeed a great deal of self-regarding and yet cajoling whimsy, which does indeed point quite away from what Oppen goes on to call 'the strength of Imagism', 'its demand that one actually *look*.' And thus, however aptly Hulme may have come to Pound's hand in 1912, when Pound wanted to assert that 'As for the future, *Les Imagistes*... have that in their keeping', none the less, by elevating this trivial and dubious piece to the status of central Imagist exhibit (for this is what it has since become), Pound opened the way to whimsical trivia as well as to the 'demand that one actually *look*'. Zukofsky and Oppen were right in 1932 to want to purge the Imagist inheritance of this weakness, and Pound by giving them his blessing virtually admitted as much.

It can still be said of course that the purge 'went too far'. Readers of Oppen's own poems – exhilaratingly sparse and 'purged' as they are – may well feel so. And those who remember and endorse Wordsworth's definition of the poet as 'a man speaking to men' may well feel that Oppen's sneer at the 'charming conversationalist' is not quite so conclusive as he means it to be. When Basil Bunting says, 'Pound has had a great influence on me of course but Wordsworth has had a steady, solid one all my life on everything',[3] he declares an allegiance that none of his

3   *Multi: Basil Bunting from the British Press*, Octaroon Book. A flyer distributed at Bunting's San Francisco reading, 1976.

American associates, not excluding Pound, would subscribe to. And it is somewhere here that one starts differentiating this English 'objectivist' from the Americans, and envisaging the possibility of a distinctively English version of this otherwise all-American movement. But first it must be emphasized that 'objectivist' is certainly what Bunting is, that he undoubtedly endorses all the positions taken up by Zukofsky and Oppen more than forty years ago. And this is something that his English readers have not taken account of. They know him as a Poundian poet – as one has been in the habit of saying, 'the only card-carrying English Poundian'. But in the preface to his *Loquitur* (1965) Bunting acknowledged 'a continual debt to the two greatest poets of our age, Ezra Pound *and Louis Zukofsky*.' The italics are mine; and in what follows I shall enquire what Bunting meant by those italicized words – not principally so as to get Bunting into perspective, but rather, as an English poet addressing other English poets, to see where English poetry has got to, and where it may go to next (at our hands, if we so choose).

And so we must go back to 'the necessity of form, the objectification of the poem' – 'as against', so Oppen goes on to say, 'the liquidation of poetry into the sentimentalism of the American socalled Imagists of the late twenties and early nineteen-thirties'. (Who *they* were, we need not now enquire, we need only note once again that Objectivism defines itself as what Imagism – at any rate, one sort of Imagism – is not.) William Carlos Williams in 1944 was talking about 'the necessity of form, the objectification of the poem', when he defined a poem as 'a small (or large) machine made of words'. And twenty years later Bunting is saying the same thing when he declares: 'A work of art is something constructed, something made in the same way that a potter makes a bowl. A bowl may be useful but it may be there only because the potter liked that shape – and it's a beautiful thing. The attempt to find any meaning in it would be manifestly absurd.'[4] For most readers, I dare say, Williams's 'machine' will seem to point one way – towards *agitprop*, perhaps, and Bunting's pot will point almost the opposite way – back towards the nineties and Oscar Wilde. But the perception of the poem as artifact rather than communiqué is not a monopoly of aestheticism; any more than 'form' is a monopoly of those who write triolets and villanelles, or verses that can be scanned:

> The lines of this new song are nothing
> But a tune making the nothing full
> Stonelike become more hard than silent
> The tune's image holding in the line.

That is Zukofsky's way of putting it, and exemplifying it too. And those

4   Bunting, loc. cit.

for whom the analogy with the musician comes easier than the analogy with the potter may set beside Zukofsky's lines Bunting's from *Briggflatts*

> It is time to consider how Domenico Scarlatti
> condensed so much music into so few bars
> with never a crabbed turn or congested cadence,
> never a boast or a see-here; and stars and lakes
> echo him and the copse drums out his measure...

Bunting's 'never a boast or a see-here' corresponds, at least in part, to Oppen castigating Hulme's 'Autumn' for 'the falsity of ingenuity, of the posed tableau, in which the poet also, by implication, poses.'

And yet 'It is time to consider...' Wouldn't Oppen have to object to that? Wouldn't he think that it established the poet merely as 'a... conversationalist'? Perhaps not. But it does strike a note that we seldom find in the American objectivists: a note that is social and public, where theirs is characteristically intimate and private. In their poems the addressee is usually in the singular: the poet is a man who speaks not to men but to *a man*. Or, to a woman – as Oppen does, touchingly:

> To find now depth, not time, since we cannot, but depth
>
> To come out safe,   to end well
>
> We have begun to say goodbye
> To each other
> And cannot say it

This is from Oppen's *Seascape: Needle's Eye* (1972), in which the only punctuation stops that appear – and those sparsely – are comma, dash, and inverted comma. The punctuation is as sparse or sparser in *North Central* (1968) by Lorine Niedecker, who was for Bunting at that time 'the best living poetess'. (Though she never published with the Objectivists, Mrs Niedecker, an exquisite poet since dead, was as surely of their company as, *avant la lettre*, Marianne Moore was.) And throughout the ten poems of Williams's sequence 'Pictures from Brueghel', in his *Selected Poems* (1969), there is not a single punctuation stop. On the other hand, merely to turn the pages of Bunting's volumes is to see the full range of punctuation stops sown at least as thickly as in normal prose; and a closer inspection will show that for the most part they have the same function as in prose, clarifying the articulate structure of sentences. This points to an acknowledgement by Bunting of the social and public institution that grammar is – an acknowledgement that his American peers (though not, incidentally, Zukofsky) mostly, or often, refuse to make.

It will be clear what these comments are tending to – to the suggestion that for the English poet the writing of poems is a public and social activity, as for his American peers it isn't. Considering that until the publication of *Briggflatts* in 1966, when the poet himself was sixty-six, Bunting had been ignored by the British public as totally as Oppen and Zukofsky and Niedecker had been by the American, this contrast is very striking. And I'm prepared to argue that this is, and should continue to be, a distinctive feature of English poetry of our time, as against American.

But this, though it is true, is something one must beware of saying at all loudly or at all often, to the English reading-public. For the sad fact is that English readers of contemporary poetry – few as they are, and perhaps just *because* they are so few – have got used to being cajoled and coaxed, at all events sedulously *attended to*, by their poets. Teachers in English classrooms have for decades now persuaded school-children and students to conceive of the reading of a poem as a matter of responding to nudges that the poet, on this showing debased into a rhetorician, is supposedly at every point administering to them. And accordingly English readers have taken to their bosoms a poet like the late John Berryman who, though an American and at times a very affecting writer indeed, does indeed nudge and cajole and coax his readers, in a way that one can be sure Americans such as Oppen and Zukofsky are offended and incensed by. Oppen flies to the other extreme when he declares, 'The image for the sake of the poet, not for the sake of the reader'; and so does Bunting when he declares, of his poem like a pot, 'The attempt to find any meaning in it would be manifestly absurd.' Neither of these declarations is worded with care, and neither is defensible as it stands. But behind them both is a conviction that is wholesome, which the English reader needs to hear about even more than the American does: the conviction that a poem is a transaction between the poet and his subject more than it is a transaction between the poet and his readers. This is to make the poet once again more than a rhetorician; and on this showing the reader, though the poet cannot be oblivious of his presence, nevertheless is merely 'sitting in on' or 'listening in to' a transaction which he is not a party to. That Bunting is more social, more public, than Oppen – this is true and significant and important; but what is more salutary for the English reader is to realize that Bunting none the less shares the Objectivists' determination to cut the reader down to size, by making him realize that he is only as it were a bystander.

The same lesson, incidentally, can be read out of Hardy. As John Bayley has said, though 'his need for praise was as great or greater than that of other artists', yet 'Hardy's anthropomorphic imagination is a substitute for... the direct intercourse of writer and reader', and accordingly, 'the way to appreciate Hardy best in his poems is to resign oneself to being cut off from him'.[5] Because of this the current vogue for Hardy's

5 'Separation and Non-communication as Features of Hardy's Poetry', *Agenda* 14: 3 (Autumn 1976), pp. 45–62.

poetry in England, though it certainly has its unfortunate sides – as when it nourishes Little Englandism, or contrives to be at once idolatrous of Hardy and condescending to him – none the less is welcome. What needs to be said – what one wishes John Bayley had said – is that in this respect Hardy is not an odd man out: that 'being cut off from' the poet one is reading is a normal experience; that it is Berryman's intimacy with his reader that is exceptional.

How intransigently Bunting holds to the poem as artifact, as verbal machine, appears in an interview he gave about *Briggflatts*. This is a very out-of-the-way document[6] – which is a great pity, since it is indispensable for penetrating that poem, however much the author might want to pretend otherwise. Here Bunting insists that his poem came to him in the shape of a schematic diagram, which he proceeds to draw for his interviewers. They cannot believe their eyes: 'Well… when you started, or say at this stage, this piece of paper, this outline, did you know that it was Briggflatts, that that was the title, that the village was the…' And Bunting interrupts: no, he knew nothing of that, the poem was there before him in its schematic blueprint 'before there was a line written or thought of'. The actual wording of the poem, it seems, actually and quite literally its *content*, was merely the filling in of the outline thus determined in advance. And yet the writing that 'fills in' is – in cadence and orchestration of sound, no less than in the associations of images – as far from aestheticism as this:

> Cobweb hair on the morning,
> a puff would blow it away.
> Rime is crisp on the bent,
> ruts stone-hard, frost spangles fleece.
> What breeze will fill that sleeve limp on the line?
> A boy's jet steams from the wall, time from the year,
> care from deed and undoing.
> Shamble, cold, content with beer and pickles,
> towards a taciturn lodging amongst strangers.

I will show my hand without more equivocation, and assert that it is writing of this quality – so compact, having no syllables to spare for nudges or tipping the wink – that English poetry needs to assimilate and build on. Only when we have done that shall we be able to deny Oppen's and Kenner's contention that the whole Objectivist endeavour is 'an American movement'. Why should we want to do that? For our own good, I think. And, heaven knows, the matter that Bunting packs into

6   *Georgia Straight* (Vancouver, British Columbia). Writing Supplement 6. (The interview was subsequently reprinted, in slightly different form, in *Agenda* 16: 1 [Spring 1978], pp. 8–19. – Ed.)

Briggflatts, the content of it, the experience that it re-creates and celebrates, is indelibly and specifically English enough to satisfy anybody. He has shown us that the achievement is abundantly possible, if only we choose to emulate it. To emulate him does not mean abandoning metre; it does not mean, in his Poundian fashion, peppering our pages with the names of Catullus and Firdausi, Dante and Villon; least of all does it mean taking over his maddening habit of supplying notes that only tease. But it does mean writing like this, about autumn twilight over an ancient battlefield in the Yorkshire dales:

> Grass caught in willow tells the flood's height that has subsided;
> overfalls sketch a ledge to be bared tomorrow.
> No angler homes with empty creel though mist dims day.
> I hear Aneurin number the dead, his nipped voice.
> Slight moon limps after the sun. A closing door
> stirs smoke's flow above the grate. Jangle
> to skald, battle, journey; to priest Latin is bland.
> Rats have left no potatoes fit to roast, the gamey tang
> recalls ibex guts steaming under a cold ridge,
> tomcat stink of a leopard dying while I stood
> easing the bolt to dwell on a round's shining rim.
> I hear Aneurin number the dead and rejoice,
> being adult male of a merciless species.
> Today's posts are piles to drive into the quaggy past
> on which impermanent palaces balance.
> I see Aneurin's pectoral muscle swell under his shirt,
> pacing between the game Ida left to rat and raven,
> young men, tall yesterday, with cabled thighs.
> Red deer move less warily since their bows dropped.
> Girls in Teesdale and Wensleydale wake discontent.
> Clear Cymric voices carry well this autumn night,
> Aneurin and Taliesin, cruel owls
> for whom it is never altogether dark, crying
> before the rules made poetry a pedant's game.

That this passage about killing comes from a poem named after a Quaker meeting-house, written by a Quaker poet who went to prison for his pacifism in the First World War, is, as they say, relevant. But this is information that we may or may not bring to the poem; it is not *in* the poem, nor necessary to it. For this poet eschews the sort of intimate relation with us in which consideration of his personal history would be to the point. Instead he aims for and achieves the hieratic tone of epic and lament, in which his own voice is indistinguishable from that of the ancient Cymric poet, Aneurin. We are as little aware of the historical identity of Basil Bunting as we are of that of Thomas Gray, the valetudinarian Cambridge don, when Gray makes over the same Cymric poem (the *Gododdin*) into eighteenth-century heroic idiom:

> To Cattraeth's vale in glitt'ring row
> Twice two hundred warriors go;
> Every warrior's manly neck
> Chains of regal honour deck,
> Wreath'd in many a golden link:
> From the golden cup they drink
> Nectar, that the bees produce,
> Or the grape's ecstatic juice.
> Flush'd with mirth and hope they burn:
> But none from Cattraeth's vale return,
> Save Aeron brave, and Conan strong,
> (Bursting thro' the bloody throng)
> And I, the meanest of them all,
> That live to weep, and sing their fall.

Bunting's achievement is greater than Gray's, because he achieves the hieratic tone not by archaic diction but by ramming his words so hard, one on the heel of the other (object on verb on subject), that no interstices are left through which his eye on the thing to be said can be deflected towards the reader, the person he is saying it to. Though it is unthinkable that George Oppen could, or would ever want to, address himself to this subject, yet this writing answers to his stringent prescriptions for Objectivist poetry; and we have seen Oppen admit as much. Elevated though it is, this passage is all poetry, there is no point at which it strays into the rhetorician's persuasive wooing of an audience. This is where English poetry has got to, it is what English poets must assimilate and go on from.

PN Review 5, 5: 1 (1977); reprinted in *The Poet in the Imaginary Museum.*

One Way to Misread Briggflatts

Briggflatts opens thus:

> Brag, sweet tenor bull,
> descant on Rawthey's madrigal,
> each pebble its part
> for the fells' late spring.
> Dance tiptoe, bull,
> black against may.
> Ridiculous and lovely
> chase hurdling shadows
> morning into noon.
> May on the bull's hide
> and through the dale
> furrows fill with may,
> paving the slowworm's way.
>
> A mason times his mallet
> to a lark's twitter,
> listening while the marble rests,
> lays his rule
> at a letter's edge,
> fingertips checking,
> till the stone spells a name
> naming none,
> a man abolished.
> Painful lark, labouring to rise!
> The solemn mallet says:
> In the grave's slot
> he lies. We rot.
>
> Decay thrusts the blade,
> wheat stands in excrement
> trembling. Rawthey trembles.
> Tongue stumbles, ears err
> for fear of spring.
> Rub the stone with sand,

wet sandstone rending
roughness away. Fingers
ache on the rubbing stone.
The mason says: Rocks
happen by chance.
No one here bolts the door,
love is so sore.

Stone smooth as skin,
cold as the dead they load
on a low lorry by night.
The moon sits on the fell
but it will rain.
Under sacks on the stone
two children lie,
hear the horse stale,
the mason whistle,
harness mutter to shaft,
felloe to axle squeak,
rut thud the rim,
crushed grit.

Stocking to stocking, jersey to jersey,
head to a hard arm,
they kiss under the rain,
bruised by their marble bed.
In Garsdale, dawn;
at Hawes, tea from the can.
Rain stops, sacks
steam in the sun, they sit up.
Copper-wire moustache,
sea-reflecting eyes
and Baltic plainsong speech
declare: By such rocks
men killed Bloodaxe.

Fierce blood throbs in his tongue,
lean words.
Skulls cropped for steel caps
huddle round Stainmore.
Their becks ring on limestone,
whisper to peat.
The clogged cart pushes the horse downhill.
In such soft air
they trudge and sing,

laying the tune frankly on the air.
All sounds fall still,
fellside bleat,
hide-and-seek peewit.

Her pulse their pace,
palm countering palm,
till a trench is filled,
stone white as cheese
jeers at the dale.
Knotty wood, hard to rive,
smoulders to ash;
smell of October apples.
The road again,
at a trot.
Wetter, warmed, they watch
the mason meditate
on name and date.

Rain rinses the road,
the bull streams and laments.
Sour rye porridge from the hob
with cream and black tea,
meat, crust and crumb.
Her parents in bed
the children dry their clothes.
He has untied the tape
of her striped flannel drawers
before the range. Naked
on the pricked rag mat
his fingers comb
thatch of his manhood's home.

On this long passage a recent commentary, designed (no doubt shrewdly) to reach the greatest number of Bunting's countrymen, reads as follows:

Briggflatts is subtitled 'An Autobiography'. We are warned not to read it as literal autobiography. In the first section Bunting peoples a Northumbrian landscape with images and then skilfully co-ordinates them. We meet the lively bull, Rawthey, and the less lively tombstone maker, reading his new inscription with his fingertips. Life, passion and 'music' are embodied in Rawthey, while death is embodied in the mason. Against the backdrop of these images, two lovers come, watch 'the mason meditate / on name and date', and generally appreciate what they see. They go home and make love before the fire, in a passage where Bunting's rhetoric gets the better of him and he produces banal effects. The lover unties 'tape / of her striped flannel drawers' and at last ' on the pricked rag mat / his fingers comb / thatch of his manhood's home'. The unfortunate rhyme and conceit, the academic poise, are totally out of keeping with the poem.[1]

The verse and the commentary thus bleakly juxtaposed, what are we to do about it? It is too late, I think, for the strategy already time-honoured, of holding the philistine up to ridicule, and trusting the common reader in time to see his way around him. We should have learned by now that the common reader has neither the assurance nor the resources to see his way around the knowledgeable philistine, least of all when that philistine is his professor, as nowadays he often is. And in this case the commentator, Michael Schmidt, has as it happens deserved rather well of the British public, in his capacities as editor and publisher. He is not a philistine, in any simple sense; but rather a man who has been extensively educated (first at Harvard, I think, and thereafter at Oxford – so the blame is shared across the Atlantic) into a frame of mind towards poetry, and a set of assumptions about it, out of which, and in terms of which, it is impossible for him to engage with what is going on in any page of *Briggflatts*. We will merely note in passing that the Rawthey is a river not the bull. We must surely deny ourselves the rhetorical pleasures of derision and invective, applying ourselves instead to discovering patiently just what unformulated and doubtless unconscious assumptions in the commentator have impelled him so wide of the mark.

And we must deny ourselves, except in passing, the pleasure of asking Michael Schmidt whether striped flannel drawers are normal underwear amid his female acquaintances, since the word 'banal' seems to imply that they are. But we can certainly ask him what circumlocution for pubic hair he would prefer to Bunting's, which he finds so 'unfortunate'. Is he of those who would call a spade a spade, and hair, 'hair'? And if he is not, how can he deny that 'thatch of his manhood's home' is a circumlocution at once accurate and elegantly ingenious, compact and yet tender? I fear that the words 'elegant' and 'ingenious' will point for others besides him to what he calls 'academic poise' – perhaps the unkindest cut of all, from Bunting's own point of view. And it is true that circumlocution has been in bad odour, as a poetic resource, ever since the Preface to *Lyrical Ballads*. But what we have here is a *kenning*, as in old English; that is to say, a sort of circumlocution that is, as a poetic form, very ancient and primitive indeed, being only a special version of that most primitive of forms, the riddle. *Briggflatts* is full of such 'kennings'; and if we applaud them as

---

1   Michael Schmidt, *An Introduction to Fifty Modern British Poets* (Pan Literature Guides, 1979).

elegant and ingenious, that implies only that elegance and ingenuity were as much valued by the Anglo-Saxon- or Cymric-speaking Briton of the allegedly Dark Ages, as by us heirs of Laforgue.

We can hardly fail to note, in this passage as in the phrase 'out of keeping', how the spectre of neo-classical decorum hovers over Michael Schmidt's responses. However, we can with more profit, to ourselves as well as to him, dwell on his observation that 'Life, passion, and "music" are embodied in Rawthey, while death is embodied in the mason.' This comment in fact takes us back to the origins of the Modern Movement, in *Bouvard et Pécuchet*, where Flaubert's couple of sublime and touching idiots are side-tracked time and again – by their readings in popularized science as by popularized aesthetics – into disregarding the infinitely various and satisfying surface of things, probing *through* that surface to arrive at significances allegedly 'deeper', and certainly much simpler. Rather than let the bull be a bull, and the mason a mason, Michael Schmidt, like Bouvard or Pécuchet, asks that each of them 'stand in for' (the currently acceptable term is 'embody' or 'incarnate', though there is always the maid-of-all-work, 'symbolize') some large abstraction like 'life' or 'death'. If we object that for Bunting as for Flaubert a bull is a bull is a bull, and a mason is a mason is a mason, Schmidt will be provoked to unhelpful thoughts about Gertrude Stein. Yet so it is: in literature or out of it, a mason is a man who pursues one particular trade, and if that trade commits him to trafficking with the dead, that traffic does not define him so as to scant the living variety of him, in his other capacities. That variety Bunting honours, even in the relatively few verses we have quoted. But for his commentator, that variety is unmanageable; and so he subscribes instead to what E.A. Burtt called (in his *Metaphysical Foundations of Modern Physical Science*) 'the postulate of an impoverished reality'; that is to say, to the unargued assumption that Nature is simpler and less bounteous than she seems. This is to suppose that Nature 'puts up a good show', or 'keeps up a splendid front'; but that her entertaintments, which seem so unflaggingly novel, are really variations on a very few basic themes, and similarly her furnishings, which seem so various, are in fact only cunningly disguised variants on a strictly limited wardrobe. But of course it is possible to believe, as Bunting seems to do, that Nature (*human* nature included) is just as inexhaustibly various, as copiously inventive for good and ill, as she seems to be. For instance she knows and provides for many ways of 'making love', from the shy caress, and the shining look exchanged, through to various sorts of copulation. And so the commentator's blunt assertion that 'they' (two children, though he doesn't say so) 'make love before the fire', quite brutally over-rides the range of possibilities that Bunting with quiet delicacy leaves open. Undoubtedly a sexual passage of some sort happens between the girl and the boy; but to say that they 'make love', appealing necessarily to what we usually understand by that expression, is to define just what Bunting tactfully leaves indefinite. And so it seems we must say that the reader who finds 'striped flannel drawers' indecorous is unable to recognize decorum when his author observes it on a matter rather more important.

It's from this point of view that we can see what Michael Schmidt means by calling the striped flannel drawers 'banal'. He means that, try as he may, he can't make these words symbolize anything beyond themselves. The words stubbornly point to that which they name, and to nothing else, to nothing 'beneath' or 'above' or 'beyond'. And we should not delude ourselves; thousands of readers besides Michael Schmidt believe that in poetry words must always do something other than this, something 'more'. These are the readers for whom it would make no sense to say that Flaubert is a very *poetic* novelist. Seventy years after Ford told Pound that today's poet must compete not only with the great poets of the past but with Stendhal and Flaubert also (and Pound passed the word to Eliot, and both Eliot and he began preaching that same gospel), Ford's lesson has not been heard in most influential circles, or else, if heard, it has not been understood.

The most baleful word in Schmidt's account is 'co-ordinates': 'Bunting peoples a Northumbrian landscape with images and then skil-fully co-ordinates them…'. It is not beside the point to remark that 'co-ordinate', as a noun, has a special and specially privileged place in the language of mathematicians. What Schmidt seems to mean by it is something like this: that the reader (and, for all we are told to the contrary, writer also) sets up in his mind two columns, one headed 'Life' and the other 'Death'; and that whatever images thereafter present themselves (blessedly vague word, that 'images') must be entered in the one column or in the other. How inadequate and obfuscating such a procedure is, as regards *Briggflatts*, will appear if we extend by a few verses our quotation from the first section of the poem:

> Gentle generous voices weave
> over bare night
> words to confirm or delight
> till bird dawn.
> Rainwater from the butt
> she fetches and flannel
> to wash him inch by inch,
> kissing the pebbles.
> Shining slowworm part of the marvel.
> The mason stirs:
> Words!
> Pens are too light.
> Take a chisel to write.

290   *With the Grain*

The slowworm has here become the boy's penis, but without scanting in the least the literal meaning that it has had at the very start of the poem, which it will later have again – as (OED) 'A small harmless scincoid lizard, *Anguis Fragilis*, native to most parts of Europe'; and the 'pebbles' have become the boy's testicles, without however in the least diminishing their status as (OED) small stones 'worn and rounded by the action of water'. When we reflect that, as small stones, pebbles are units of that material which the mason shapes and incises so as to honour the dead, this kenning forces us to realise how hopeless it is to approach this poem by way of sorting its images into 'lively' and 'deathly'. The life is *in* the death, and *vice-versa*; as the poem itself has told us, quite explicitly:

> Decay thrusts the blade,
> wheat stands in excrement
> trembling. Rawthey trembles.

What Rawthey trembles at isn't fear of death; he trembles with erotic excitement, sparked to it precisely by the 'deathly' images of decay and excrement. And yet that isn't quite right, either: fear of death is part of erotic excitement, and *vice-versa*. Once we take 'lively' and 'deathly' as mutually exclusive categories, we have closed our minds in advance to just the perceptions that this poem is designed to explore and enforce.

Our purpose – let us remind ourselves – is not to score points, nor to exercise a facile and self-serving derision. The purpose is diagnosis – of a condition like Michael Schmidt's, from which it is impossible to engage with one of the great poems of our time. It's in this spirit that one enquires how Schmidt came to entertain a set of assumptions that so conclusively shut him off from Bunting's poem. And the answer, I believe, comes on the next page of his commentary, when he is commenting on a phrase from the second section of Bunting's poem, 'Schoenberg's Maze', and on the allusion to the Minotaur in the last lines of that section: 'The image of the labyrinth – Muir's image for the mind – comes into play.' Why this abrupt invocation of a poet surely as unlike Bunting as it is possible to imagine? I think the answer is plain: Edwin Muir is one poet with a respectable reputation from Bunting's lifetime who certainly did subscribe to 'the postulate of an impoverished reality'. His use of symbols like the labyrinth (*fixed* symbols at the opposite pole from the fluid and provisional symbols of the *symbolistes*) can only make sense on that postulate. And to some of us – for at this point one has to take sides – it is precisely this in Muir which makes him a poet of the second order at best. It is unfortunate that one cannot make the case that needs to be made for Bunting without, at least in the present context, denigrating Muir, who was a harmless and amiable man and indeed something more, for it was he, collaborating with his wife, who introduced the English-speaking world to Kafka. (That Kafka's world, the world of German expressionism, was Muir's point of departure, doubtless helps to explain how he could for his own purposes afford to ignore the Flaubertian French challenge thrown down by Ford Madox Ford. Another less readily explicable puzzle is how Eliot, as elderly poet-publisher, came to sponsor Muir.) At any rate a reader who trusts or admires Muir's platonic or platonizing intelligence, who thinks that that is the characteristically *poetic* intelligence (and there are many who do think so – Kathleen Raine for one) will, like Michael Schmidt, just not *see* how a poetic intelligence like Bunting's moves through and among his images. What will baffle them is that Bunting's images are always of particulars – 'striped flannel drawers', 'pricked rag mat'; and that they have to be so because only in that way can the poet relish and celebrate the inexhaustible plentitude of particulars *in nature*. By the same token (since Muir is enough of a poet to be all of a piece) the ear which takes as a poetic norm the deliberate iambic mellifluousness of Muir's verses just can not *hear* the sharper notes of Bunting, and his more dancing transitions from sound to sound; will indeed, as I'm afraid Michael Schmidt does, hear one of the loveliest sequences in *Briggflatts* as 'near doggerel'.

And the conclusion? Perhaps only this: that the resistance to Bunting's poetry, on both sides of the Atlantic but particularly in England, is not always and in every case the product of obtuseness and/or bad faith. The obstruction may be, and in some cases is, philosophical. Which doesn't in the least absolve us, who champion Bunting, from asserting that the philosophy which would debar him is false, and below what the plentitude of nature deserves and demands.

Basil Bunting: Man and Poet, edited by Carroll F. Terrell (Orono: National Poetry Foundation, Inc., 1981).

Basil Bunting and his Masters

Thomas Warton Lecture on English Poetry, delivered 14 November 1990

My aim is modest. I intend merely to endorse and amplify two sentences written some years ago by Kenneth Cox: 'Bunting's taste was formed early: he had a lot to discover but little to unlearn. His revaluation of the canon was more radical than Pound's and less erratic.' This was Mr Cox's word to the wise. And one might expect that the wise would have taken note. In that case there would be no need for me or any one else to dot the 'i's and cross the 't's. However, where Bunting is concerned such expectations have been many times disappointed. And for that matter, the exceptionally just and independent and learned criticism of Kenneth Cox has never been collected, but must be sought for in the relatively out-of-the-way journals that over the years have given him a hearing. In this case the journal is the twice-yearly, admirably capacious magazine *Bête Noire*. This is published from Hull, that is to say, from north of the Trent: and it is noticeable how many of the journals which pay attention to the pugnaciously Northern poet Bunting are themselves from the North Country – a cogent reason, one surmises, why words to the wise often fail to reach them if their wisdom is that of the metropolis, or of Oxford and Cambridge. It is, I acknowledge, not altogether a matter of received wisdoms but of sensibility, particularly auditory sensibility: a lot of Home counties readers simply cannot hear, as Bunting knew they would not, the music he makes of vowels and consonants given a North Country intonation.

However, it is not my intention to explore the gulf, not political but cultural, between the North of our small country and the South. My humbler aim is to explore and vindicate Kenneth Cox's claim for Bunting that 'his revaluation of the canon was more radical than Pound's and less erratic.' It would be a very innocent person who would ask why Bunting's view of the canon is here differentiated from Ezra Pound's rather than, say, T.S. Eliot's. Those who seek to marginalize the achievement of the author of *Briggflatts* have characteristically done so, as they do still, by presenting Bunting as a slavish disciple of Ezra Pound. In this way, even those who do not nurse a special animosity for Pound (or do not care to confess as much) can still convict Bunting of 'slavishness'. And this is the charge that I, like Kenneth Cox, would absolve him from.

Certainly Basil Bunting loved and admired Pound, as man and friend no less than as writer. But now that we have in print a sufficient body of Bunting's judgements on other writers made both publicly and in private – opinions culled and assembled I'm afraid rather more by Americans and Australians than by us British – we can see that not only did Bunting admit debts to both Eliot and Yeats as well as to Pound; but far more importantly he was in the habit of measuring himself constantly and consistently against poets from long before 'modernism' was thought of. I mean to list these names from the sometimes remote past to which Bunting pays homage, tentatively explaining where I can, honestly confessing my incapacity where I can't (and asking to be enlightened by others). What may emerge is Bunting's personal *pantheon*, significantly different from Pound's or any other's – but with this crucial qualification: this will not be a list of, as Bunting saw it, the world's greatest poets, but of those poets who had instructed him; not 'the master-poets of the world', but 'masters' in a more manageable and semi-technical sense – master artificers in whose notional *ateliers* he, Bunting, had served his apprenticeship and learned his trade. He made the distinction himself in relation to no less a name than Homer; Bunting did not challenge in the least the pre-eminence of Homer in the annals of poetry, merely he testified that, so far as he could see, Homer had been of no particular use *to him* in his writing. In making such a distinction Bunting was every inch a professional poet; and it may as well be said at once that those who prefer their poets to be amateurs, doing they know not what, will find Bunting indigestible.

It is convenient, though it risks giving the wrong impression, to start by listing those poets of the English language, writing in England or at least in Great Britain, to whom Bunting declared himself most indebted. Among such poets, Bunting has written or spoken admiringly of Dryden, Burns, Swinburne, D.G. and Christina Rossetti – in each case specifying some of their works rather than others. But none of these, so far as I can see, is accorded the veneration that he consistently reserves for just three names: Thomas Wyatt, Edmund Spenser, and William Wordsworth. Conjoining the first two of this trio – Wyatt and Spenser – already moves us outside the ambit of received opinion. For long before the late C.S. Lewis famously or notoriously distinguished in Elizabethan poetry between the 'drab' and the 'golden' (Wyatt belonging with the drab, Spenser with the golden), it had become received opinion that one could esteem one of these poets only at the expense of the other. Wyatt, we were told, was colloquial and dramatic whereas Spenser was 'ornamental'. But Bunting, if he was aware of such distinctions (as doubtless he was), ignored them. For him Wyatt was great not because he was colloquial and dramatic but because he composed to accompaniment on the lute:

In Tudor music composers were fond of beginning a note just before where we now place the bar and carrying it on over the bar. The technical term for this is syncopation. The effect is to displace a stress or lose it altogether. Wyatt uses this principle very often. If you read carefully, you'll find it used in some of Shakespeare's songs and here and there in other Elizabethan song-writers... But it vanished from music, or at least became less prominent in music, particularly popular music, soon after Elizabethan times and did not revive until this century in verse, except among a few highly sophisticated writers.

Less dauntingly technical, more expansive and enthusiastic, was what Bunting said in a 1977 interview where he compared Wyatt with Thomas Campion whom (he made clear) he greatly esteemed:

Before Campion's day there was Wyatt who is a great poet, a much greater poet than Campion, but we don't possess his musical settings. His court must have been an astonishing one. There was King Henry VIII, himself a competent poet and a competent composer, responsible for tunes we still sing, responsible for poems which are still readable, and with a queen whom he had chosen, not for beauty (she had very little), but because she was the wittiest and best-educated woman in Europe – Anne Boleyn. And there was Wyatt, who had intended to marry Anne Boleyn before the king took to her, and all of them with their lute in one hand and somebody with a pen beside them, writing it all down while they composed poems. That was the way to do it, and that's the way Wyatt did it. Right up to 1640 you can say that a poet wasn't a poet unless he was capable of playing a musical instrument and composing his poems to that. And that applies to the young Milton.

We may suspect that this is a romanticized or idealized account of the murderously insecure court of Henry VIII. And – perhaps more to the point – we may rightly complain that we are given no grounds for agreeing that Wyatt is 'a much greater poet than Campion'. (We may concede that he is, but Bunting hasn't specified the grounds on which we may think so.) It remains true that, so far as I can see, no one can prove that the relation between Wyatt's poetry and his lute-playing is other than what Bunting pretends.

Spenser, in Bunting's sense of the matter, is great precisely because he broke that close relation between poetry and music which Wyatt took for granted, as it was taken for granted as late as the nonage of Milton:

Spenser... invented a new thing which has given a complexion to English verse ever since... Spenser made the words produce their own music, instead of depending on the musician to do it. It was utterly astonishing to his contemporaries. There's an account in one of Ludowick Briskett's letters of a poetry reading at some village outside Dublin where Spenser read some bits of THE FAERIE QUEENE. They were extremely astonished and worried and called on Spenser to justify doing this sort of thing.

Bunting sees Spenser — he makes the analogy more than once — as the Ezra Pound of his age. The analogy was certainly lost on Pound, as on most of Pound's admirers to the present day. Yet the analogy has its force, particularly if we look where Bunting wants us to, to Spenser's *Shepheardes Calender*. 'Spenser began,' so Bunting says, 'just as Ezra Pound began, by trying every possible mode that was known to poetry, seeing what could be done in it. In *The Shepheardes Calender* you have a wonderful collection of possibilities which served English poets for nearly 300 years after Spenser wrote it, and which contained some poems which are exceedingly beautiful in themselves: the "November Eclogue" for instance.' More than once Bunting associated Spenser with Pound in a way less complimentary to either of them: Spenser's *Faerie Queene*, he thought, suffered just as Pound's *Cantos* did, from being composed over a span of years in which historical change was more rapid and far-reaching than either poet had bargained for, or could artistically control. But Bunting's debt to Spenser, if we may believe him, went deeper and was far more intimate. In 1982 a couple of Australian scholars asked Bunting, through the mail: 'In the original drafts of *Briggflatts* were you working in terms of a narrative?' He replied:

> A very short narrative — nine stanzas — was needed to set the key for *Briggflatts*. For the rest, I'd learned from Spenser that there's no need to tell the reader what he can see for himself. Perhaps that assertion might puzzle trudgers through *The Faerie Queene*; but consider the 'Amoretti-Epithalamion' volume. No reconciliation after the tiff, the sequence ends in sadness. Then two pages of time filling. Then straight into the greatest of all processional hymns. The reader feels an enormous elation, which wouldn't be there if he's had to read all the details of making up. Many times I've read it and still I almost cry aloud with delight. Why waste such possibilities, whether for delight or for something different?

Spenser's 'Amoretti' and 'Epithalamion' were indeed printed together, in 1595, the year after Spenser married Elizabeth Boyle. I'm not clear how Spenser scholars today regard the notion that the poems in this volume constitute a narrative of the poet's courtship crowned by his marriage. I sympathize with those who might say that, since the question cannot be answered, speculation about it is fruitless; moreover, that the question is raised only by those who have a simple-minded idea of how an artist's experience feeds into, and is transformed by, his art. Bunting was not simple-minded; though he subtitled *Briggflatts* 'An Autobiography', he was at pains to say that the love-story told in the poem does not recount occurrences so literally as would be required by a deposition in a court of law. In any case, even if Bunting misconceived these Spenser poems, his misconception (it appears) provided him with the structure for his most ambitious poem – a structure that has baffled and intrigued many who have disregarded this plain directive from the author. I need hardly point out that Spenser's poetry does not, either as a whole or in part, figure so largely in any other modernist's scheme of things – not in Pound's, not in Eliot's, not in Wallace Stevens's, not even in Yeats's.

Bunting's habit, when he applauded a poet of the past, was to base his claim on something off-centre from the accredited monumental centre-piece. This shows up very strikingly in respect of the third of his English 'markers': Wordsworth. He exhorted his Australian interlocutors;

> Look at the narrative complexity of 'The Brothers'. Wordsworth could tell a story better than anyone in English at least since the middle ages. His humour, so utterly English, so like Chaucer's. The splendour of his sound, lost unfortunately on people who insist on reading him in the pronunciation of southern English. His economy (not always exercised, but usually). And so on... He wrote too much, not all at one level, but the best, say, three-quarters of his work seems to me indispensable.

Here surely Bunting doth protest too much. Wordsworth is mostly *economical*? As much as three-quarters of his work is 'indispensable'? Surely not. Yet Bunting is surely right about Wordsworth's humour. There are accounts of how Bunting had a student audience rolling in the aisles on account of 'The Idiot Boy'. And there is indeed much under-stated humour in the poem that he singles out, 'The Brothers', a very perplexing fable about the relation between the community (or 'the collective') and the individual. Wordsworth the moral sage extolled by Matthew Arnold, the author of *The Prelude*, fades out of sight behind Bunting's Wordsworth, the sly story-teller with a Cumbrian accent.

Bunting offered a more measured and more acceptable, because more general, estimate of Wordsworth, in an interview he gave in 1977:

> ...Wordsworth, who seems to me one of the very greatest poets certainly – as a narrative poet, the best we have in English. That's not usually noticed, I think, but it's true. I'm afraid Wordsworth is mostly misrepresented as part of the Romantic movement because he was a friend of Coleridge who was the father of the Romantic movement, the real founder of it. But Wordsworth is really the culmination of the 18th century. All the things they were feeling for and trying for

throughout that century he suddenly brings to perfection. You have in him, besides the realism, the acme of the discursive poem that the 18th century was always busy with.

This is a view of Wordsworth that was contended for by others in Bunting's lifetime, notably the late F.W. Bateson. And I may as well come clean, and confess that I think Bateson and Bunting were right about this great poet. Romanticism is, and has always been, a stumbling-block in our understanding of Wordsworth at his true worth. Bunting launched no philippics against Romanticism, because it was not his way to deal in such abstractions. But his notable coolness towards William Blake, and his irritable dismissing of nineteenth-century poetry apart from the nonsense-poems of Lewis Carroll, the translations of the *dolce stil nuovo* by Rossetti, and the metrical *bravura* of his fellow-Northumbrian Swinburne, tell their own tale. In his view, all Romantic theories of poetry were tainted by what was for him the ultimate heresy: self-expression. Eliot and Yeats and Pound all bought into and temporized with that heresy in a way that Bunting could not condone. And that is why an eighteenth-century Wordsworth figured largely in his pantheon as notoriously he did not in Pound's or Eliot's or Yeats's.

I turn now, in considerable distress, to two bodies of poetry of intimate interest to Bunting, as to which I must declare myself incompetent. The first such *corpus* comprises the poems of Manuchehri and Firdausi and other poets esteemed as classical in Persian and Arabic. The momentousness of these for Bunting is more than literary: he married an Iranian lady, and his sympathy with an Iranian way and quality of life is evident throughout his poetry, at its most generously explicit in the slim volume he made out of his Second World War experiences, *The Spoils* (1951). This is a matter that may be thought topical just now, when we seem poised to unleash on the Persian Gulf dogs of war more mordant than ever before. In any case, Bunting nowhere represents his Persian sympathies as in any way exotic; he is not in that sense an Orientalist. He does not offer classical Persian culture – for instance in architecture any more than in literature – as making good what is lacking in Western European culture. What he admires in Manuchehri and Hafiz and Firdausi, as in the architecture of Isfahan, is not offered to us as a challenge; the notion of 'Eurocentrism' as a condition we inherit and should seek to correct, is to him quite alien. What he learns from Firdausi is what he learns, or had learned, from Spenser. The iron laws that govern poetic composition are the same under Islam as within Christendom.

The other body of ancient precedents as to which I must plead ignorance is that of Old English, Old Norse, and Northumbrian Cymric. Here fortunately we have help, in an admirable essay by Andrew McAllister (in *Bête Noire* 2/3, Spring 1987). By citing at all points chapter and verse McAllister shows how intimately each of these archaic strands is woven into the texture of *Briggflatts*. And so he earns the splendid flare of partisanship that he ends with: 'it is a poem which performs one of the most important tasks of our day... appropriating from language and social history the identity and self-respect necessary to any region or culture which would set itself in opposition to the feckless and feculent hegemony perpetrated these nine hundred years from the southeast.' The learned and Latinate 'feculent', alliterating so sonorously with the Scotticism 'feckless', betrays McAllister into proving, even as he seems to deny it, how North and South-east have co-operated in the making of our language and our literature. And Bunting is aware of that, as some of his intemperate admirers are not.

Bunting indeed must be thought a thoroughly *Latinate* poet – in the crucial sense that he seems never to have doubted that Roman Latin and its derivatives (the Romance languages) were the principal conduits through which was transmitted to him the sort of poetry that he sought to perpetuate and further adorn. If this should seem something that can go without saying, it is not so. For Bunting, fiercely and often resentfully aware of the North European poetic traditions that had been and still were marginalized in public esteem, there was every temptation, which others in that situation had succumbed to, to try to locate a centre for Western European poetic culture somewhere in Germanic or Scandinavian Europe. If that alternative ever presented itself to Bunting, he dismissed it out of hand. It helped that he had spent as many years among Italian-speakers and Spanish-speakers as among speakers of Persian. For him the centre, if 'centre' in this perspective has any meaning, was still the Mediterranean. Accordingly, his dealings with the ancient Latin poets constitute a matter of the first importance. Those dealings prompt two overwhelming questions: why did Bunting consistently prefer Lucretius to Eliot's marker or 'banker', Virgil? and why, among lyrical poets, did Bunting consistently prefer Horace before (Pound's favourite) Propertius, and (Yeats's favourite) Catullus?

The very conspicuous preference for Lucretius over Virgil opens up very long historical-cultural perspectives which I have adumbrated in another place, and will not now rehearse. Very briefly Bunting, as a heterodox but never formally alienated member of the Society of Friends, was a non-conformist churchman who could not fail to be affronted by T.S. Eliot's attempt to enlist Virgil, on the score of the Pollio eclogue, as an apologist for the Anglo-Catholic reading of ecclesiastical history. This argument, though I believe that it alone accords with the recorded facts, is as unwelcome to those who would make of Bunting a secular humanist as to Roman Catholic or Anglo-Catholic apologists. Bunting was a religious poet; and his religion was in large part that of Lucretius, whom we certainly misread if we see in him a secular humanist born several centuries before his allotted time. Lucretius's materialism/epicureanism was not, in his time and place, irreligious.

This matter of Lucretius, who is a presence in Bunting's verse as well as in his conversation, opens up what may be legitimately considered Bunting's *ideology*. And anxious though I am to follow Bunting himself in discussing poetry only in its own terms, yet his honourable reluctance to transgress those self-imposed limits has led to the misconception that he had no ideology, for instance no politics and no philosophy of history. This is quite wrong. As a responsible temporary citizen of societies like Iran and the Canary Islands under General Franco, as well as of the UK, Bunting had arrived at firm political opinions and sentiments. He set great store, we may say, by bloody-mindedness; by the right and duty of the individual to mutiny against an imposed consensus, inside a State or a Church or a Trade Union. This is a stance often affected by irresponsible bohemians; and there are colourful anecdotes, particularly about Bunting's youth in Paris, which taken by themselves suggest that Bunting's ethics and politics were those of bohemia. But Bunting's attitudes were far more firmly based than that, especially in his historic awareness of the civic and religious tradition which nurtured him, which he honoured by naming his most ambitious poem, *Briggflatts*, after an ancient Quaker meeting-house. With impressive quietness, very late in his life, he remarked of Eliot, Yeats and Pound: 'What these poets and many other writers really had in common was a love of order' – a love, he goes on to acknowledge, 'shared with Dante and Shakespeare and probably far more than half of the world's great poets...' This is a love that, he implies, he cannot share – which does not mean that he is in favour of disorder, of anarchy, only that he looks for an order in society far more flexible, less overbearing, than what Eliot and Yeats and Pound dreamed of and tried to will into being.

Of course, no linguistic or poetic procedure, still less any conspicuous change in such procedures, is without ideological implications. 'Horatian' is a term we apply to a way of life practised or recommended, as readily as to a way of constructing and conducting a poem. However, Bunting's other Roman, Horace, is recommended to us in terms not ideological at all but strictly technical. The Horace whom he admires is, it should be noted, the lyrical Horace: the poet of the *carmina*, not of the *sermones* (satires and epistles). Why is it Horace rather than Catullus (as with Yeats) or Propertius (as with Pound) who is pre-eminent for Bunting among Roman lyrical poets? One main part of the answer is: Horace's grammar. Thus, he tells the Australians in 1982: 'Young, I liked Horace's way of changing the whole mood of a poem in a single line. Now I am astonished at the feats he was able to perform with Latin syntax.' It was along the same lines that Bunting in 1948 admonished Louis Zukofsky:

Horace works wonders with a word order which was crabbed even to his contemporaries, as one may see by reading Lucretius and Ovid on either side of him in time. It is not right to banish such effects, which have their place, one I think too much neglected now, even though we and especially I follow Yeats's example of plain diction and plain syntax.

And this must be taken along with a remark later in the Australian interview: 'Certainly Pound was right to say that poetry ought to be written at least as well as prose. Translated, that should mean: Learn syntax.'

But this is extraordinary! For among the modernists whose names are most often coupled with Bunting's, such a respect for syntax, for the grammar of the simple sentence, is conspicuous by its absence. Particularly is this true of his American peers and co-workers. The command of syntax by William Carlos Williams is rudimentary; George Oppen comes to distrust it completely; and Pound himself in *The Cantos* treats it as, at all points, dispensable. It is a very large and intractable subject this, as I learned nearly forty years ago, writing a book called *Articulate Energy*. For present purposes, it is enough to remark that very few of the modernist poets, at least in English, write at all often *in sentences*. (Yeats is the great exception, as Bunting was at pains to point out to Zukofsky, who took the point or else endorsed it, for he too wrote verse that mostly can be parsed.) Bunting, apart from a youthful aberration in his 'Villon', always writes in sentences, though his conciseness – especially his excision of needless connectives – obscures the fact, even for his admirers. It is a salient feature of his poetry, which in this respect is deeply conservative. And this stylistic conservatism he learned, by his own account, chiefly from Horace.

Instead of proceeding at once to explore other places where Bunting fed from Latinate or Romance sources – from Dante in Italian, and Malherbe in French – this seems a good time to grasp the nettle of Bunting's relations with the tradition of American poetry. Because he spent so much of his life outside Great Britain, and also because sixty years ago he was the sole non-American member of the poets' group who called themselves 'Objectivists', it has always been possible for ill-disposed people to present him as essentially an American poet who merely happened to carry a British passport. This is possible only to those who regard Northumberland as nearer, culturally and in imagination, to Nantucket than to Sussex; and unfortunately such people exist. In fact Bunting's relations with American poetry were always fraught and vexed, though one must read between the lines to discern this. It was American, not British, opinion that accorded Bunting as much recognition as he came by in his lifetime; and it was mostly American friends and correspondents who assured him through his worst times that he was not forgotten. Accordingly, he had every reason for being tender towards American poetry. On the other hand his dislike of the self-expressive strain in Romantic theories could not help but set him at odds with most American justifications of their poetry, since these recognize effectively no precedents earlier than the Romantic Movement. The strain shows up, if we look at all closely, in what Bunting has to say about his one-time Objectivist colleague, William Carlos Williams. Though Bunting obviously regarded Williams with affection, and pays him compliments wherever he can, it is plain that he could not endorse the very high valuation now generally accorded to Williams in the United States. He is particularly severe on *Paterson*, Williams's attempt at a sort of epic. And there is a more illustrious name about which he pleads inconspicuously to differ: Emily Dickinson. Her eccentrically sparse punctuation permits and invites syntactical uncertainties such as Bunting the Horatian could not approve. He preferred to her the obscure and humble mid-Westerner Lorine Niedecker, who was sustained though long years by letters from Zukofsky and Bunting and a couple of others. If Bunting had a pupil in poetry apart from Tom Pickard in this country, it was probably Ms Niedecker.

Even the one American poet of the past whom Bunting commended loud and often – I mean, Walt Whitman – seems to me not a clear-cut case. Bunting told the Australians that he did not write *vers libre*:

'Free verse' is a French 19th century term, at first mere slackening of the very strict conventions of their alexandrines, which has gradually degenerated into bad prose chopped up. That gets confused with verse that is derived from Walt Whitman (mostly by Pound and me) which is contrived by modifications of the musical phrase, which seems 'free' to people who don't have ear enough to detect the principle. Quantity is no doubt one element in it – there are semibreves as well as crochets etc. in the music. To write purely quantitative poems in English... is very difficult because the stress in English is so strong that people, at least in the south of England, don't notice anything else. Besides, the stress sometimes modifies the quantity. English phrases with stress on a short syllable are not common. But a poet ought to be always aware of the quantities and it is very good exercise to imitate quantitative patterns.

This certainly seems to mean that Bunting counted Whitman among his masters. And if I confess that I've never been able to match up these sentences with any passage of Bunting's verse, that may be taken to prove only that I 'don't have ear enough'. What may be more betraying is that the Whitman poem that Bunting always cites is 'Out of the Cradle Endlessly Rocking', which anyone can see is very untypical in being almost regular and scannable dactylic measure. Bunting told Eric

Mottram that when he was fifteen years old he was sought out by Whitman's friend Edward Carpenter, on the strength of a prize essay he had written on Whitman, 'a more or less national prize – a national prize for Quaker schools.' That would have been in 1915, when Edward Carpenter's vigorous propaganda was making Whitmanesque poets out of writers only a few years older than Bunting: Ivor Gurney, Edward Thomas, D.H. Lawrence. The enterprise was discontinued when this generation of poets died; Bunting looks like a lone and eccentric survivor from that climate of opinion.

About Bunting's masters in the Romance languages it seems I shall have to be brief. It may appear that his devotion to Dante can go without saying, but we forget that there have been generations of English poets, and not so long ago at that, for whom *The Divine Comedy* was by no means required reading; Father Gerard Hopkins thought it manifestly unserious when set beside *Paradise Lost*. Bunting testified: 'When I became acquainted first with the work and then with the persons of Pound and Eliot, what astonished me and made me so enthusiastic was that here were men who were doing and had been doing all the time… the things which I had painfully worked out for myself were the things necessary to do with poetry, but we'd arrived by quite different roads at this conclusion. Only a very small part of my road to these ideas coincides with Pound's road or Eliot's road. The chief part of that would be that we were all three very enthusiastic readers of Dante.' Eliot's concept of Dante depended, as we have seen, on a view of historic Christendom such as Bunting could not share; and Pound of course came to *The Divine Comedy* from outside Christendom altogether. If Bunting seems to insist too loudly on his independence from the two older poets, these radical divergences among them must be borne in mind.

I have now spoken for the best part of an hour about a poet, without speaking a single line of his verse. That is not my usual practice, nor a procedure that I commend. But I have not been offering an introduction to Bunting's poetry, nor trying to win new readers for it. I have done that in other places. On this occasion I have assumed that Bunting's status as a poet of the first importance is by now, or ought to be, assured; and I have been concerned rather to define what sort of poet he is. That sort should now be clear; unlike say Hardy or Yeats, poets who do not require that we revise the canon, Bunting belongs with Pound and Eliot (and Wordsworth), poets who do make that demand of us. The demand that Bunting makes is seen at its most intransigent when we turn to the last and most surprising of Bunting's declared masters: François de Malherbe (1555–1628), whom he was extolling in *The New English Weekly* as early as 1932. Only six years before that St John Lucas, introducing a revised and expanded version of his *Oxford Book of French Verse* (originally 1907), had written of 'the cold cleverness of Malherbe'. And fifty years later

D.G. Charlton was still telling British readers of Malherbe: 'however, even in practice, he was seldom more than a conscientious craftsman'. It was in the face of a consensus thus unquestioningly based on a romantic idea of the lyrical afflatus that Bunting first found, and then declared (as late as 1969), Malherbe among his masters. There is a great deal that could and should be said about this. I will throw out only two hasty observations: first Bunting saw himself as a lyric poet, vigorously scotching for instance any suggestion that in *Briggflatts* he had indulged epical ambitions; but secondly, it seems certain that he conceived of 'lyric' in uncompromisingly pre-romantic or anti-romantic terms. We can get access to his lyricism out of Horace and Malherbe, or Spenser and Wyatt, sooner than out of John Keats. And yet it was – was it not? – the Romantic Movement that notably demanded attention for those Celtic and Scandinavian poets of long ago whose cadences are lovingly re-created in *Briggflatts*. How can this be? Not for the first time I confess myself out of my depth; but the possibility surely arises that we misconstrue bardic and skaldic poetry if we read it too much through the spectacles of folklorists and antiquaries of two hundred years ago. Bunting's canon comprehends Taliessin *and* Horace, Manuchehri *and* Malherbe; it is more radical than Pound's and more consistent, because even more than Pound Bunting honours that status of 'conscientious craftsman' which the romantically inclined will always speak of slightingly.

The Uncollected Bunting

Basil Bunting, *Uncollected Poems*, edited by Richard Caddel (Oxford: Oxford University Press, 1991)
Victoria Forde, *The Poetry of Basil Bunting* (Newcastle-upon-Tyne: Bloodaxe Books, 1991).

Music! Not 'the music of verse', whatever that flabby locution may be taken to mean; but music of an authenticated kind – sonatas, quartets, sonatinas. Basil Bunting himself at times, and more insistently his few but fervent devotees, would put his poetry out of bounds to those who do not share his and their enthusiasm for chamber music. I don't know where that leaves readers like me, who, cursed with a poor ear, are as unmoved by Arcangelo Corelli as by Miles Davis, and yet find something in Bunting's poetry that we find nowhere else. Are we fooling ourselves? Or are there indeed ways into this poetry different from that chamber-music way which he seemed to prescribe?

Corelli (born 1653, died 1713, having composed five books of twelve sonatas each) is not a name at random. For the elderly and failing poet wrote to Victoria Forde in 1973 about the poem in sonata form that he was never to complete: 'My difficulty may be to hide the myths in something more ready to the contemporary mind. Corelli would have seen in them types of the resurrected God, but he wouldn't have underlined that. It would have been hidden in jigs and long, long notes that you can take merely for delights.' It's hard to escape the implication that those of us who respond to Bunting's poem are receiving at most a second best to what we might get from Corelli's music, could we but hear it aright. I refuse the implication, for obvious, mutinous reasons. Since music cannot be paraphrased, who can say that it is intelligible? Disabled as I am by my musical obtuseness, I must protest that intelligibility becomes possible only when we deal with, not notes and chords, not rhythms and cadences, but *words*. Bunting, when pushed to the wall, would admit this; but never did he admit it readily.

What he wrote to Victoria Forde reveals in the first place that he conceived himself to be dealing with 'myth' or 'myths'; secondly, that he conceived both Corelli and himself to be occupied with the 'resurrected God'. The matter of myth can be dealt with in short order. Unlike his associates and (in part) mentors, Eliot and Pound and Yeats, Bunting did not nourish himself or his poetry out of Freud's *Totem and Taboo* or Frazer's *Golden Bough*. In so far as such works seemed to vindicate ancient myths as repositories of wisdom, they interested him little. And the 'myth' that he refers to in relation to this poem boils down to a shipboard acquaintance with a young woman who, because the non-sexual encounter coincided with the emergence of a new moon and a striking apparition of the planet Jupiter, fixed herself in his mind as 'daughter of the moon'. Recovering a mythic significance for the moon is the difficulty he envisages in pushing his poem further; and it amounts to no more, though also no less, than re-invigorating the well-worn trope for the moon: Queen of the Night.

The matter of 'the resurrected God' is more difficult. Some early enthusiasts for Bunting wanted to promote him as dauntlessly secular and agnostic. But as documents have come to light, this position has become less and less tenable. Now it is generally accepted that he was, in intention and in fact, a religious poet. So long as the religion in question is that of Lucretius – to whom, indeed, Bunting was devoted – not much harm is done to the secularist case. But 'the resurrected God' narrows the options to certain specific religions, notably Christianity. And sure enough, Bunting never repudiated his allegiance to the Society of Friends.

The poem in question, added to the Bunting canon by Richard Caddel as editor of *Uncollected Poems* and by Victoria Forde as the old poet's *confidante*, comes in three sections, which we may as well call stanzas. First, this:

> Such syllables flicker out of grass:
> 'What beckons goes'; and no glide lasts
> nor wings are ever in even beat long.
> A male season with paeonies, birds bright under thorn.
> Light pelts hard now my sun's low,
> it carves my stone as hail mud
> till day's net drapes the haugh,
> glaze crackled by flung drops.
> What use? Elegant hope, fever of tune,
> new now, next, in the fall, to be dust.

The distinctively Bunting note is struck in the fifth and sixth lines; which read, put into prose, 'Light pelts down hard, now that my sun is low; it carves my stone as hail carves, or might carve, mud.' The grammar of the English sentence is at no point transgressed; instead every omission which that grammar permits is taken advantage of. We call this conciseness, which it is; but we might do better to call it 'speed', speed through the sentence and so, as sentence follows sentence, speed through the poem. This is what makes Bunting difficult, though he wouldn't admit he was:

we are not used to having to move so fast – not to 'catch on', but simply
form one sentence or verse-line to the next. (To be sure, the pace can be
slowed down, quite dramatically; as in the last line here, with its three
commas.) There is music here of a sort that even a musical ignoramus can
recognize – as in 'even beat long', which enacts what it says, the long
syllables retarding what – speed again! – had begun so fast just before in
the thin light vowels of 'syllables' and 'flicker'. A particular felicity and
audacity is in how the birds, already evoked in 'glide', 'wings' and 'beat'
without needing to be named, are nevertheless named in the fourth line.

The poem continues:

> Wind shakes a blotch of sun,
> flatter and tattle willow and oak alike
> sly as a trout's shadow on gravel.
> Light stots from stone, sets ridge and kerf quick
> as shot skims rust from steel. Men of the north
> 'subject to being beheaded and cannot avoid it
> of a race that is naturally given that way'.
> 'Uber sophiae sugens' in hourless dark,
> their midnight shimmers like noon.
> They clasp that axle fast.

Peter Quartermain, who seems to have been in Bunting's confidence no
less than Victoria Forde, quotes the poet writing in 1964 (presumably in
a private letter): 'I owe poems to… Cooper Stephenson, who was killed
in the great battle of March 1918, the closest of all friends I've had; and
to Peggy Greenbank and her whole ambience…' The debt to Peggy
Greenbank was discharged in *Briggflatts*; whereas Quartermain seems sure
that the verses before us are as much as ever got written of the poem for
Cooper Stephenson. If so, this explains the otherwise egregious invocation of 'men of the north'. For Quartermain says of the poem for
Stephenson: 'it, too, would be a Northern poem, and would include the
Cliffords and the Percys and the Rising of 1569'. I wish someone would
explain 'Uber sophiae sugens'; but the other passage in quotation-marks
need not be a true quotation at all. For it serves its purpose by introducing, with its suddenly formal and yet gruesomely throw-away diction,
a sardonic note; and this signals the thematic turn-around in the poem –
from celebration of early summer light to valuing its opposite, the blackness of the night.

Accordingly, the last stanza runs:

> Those who lie with Loki's daughter,
> jawbones laid to her stiff cheek,
> hear rocks stir above the goaf;
> but a land swaddled in light? Listen, make out

lightfall singing on a wall mottled grey
and the wall growls, tossing light,
prow in tide, boulder in a foss.
A man shrivels in many days, eyes thirst for night
to scour and shammy the sky
thick with dust and breath.

Victoria Forde usefully glosses 'Loki's daughter', and her whole discussion is invaluable. The rare word 'goaf' is brilliantly apt for the level in Loki's underworld where the slain in battle lie close to her; for it means (*Chambers Dictionary*) 'the space left by the extraction of a coal-seam, into which waste is packed' – is not Cooper Stephenson part of that packed waste? This is mercilessly pagan. And yet Sister Forde quotes Bunting's own gloss on the closing lines: 'As for God's graces, what can we see except in the dark? Daylight is opaque, like water we've washed our hands in.'

This poem, the finest of the thirty-four that Caddel has dug out for us (yet by no means a solitary brilliant thing out of detritus), we are asked to regard as incomplete. Plainly it is so, in the sense that a sonata is required to incorporate several movements. Moreover, we can only be wistful about the north-country history that might have adorned those later movements which Bunting, penurious and harassed to the end, never found the time and ease to write. Yet I experience it as complete and splendidly satisfying, the more readily perhaps because my grasp of the formal completeness of sonatas is so uncertain. Bunting demands close attention, and at last he is getting it, from Victoria Forde and Caddel and others. But it is the sort of attention that we give to poetry, not to music.

Times Literary Supplement, 25 October 1991.

God and Basil Bunting

Peter Makin, *Bunting. The Shaping of his Verse* (Oxford: Clarendon Press, 1992).

In 1986 I was commissioned by the *TLS* to write a brief article, 'God in recent poetry'.[1] I took the opportunity to make a plug for a poet and a poem that I thought, as I still think, scandalously under-esteemed. The poet was Basil Bunting, and the poem was his *Briggflatts* (1965). Because of the frame of reference that I was committed to (though for more pressing and personal reasons also), I dwelt on a passage in the middle section of *Briggflatts* which tells, drawing on Persian sources, how Alexander of Macedon, climbing a sacred mountain alone, encountered the angel Israfel:

> scrutinizing holds, while day lasted,
> groping for holds in the dark
> till the morning star reflected
> in the glazed crag
> and other light not of the sun
> dawning from above
> lit feathers sweeping snow
> and the limbs of Israfel,
> trumpet in hand, intent on the east,
> cheeks swollen to blow
> whose sigh is cirrus: Yet delay!
> When will the signal come
> to summon man to his clay?

Of these verses I asked: 'From whom but God can the signal come, to direct Israfel to sound the trump that will bring about the end of the world? The image of the angel with the trumpet forever at his lips, and his cheeks forever distended to blow into it, is appalling, and yet in a

---

1 *TLS*, 23 May 1986, p. 589. Davie cannibalized a good deal of this article for more than one chapter of his *Under Briggflatts: A History of Poetry in Great Britain, 1960–1988* (Manchester: Carcanet Press, 1989). The argument was continued a further article, 'Nonconformist Poetics: A Response to Daniel Jenkins', *The Journal of the United Reformed Church History Society*, 3: 9 (Oct. 1986). – Ed.

weird way comforting. The world can end at any time, before the next
tick of the clock; it is entirely at God's disposal, and so our lethal child's
play with nuclear toys has not the apocalyptic consequences that we scare
ourselves with. This is an orthodox because necessary inference from the
Christian's understanding of God, as from the Muslim's – or indeed, one
supposes, anyone else's.'

This appeared on 23 May 1986. On 20 June appeared a letter from
Richard Caddel appealing to Bunting's 'open and often repeated scepti-
cism' so as to suggest that Bunting 'would... be horrified at Davie's
deduced moral from *Briggflatts*'. And on 1 August was printed a letter
from Peter Makin which, while disowning Caddel's hint that Bunting
might have been an atheist, accused me of looking for evidence of
Bunting's religious beliefs to his prose, in interviews he gave, rather than
to his verse. But of course it was thirteen lines of *verse* by Bunting that I
cited to make my case.

Caddel and Makin were at one in citing, to rebut my argument that
Bunting recognized a God, two lines near the end of *Briggflatts*:

> Furthest, fairest things, stars, free of our humbug,
> each his own, the longer known the more alone...

But of course – a point I have tried to make in my own verse (*To Scorch
or Freeze*) rather than in polemical prose – the stars, however far from us
in space and time, still do not dwell in Eternity, which is the dimension
in which we look for God. The stars figure for us, as for generations
before us, as emblems of infinity; but Infinity (constantly encroached on
anyway, as we learn to measure more and more) in any case, necessarily
and logically, falls short of Eternity. God is, by definition, eternal; and the
stars aren't. So any reading of *Briggflatts* that comes to rest on 'Furthest,
fairest things, stars' falls short of accommodating what the poem itself has
set in motion.

Richard Caddel, who is my friend, has – while never recanting his
views on Bunting's religious disposition – turned to serving Bunting's
memory in ways that do not impinge on this vexed matter. Such service
is done by his excellent and necessary edition of Bunting's uncollected
poetry,[2] as is his fostering, with Diana Collecott, of the Bunting archive
in Durham University Library.[3] Peter Makin, whom I have never met but
greatly esteem for his *Pound's Cantos* (1985), cannot thus evade the question. His admirably learned and vigorous book lifts Bunting Studies, a
puny enterprise until now, to an unprecedented level of seriousness. (This

2   Basil Bunting, *Uncollected Poems*, edited by Richard Caddel (Oxford: Oxford University
Press, 1991).
3   A special issue of the Durham University Journal, celebrating the 95th anniversary of
Bunting's birth, was published in March 1995.

doesn't mean however that Victoria Forde's pioneering study[4] can now be disregarded; Bunting in his last years confided in her by letter, and this makes her testimony irreplaceable.) Obviously I was eager to see how Makin has dealt with the thirteen lines of verse that I isolated in 1986. He does so by paraphrasing: 'Alexander, the great quester, turns out to be a great fool. All he finds is an angel with a trumpet, magnificent beyond his comprehension, expressing a truth beyond his control: that the ending (and the beginning?) of this cosmos are of *it*, not of us'. To my word, 'God', Makin prefers an italicized '*it*' – which lets us in for the surely very difficult conception that this '*it*', having inaugurated itself, will in due course bring itself to an end.

Bunting himself was quite ready to speak of 'the voice of God', though chary of doing so – chiefly, I suspect, for fear of raising the hackles of such as Richard Caddel and Peter Makin. Makin, as a scrupulous scholar, has to cope with the difficulty that 'God' was a meaningful word in the vocabulary of the poet, though it's meaningless for the critic, Makin himself. His way of coping is to devote several fascinating pages to the ancient saints whom Bunting names, seemingly with approval, near the end of *Briggflatts*: Columba, Columbanus, Aidan, Cuthbert. The trouble is that the information we have about these virtually legendary persons is nothing more than scanty folklore. And with St Columbanus Makin doesn't even try. In recompense he gives us a strikingly confident and peremptory portrait of St Wilfrid: 'a man remarkable for lack of delight, humility, and ability to let live; for the amassing and flourishing of wealth as a source of influence; for a fuss about chronology and historical data as sources of authority; for addiction to rule-making and to territory, bellicosity, and arrogance'. Anglo-Saxonists must tell us what grounds there are for this disparaging portrait; so far as I can see, Makin has no more reliable source for St Wilfrid than he had for St Cuthbert. But as a bogey-figure Wilfrid is for Makin indispensable. If we believe the Venerable Bede, Wilfrid was a spokesman at the Synod of Whitby for the Roman connection that there triumphed over the Irish-Ionan church which had nurtured Columba, Aidan and Cuthbert, which had previously been dominant in Northumbria. Wilfred can thus be made to embody all those ecclesiastical proclivities (theology, 'rule-making', fuss about 'historical data') which the earlier saints had no use for. And thus Columba, Aidan and Cuthbert can be presented as, in seventh-century Northumbria, Franciscans or Quakers born centuries before their time. This may indeed have been, as Makin wants us to believe, Bunting's view also; but the hard evidence is hard to find, and the polemical opposition of Aidan and Cuthbert on the one side, ranged against Wilfrid and Bede on the other,

---

4   Victoria Forde, *The Poetry of Basil Bunting* (Newcastle-upon-Tyne: Bloodaxe Books, 1991).

seems to be all Makin's doing, not Bunting's at all. In this way 'God' can be allowed into Peter Makin's discourse, but only on the understanding that he is Cuthbert's remarkably nebulous God, not the God of Wilfrid or of subsequent ('Roman') centuries. I wrote in 1986 about Peter Makin that 'he wants us and our poets to have religious feelings but not religious conceptions' and my reading of *Bunting. The Shaping of his Verse* doesn't change my mind. An irreligious reader meets a religious poem: the outcome, inevitably, is stalemate.

Of course it's not true that Peter Makin's evident discomfort with institutional Christianity entirely vitiates his treatment of Bunting. Bunting, as a life-long Quaker, had his quarrels with that institution, as for historical reasons all Quakers have; and to that extent the poet and his critic are at one. All the same, some of Makin's most sparkling excursions – I think particularly of an illustrated digression into art-criticism, contrasting the illuminations of the Lindisfarne gospels to those of the Codex Amiatinus, done at Bede's monastery in Jarrow – do undoubtedly have the air of distracting us from the main issue. Of course many readers, including Peter Makin, will deny that the main issue is whether Basil Bunting was, or was not, Christian.

Poetry Review, 83: 1 (Spring 1993).

III

With the Grain

1.

Why, by an ingrained habit, elevate
  Into their own ideas
Activities like carpentry, become
  The metaphors of graining?
Gardening, the one word, tilth? Or thought,
  The idea of having ideas,
Resolved into images of tilth and graining?

An ingrained habit... This is fanciful:
  And there's the rub
Bristling, where the irritable block
  ·Screams underneath the blade
Of love's demand, or in crimped and gouged-out
  Shavings only, looses
Under a peeling logic its perceptions.

Language (mine, when wounding,
  Yours, back-biting) lacks
No whorl nor one-way shelving. It resists,
  Screams its remonstrance, planes
Reluctantly to a level. And the most
  Reasonable of settlements betrays
Unsmoothed resentment under the caress.

2.

The purest hue, let only the light be sufficient
  Turns colour. And I was told
If painters frequent St Ives
  It is because the light
There, under the cliff, is merciful. I dream
  Of an equable light upon words
And as painters paint in St Ives, the poets speaking.

Under that cliff we should say, my dear,
  Not what we mean, but what
The words would mean. We should speak,
  As carpenters work,
With the grain of our words. We should utter
  Unceasingly the hue of love
Safe from the battery of changeable light.

(Love, a condition of such fixed colour,
  Cornwall indeed, or Wales
Might foster. Lovers in mauve,
  Like white-robed Druids
Or the Bards in blue, would need
  A magical philtre, no less,
Like Iseult's, to change partners.)

3.
Such a fourth estate of the realm,
  Hieratic unwinking
Mauve or blue under skies steel-silver,
  Would chamfer away
A knot in the grain of a streaming light, the glitter,
  Off lances' points, that moved
A sluggish Froissart to aesthetic feeling.

And will the poet, carpenter of light,
  Work with the grain henceforward?
If glitterings won't fetch him
  Nor the refractory crystal,
Will he never again look into the source of light
  Aquiline, but fly
Always out of the sun, unseen till softly alighting?

Why, by an ingrained habit, elevate
  Into the light of ideas
The colourful trades, if not like Icarus
  To climb the beam? High lights
Are always white, but this ideal sun
  Dyes only more intensely, and we find
Enough cross-graining in the most abstract nature.

Sewanee Review, 67: 1 (Winter 1959); first collected in *New and Selected Poems* (Middletown, Connecticut: Wesleyan University Press, 1961).

Art and Anger

On 21 and 22 May 1970, the Program in Creative Writing of the University of California at Irvine, together with the graduate division of the Department of English there, sponsored a conference under the rubric, 'Art and Anger'. In the leaflet which the sponsors distributed to participants, they declared:

> This conference will explore the connections between literature and social upheaval: between the act of writing a poem and acts of irrational violence. Connections run deep. The poet has a stake in the irrational, in the forces which both create poetry and destroy social order; the poet also has a stake in preserving social order and his cultural heritage. The violence of social and psychological change may provoke his Muse to descend and stimulate him to write; but his language, his form, and his entire mode of expression derive from culture. He knows that culture and social order exist by virtue of repression; he also knows that the poet breaks through repression. Hence a dilemma: a challenging set of paradoxes.

I began my contribution by quoting famous verses from the Second Dialogue of Alexander Pope's 'Epilogue to the Satires' (1738):

> Ask you what Provocation I have had?
> The strong Antipathy of Good to Bad.
> When Truth or Virtue an Affront endures,
> Th'Affront is mine, my friend, and should be yours.
> Mine, as a Foe profess'd to false Pretence,
> Who thinks a Coxcomb's Honour like his Sense;
> Mine, as a Friend to ev'ry worthy mind;
> And mine as Man, who feel for all mankind.
>   *F.* You're strangely proud.
>   *P.* So proud, I am no Slave:
> So impudent, I own myself no Knave:
> So odd, my Country's Ruin makes me grave.
> *Yes, I am proud: I must be proud to see*
> *Men not afraid of God, afraid of me:*
> Safe from the Bar, the Pulpit, and the Throne,
> Yet touch'd and sham'd by *Ridicule* alone.

Anger? Surely. And 'art'? Superbly; though the anger can afford to be thus superbly explicit only because (1) this is an old and famous poet justly calling upon the evidence of a lifetime's witness to the social responsibility of himself as poet; and (2) he writes in and for an age in which fear of God was a religious duty constantly inculcated and immediately experienced (so that what looks like pride, and declares itself such, is really humility, in that it is only the utterly depraved, the merest scum of society, who – since God's wrath cannot touch them – may be stung by that less than God-like thing, a poet).

But if this is my touchstone of the relation between Art and Anger at is most splendid and admirably fruitful, I'm at a loss to know how to get from this to what (it seems) we are expected to discuss under this rubric; 'the connections… between the act of writing a poem and acts of irrational violence'. *I deny that any such connections exist*; and if Pope's lines may represent angry art at its most splendid and most moving, they move me away from rather than towards any sympathy with 'acts of irrational violence'.

Again, it is suggested to us that 'the poet has a stake in the irrational, in the forces which both create poetry and destroy social order; the poet also has a stake in preserving social order and his cultural heritage.' Still going by Alexander Pope as my mentor and exemplar, *I deny the first stake, and affirm the second.* For Pope's anger – pre-eminently in the *Dunciad*, but consistently throughout his career – was directed against those who threatened social order and would squander the cultural heritage – and indeed it is his consistent tenacity in directing his anger always (as he saw it) at these targets, which makes his lifelong anger heroic. (To be sure, when we speak of 'social order' in this case, we do not mean the law and order of the current political 'Establishment'. For in the poems from which I've quoted, as in others for twenty years before, Pope's main target is the effective first executive of the English state, the king's first minister, Robert Walpole. The head of state may be the worst enemy of social order in that state – as some people believe is the case in the United States at the present day [1970]. All the same, the poet's anger is on behalf of order and against disorder – even, or especially, when the worst fomenter of disorder is the man who should be keeping order.)

Let me jump ahead at once to the hardest of the sayings which come to me from this example of angry art, and from others which come to mind – that the act of poetry is by necessity and of its nature in the profoundest sense *conservative*. Or – to reverse the proposition and make it more challenging still – that a revolutionary poet is a contradiction in terms. (When Pound and Yeats ceased to be conservatives and spoke as revolutionaries, they turned out to be revolutionaries of the right, i.e., fascists. They damaged their art and betrayed their vocation.)

The poet, we are reminded, knows that 'his language, his form, and his entire mode of expression derive from culture.' Yes, indeed! And revolution, as we have known it in our century (as distinct from what the Americans knew in 1776 or even the French in 1790), is not a bid to revitalize and redirect the inherited culture, but a bid to cancel it out, to obliterate it or rule it out as irrelevant, and to start *afresh*. And the poet has too much stake in the inheritance – first and foremost, in that inheritance which is his language – to lend himself to that sort of 'fresh' start. He cannot imagine it; and it is his duty that – as against the philosopher, for instance – what he cannot imagine, he will not conceive.

But I'm more interested in trying to distinguish anger from other manifestations that are often confused with it, and from which indeed (in the case of particular works of art) it is hard to distinguish it. I have in mind, in the first place, *hatred, rancour*, and *indignation*. Anger, I believe (and may even say that I know from experience), nourishes art; it makes for a clean discharge of emotional energy, articulately. Hatred and rancour, on the other hand, are 'a slow burn' – the man who experiences them learns to live with them, grows habituated to them, grows to need them and to depend on them, to like these feelings and to luxuriate in them. Accordingly hatred and rancour do not impel a person to discharge his feelings in action or in the poet's act of speech. They nourish neither action nor art; instead they nurse themselves, stoke their own fires; they are inward-turning, self-regarding, and self-nourishing; the last thing they want is to be discharged. Accordingly I take hatred and rancour to be profoundly and essentially anti-artistic. And the point is worth emphasizing because lots of people plume themselves on feeling anger when what they are really feeling is a sterile hatred or a mean rancour. And here I may be allowed to speak with some special and mournful authority, as an Englishman – i.e., as citizen of a country where class hatred, under the specious disguise of class solidarity, is daily offered as a civic virtue and a social duty. As for *indignation*, though I bow to the traditional ascription of *saeva indignatio* to the time-honoured form of Juvenalian satire, and accordingly I am sure that indignation can nourish art and action as anger can, yet I believe that as indignation is directed more at actions, policies, and institutions than at persons (as anger is), indignation is, even more than anger, liable to be confounded with the sterile emotions of rancour and hatred.

Indignation, like anger, is a flash point, not a slow burn like rancour. But, unlike anger, indignation can always find occasions. And I would ask in all sincerity of those who share my indignation at the invasion of Cambodia whether the feeling of righteous indignation which we experience (however righteous, however just) isn't in the long run *luxurious*. How simple life is, when we have, and know we must keep as a political duty, feelings of indignation and outrage! In such a psychological situation, how much that is ultimately more baffling and ambiguous in our mental lives can be disregarded or suppressed or put on the back burner! Once we've experienced this blessedly simplified state, don't we feel the temptation to prolong the condition, pharisaically seeking out other things to be indignant about? It is a hard thing to acknowledge; but we can get to like our indignations, and to rely on them as on a drug. The artist has the duty to resist such seductive simplifications of his mental and emotional life; and to insist that human consciousness, though it comprehends political consciousness, transcends it. The only poem that I know which deals with this issue, glancingly, is a British poem by Kingsley Amis, 'After Goliath'.

Second Thoughts (1977)

To take up this subject after seven years is to recognize with a shock what a difference those years have made. In 1970, under the Nixon presidency, as the United States was brutally and precipitately extricating itself from the ruins of its intervention in Southeast Asia, the connection between art and anger was of immediate concern for American poets and many of their American readers; because poems of 'protest' – against the national policy, or else (more rarely) in support of that policy against internal protesters and dissidents – were in many cases the only poems that responsible poets felt able to write, or justified in writing. Seven years later it is as if that climate of sentiment had never been; and once again it is easy for people to suppose that anger never feeds art, or that it does so very seldom – in which case 'Art and Anger' will seem to be an out-of-the-way topic, of (as they say) mainly academic interest.

However, I don't find it so – if only because the angers that I feel are prompted, as they always were, by the United Kingdom, rather than the United States; in particular by the arrogant rationalism and authoritarianism of British socialism, which is even more menacing and disgraceful in 1977 than it was in 1970. (Not that the distinction need be pressed very far; as words like 'rationalism' and 'arrogant' may suggest, the temper of mind of British administrators is at bottom the same as what affronted Americans in the slide-rule planners and strategists who forced them deeper and deeper into the bog of Vietnam.) Of the poems I have written since 1970 not many, but a few, have been fed by anger; and my British readers seem to resist and resent such poems even more than they used to do. I can't pretend to be surprised that what I take to be anger and indignation is interpreted by them as rancour and resentment; but at all events the matter for me isn't 'academic' at all, but as compelling now as it was in 1970.

At the end of the first book of his *Philosophical Inquiry into the Origin of our Ideas of the Sublime and Beautiful*, Edmund Burke, having discoursed on Joy and Grief and Fear and Love and one or two other passions, decides that these are 'almost the only ones which it can be necessary to consider', the only ones worthy 'of an attentive investigation'. It is surprising and it must be significant that, writing so soon as he did after the death of Pope, a great poet of anger, Burke neither at this point nor elsewhere in his treatise considers among the passions either anger or indignation. If we look in his pages for any acknowledgement of the effect made on us by

> Yes, I am proud; I must be proud to see
> Men not afraid of God, afraid of me

we come nearest to it at 1, xvii, when Burke says:

> Hence proceeds what Longinus has observed of that glorying sense of inward greatness, that always fills the reader of such passages in poets and orators as are sublime.

But the connection is accidental and illusory, for Burke and Longinus are speaking of a sentiment aroused in the reader, not of a sentiment avowed by the poet, as Pope avows it here. And indeed, there can be little doubt that Burke would have concurred with his contemporaries – with Thomas Warton, and with even so great an admirer of Pope as Dr Johnson – in denying to Pope any touch of 'the sublime'. This would be inevitable, given Pope's clarity and on the other hand Burke's insistence that 'the sublime' abhors clarity, being at home rather in the indistinct and the murky.

It was this in Burke that provoked another great poet of anger, William Blake, to explode in the margin of his copy of Reynolds's *Discourses*: 'Obscurity is Neither the Source of the Sublime nor of anything Else.' I am sure that Blake was right, and indeed I would say that because of its insistence to the contrary Burke's *Philosophical Inquiry* is, unintentionally, one of the most mischievous books ever written by a man of genius.

This will raise a smile. Isn't Burke's treatise merely a historical curiosity, which none of us needs to get heated about? I think not; though there are parts of it, notably Book Four, which indeed are now merely quaint, most of the time Burke is articulating mistaken ideas which have done vast damage ever since his time, and are rampant today. If 'sublime' and 'beautiful' are terms that we no longer find much use for, the reason is, I suspect, that in our apprehension of the arts – at any rate, of literature – what Burke called 'the sublime' has long ago overborne 'the beautiful'. For us the beautiful means the pretty, the graceful, and the effeminate – a disastrous scaling down such as Burke in his book is quite manifestly (and, one must suppose, consciously) instigating or promoting. In a famous passage, where Burke is extolling sublimity in a passage from Milton, who is for him consistently and pre-eminently the English master of 'the sublime', he writes:

The mind is hurried out of itself, by a crowd of great and confused images; which affect because they are crowded and confused. For, separate them, and you lose much of the greatness; and join them, and you infallibly lose the clearness. The images raised by poetry are always of this obscure kind.

And in another passage, following his ancient authority Longinus in going for sublimity to the Hebrew scriptures, Burke comments on some verses from the Book of Job:

We are first prepared with the utmost solemnity for the vision; we are first terrified, before we are let even into the obscure cause of our emotion; but when the grand cause of terror makes its appearance, what is it? Is it not wrapt up in the shades of its own incomprehensible darkness, more awful, more striking, more terrible, than the liveliest description, than the clearest painting, could possibly represent it?

Take these two passages together, and do they not express what we experience – and what our children are glad to experience – in reading the *Ariel* poems of Sylvia Plath? There the poet is clearly expressing some vast dissatisfaction with herself and the terms of her life. But if that is clear, nothing else is. Plainly the *Ariel* poems are somehow angry poems; but what occasions the anger, what the anger is directed at – this is never clear. This possibility is mooted, and then another one, and then another, 'a crowd of great confused ideas'. And apparently we like it that way; this is the sublime, and the sublime is what we like. What is plain is that a Plath poem is not, either for the poet or her readers, a clean discharge of the angry energies that went into its making. The poet pathetically admitted as much by killing herself. And so what emerges from the poems is ultimately *not* anger, but rancour, the slow burn, the gas oven. And surely the same is true of that other suicide, a far more winning and inventive writer, the late John Berryman; with Berryman too, it was the inability to focus his angers, to locate them, define them, and discharge them, which won him readers and compelled his suicide. He too in his jokey way 'affected the sublime', and was esteemed by a public that despised beauty but was entertained by the sublime – all the more of a thrill if it claimed the life of the entertainer. The sublime, it turns out, is murkier than Edmund Burke could know. Disaffection, resentment, acedia, malaise, 'alienation' – all those fashionable conditions, precisely because in all of them the sufferer 'doesn't know what is wrong with him', produce in art 'the sublime'. Anger, on the other hand, and indignation, because they drive towards clarity and depend upon achieving it, belong in the other category, 'the beautiful'.

With the indistinct duplicities of a Plath or a Berryman, compare the clarity of an epigram by Yeats:

Parnell came down the road, he said to a cheering man:
'Ireland shall get her freedom and you still break stone'.

That is the note of:

> Yes, I am proud; I must be proud to see
> Men not afraid of God, afraid of me.

And it is surely obvious why Yeats and Pope raise the modern reader's
hackles, as Plath and Berryman don't. In Yeats and Pope the anger is
more than half contempt. This has to be so, if the anger is to be cleanly
and completely discharged; the occasion of the anger is consumed clean
away, never to be thought of again. We may contrast a greater poet than
Plath or Berryman, Yeats's friend Ezra Pound. Throughout the *Cantos*
what is felt for Roosevelt and the Jews is never, strictly speaking, anger;
the emotion never is, nor could it be, discharged – because the malefac-
tions alleged against them are never focused with clarity, but come to us
only as 'a crowd of great and confused ideas'. We speak only loosely and
misleadingly if we say that what Pound feels for Franklin Delano
Roosevelt or Sir Basil Zaharoff is anger and contempt. If that were really
what he felt, his hostility toward them would not rankle as it does
through more than one hundred cantos and more than forty years. The
Cantos are perhaps, or this side of them is, sublime; it cannot be beautiful.
And my impression is that even by Jews and American Social Democrats
Pound will be forgiven sooner than Yeats or Pope will – because the
sublime is self-confessed muddle, and thereby democratic, whereas what
Yeats and Pope feel and express is, along with anger, contempt. And in
democracies contempt is unforgivable, as ultimately hatred isn't.

When Burke's friend Dr Johnson, more than twenty years after the
Philosophical Inquiry, undertook to write a life of Pope, he did not principally see Pope as a poet of anger. And indeed many other passions besides
anger nourished Pope's art. Nevertheless, as Jean Hagstrum showed us
long ago, Johnson's polemical endeavour through that one of his *Lives of
the Poets* was to present Pope as throughout a poet of 'the beautiful',
without 'the sublime' and 'the pathetic' and yet no worse for lacking
them. This is the true meaning of Johnson's famous rhetorical question:
'If Pope be not a poet, where is poetry to be found?' And if for us Pope
is far more conspicuously a poet of anger than he was for Johnson, none
the less Johnson's argument holds good. Anger is beautiful; and the art
that anger feeds is crisp and clear and bright, not the hulking and nebulous immensities of 'the sublime'.

Trying to Explain (Manchester: Carcanet Press, 1980).

The Rhetoric of Emotion

Somewhere, perhaps in many places, a distinction has been drawn between 'emotion' and 'feeling'. Certainly a distinction there is, and no very fine one. I find in myself, when I think of the verbal arts, a disposition to talk of 'feeling'. Who does not prefer 'feel' to the appalling verb, 'emote'? Not only is feeling anchored in the immediacy of sensuous apprehension, tactile in the first place; but also, because it can mean 'groping', it fits those artifacts that we want to applaud as 'sensitive', as (precisely) *tactful*. Either way, 'feeling', far more than 'emotion', reminds us that art is a matter of response, and of response not to etiolated 'stimuli' but to something as substantial, as intact in its own always surprising contours, as the pebble that a blind man's hand has picked up from the beach, and now explores in order to know. Just so, surely, does a good poem or story explore, respectfully and patiently, the somehow foreign body which has provoked it.

And so, if we turn now to 'emotion', we have to start by scotching some of the misapprehensions which the less satisfactory word brings with it. The first of these comes about because of the lack, in 'emotion', of that tentative exploratory character that we have just applauded in 'feeling'. Because of this lack there arises the misapprehension that, other things being equal, a poem or story will be better if the emotion which it embodies or controls or conveys is strong, is powerful, is intense, is over-mastering (for the reader, if not for the writer). 'Feeling' shows, or it ought to show, that this is not true; and this misapprehension darkens counsel and indeed experience to the point where we cannot distinguish between disturbed and alerted emotion on the one hand, and jangled nerves on the other. 'Emotion', unlike 'feeling', provides no safeguards against sensationalism – against, that is, the intense though mostly shallow experiences which, outside of art, make us vomit or put us in a state of shock. And sure enough, do we not commonly hear pieces of literature applauded because, so it is said, the emotions which they convey are 'visceral'?

Another misapprehension we have come across already; the reader who thinks about literature by way of emotion rather than feeling is likely to deny or ignore the fact that the provocation for a poem or a story comes to the artist always 'from outside'. At least in some cases, such a reader will argue, the artefact is self-generated out of some need or impulse in the consciousness of its creator. If we want to deny this, we do not have to espouse some literary equivalent of representationalism; we do not have to assert that every poem or story has 'a subject', though of course most of them do. 'Subject' is not the point. For in literature one element is *always* foreign to the writer when he begins writing, as to the reader when he begins reading or the listener who begins listening; it is language, the medium itself. There are very many bad poems and stories, and a few very good ones, in which the emotion expressed or conveyed is predominantly or even exclusively provoked by and responsive to the medium itself, sounds and meanings and their interactions. The possibility of this is allowed for when we speak of 'feeling', but only distractingly and with difficulty when we speak of 'emotion'.

This thinning-out of the artistic medium, to the point where as an independent entity in the artistic transaction it virtually evaporates from the reader's mind, is a danger whenever we approach art with expectations of 'emotion'; but it becomes all but inevitable when we couple emotion with rhetoric as I have done in my title. For 'rhetoric', though it has other more recondite meanings, is centrally and normally apprehended in literary theory as a set of coded signals sent by speaker to auditor, hence by writer to reader, to cue the hearer or the reader into… into what? In the strictest theories of rhetoric the hearer was to be *persuaded*; that is, he was to be induced or compelled to a conviction, and ideally into a conviction that would issue in a course of action. But conviction is different from assent, just as rhetoric is different from logic. Conviction is assent plus emotion, and the emotion is provoked in the hearers by the speaker, who inflames for instance their indignation so as to set their feet running and their fists clenching as they rush away into action, snatching up stones as they go.

Thus the orator works by provoking and inflaming emotion. But the signals which he makes are cues not to emotion but to action. The emotion is the means to that active end; and for the transaction to be most effective, the auditor should be aware of being impelled to a conviction which must issue in action, not at all of being inflamed into a state of emotion. In rhetorical art on the other hand, though the theory often maintains the pretence (for instance, in theories of satire) that action is the end, in practice the emotional inflammation is the need aimed at by poet and reader alike. Thus in rhetorical literature the signals are cues not to action but emotion; and since the audience, if it is at all sophisticated, recognizes these as the terms of the contract, there is an unpleasant flavour of masturbation about the whole transaction. 'Oh,' says the compliant reader, 'he wants me to feel indignant, does he? Very well, I think I can manage that.' And he duly manipulates himself into the state required of him. Getting the cues and responding to them is what such a reader

understands as experiencing literature; and he finds it enjoyable, since he
is getting something for nothing. He experiences emotion without
having to suffer its occasion or act upon its prompting.

Whether from distaste at this or for other reasons, responsible English
writers both in theory and practice abandoned this rhetorical art a long
time ago. For the poets it was relatively easy to do so, and they made the
renunciation early; certainly the young Wordsworth is already a poet of
feeling, not a rhetorical manipulator of readers' emotions. For storytellers,
for a Dickens or a Thackeray, so much more hopeful of and dependent
upon a large public, it was harder – and in both these writers, as is generally conceded, pages of feeling and pages of rhetoric lie side by side. In
English verse however it might be maintained that Thomas Gray was the
last serious and greatly gifted poet to practise a rhetorical art. (And it needs
to be said that rhetorical art can be great art – for the 'Elegy' is rhetorical
in its own way no less than Gray's Pindaric Odes.)

Yet the readers of English poets of today – our critics and also, most
plainly and damagingly, our educators – still act as if poetry were a rhetorical art, and approach Roy Fisher as if he were Thomas Gray. Our
schoolchildren are trained to read poems as if they were coded signals
giving them cues about what and how to feel. The reader looks at the
poem published yesterday to see what signals the poet is sending him,
whereas the poet if he is any good is not flying any signals at all but feeling
his way into or around a fragment of life. The reader may listen in if he
wants to, but he is not being addressed. Of course if he attends closely he
in effect enlists in the exploring expedition, and can partake of the
discovery that is made. For instance: 'The wan moon is setting behind the
white wave, / And Time is setting with me, oh.' If Burns in these lines is
flying rhetorical signals, he is using a code which has been cracked too
many times for the addressee of 1972 to trust it; unless he is unsophisti-
cated, that reader will be unwilling, if not indeed unable, to comply with
what seems to be the directive thus signalled, unable to drum up in
himself the passionate wistfulness that seems to be asked for. But suppose
there is no addressee? Yeats supposed there was not, saying of these lines:

> Take from them the whiteness of the moon and of the wave, whose
> relation to the setting of Time is too subtle for the intellect, and you
> take from them their beauty. But, when all are together, moon and
> wave and whiteness and setting Time and the last melancholy cry, they
> evoke an emotion which cannot be evoked by any other arrangement
> of colours and sounds and forms.

An emotion, Yeats acknowledges, is evoked – but not to the end that
members of Burns's public shall eat their emotions' cake and have it, but
to the end that a certain pattern of relationships may be explored and
known, a pattern which, since it is 'too subtle for the intellect', can be

explored only through emotion and known only *as* emotion.

Thus what looked like an all too recognizable signal, that 'oh' which Yeats called a 'melancholy cry', is not a signal to the reader at all. The same threadbare flag may have been flown as a signal by poorer and more vulgar writers than Burns, but when Burns hoists it, it signals nothing but itself. And so its being threadbare does not matter.

Many complications remain. For it may indeed be true that it is two hundred years since a poem in English could be both rhetorical and great. But throughout that period inferior poems have been rhetorical, or they have been nothing. Mostly they have been nothing, of no account one way or the other. But some of Swinburne, much of Kipling, most of Rupert Brooke – this is poetry which has flown its rhetorical signals very clearly and vividly; and the signals have been read and complied with, eagerly, by thousands on thousands. Why not? I call such poetry inferior – inferior in kind; but certainly not shameful, not (in any sense that matters) depraved or depraving. Poetry comes in kinds, and some kinds are inferior to others.

The trouble is – and how often one has heard it said! – that the bad drives out the good, the inferior shoulders aside the better. And this too may be misunderstood. One does not mean that thousands have been reading Kipling when they ought to have read Hardy, Rupert Brooke when they ought to have read Edward Thomas. What happens is more complicated. Because, as we saw with the distich of Burns, rhetorical and non-rhetorical poems fly the same flags (words and arrangements of words), non-rhetorical poets can be, and most often are, read as if they were rhetoricians. They can be made to seem to be sending signals when they are doing nothing of the sort. A kind of directive, even, can be decoded from them – though not of course anything like so clear and ringing a directive as those of the rhetoricians; and so Hardy's 'Channel Firing' might be read, and doubtless has been, as a creditable but muffled attempt at what the war-poems of Kipling did better.

And so, through one generation after another in the present century, serious poets can be seen going to very great lengths indeed to advertise that they are not rhetoricians, and for their pains either finding themselves unread or else transformed by the public into rhetoricians after all. T.S. Eliot insisted time and again that *The Waste Land* was not a directive to the reader to feel thus and thus about the twentieth century. (Pound's *Cantos* in large part was; but Pound broke the other half of the rhetorical artist's contract by insisting that the feelings 'drive through to action'.) Hardy in baffled fury insisted time and again that his poetry was not a directive to feel thus and thus (rancorously, bitterly) about the Universe. It was all to no avail. And yet the poets' remonstrances were not merely in what they said about their poems, they were *inside* the poems. For the grotesque corrugations of Hardy's diction, the discontinuities of Eliot, were surely intended to advertise: 'No signals are being sent.' It was all no use; signals were somehow received and read, and in the end in many quarters cherished all the more for having been so hard to decode and misconstrue. The public had to treat these poems as signals in code, because that was the only way that the public knew, or was ever told, about how to treat any poetry at all.

So insecure is a man's sense of himself, so threatened does he feel if he is overlooked or merely tolerated rather than directly addressed, that many or most of us will twist and turn with unflagging energy and resourcefulness, rather than admit to having been present at certain trans-actions to which our presence or absence was a matter of indifference. Nothing else can explain our tenacity when we seek to transform the transactions of art into transactions of rhetoric. The same logic operates not only *in* Freudian thought, but behind it and beneath it: 'If she abuses me to my face, that shows she cares about me...'; 'He so conspicuously takes no notice of me that he must be acutely aware of me...'. Just as hate thus becomes the mirror-image of love, unconcern of concern, so an addiction to rhetoric creates, or at least welcomes and eagerly accommo-dates, anti-rhetoric. The haughtier the artist, the more we love him, the more eagerly do we apply ourselves to show that his hauteur towards us is only the mirror-image of his needing us. I do not know how else to explain what is surely one of the most extraordinary manifestations of Anglo-American culture over the last fifty years – the way in which Joyce and Pound and Yeats, the artists who with most conspicuous hauteur rejected our culture, have become its darlings, instituted as such academ-ically. Somewhere surely, in someone's breast, there is a triumph of revenge: 'Ah, so you thought you'd got away, did you? On the contrary every struggle you make to escape our nets only limes you in them more securely!'

Of course this is only a particular instance of a general phenomenon: the effectiveness with which the packaging industries have taken over and familiarized, from the literary arts as from others, stylistic dispositions that were meant to preclude any packaging at all. For some years now, for instance, some British poets have been practising an anti-rhetoric of preg-nant terseness. But this will not save them; Leonard Cohen has been writing *haiku* for years. Turn and twist as he may, nowadays the serious artist feels the rhetorician's breath hot at his heels, more pressingly than ever before. And this is a creeping disease: not only has the writer failed up to now to find an anti-rhetoric that is really prophylactic, one that cannot be construed as the mirror-image of rhetoric, but the attempt to find it has sapped and deflected the energies that should be directed intently on his proper business. The search for devices that will *not* cue the reader into having emotions is more exhausting and distracting than the search for devices that *will*. And the energy that goes into such a search is in the end inescapably rhetorical energy, rather than poetic. For an anti-rhetoric *is* a rhetoric; the would-be transparent envelope is a specially sophisticated sort of packaging.

This throws a new and topical light, for instance, on Pound's celebrated remark about free verse – that 'no verse is really free for the man who wants to do a good job'. This can still mean what Pound intended to convey – that a writer who casts free of the crutch of metre has to be that much more attentive to the rhythms that he can summon up to sound in his inner ear. But in the understanding of the public, one of the things that free verse claimed to be free from was rhetoric; from that point of view, free verse was an anti-rhetoric in itself. And now that there is no excuse for not realizing that anti-rhetoric is rhetoric in mirrored reverse, free verse has to be seen to be a convention as constricting (though also as liberating) as the iambic pentameter it was once intended to supplant. Poets will continue to practice free verse, but there is no excuse for their doing so in the spirit of D.H. Lawrence, who thought that by doing so he had escaped all the fowlers' nets of rhetoric.

What seems more likely, however, and more promising, is a rediscovery by poets of the usefulness of the iambic pentameter and other metrical forms – not in the casually loosened versions that have been practised for years by Philip Larkin and others, but in all their traditional rigour. For the prophylactic against rhetoric which promises most nowadays is likely to be not avant-garde but quite the reverse. There is for instance Thom Gunn's, in 'Moly':

> Oh a man's flesh already is in mine.
> Hand and foot poised for risk. Buried in swine.
>
> I root and root, and think that it is greed.
> It is, but I seek out a plant I need.
>
> Direct me gods, whose changes are all holy,
> To where it flickers deep in grass, the moly.

Far more than any *avant-garde* terseness or discontinuities, Gunn's metre and his rhymes, so determined to draw attention to themselves, deter the reader who wants poetry to cue him how to feel. And the cries of injured frustration which greeted the collection, *Moly*, show that in the short run Gunn has succeeded. 'Without exception,' declared one reviewer, 'the Moly poems are dead' – dead, that is (so we may infer) to the presence of this reader, who was waiting to be 'moved'. Trying again, the reviewer (it was Michael Fried) expostulated: 'Their failure is not essentially a feature of tone. They do not *smell*.' Did Sidney's poetry 'smell'? Did Shakespeare's, in those scenes of *A Midsummer Night's Dream*, where the rhymes are as clangingly obtrusive as Gunn's on 'holy' and 'moly'? The art that refuses to conceal itself runs an insurmountable wire fence between itself and the reader; the reader may look through the wire mesh, but he cannot join in, except by the exercise of a sympathetic imagination. He cannot smell what is going on; he can only see it. And that is an affront that the reader finds too gross to stomach, if he has been schooled in a rhetorical theory of literature so as to think that the writer's prime duty is to him, the reader, rather than to his own experience, his own subject.

Thom Gunn gives peculiar offence because the subjects that he treats with this aggravating coolness are precisely those which the modern reader supposes he has a special right to feel tempestuously or intensely about. All of *Moly* is concerned, in one way or another, with drug-taking. And when Gunn in another poem in *Moly* presents the spiel of a San Francisco drug-pusher in a form strikingly reminiscent of Herrick's 'Cherry Ripe' or Dowland's 'Fine Knacks for Ladies', what can he be implying, if not that this traffic, which has called up so much agitated emotion for and against, is no more sensational than the trade that was plied by many a Jacobean Autolycus? On the grounds of private morality, of personal hygiene and civic order, we may or may not agree with him; but that is another question. By purely formal means, in particular by highly conscious use of one of those ready-made forms which vulgar modernism declared to be illegitimate and exploded, Gunn has presented for cool contemplation one 'burning topic' and one possible attitude towards it. And in doing so, *in order to do so*, he has avoided both rhetoric and the anti-rhetoric that is merely rhetoric inverted. We are not to 'feel'; we are, for a change, to think.

In Gunn's own development this represents – for him, and for us if we choose to follow him – a penetration behind the ambiguous and magnetic figure of John Donne, into the Renaissance poetic out of which Donne sprang, and from which he diverged. In particular it represents a creative penetration of Shakespeare. Does Shakespeare cue the playgoer how to feel about the spectacles he presents in *A Midsummer Night's Dream*, in *As You Like It,* in *Much Ado About Nothing*? Surely, after all that the commentators have pretended to the contrary, the very titles – together with many internal features – show that Shakespeare did no such thing; that with a smiling arrogance he refused to cue our emotions, and threw his refusal in the playgoers' faces. Dr Johnson, who preferred Shakespeare's comedies to his tragedies, did not feel affronted; but it seems that we do. And indeed our fussiness about 'tone' (most baleful and most insular of all I.A. Richards's bequests to us) reveals us as more locked into a rhetorical theory of literature than ever Dr Johnson was.

Times Literary Supplement, 29 September 1972; reprinted in *The Poet in the Imaginary Museum*.

George Steiner on Language

George Steiner, *After Babel: aspects of language and translation* (London: Oxford University Press, 1975).

Some months ago there appeared, in the first issue of the *New Review*, a long letter from George Steiner explaining in effect why he could not respond to the editor's invitation to write for that journal. Though it must have seemed to many people that Steiner lost control of his argument at certain points, yet his wounded diatribe about the present state and future prospects of British literary culture must have struck nearly everybody as a document of the first importance, exceptionally brave, penetrating, and vulnerable; just as the printing of it, so damaging as it was and was meant to be, was an act of exceptional courage on the part of the editor, Ian Hamilton. Among Steiner's accusations was this:

> An unmistakable thinness, corner-of-the-mouth sparsity, sour fastidi-
> ousness, have developed in the English intellectual literary tone. The
> age is less one of anxiety than of envy, of hopeful malice, To borrow
> an image from a French children's story, the thin grey ones, the steely
> trimmers, hate the round warm ones. They deride the messiness of
> intense presence, of intense feeling which they call 'flamboyance'.
> They come with tight lips and deflation.

Because any reviewer faced with a book as big as *After Babel* may feel the need to establish his own position, if not his credentials, I may say that I recognize the tone that is defined by Steiner in his first two sentences and that I want quite vehemently to dissociate myself from its 'hopeful malice'; but that, on the other hand, in the terms provided by the French children's story, I recognize myself – not perhaps without some fatuous complacency – as one of the 'steely trimmers'. Whether I can thus eat my cake and have it is, of course, open to question. But I think I owe it to Professor Steiner thus to declare my hand, more particularly since he has lately been as good as his disparaging word, and has removed himself from the British literary scene to Geneva, for reasons which I understand.

I am provoked to think first about earnestness, 'being in earnest'. If Dr Johnson was wrong and naïve in his famous refusal to consider that Milton in *Lycidas* might have been in earnest (because, Johnson thought,

the use of the pastoral convention precluded it), must we suppose that
whatever we take as signs of earnestness in either speech or writing are in
fact wholly conventional signs, ultimately arbitrary? Surely we must. For
we perceive clearly that what are signs of earnestness in one language are
signs of flippancy in another. The difference between British and
American English is striking in this respect, and from this and many other
points of view British and American must be considered as distinct
tongues, though it is not to George Steiner's purpose so to consider them.
However that may be, the difficulty that some British readers have had in
'taking Steiner seriously' – a difficulty which he is aware of and resents,
which he is still trying to remove by trying a new 'register', a new style –
surely derives, though I'm not sure he realizes it, from his trilingualism, a
condition which he presents to us in this book as being, to all intents and
purposes, innate. Though we can accept without demur his contention
that he is lexically, grammatically, and in deeper ways, too, a native
speaker of each of his three languages – French, German, English – I
think a consideration of his career as a writer (also, I would guess, as a
public speaker) would show that *rhetorically* one of his languages, British
English, is *not* native to him. But of course, once we move into the
rhetorical dimension of language, we know no longer whether we are
speaking of a style of speech or a style of thought; and so some people
might want to say that Steiner, though he speaks and writes an English
without gallicisms, none the less *thinks* like a Frenchman – for 'earnest' is
a word that can go with 'thought' no less than with 'feeling' or 'speech'.

In one language community at some one time, a terse pithiness, a dry
or casual tone, and a conversational or colloquial vocabulary are taken for
signs that a writer is in earnest; in a neighbouring language community,
or in the first language at another period, earnestness is signalled on the
contrary by copiousness, by 'hammering home' (i.e., saying one thing in
different ways, many times over), by an excited or urgent tone, and by a
vocabulary that darts or ranges all the way from the racy to the ornate and
the proudly erudite. In so far as the accepted signs of earnestness in
current English are pithiness, dryness, casualness (and in fact there are
probably English-speaking circles where these signs are *not* accepted, and
perhaps never have been), George Steiner is still in this book using a
foreign rhetoric, one that the steely trimmers among us have been conditioned to distrust. True, Steiner has dried out of his style the effects of
restless and lurid chiaroscuro which characterized earlier books like
Language and Silence and *In Bluebeard's Castle*; and to my English-condi-
tioned taste this is sheer gain. But he is still an eloquent, ornate and *driving*
writer, above all a copious one. It is important that as English readers we
overcome our conditioned prejudice against such copiousness; overcome,
for instance, our feeling that Steiner's book as a whole, and each of its six
massive chapters, could and should have been shorter. For we must

suppose Steiner, in this book, to be entirely in earnest. We must do this for our own good, not in charity to him – simply because he is saying things we cannot afford not to take note of, and in doing so he is challenging reputations so formidably influential among us as Noam Chomsky's and J.L. Austin's. Moreover, these reputations were made and are maintained in fields quite other than the field, comparative literature, in which Steiner might feel himself professionally 'safe'; and so this too we must salute as a sign of earnestness – Steiner has been either brave or rash, he has been at all events *bold*.

Because his style is copious, this author is at one and the same time seductively quotable, and yet not easily quotable *to some purpose*. After tearing my hair a good deal, I excerpt the following passages to represent what I register as his central and most salutary contention. He is speaking of the ancient Greeks, and their view of the relation between truth and language:

> One need only recall the enchanted exchanges between Athene and Odysseus in the *Odyssey* (XIII) to realise that mutual deception, the swift saying of 'things which are not' need be neither evil nor a bare tactical constraint. Gods and chosen mortals can be virtuosos of mendacity, contrivers of elaborate untruths for the sake of the verbal craft (a key, slippery term) and intellectual energy involved. The classical world was only too ready to document the fact that the Greeks took an aesthetic or sporting view of lying. A very ancient conception of the vitality of 'mis-statement' and 'mis-understanding', of the primordial affinities between language and dubious meaning, seems implicit in the notorious style of Greek oracles. ...
>
> In short, a seminal, profound intuition of the creativity of falsehood, an awareness of the organic intimacy between the genius of speech and that of fiction, of 'saying the thing which is not', can be traced in various aspects of Greek mythology, ethics, and poetics. ... But from Stoicism and early Christianity onward, 'feigning', whose etymology is so deeply grounded in 'shaping' (*fingere*), has been in very bad odour.
>
> This may account for the overwhelming one-sidedness of the logic and linguistics of sentences. To put it in a crude, obviously figurative way, the great mass of common speech-events... does not fall under the rubric of 'factuality' and truth. The very concept of integral truth – 'the whole truth and nothing but the truth' – is a fictive ideal of the court-room or the seminar in logic. Statistically, the incidence of 'true statements' – definitional, demonstrative, tautological – in any given mass of discourse is probably small. The current of language is intentional, it is instinct with purpose in regard to audience and situation. It aims at attitude and assent.... We communicate motivated images,

local frameworks of feeling.... We speak less than the truth, we fragment in order to reconstruct desired alternatives, we select and elide.
It is not 'the things which are' that we say, but those which might be,
which we would bring about, which the eye and remembrance
compose... Information does not come naked except in the schemata
of computer languages or the lexicon. It comes attenuated, flexed,
coloured, alloyed by intent and the milieu in which the utterance
occurs (and 'milieu' is here the total biological, cultural, historical,
semantic ambience as it conditions the moment of individual articula-
tion).

We may pause here for a reflection that will seem spiteful, but is not. To
put it demurely, the conveying of accurate information has never been
one of the things for which we have valued Steiner's writings; and before
I am through I shall have to notice an instance of misinformation in this
very book. But the conveying of information is not – so Steiner powerfully argues – anything but a marginal and highly specialized function of
language. And so the passage just quoted can be seen as exculpation, self-
justification, very adroit and telling.

The direction of Steiner's argument is in any case very clear:

In brief: I am suggesting that the outwardly communicative, extrovert
thrust of language is secondary and that it may in substantial measure
have been a late socio-historical acquirement. The primary drive is
inward and domestic.

Each tongue hoards the resources of consciousness, the world-
pictures of the clan. Using a simile still deeply entrenched in the
language-awareness of Chinese, a language builds a wall around the
'middle kingdom' of the group's identity. It is secret towards the
outsider and inventive of its own world. Each language selects,
combines and 'contradicts' certain elements from the total potential of
perceptual data. This selection, in turn, perpetuates the differences in
world images explored by Whorf.... There have been so many thousands of human tongues, there still are, because there have been,
particularly in the archaic stages of social history, so many distinct
groups intent on keeping from one another the inherited, singular
springs of their identity, and engaged in creating their own semantic
worlds....

Most probably there is a common molecular biology and neuro-
physiology to all human utterance. It seems very likely that all
languages are subject to constraints and similarities determined by the
design of the brain, by the vocal equipment of the species and, it might
be, by certain highly generalized, wholly abstract efficacies of logic, of
optimal form, and relation. But the ripened humanity of language, its

indispensable conservative and creative force lie in the extraordinary diversity of actual tongues, in the bewildering profusion and eccentricity (though there is no centre) of their modes. The psychic need for particularity, for 'in-clusion' and invention is so intense that it has, during the whole of man's history until very lately, outweighed the spectacular, obvious material advantages of mutual comprehension and linguistic unity....

It follows... that the poem, taking the word in its fullest sense, is neither a contingent nor a marginal phenomenon of language. A poem concentrates, it deploys with least regard to routine or conventional transparency, those energies of covertness and of invention which are the crux of human speech.

With that last resounding contention, it comes clear how the whole ambitious arc of Steiner's argument – it has taken him over two hundred pages to get to this point – should have arisen out of his professional field of comparative literature to which, at this point, it returns. And it may be thought that we have heard this before, from other scholars and teachers with a vested interest in the study of literature, rather than linguistics or philosophy, communications theory or semiotics or computer science or three or four other disciplines which nowadays set their sights all or some of the time on the phenomenon of human language. But in fact there is a notable difference between this sentiment as we hear it from Steiner and as we have heard it from others. For in the first place those two hundred pages have not been wasted, but have been spent by this literary scholar in reviewing those other studies, one after another, so as to substantiate his charge that all are characterized by 'overwhelming one-sidedness'. In the second place he has insisted that the condition of the polyglot is – not statistically, of course, but logically – more normal than the monoglot condition, for any responsible study of language. And the truth is (though this is my point, not Steiner's) that this is no more of a challenge and a reproach to current habits in linguistics and linguistic philosophy, than it is to much or most study of language under the auspices of literature – where indeed a sort of linguistic chauvinism has lately become not just common practice but, in some energetic circles, positively a required duty.

Moreover, the central perception – that the function of human languages is, quite properly and necessarily, more to conceal than to reveal – reaches out into quite other areas. Hannah Arendt, for example, discussing in *Of Violence* what changes *engagés* into *enragés*, decides, 'it is not injustice that ranks first, but hypocrisy...' And, maintaining that a resort to violence from these motives is 'not irrational', she declares, 'words can be relied on only if one is sure that their function is to reveal and not to conceal.' But Steiner contends, and so far as I am concerned he proves, that the assurance which Hannah Arendt here asks for on behalf of the *enragés* is one that can never be given. For their 'hypocrisy' we should read 'duplicity', and a duplicity which is of the nature of human language as such, since nothing else explains the multiplicity of tongues that humankind does speak. Thus the *enragés* are asking for the impossible. But, in the first place, they could have been brought to ask for it by listening to linguisticians and philosophers, even (I'm afraid) to literary critics; and second, they would, if they were sincere and intelligent, be less likely to ask for this impossibility if they knew something other than a monoglot culture. (Moreover, in an extended but justifiable sense, our culture is becoming more completely monoglot with each year that passes. The legitimizing of the four-letter words in the name of sexual revolution – their newly public currency hailed as enlightenment – plainly represents a deliberately covert language made overt and public.)

As regards poetry, while Steiner's argument obviously and powerfully validates poetry that is hermetic and arcane, it does not elevate it over a poetry that aspires to be limpid and readily accessible, even readily translatable. (Steiner establishes – indeed, it is the first point he makes, and abundantly demonstrates – that to gain *access* to calculated utterances in one's native tongue itself involves, very crucially, acts of translation.) If language of its nature covers up as much as it opens out, the poet who aspires to be lucid will find necessarily, in his medium, enough to frustrate that aspiration – as many a poet can mournfully testify, having seen what he took to be as plain as a pikestaff converted, by reasonably attentive readers, into something as gnarled and convoluted as a yew tree. Steiner doubtless would agree to this, and yet his heart might not be in it. For he is, as he always was, excited by extreme situations in art and by the extremists who provoke and contrive them. Thus we do not have to wait long, after he has descended to particular cases of interlingual translators and translations, before we find him saying: 'But Hölderlin pressed further. He was trying to move upstream not only to the historical springs of German but to the primal energies of human discourse.' Though his examination of Hölderlin as translator and Broch as self-translator establishes quite fairly his challenging and crucial contention that 'literalism is not, as in traditional models of translation, the naïve, facile mode but, on the contrary, the ultimate', nevertheless some readers may detect a foreign style of feeling, too much of 'the messiness of intense presence', in the evident excitement with which Steiner approaches all cases of 'pressing further'.

This foreignness might be defined by saying that Steiner is rather seldom concerned that translation be *serviceable*. And yet, to this too there are exceptions. It is just hereabouts, in his chapter five, that he provides several scintillating yet wholly self-explanatory pages which could and should be put in the hands of any translator, from the merest beginner to the most professionally accomplished, pages concerned simply with French, German, and English at the level of the tourist's phrase book, demonstrating how it is impossible to translate 'I like swimming' or 'it looks like rain' or 'the child has been run over' without 'falsification' – that is to say, without running one's head at once into the inherent biases not just of French language, German language but of French *culture*, German *culture*. The touching thing here – though in fact the poignancy informs the whole book – is that Steiner, whose trilingualism shows him how 'impossible' translation is, nevertheless affirms that it must be possible because it is necessary, with a necessity that is inherent in the human condition.

He says that *After Babel* originated in the *Penguin Book of Modern Verse Translation*, which he edited in 1966. If we look back at his introduction to that anthology, we see that on certain crucial issues he has changed his mind. This is high praise, of a sort that one cannot often give – least of all to a writer who conceives of himself as embattled, as Steiner plainly does. To look again, to think again, to allow that certain objections are just – this is particularly difficult and honourable in someone who feels himself isolated, and under attack. Thus, in *After Babel*, we are no longer told that 'the period from Rossetti to Robert Lowell has been an age of poetic translation rivalling that of the Tudor and Elizabethan masters'; and in fact we now come across references to Lowell that are sharply disparaging, as well as many that are admiring. More momentously, Steiner has abandoned the working definition of 1966, when he declared (his italics):

> I have taken translation to include *the writing of a poem in which a poem in another language (or in a earlier form of one's own language) is the vitalizing, shaping presence; a poem which can be read and responded to independently but which is not ontologically complete, a previous poem being its occasion, begetter, and in the literal sense raison d'etre.*

The trouble with such a definition is not that it is demonstrably wrong (for of course it isn't) but that it is *useless*; it comprehends too much, excludes too little, for it to be a serviceable tool in any circumstances one can conceive of. And what is the point of a working definition that can never be set to work? In *After Babel* Steiner has retreated to the common-sense position that (however many borderline cases crop up, as of course they do) there is translation properly or strictly considered, and on the other hand – across a frontier which exists, though we cannot always find it – all those other traffickings between poems which we gesture at in words like 'running allusion', 'imitation', 'adaptation', 'parody', 'pastiche', 'burlesque', 'variation'. Of course there's no need for him to give up his fervent interest in these transactions. He devotes his last chapter to them, arguing eloquently and movingly that the progeny through the centuries of forms and themes first defined for the most part in ancient Greece (he traces some of the lines of descent) constitutes a continuity and integrity in western Europe from at least the fifth century BC to at least the twentieth century AD. (About the twenty-first he has alarming apprehensions, which it is hard not to share.) Though to a student of literature this phase of his argument is less novel and arresting than earlier stages, here too is much that is instructive and provocative – notably a brief but exhilarating treatment of musical settings for poems as being in some sense (and who can deny it?) *translations* of those poems. Nor should anyone want to deny Steiner his conviction that all these transactions – imitations, parodies, 'settings' – are kinds of translation, in the sense that the areas they denote are what we get into as soon as we cross the frontier from translation proper. We might even concede that the distinction between 'translation' and 'imitation' is a distinction merely of convenience. But 'convenience' matters – *our* convenience, as readers and thinkers, as translators and poets. This is what one means by asking that any discussion of these baffling maters be *serviceable*; and the discussion in *After Babel* is serviceable, as the discussion in the Penguin anthology wasn't, and couldn't be.

It should be clear by now that I greatly admire the intellectual venture which this book represents – so boldly sustained, so vulnerably extended; that I esteem it as of quite another order from Steiner's earlier writings, or from such as I have read. That said, I must point out how difficult he makes it for his admirers. Probably he has been at more pains to protect himself in the many areas he invades where I cannot check on him, than in the area of concerns which, as it happens, we share. But it is on page fifteen – as early as that, in a book of nearly five hundred pages – that I find him writing as follows, of our alleged inability nowadays to respond fairly to D.G. Rossetti, Swinburne, Lionel Johnson, and others of their generations:

> Much more is involved here than a change of fashion, than the acceptance by journalism and the academy of a canon of English poetry chosen by Pound and Eliot. This canon is already being challenged; the primacy of Donne may be over, Browning and Tennyson are visibly in the ascendant. A design of literature which finds little worth commending between Dryden and Hopkins is obviously myopic.

Here, though I hate to say it, just about everything is wrong that could be. In the first place, neither Eliot nor Pound *did* choose or establish 'a canon'. It is not, one might say, an activity that poets are prone to. Whatever phantasmal canon may be thought to be currently established among us, or to have been so established until lately, was defined and disseminated not by Pound nor by Eliot, but by their mostly academic epigones, who have systematized and made categorical certain animadversions and preferences thrown out by the two poets in passing, or at any rate in the context of highly specific occasions. Secondly, in so far as there has come into being by this process a Poundian and an Eliotic 'canon', they diverge radically: whereas an Eliotic canon would indeed exclude Swinburne, Rossetti, and Lionel Johnson, a Poundian canon would in fact find an honourable place (though not equally honourable) for each of these poets and for the poetic idiom which each of them stands for. Thirdly, the astrological metaphor – 'Browning and Tennyson are visibly in the ascendant' – should not obscure the fact that what Steiner is talking about is precisely what he denies, 'a change of fashion'. To be specific, the novel interest and pleasure that some of us can now take, thanks to Christopher Ricks, in certain poems of Tennyson rests immediately on our no longer having to repudiate the idea that Tennyson is of the company of Virgil and Milton; we see and can relish what a past poet has to offer, only when inflated claims for him have been exploded. As for 'the primacy of Donne' and 'a design of literature which finds little worth commending between Dryden and Hopkins', surely these chimeras never existed outside the heated imagination of George Steiner. Barbarianized as we are, surely no one even remotely reputable ever claimed for Donne 'primacy' over Shakespeare or Chaucer? And who ever found 'little worth commending' between Dryden and Hopkins? How much is 'little'? Is Wordsworth 'little'? How much of Wordsworth is 'little'? One has only to phrase these questions to see that we are moving in a world of what is *à la mode*, not at all in a world of responsible intellectual endeavour.

The truth is that George Steiner, now as in the past, can veer disconcertingly from genuine intellectual elevation and rigour to what one can only call *vulgarity*. Somewhere in his head there is the image of a mittel-European or else mid-Atlantic bourse, where every living writer, as well as many dead ones, is quoted at a certain selling price; and for these 'quotations' Steiner has an unaccountable respect. His word for them, sometimes, is 'canonical'. Pound's *Cantos*, it seems, are still going dirt-cheap (a 'laboured, ultimately sterile exercise'); on the other hand, Pound's *Homage to Sextus Propertius* still commands a high price – though as a translation, which it surely isn't, but rather a quite deliberate, highly inventive, and instructive *travesty*. In any case it is this stock-exchange fantasy which accounts, in *After Babel*, for such bizarre parentheses as 'Paul Celan, almost certainly the major European poet of the period after 1945'; or, 'the modal completeness of French literature (major performances in every genre)'. It explains too, in Steiner's letter to the *New Review*, the lordly interjection, 'No one since D.H. Lawrence being at once "English English" and, beyond cavil, of world rank' – a ticker-tape read-off which reappears, in *After Babel*, as a rhetorical question: 'Has there been an "English English" author of absolutely the first rank after D.H. Lawrence and J.C. Powys?' What is sad about this last instance is that Steiner, when handing down this judgement, is in no sense swimming against the tide but, on the contrary, as he must realize, is the spokesman for an inert consensus. For thirty years at least the English have been telling themselves that they neither have, nor can expect to have, writers of the status of D.H. Lawrence – precarious as *that* status is, in all conscience. And by now that proposition, parroted unthinkingly through several generations, has most of the characteristics of a self-fulfilling prophecy. What is even more mournfully comical is that this predetermined view of 'English English' writing, voluntarily subscribed to by Steiner, appears to originate in just that 'corner-of-the-mouth sparsity, sour fastidiousness' which he declares himself at odds with, and unable to stomach. For my part, in so far as I can give any substance to the notion of 'world rank' or 'first rank', I do so by recalling opinions that I have heard expressed by non-British people who have shown themselves to be both informed and exacting readers of English; and on that basis I report – for what it is worth, which is little – that four or five of my 'English English' contemporaries, some writing verse, some prose, seem to be generally accorded the rank that Steiner would deny them.

All of this is a pity, but in the last analysis it isn't important. George Lukács, writing *The Historical Novel*, muddles one Walter Scott novel with another, and is only intermittently and imperfectly aware that the history of Scotland and the history of England differ. And what could be more vulgar, in the bleakest sense, than for Lukács in the 1950s to have lent his investigations of literary genre and literary history to the specious purposes of a 'common front for peace', under the sinister auspices of Picasso's dove-with-olive-branch? Never mind! Lukács belongs securely in a tradition of high-flying speculation about literature, which we costive islanders cannot afford not to profit by. In such cases the chain of reasoning is emphatically *not* as strong as its weakest link. George Steiner belongs in that tradition also; and with this eloquent and earnest book he earns a place in it as securely as Lukács.

Times Literary Supplement, 31 January 1975.

Epistle. To Enrique Caracciolo Trejo

(Essex)

A shrunken world
Stares from my pages.
What a pellet the authentic is!
My world of poetry,
Enrique, is not large.
Day by day it is smaller.
These poems that you have
Given me, I might
Have made them English once.

Now they are inessential.
The English that I feel in
Fears the inauthentic
Which invades it on all sides
Mortally. The style may die of it,
Die of the fear of it,
Confounding authenticity with essence.

Death, an authentic subject,
Jaime Sabinès has
Dressed with the yew-trees of funereal trope.
It cannot be his fault
If the English that I feel in
Feels itself too poor
Spirited to plant a single cypress.
It is afraid of showing, at the grave-side,
Its incapacity to venerate
Life, or the going of it. These are deaths,
These qualms and horrors shade the ancestral ground.

Sabinès in another
Poem comes down
To the sound of pigeons on a neighbour's tiles,
A manifest of gladness.

Such a descent on clapping wings the English
Contrives to trust
No longer. My own garden
Crawls with a kind of obese
Pigeon from Belgium; they burst through cracking branches
Like frigate-birds.

Still in infested gardens
The year goes round,
A smiling landscape greets returning Spring.
To see what can be said for it, on what
Secure if shallow ground
Of feeling England stands
Unshaken for
Her measure to be taken
Has taken four bad years
Of my life here. And now
I know the ground:
Humiliation, corporate and private,
Not chastens but chastises
This English and this verse.

I cannot abide the new
Absurdities day by day,
The new adulterations.
I relish your condition,
Expatriate! though it be among
A people whose constricted idiom
Cannot embrace the poets you thought to bring them.

Times Literary Supplement, 9 May 1968; first collected in *Collected Poems, 1950–1970* (London: Routledge and Kegan Paul, 1972).

Index